# Philippine Security in the Age of Terror

National, Regional, and Global
Challenges in the Post-9/11 World

# Philippine Security in the Age of Terror

## National, Regional, and Global Challenges in the Post-9/11 World

## ROMMEL C. BANLAOI

**CRC Press**
Taylor & Francis Group
Boca Raton London New York

CRC Press is an imprint of the
Taylor & Francis Group, an **informa** business

AN AUERBACH BOOK

CRC Press
Taylor & Francis Group
6000 Broken Sound Parkway NW, Suite 300
Boca Raton, FL 33487-2742

First issued in paperback 2018

ISBN-13: 978-1-4398-1550-2 (hbk)
ISBN-13: 978-1-138-37420-1 (pbk)

### Library of Congress Cataloging-in-Publication Data

Banlaoi, Rommel C.
　　Philippine security in the age of terror : national, regional, and global challenges in the post-9/11 world / Rommel Banlaoi.
　　　　p. cm.
　　Includes bibliographical references and index.
　　ISBN 978-1-4398-1550-2 (hbk. : alk. paper)
　　1. Philippines--Politics and government--21st century. 2. National security--Philippines. 3. Security, International--Philippines. 4. Terrorism--Philippines. 5. Philippines--Foreign relations. I. Title.

DS686.614.B36 2010
355'.0330599--dc22                                                                2009028150

Deeply dedicated to:

My wife, Grace Quilitorio-Banlaoi,

for her unfailing love, patience, and understanding…

My children, Rome Melchizedek and Ronaiah Gail,

for the inspiration and joy of parenting…

My mentor, Dr. Clarita Carlos, for being my model academic…

My parents, Rizalino Gallardo Banlaoi (deceased) and Lolita Capudoy Banlaoi,

for teaching me how to be a strong person…

and

My students, who continue to make me relevant as a scholar!

# Contents

## SECTION III GLOBAL, REGIONAL, AND MULTILATERAL SECURITY ISSUES

# Preface

The study of Philippine security generated a tremendous amount of interest in the academic and policy-making communities after the end of the cold war, particularly in the aftermath of the September 11, 2001 (9/11) terrorist attacks. Many issues that were once viewed as "social" or "public" issues have been recently labeled as "security" issues, especially when they have a significant effect on the vital interest of the state and the welfare of human beings. Even topics of human rights have been deeply incorporated in the discourse of human security. Food production is now being analyzed in the context of food security; environmental degradation is part of environmental security; and economic and political issues have become economic and political security issues.

In the past, particularly at the height of the cold war, security discourse was the exclusive domain of the military sector. Now, security has become so broad and comprehensive that it encompasses many sectors, including: political, economic, social, cultural, environmental, and others. Though there are numerous related books, journals, occasional papers, and publications related to the study of Philippine security in its various dimensions, it is lamenting to note that no single book to date has been published that examines the widening and deepening scope of Philippine security. This book is my humble, yet daring, attempt to discuss Philippine security in the context of national, regional, and global security challenges after 9/11. It is a product of my long, frustrating search for a single volume that covers the many facets of Philippine security in this age of global terrorism.

Divided into three sections, this book is a collection of my published works and articles related to the study of Philippine security. Each chapter has been carefully updated and rigorously revised to make the data and analysis more current, informative, and relevant to the present and future needs of readers from the academic community, government agencies, policy-making institutions, media, and the wider public, not only in the Philippines but also in other countries interested in the Philippine security situation.

Section I discusses national security issues confronting the Filipino nation. It is composed of seven independent chapters. Chapter 1 examines the problematic concept of Philippine security using the framework of identity politics. It argues that the contested concept of Philippine national security can be rooted in the controversial issue of Philippine national identity. National security in the Philippines, though people-oriented in theory, remains state-centric or regime-focused in practice. As a result, national security has become a comfortable excuse of "oligarchs" in government to perpetuate themselves into power. In short, Philippine security is parochially viewed as elite security or regime security.

Chapter 2 expounds this issue by highlighting the dilemma of the Philippine state in building a Filipino nation in the era of globalization. It contends that the Philippine state enormously suffers the predicament of nation-building because the state itself is captured by the "few" selfish elite who prioritize personal and family interests at the great expense of national interests. As a result, the Philippines has developed a weak state that strongly exacerbates rather than ameliorates the immense insecurities of the Filipino people. The weakness of the Philippine state mirrors the parochial view and sometimes repressive practice of Philippine national security.

Chapter 3 describes threats to Philippine security emanating from radical Muslim terrorist groups and examines the response of the Philippine government to these threats. The chapter concludes by highlighting the reality that Muslim radicalism in the Philippines has deep historical, economic, social, and political roots requiring a more nuanced security policy response. Chapter 4 focuses on local government response against terrorist threats in the Philippines. It argues that national efforts must be complemented by local actions to provide a more holistic antidote to terrorism.

Chapter 5 deals with the role of the military in Philippine democratization. It provides discussions on the factors and forces that encourage the military to intervene in politics and how military intervention challenges national security in a society undergoing painful democratic consolidation. To prevent the military from pursuing political adventurism and contain the armed forces from partisan politics, democratic control is deemed imperative. Chapter 6 elaborates the concept of democratic control through the concept of security sector governance. It argues that good governance of the security sector is necessary to prevent the military from intervening in partisan politics.

Chapter 7 concludes Section I by underscoring the role of elections in promoting national security. It contends that election is a bedrock of democracy. The infirmities of Philippine elections result in the weakness of Philippine democracy, which in turn, creates a condition for the emergence of various internal security threats. Reforming the Philippine electoral system is imperative for Philippine democracy to flourish. A vibrant democracy will provide a political environment conducive to promoting national security.

Section II, composed of three interrelated chapters, moves from national security to bilateral security issues. Chapter 8 examines the role of Philippine–American relations in the global campaign against terrorism. It underscores the fact that threats from global terrorism have reinvigorated the once-ailing Philippine–American security alliance. The Philippines has become a major ally of the United

States in the fight against global terrorism. Chapter 9, however, explains that Philippine–American relations shall not sacrifice Philippine relations with China, which is a rapidly growing Asian power. Thus, this chapter urges the Philippine government to sustain friendship and enhance cooperation with China on defense-related matters without creating unnecessary discomforts to the United States. The fight against terrorism also requires the Philippines and China to work together in pursuit of common security interests. Chapter 10 examines Philippine defense security relations with Australia. This chapter emphasizes the role of Australia in promoting Philippine security. It argues that convergent security interests and cultural familiarity provide fertile ground for Australia and the Philippines to broaden their defense ties.

Section III of this anthology devotes six independent chapters to the examination of Philippine security in the context of selected global, regional, and multilateral security issues. Chapter 11 provides a general overview of global security issues and concerns after 9/11. It demonstrates that the threat of global terrorism creates mixed reactions among states in the international community. Though combating terrorism has become a global priority, the pre-9/11 security issues persist. As such, nothing has fundamentally changed in the global security architecture since 9/11. What has changed is a greater emphasis of states to combat international terrorism.

Chapter 12 is an example of how old security issues could still affect many states after 9/11. It provides a security outlook in the maritime domain of Southeast Asia, focusing on the problem of piracy and its nexus with terrorism. While regional cooperation is needed to combat maritime security threats, building the national capabilities of littoral states is equally important to address these threats. Chapter 13 extends the discussions of maritime security issues in Southeast Asia to the Indian Ocean. It argues that maritime security issues bring the waters of Southeast Asia and the Indian Ocean into the same regional maritime security complex. The maritime domain also intensifies the security convergence between Southeast Asia and South Asia.

Chapter 14 focuses on regional cooperation to address a myriad of issues confronting the broader Asia–Pacific region. It examines the role of the ASEAN (Association of Southeast Asian Nations) Regional Forum (ARF) in the process of security-community building in the region. It also draws upon lessons from Europe to highlight issues and challenges of security-community building in the Asia–Pacific region. Chapter 15 examines security cooperation and conflict in Southeast Asia after 9/11. It describes how the war on terrorism has greatly affected interstate cooperation in the region. Yet, the ASEAN Way continues to serve as the overarching framework to promote regional cooperation and to prevent regional conflicts in Southeast Asia. Chapter 16 ends the volume by describing the evolution of security cooperation in Southeast Asia and takes stock of ASEAN achievements in this area spanning four decades of its existence. This concluding chapter also identifies some challenges facing ASEAN as it aspires to become a regional organization with a coherent regional security agenda. It finally examines the role of the Philippines in the pursuance of security cooperation in Southeast Asia using ASEAN as the major platform.

Though this collection of essays attempts to examine the many facets of Philippine security from national, regional, and global perspectives, it does not have the pretension of covering all strategic and foreign policy issues impinging Philippine security. For example, this volume has limited discussions on the Local Communist Movement (LCM), which is the main threat to Philippine internal security, because many works have been published on the topic.[1] There are also limited discussions on Philippine bilateral security relations with India, Japan, and Russia — three major powers that can affect Philippine security. The volume also has little discussion on the Asia–Pacific Economic Cooperation (APEC), East Asia Summit (EAS), and the United Nations. Another book or volume is therefore needed to systematically analyze these issues relevant to Philippine security. Despite its limitations, this volume can provide students, policymakers, researchers, and the general public with a valuable, ready sourcebook on topics that have tremendous repercussions on Philippine security.

This anthology of previously published papers reflects the author's diverse interests as a scholar of politics, security studies, terrorism research, foreign policy, and international relations. It documents the author's intellectual journey as an observer, analyst, and commentator of Philippine security predicaments. Though essays in this volume are written independently of one another, they are all closely interrelated and are strongly bound by a common goal to promote Philippine security in the age of global terrorism.

## Endnote

1. See, for example, Patricio N. Abinales, *Fellow Traveller: Essays on Filipino Communism* (Quezon City: University of the Philippines Press, 2001); Kathleen Weekley, *The Communist Party of the Philippines: 1968–1993* (Quezon City: University of the Philippines Press, 2001); Joel Rocamora, *Breaking Through: The Struggle within the Communist Party of the Philippines* (Pasig City: Anvil Publishing, Inc., 1994); Gregg Jones, *Red Revolution: Inside the Philippine Guerilla Movement* (Boulder: Westview Press, 1989); and Alfredo B. Saulo, *Communism in the Philippines: An Introduction* (Quezon City: Ateneo de Manila University Press, 1969).

# Acknowledgments

This book is a product of the generous support, assistance, and encouragement of many people and institutions.

In preparing this book, I need to admit to having sacrificed most of my quality time with my family, friends, and colleagues. But I am truly blessed to have a family that fully understands my intricate profession as a serious academic. I am also grateful to have friends and colleagues who, despite their disagreements with some of my views, continue to support my scholarly pursuit.

I am particularly indebted to Dr. Ruben F. Ciron, then Assistant Secretary of National Defense, who allowed me to enjoy my time to prepare this book during my stint in his office as a consultant for plans and programs. My assignment to his office at the Department of National Defense was truly intellectually enriching, though physically exhausting. His nurturing, spiritual attitude inspired me to be a productive scholar and provided me several opportunities to help the defense establishment in strategy formulation, policy development, and administrative supervision in order to humbly contribute to the promotion of Philippine national security.

I wish to acknowledge the Philippine Studies Association, Inc. (PSA), especially Dr. Bernardita R. Churchill, for the privilege of preparing a paper that has become Chapter 1 of this book. Thanks also to Dr. Paul Mathews of the University of Western Sydney in Australia for publishing the original version of Chapter 1 in *Pilipinas: A Journal of Philippine Studies*.

I thank Dr. Yoichiro Sato of the Asia–Pacific Center for Security Studies (APCSS) in Hawaii for the wonderful editing of my original paper that is now Chapter 2. This chapter was originally published in Dr. Sato's edited volume *Growth and Governance in Asia*, published by APCSS. My fellowship at APCSS in 1999 also contributed immensely to the broadening of my knowledge on security studies. I owe a great deal to Dr. Carlyle Thayer for becoming my mentor during my stay at APCSS. It was Dr. Thayer who encouraged me to pursue Southeast Asian security studies based on my knowledge of European security studies. I gained my knowledge of European security when I became a visiting scholar in 1997 at the University of Leiden in the Netherlands, for which I am grateful to Dr. Neils Blokker, my supervisor at that time.

My deep appreciation also goes to a dear friend, Dr. Andrew Tan, now with the University of Sydney. Chapter 3 of this book originally appeared in his edited volume *Handbook on Insurgency and Terrorism in Southeast Asia*, published by Edward Elgar Publishing, Limited.

I thank the Konrad Adenauer Striftung (KAS), the Hans Seidel Stiftung (HSS) and the Friedrich Ebert Stiftung (FES) for the opportunity to write papers that have become Chapters 4, 5, and 6 of this anthology. Chapter 4 is based on the original paper that I presented to an international conference organized by KAS and the Local Government Development Foundation (LOGODEF). Chapter 5 is drawn from the paper I prepared for a conference organized by HSS and the Foundation for Communication Initiatives (FCI). Chapter 6 is culled from the paper I presented in a conference organized by FES and the Institute of Defense and Strategic Studies (IDSS), now called S. Rajaratnam School of International Studies (RSIS). I also thank Emmanuel Dubois, general manager of *Asian Affairs*, for the opportunity to write an article that is now Chapter 7.

I convey my sincerest gratitude to the Institute of Southeast Asian Studies (ISEAS) in Singapore for publishing my articles in *Contemporary Southeast Asia*. These articles have become Chapters 8 and 10. I am also grateful to the Centre of Asian Studies (CAS) of the University of Hong Kong for the invitation to present a paper that is now Chapter 9. I wish to extend my deepest thanks to General Alexander Aguirre, Chairman of the Strategic and Integrative Studies Center, Inc. (SISC), for the support to write a paper that appears as Chapter 11 of this collection.

Many thanks are also due to Joshua Ho and Catharine Zara Raymond for the competent editing of my article that is now Chapter 12. This chapter originally appeared in their edited volume, *The Best of Times, The Worst of Times: Maritime Security in the Asia–Pacific*, published by World Scientific Publishing. Sincere appreciation also goes to Lt. General V.R. Raghavan and Dr. Lawrence Prabhakar for the opportunity to write a paper that is presented as Chapter 13. This chapter is a product of a conference held in Chennai, India, in December 2006, and is published in a book entitled *Maritime Security in the Indian Ocean Region: Critical Issues in Debate*, published by McGraw-Hill.

I am also very grateful to Dr. Clarita Carlos of the University of the Philippines for her nurturing attitude to young scholars like me. One of the many products of her nurturing attitude became Chapter 14 of this book. Among the many academics I have worked with, Dr. Carlos was the only one who left an indelible ink on my scholarly pursuit. She has been my mentor since my undergraduate years at the University of the Philippines. Were it not for the continuing mentoring of Dr. Carlos, I would not have traversed the path less traveled by scholars. I owe her my intellectual umbilical cord.

I also thank Dr. Amitav Acharya, then from Nanyang Technological University (NTU), and Dr. Lee Lai To of the National University of Singapore (NUS) for including my work in their edited volume, *Asia in the New Millennium*, published by Marshall Cavendish Academic. This work is now Chapter 15. Finally, Chapter 16 was originally published in Mandarin at the academic journal of Jinan University, China, and I sincerely thank Dr. Cao Yunhua of the Department of International Relations for the great intellectual engagement and supervision.

Of course, this book would not be put into print without the generous assistance of Mark Listewnik and Linda Leggio of Taylor & Francis Group. I convey my sincerest gratitude to them.

Most of all, I owe enormous debt to my dear wife, Grace, whose unfailing love gives me the intellectual, moral, and physical energy to pursue my scholarly endeavors amidst the pressures of parenting. Because of my tremendous passion as a full-time researcher, scholar, and educator, my wife sometimes calls me a "part-time husband" and a "part-time father." But I thank my children, Zed and Zoe, for the enormous joy of child-rearing. My children always give me hope of a brighter and more secure future for the Philippines.

Readers should be strongly reminded by the usual caveat that this book articulates my personal academic perspectives and expert opinion and not the official positions of the many people and institutions I have mentioned and acknowledged. If there are factual errors or lapses in my judgment, I need to emphasize my personal accountability.

Finally, I thank the Lord Almighty for endowing me with the wisdom to enjoy the journey of a scholar. Though my profession is not financially rewarding, it is spiritually fulfilling and enriching. I offer this work to Him, who is the main source of our security. To God be the Glory!

# About the Author

Rommel C. Banlaoi is the Chairman of the Board and the Executive Director of the Philippine Institute for Peace, Violence and Terrorism Research (PIPVTR) and head of its Center for Intelligence and National Security Studies. He is also a Senior Fellow of the Yuchengco Center of De La Salle University, Manila, where he heads its Regional Security and Foreign Relations program.

A former professor of political science at the National Defense College of the Philippines (NDCP) where he became Vice President for Administration and Assistant Vice President for Research and Special Studies, he also served as assistant professor in international studies at De La Salle University, instructor in political science at the University of the Philippines (Los Baños), university research associate at the University of the Philippines (Diliman), and Director for Research and Publications of the World Citi Colleges (WCC). He is currently the Chairman of the Board of Directors of the Council for Asian Terrorism Research (CATR), the largest network of terrorism think tanks in the Asia–Pacific; and was a founding director of the Mayor's Development Center (MDC) of the League of Municipalities of the Philippines (LMP).

Professor Banlaoi frequently lectures at the Command and General Staff College (CGSC) of the Armed Forces of the Philippines (AFP), the Intelligence Training Group (ITG) of the Philippine National Police (PNP), Foreign Service Institute (FSI) of the Department of Foreign Affairs (DFA), and other military and police training institutions. He is a member of the International Studies Association (ISA), the Asian Political and International Studies Association (APISA), the International Institute for Strategic Studies (IISS), the Philippine Political Science Association (PPSA), the Philippine Studies Association (PSA), and the Philippines Association for China Studies (PACS). He has provided consulting services to the Philippine Department of National Defense, National Counter-Terrorism Action Group (NACTAG), and other agencies of the Philippine government.

He is happily married to Grace Quilitorio Banlaoi and is blessed with two children: Rome Melchizedek and Ronaiah Gail.

# Also by Rommel C. Banlaoi

*Transnational Islam in South and Southeast Asia: Movements, Networks and Conflict Dynamics*, coauthor (Seattle, Washington: National Bureau of Asian Research, 2009).

*Al-Harakatul Al-Islamiyyah: Essays on the Abu Sayyaf Group,* revised and updated edition (Quezon City: Philippine Institute for Peace, Violence and Terrorism Research, 2009).

*The Philippines and Australia: Defense and Security Cooperation against Terrorism* (Quezon City: Philippine Institute for Peace, Violence and Terrorism Research, 2008).

*Security Aspects of Philippines–China Relations: Bilateral Issues and Concerns in the Age of Global Terrorism* (Quezon City: Rex Book Store International, 2007).

*Defense and Military Cooperation between the Philippines and China: Broadening Bilateral Ties in the Post-911 Era* (Taipei: Center for the Advancement of Policy Studies, 2007).

*War on Terrorism in Southeast Asia* (Quezon City: Rex Book Store International, 2004).

*Electoral Reform in the Philippines: Issues and Challenges*, coauthor (Makati City: Konrad Adenauer Foundation, 2004).

*The ASEAN Regional Forum, the South China Sea Disputes and the Functionalist Option* (Quezon City: National Defense College of the Philippines, 2001).

*Security Cooperation in the ASEAN Regional Forum and the European Union: Lessons Learned* (Quezon City: National Defense College of the Philippines, 2001).

*The Amsterdam Treaty and the European Union's Common Foreign and Security Policy* (Quezon City: Center for Asia Pacific Studies, 1999).

*Political Parties in the Philippines: From 1900–Present*, coauthor (Makati City: Konrad Adenauer Foundation, 1996).

*Elections in the Philippines: From Pre-Colonial Period to the Present*, coauthor (Makati City: Konrad Adenauer Foundation, 1996).

# NATIONAL SECURITY ISSUES

# Chapter 1

# Identity Politics and Philippine National Security in the Age of Terror*

## Introduction

Though much talked about in the academe, media, and government, national security remains one of the neglected areas in Philippine studies and an underdeveloped field of scholarly research in the Philippines. Sadly, national security is only treated as "special studies" in major academic disciplines, particularly in political science and international relations. With the securitization of many issues confronting states and human beings, this chapter urges Filipino academics and scholars to seriously engage in national security studies debate to enable them to provide useful scholarly inputs to national security policy development and decision making.

The main objective of this chapter is to examine the national security predicaments of the Philippines in the context of identity politics. It attempts to critically analyze the Philippine government's perspectives of national security using Critical

* Revised and updated version of a paper originally published with the title "Identity Politics and National Security in the Philippines" in *Pilipinas: A Journal of Philippine Studies*, Vol. 42 (March 2005), pp. 25–45. An earlier version of this paper was presented to the 4th National Philippine Studies Conference held at Golden Pine Hotel and Restaurant, Baguio City, September 17–18 2004.

3

Security Studies (CSS) and the Copenhagen School of security as main frameworks of analysis.[1] The end state of this paper is to depart from a state-centric analysis of national security and adopt a more people-centric analysis by making the people, rather than the state, as the referent object of national security studies and policy-making in the Philippines.

This chapter contends that national security problems of the Philippines remain largely internal in nature. These internal security problems are comprehensive and rooted in long conflicts over the identity of the Philippine nation–state. Thus, identity politics provides an alternative explanation of Philippine national security predicaments. This alternative explanation can be a firm basis of a Philippine national security policy that can promote the aspirations and interests of the Filipino people.

## The Problematic Concept of Security

It is customary to view security as a state of being free from danger and injury or a state of being safe from harm. Others view security as the absence of threats or the ability to overcome these threats. But a more scholarly definition makes security a highly contested concept.[2] Security is a very problematic concept in political science and international relations because scholars and practitioners do not have a shared understanding of the meaning of "security".[3] There are scholars advocating a *limited* or *bounded* definition, while there are those who advance a *broader* or more *expanded* definition.

A limited definition of security is based on the traditional notion that the state is central to the whole concept of security.[4] The state is the primary political community and player and therefore the main referent of security.[5] This limited definition of security is apparently anchored on the realist school, which views the state as the principal player in domestic and international politics.[6] From this perspective, the security of the state rests on its ability to develop a strong external defense defined in terms of military power, which, on the other hand, is measured in terms of possession of a huge arsenal of weapons as well as recruitment and training of troops for war-fighting missions. In short, some scholars traditionally define security in geopolitical terms, encompassing issues of nuclear deterrence, balance of power, and military strategy.[7] Scholars adhering to the narrow definition of security are those interested in military statecraft and strategic studies.

Other scholars, however, have challenged this limited definition of security, arguing that security is a broad concept that goes beyond its military dimension.[8] Security also means the security of the environment (environmental security), the security of the people (human security), and security from hunger (economic security), among other definitions. Southeast Asian academics call this concept "comprehensive security."[9] The concept of comprehensive security regards the traditional definition of security as an insufficient conceptual tool to describe the security predicaments of developing countries. The limited definition can only best describe the security predicaments of developed countries where the concept of statehood has already been settled. Because statehood is not a source of domestic political contestation, developed countries can, therefore, pay attention to external defense.

In many developing countries, however, the role of the state is highly contested and is not even seen as an effective provider of external defense.[10] The state in some developing countries is, in fact, viewed as an oppressor and a producer of insecurities.[11] Insecurities of the people in the developing world are also located in the arduous processes of state making, which is considered fragile, distorted, and incomplete.[12] Since the process of state making in the developing world is far from complete, security threats are largely internal, rather than external.[13] Thus the state, in some cases, has become a threat to the national security of the people in the developing world.

## Frameworks for Analysis

To grapple with the concept and practice of Philippine national security, this chapter uses a combination of the CSS and the Copenhagen School as frameworks of analysis.

CSS is a coherent critique of traditional security studies. Conceptualized by Keith Krause and Michael Williams, this approach articulates strong dissatisfaction with the orthodox security studies and expresses high disillusionment with the agenda of mainstream security studies.[14] Rather than focusing on the military dimension of security, CSS pays greater attention to individuals, community, and identity. A variant of CSS focuses on the idea of human emancipation. Otherwise known as the Welsh School of Security initiated by Ken Booth, this variant contends that only a process of emancipation can make the prospect of security more likely and relevant.[15] This chapter uses CSS to analyze identity politics and national security in the Philippines.

Identity politics approximates the various assumptions and argumentation of the CSS insofar as the issue of identity is concerned. Identity politics is a progressive and critical analytical perspective that recognizes the reality that in a given society, some social groups desolately experience oppression and marginalization. The state and the dominant group it represents are viewed as perpetuators of oppression and marginalization of these social groups. These oppressed and marginalized social groups are powerless and hence are often victims of state violence and social exploitation. Identity politics, therefore, struggles against injustices, and it clamors for the politics of difference to emancipate or liberate the marginalized sectors from the clutches of state oppression and social exploitation.[16] The following words have succinctly captured the main philosophical idea of identity politics:

> The laden phrase "identity politics" has come to signify a wide range of political activity and theorizing founded in the shared experiences of injustice of members of certain social groups. Rather than organizing solely around ideology or party affiliation, identity politics typically

concerns the liberation of a specific constituency marginalized within its larger context. Members of that constituency assert or reclaim ways of understanding their distinctiveness that challenge dominant oppressive characterizations, with the goal of greater self-determination.[17]

Related, but not similar, to the CSS is the Copenhagen School of security. The Copenhagen School emanates from the work *Security: A New Framework for Analysis*, written by Barry Buzan, Ole Waever, and Jaap de Wilde of the Conflict and Peace Research Institute (COPRI) based in Copenhagen, Denmark. The Copenhagen School regards security as a particular type of politics applicable to a wide range of issues: social, economic, military, economical, and ecological. It even argues that all security is political because all threats and defenses are constituted and defined politically.[18] These processes of constitution and definition make security a socially constructed concept. Who is security for and what should they be secured against? What component of security should we be concerned with, and how can this security be attained?[19] These are essential questions that come to mind when viewing security as a product of social construction from the point of view of the Copenhagen School.

The Copenhagen School is cognizant of the limited versus broad divide in security studies. But it subscribes to the broader definition and identifies five general categories or sectors of security: military security (military sector), environmental security (environmental sector), economic security (economic sector), societal security (societal sector), and political security (political sector). Among these categories, the Copenhagen School regards the political sector as all-encompassing because societal, economic, environmental, and military security in a sense mean "political–societal security," "political–economic society," and so forth.

Although the traditional concept of politics means the "affairs of the state" (from the word *polis*), the Copenhagen School defines politics as "the shaping of human behavior for the purpose of governing large groups of people." [20] The shaping of human behavior may be in the form of the Weberian concept of institutionalization of rule and stabilization of authority. [21] The shaping of human behavior may also be in the form of Ernesto Laclau's concept of "political," which is the upsetting of stabilized patterns.[22] From these two perspectives, security is inevitably a political practice.

An important contribution of the Copenhagen School is its differentiation of *nonpoliticization*, *politicization*, and *securitization*. A public issue is nonpoliticized when an issue is not elevated to public debate. An issue is politicized when it becomes "part of public policy, requiring government decision and resource allocations or, more rarely, some other form of communal governance."[23] When an issue "is presented as an existential threat, requiring emergency measures and justifying actions outside the normal bounds of political procedure," it becomes securitized.

This chapter also uses the Copenhagen School's concepts of politicization and securitization and the CSS's concept of emancipation to describe identity politics and national security in the Philippines. In the realm of identity politics, the referent of security is arguably the people. The national identity of the people defines national security. The problematic concept of national identity also makes the concept of national security highly problematic. Conflicts over national identities also create various insecurities that can inevitably result in internal armed conflicts and many forms of domestic political violence.

In most developing countries, like the Philippines, people come into conflict with each other over issues related to national identities.[24] According to the Copenhagen School, conflicts over national identities make the concept of national security in the developing world highly contested and problematic. Since the state is the main securitizing player, the dominant ethnic or elite group capturing the apparatuses of the state usually defines and determines the state's national security. The elite determine what constitutes national security. Thus, national security in developing countries usually means state security. Since most states in the developing world are weak states[25] — meaning they are captives of the parochial interests of the elite — state security means regime security. More often than not, regime security means the legitimacy of the regime in power. The elite in many developing countries erroneously treats "regime security" or "regime legitimacy" as synonymous with "national security."

Regime security is the core of the Copenhagen School's concept of political security defined as the organizational stability of social orders.[26] The heart of the political sector, on the other hand, is made up of threats to state sovereignty. Whom state sovereignty is for is another problematic issue. But political threats to sovereignty are made to (1) internal legitimacy of the political unit, which relates primarily to ideologies and other constitutive ideas and issues defining the state, and (2) the external recognition of the state — its external legitimacy.[27]

If the great number of the people does not regard the regime as legitimate, then the elite in power are likely to face a difficult political challenge. That challenge is likely to require activity outside normal politics — that is, the use of extraordinary measures.[28] When the populace utilizes extraordinary measures to challenge the legitimacy of the regime in power (for example, storming government buildings to overthrow the elite or regime), the government can securitize this move to prevent the prevailing regime from collapsing.[29] When regime survival is at stake, extraordinary measures from the population can be declared security threats. The elite in power can also use the extraordinary power of the state by exercising its prerogative to use force to surmount the state-defined security threats.

Crucial to the creation of legitimacy for the nation and state is the establishment of a shared national identity. The failure of the regime in power to establish shared norms and values (a shared identity) in the ethnically diverse body politic makes its own legitimacy highly questionable. This situation can ignite the incidence of resistance and violence in the cities and the countryside. When the dominant group refuses to accept the identity of a minority group, the latter can safeguard its identity through the normal political process (politicization). In this case, the identity issue remains a public issue and not a security issue. When a minority group pursues its identity through extraordinary means (rebellion, insurrection, coups, and so forth), the state can securitize the issue and declare this group a security threat from the point of view of the state. This state action, however, can be a threat to societal security from the vantage point of the people.

The Copenhagen School and the CSS assert that security (that is, societal security) is about collectives and their identity.[30] Threats to identity are always a question of the construction of something as threatening some "we" — and often thereby actually contributing to the construction or reproduction of "us." According to the Copenhagen School, "Any we identity can be constructed in many different ways, and often the main issue that decides whether security conflicts will emerge is whether one or another self-definition wins out in a society."[31] The elite of the dominant ethnic group is often the source of societal security threats by enforcing a definition of "national identity" in accordance with its own ethnic identity.[32]

## National Security in the Philippines: Concept, Formulation, and Organization

A reference paper prepared by the Office of the National Security Adviser (NSA) and the National Security Council (NSC) secretariat defines Philippine national security as "a state or condition where our most cherished values and beliefs, our democratic way of life, our institutions of governance and our unity, welfare and well-being as a nation and people are permanently protected and continuously enhanced."[33] This definition has evolved from a highly state-centered notion of national security to a more society-oriented approach.[34] On the basis of this definition, it identifies seven fundamental elements that lie at the core of and therefore further amplify "our definition of national security" and at the same time, "they constitute the most important challenges we face as a nation and people," to wit:

> The first and foremost element is socio-political stability. We must achieve peace and harmony among all Filipinos, regardless of creed, ethnic origin or social station. The government and the people must engage in nation building under the rule of law, Constitutional democracy and the full respect for human rights.
>
> The second is territorial integrity. We must ensure the permanent inviolability of our national territory and its effective control by the Government and the State. This includes the preservation of our country's Exclusive Economic Zone (EEZ) and its protection from illegal incursions and resource exploitation.
>
> The third is economic solidarity and strength. We must vigorously pursue a free-market economy through responsible entrepreneurship based on social conscience, respect for the dignity of labor and concern

for the public interest. We must perpetuate an economic regime where the People take command of their own lives, their livelihood and their economic destiny.

The fourth is ecological balance. National survival rests upon the effective conservation of our natural environment in the face of industrial and agricultural expansion and population growth. We must promote sustainable development side by side with social justice.

The fifth is cultural cohesiveness. Our lives as a people must be ruled by a common set of values and beliefs grounded on high moral and ethical standards, drawn from our heritage and embodying a Filipino identity transcending religious, ethnic and linguistic differences.

The sixth is moral–spiritual consensus. We must be propelled by a national vision inspired, and manifested in our words and deeds, by patriotism, national pride and the advancement of national goals and objectives. The seventh is external peace. We must pursue constructive and cordial relations with all nations and peoples, even as our nation itself must chart an independent course, free from external control, interference or threat of aggression.[35]

From the foregoing, the Philippine government apparently articulates a comprehensive view of national security encompassing political, military, sociocultural, economic, ecological and diplomatic dimensions. This is consistent with the broad concept of national security articulated by the CSS and the Copenhagen School. The Philippine government's view of national security, however, remains very problematic both in theory and in practice. The Philippine government's definition of *national security* assumes that the Philippine state has an uncontested notion of a Filipino nation. In reality, however, the perception of a "Filipino nation" remains divided because there is the "nation" of the elite and the "nation" of the masses.[36] There is also the "nation" of the dominant group and the "nation" of marginalized indigenous communities in the Philippines. There is even a tri-people concept of the Filipino nation composed of the Christians, Muslims, and *Lumads* (indigenous communities). Apparently, the Philippine government's definition of national security reflects a dominant Christian elite view of a Filipino nation. Its concept of national security, therefore, is elitist in orientation.

The organization of the NSC mirrors the elitist orientation of Philippine national security. Based on its organizational setup, the NSC consists of three main offices: the Council Proper, the Office of the NSA, and the NSC Secretariat (see Figure 1.1).[37]

From these three main offices, the Council Proper is the highest policy-making body consisting of the president as chairperson. Other members of the Council come from the Cabinet, the Philippine Senate and House of Representatives, past Philippine presidents, and other eminent persons from the private sector that the president may designate from time to time. In short, the membership of NSC alone

**Organization for National Security in the Philippines**

**Figure 1.1 Organization of the National Security Council. (From the National Security Council Secretariat, 2001.)**

reveals its elitist character. Although Executive Order No. 34, dated September 17, 2001, redefines the NSC membership, officers or members from the civil society or cause-oriented groups have not been represented. Marginalized sectors also remain unrepresented in the NSC.

One problematic aspect of national security in the Philippines is the central role of the Philippine state. Although President Gloria Macapagal Arroyo advocates the rhetoric of a "strong republic," the Philippines remains a weak state because its apparatuses remain under the control of powerful elite representing a landed family, clan, or business group.[38] A weak Philippine state results in the "politics of privilege"[39] or "crony" capitalism.[40] Under a weak Philippine state, national security essentially means the security of landed family, clan, or business groups. Threats to national security, therefore, are those threats to the power and interests of landed family, clan, or business groups. Using the Copenhagen School, national security in the Philippines is, in practice, the security of the regime in power. Thus, national security in the Philippines has been understood as a defense against internal challenges to the government and to the political system it perpetuates.[41]

Other conceptual and operational issues in the government's definition of national security are the concept of the "people" and the idea of "our cherished values and beliefs." Who are the people, and whose "cherished values and beliefs" is the Philippine government trying to protect? Although the government's definition of national security may be inclusive of all Filipino people regardless of economic status and ethnic origins, the Philippine government's practice of national security, however, tends to exclude and marginalize other people. The practice of Philippine national security is targeted against other people, particularly those "separatist" ones. Moreover, although the Philippine government's definition of national security talks about "our cherished values and beliefs," its practice of national security tends to exclude the cherished values and beliefs of other people like those of the *Bangsamoro* people, the indigenous communities, and those Filipino people whose cherished values and beliefs are anchored on socialism and other ideologies that run counter to the ideologies of the State and the dominant group it represents.[42]

## The Practice of National Security in the Philippines

Although Philippine national security has become more society oriented (societal security) in theory, its practice of national security, however, remains State centered and threat oriented (political security). The National Internal Security Plan (NISP) formulated by the now defunct Cabinet Oversight Committee on Internal Security (COCIS) indicated the State-centered and threat-oriented practice of Philippine national security. Even the enhanced version of the NISP did not change this orientation. The NISP identifies three major internal security threats in the Philippines: the Local Communist Movement (LCM), the Southern Philippines Secessionist Group (SPSG), and the threat posed by terrorism to include the Abu Sayyaf Group (ASG). Common among these threats groups is their strategic intention to challenge the legitimacy of the Philippine state.

The LCM refers to the threat posed by the New People's Army (NPA). The Philippine government renamed the LCM to Communist terrorist movement (CTM) in the aftermath of 9/11 terrorist attacks. According to the 2008 estimate of the Armed Forces of the Philippines (AFP), NPA strength was placed at 5,761 combatants, compared with the 2002 figure of 9,257 (see Figure 1.2). The NPA has affected around 1,919 from a total of 42,000 barangays (villages) nationwide.

The Department of National Defense (DND) states that the NPA remains capable of organizing the masses and establishing organs of political power at the grass roots through infiltration, coercion, and intimidation. Intelligence sources even state that the NPA has the capability to undertake selective terrorist actions and guerrilla operations against high-impact targets to create an atmosphere of instability and hopelessness in the countryside, the hotbed of Communist insurgency. Police sources also state that the NPA can conduct agitation-propaganda by exploiting popular issues to provoke the populace and distort public perception. The NPA also has a strategy of riding on the peace and electoral processes to consolidate

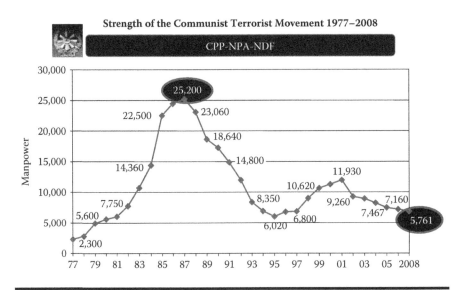

**Figure 1.2 Strength of the Communist Terrorist Movement, 1977–2008. (From the Office of the Deputy Chief of Staff for Intelligence, 2008.)**

its forces and expand its areas of political influence. It has also infiltrated and agitated various sectoral groups including the government bureaucracy. It has also utilized the mass media to exploit social issues for its propaganda campaign. The NPA problem has been threatening the legitimacy of the Philippine government for more than three decades. Because of the seriousness of the threat posed by the CTM, President Arroyo announced her plan to crush the Communist insurgency in 2010. Though analysts find this plan unrealistic, the government committed P1 billion Philippine pesos for acquiring military equipment and undertaking development projects in a two-pronged approach to crushing the almost four-decade-old Communist insurgency. The Arroyo administration announced that it would use excess money from the 2007 national budget allotment write-off to finance military and police offensives to crush the Communist NPA. President Arroyo also promised more than P75 billion to prop up the distressed economy in Northern Luzon, long a hotbed of the Communist insurgency.

The SPSG refers primarily to the threat posed by the *Moro* Islamic Liberation Front (MILF). The Philippine National Police (PNP) reported in the first quarter of 2009 that the MILF strength was placed at around 11,500 (see Figure 1.3). Considering its present strength and resources, the MILF can still conduct terrorist actions and limited guerrilla operations. It can also engage in criminal activities. According to military intelligence sources, the MILF is still capable of recruiting and training new members. It can finance its recovery campaign and procurement of firearms from its forced taxation and extortion activities, kidnap-for-ransom operations, and foreign funding through Islamic nongovernmental

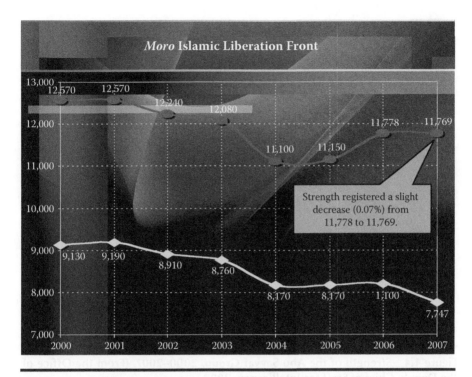

**Figure 1.3 Strength of the *Moro* Islamic Liberation Front, 2000–2007. (From the Philippine National Police Intelligence Group, 2008.)**

organizations (NGOs). It can also exploit the peace process to gain concessions, as well as manipulate the media for its propaganda campaign. The uncovered linkage of MILF elements with the Jemaah Islamiyah, an al Qaeda–linked terrorist organization, is also a major source of internal security concern.[43] In 2008, there was the breakdown in the peace talks between the government and the MILF because of the controversy on the Memorandum of Agreement on Ancestral Domain (MOA-AD).[44]

Finally, local terrorism refers primarily to the threat posed by the ASG (Figure 1.4).[45] Based on the 2008 Threat Assessment of the AFP, the strength of the ASG was reduced to 383 members from its strength of 522 before the start of "Oplan Ultimatum" on August 1, 2006. The reduction of ASG forces was attributed to the continuing hot pursuit against the terrorist group. Though the strength of the group has been reduced, the AFP still considers the ASG as number one in the list of terrorist groups operating in the Philippines. The ASG is still capable of mounting terrorist attacks and conducting kidnapping activities.[46]

Though intelligence reports state that the ASG is already a spent force because of the capture and neutralization of some of its political leaders, it still has the capacity to exploit the Islamic religion to recruit members and solicit support.[47]

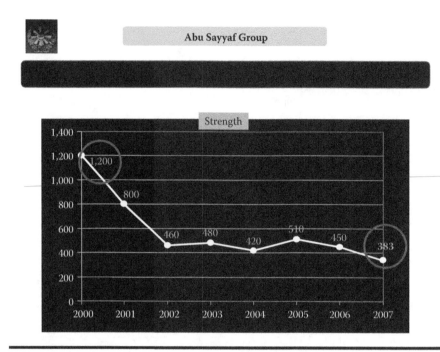

**Figure 1.4    Strength of the Abu Sayyaf Group, 2000–2007. (From the Office of the Deputy Chief of Staff for Intelligence, 2008.)**

Its cellular structure makes detection difficult; thus, it can still launch terrorist activities such as kidnapping and bombing operations far from its traditional areas of operation.[48] The ASG is also highly elusive due to its seaborne capability and its familiarity of terrain. The ASG has also been able to sustain itself through its clan/family support and informal alliances with the other secessionist groups in the Southern Philippines. The ASG members have also built capabilities to wage maritime terrorist attacks in Southern Mindanao, particularly in the Island of Solo and Tawi-Tawi.[49]

In January 2007, the AFP confirmed the deaths of Khadaffy Janjalani and Abu Sulaiman (Jainal Antel Sali, Jr.) as a result of this military offensive. Despite the killing of its key leaders and the reduction of its strength to 383 at the end of 2007, the AFP still considers the ASG as the number one terrorist threat in the Philippines because of its continuing intent and capability to wreak havoc. The ASG is believed to be currently headed by Yasser Igasan, a younger and more idealistic leader.

To surmount these three major threats to internal security, the Philippine government has adopted the Strategy of Holistic Approach (SHA) as the grand strategy to overcome insurgency problems (see Figure 1.5). The SHA consists of four major components: (1) political/legal/diplomatic, (2) socioeconomic/psychosocial, (3) peace and order/security; and (4) information.[50]

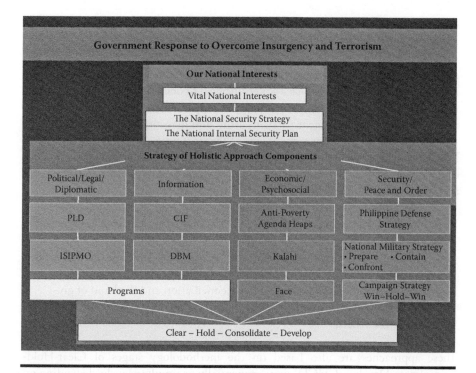

**Figure 1.5 The Strategy of Holistic Approach. (From the Cabinet Oversight Committee on Internal Security, July 2004.)**

The political/legal/diplomatic component pushes for "political reforms and institutional development to strengthen democratic institutions and empower the citizenry to pursue personal and community growth." This component aims to develop and propagate Philippine democracy to "confront the communist ideology." The cornerstone of this particular component is the peace process based on the "Six Paths to Peace" formula:

■ Pursuit of social, economic, and political reforms.
■ Consensus-building and empowerment for peace.
■ Peaceful, negotiated settlement with the different rebel groups.
■ Programs for reconciliation, reintegration, and rehabilitation.
■ Conflict management and protection of civilians caught in armed conflict.
■ Building and nurturing a climate conducive to peace.

The socioeconomic/psychosocial component, on the other hand, aims to alleviate poverty in the country through the acceleration of development programs of the Philippine government. This component also aims to develop and strengthen "a spirit of nationhood among the people, which includes developing national character/identity without losing cultural integrity."

The peace and order/security component aims "to protect the people from the insurgents and provide a secure environment for national development." More importantly, this component has the specific goal of denying the insurgents "access to their most important resource — popular support." This particular component aims to confront the insurgent party, its army, and mass organization.

Finally, the information component is the integrating component in the SHA. It "refers to the overall effort to advocate peace, promote public confidence in government and support government efforts to overcome insurgency through tri-media and interpersonal approaches."

The operational aspect of the SHA is the "left-hand" and "right-hand" approaches. In an interview, President Arroyo explains these approaches in the following words:

> How do we address this problem [of] insurgency? Through the right-hand and left-hand approach. [The] right hand is the full force of the law and the left hand is the hand of reconciliation and the hand of giving support to our poorest brothers so that they won't be encouraged to join the rebels.[51]

These approaches are also based on the methodology stages of Clear-Hold-Consolidate-Develop (CHCD) done sequentially or simultaneously, depending on the specific situation of a particular area in the Philippines.

The Clear stage aims to decisively defeat main armed groups in the Philippines with the AFP and the PNP as lead agencies.

The Hold stage aims to protect the people, defend the communities, and secure vital facilities and installations in the cleared areas with AFP, PNP, civil voluntary organizations (CVOs) and Civilian Armed Forces Geographic Units (CAFGUS) as lead agencies.

The Consolidate stage aims to reestablish government control and authority in contested areas with local government units (LGUs), NGOs, and people organizations (POs) as principal players.

Finally, the Develop stage aims to sustain the delivery of basic human development services to the people to address the root causes of insurgency in the country. In this stage, all concerned agencies of government play a developmental role.

In 2006, the Philippine government replaced the SHA with the strategy of "whole-of-government" (WOG) approach against terrorism and insurgency. Like the SHA, the WOG aims to address the root causes of security challenges facing the Philippine state (Figure 1.6). But the WOG pays greater attention to non-military means to defeat terrorism, which includes job creation in the rural areas, provisions of social services and infrastructure to communities, strengthening good governance at the national and local levels, and establishment of an effective local judiciary system.[52]

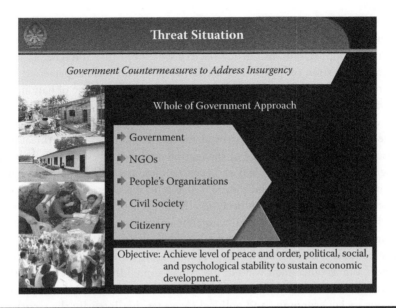

**Figure 1.6    The Whole-of-Government Approach. (From the Office of the Deputy Chief of Staff for Intelligence, 2008.)**

## Identity Politics and the Roots of Insurgency

Apparent from the practice of national security in the Philippines is the government's preoccupation with combating insurgency threats.[53] Although the government's SHA or WOG approach claims that it adopts a holistic, or whole-of-government, approach to counterinsurgency, it is, however, predominantly military in orientation. The SHA's operational methodology of CHCD is a predominantly military approach based on a counterinsurgency doctrine developed by American scholars.[54] The NISP, itself, admits that this counterinsurgency approach was effective in dismantling the *Partido Komunista ng Pilipinas* (Communist Party of the Philippines) in the 1950s during the time of President Ramon Magsaysay. Edward Lansdale of the Central Intelligence Agency (CIA) assisted Magsaysay in the implementation of this counterinsurgency approach.[55]

From an identity politics perspective, insurgency "threats" are symptoms of insecurities rather than causes of insecurities in the Philippines. Insurgency problems have root causes embedded in the identity problem of the Philippine nation–state exacerbated by the politics of social exclusion and socioeconomic marginalization of some sectors. By addressing the symptom rather than the cause of insurgency problems, counterinsurgency operations of the Philippine government aggravate rather than alleviate the problem of insecurities in the country.[56]

Thus, from the perspective of identity politics, the Philippine practice of national security has become an oppressive rather than a liberating tool where the "welfare and well-being" of the broad masses of Filipino people "are permanently protected and continuously enhanced." One peace advocate candidly observes that the Philippine government's approach to insurgency "lacks a sense of history and tends to focus in its operationalization on preserving the status quo from various perceived threats and threat groups."[57] Hence, the Philippine government's practice of national security is very conservative. It aims to primarily preserve the status quo, the main objective of which is to legitimize the regime in power (political security).

The Philippine state securitizes the challenges posed by so-called threat groups because they defy the legitimacy of the regime in power. They are threats because these groups menace the political and economic interests of the dominant groups capturing the apparatus of the state. From the perspectives of the threat groups, however, the Philippine state has become a threat to their security (societal security) through the government's counterinsurgency operations. The government's use of force against these threat groups endangers their ways of life. Thus, these threat groups make their own securitizing move by waging arms against the government to protect and advance their ways of life. These contending perspectives of threats and insecurities from the perspectives of the state and the threat groups create enormous social, economic, and political cleavages that intensify the security predicaments in the Philippines.

From the perspective of identity politics, insurgency problems persist in the Philippines because of the utter failure of the Philippine government to effectively address the cultural and social roots of rebellion, whether Communist or Islamic. While the present counterinsurgency campaign of the Philippine government can provide a short-term military solution to this internal security threat, a long-term comprehensive approach that addresses the root of Philippine insurgency is imperative. Filipinos who have joined insurgency movements in the Philippines have often done so "to seek the security that the state has failed to provide."[58] The Communist insurgency, for example, is rooted in the problem of economic injustices committed to peasant Filipinos in the countryside. Most NPA members belong to the peasant sector. About 75% to 90% of the Filipino peasants are landless, while the rest own or lease an average of one-half to one hectare.[59] The national peasant situation in the Philippines reveals that a maximum harvest of 40 to 100 cavans of palay is obviously not enough to sustain the daily needs of a farmer's family, and even more, to sustain the production costs of his farm in the next planting season.[60] Landlessness and economic deprivations lead them to utter desperation and ignite them to join the insurgency movement as a securitizing move to protect them against the oppression and exploitation of families with land.

The Muslim insurgency, on the other hand, is rooted in the injustice to the *Moro* identity.[61] Muslim insurgency in the Southern Philippines has long historical antecedents emanating from political, economic, and social causes.[62] Some Muslim Filipinos joined the Islamic insurgency because the Philippine State could not guarantee their freedom to govern themselves in their own way, according to their customs, traditions, and precepts of their religion.[63] Some Muslim Filipinos even resorted to terrorism to display their defiance to the regime in power.[64] As a matter of fact, Filipino Muslims have nurtured a sense of separatism (or what *Moro* calls "struggle for national liberation") for most of their history in the Philippines.[65]

Filipino Muslims struggled against Spanish, American, and Japanese colonialism for almost 400 years. Since the Philippines gained its independence in 1946, Filipino Muslim separatists have continued their struggle against what they call "Imperial Manila." To provide a just and lasting solution to the problem of Muslim insurgency in the Philippines, there is, therefore, a need to recognize the identity and way of life of Muslim Filipinos. The MILF advocacy, in fact, is anchored on identity politics as it urges the Philippine government to facilitate and ensure the establishment of a "system of life and governance suitable and acceptable to the *Bangsamoro* people."[66] The MILF is presently waging an arms struggle against the government as a securitizing move to protect the *Bangsamoro* identity. According to the late Hashim Salamat of the MILF, "Perhaps the *Bangsamoro* struggle for freedom and self-determination is the longest and bloodiest in the entire history of mankind."[67]

The lingering socioeconomic problems in the Philippines also aggravate the insurgency situation in the Philippines. The poverty situation is worsening, with over 40% of the Philippine population living below the poverty threshold or poverty line.[68] The National Statistics Coordination Board (NSCB) defines the poverty line as "the minimum income required to meet the food requirements and other nonfood basic needs." Based on the latest NSCB record, the annual per capita poverty threshold was estimated at P11,906 (around US$200) in 2002, a 2.5% increase over the 2000 threshold of P11,620. With this threshold, according to NSBC, a family of five members should have a monthly income of P4,961 (around US$90) to meet its food and nonfood basic needs. The worsening state of Philippine poverty creates a conducive environment for some people to join or support the country's insurgency movements. From this perspective, poverty and not insurgency is the greatest threat to Philippine national security.

The Philippines has also been suffering from a chronic budget deficit. It posted a budget deficit of P64.7 billion for the first four months of 2004 alone. During the first quarter of 2009, there was a 1.2% increase in the budget deficit. The ballooning foreign debt aggravates the budget crisis. According to the Freedom from Debt Coalition (FDC), a cause-oriented organization, Philippine total debt has reached an alarming figure of US$96 billion, including both public and private borrowings, foreign and domestic.[69] More than 31% of the national budget has been earmarked to debt servicing. Economists project that a rise in foreign interest rates would make repayment even more cumbersome and such scenario "would thrust the Philippines into a financial crisis of Argentinean proportions."[70] The seemingly unabated economic problems of the Philippines attract the marginalized sectors of the Philippine society to join insurgency movements. The failure of the Philippine government to alleviate the country's economic situation also unleashes the idea of the State as a "threat" to people's security.

## Toward a People-Oriented National Security Paradigm for the Philippines: Prospects for Human Security

To promote a more people-oriented national security paradigm for the Philippines and to provide a more comprehensive and truly long-term solution to the insurgency problem, the concept of human security is worth looking into.

Human security departs from a state-centered concept of security. Human security focuses on the security of the humanity rather than the security of the state. Instead of wasting government resources to fight insurgency, human security upholds the use of government resources to satisfy human needs and fulfill human aspirations. Human security is concerned with safeguarding and expanding people's fundamental freedoms. It is focused as much on protecting people from risks and pervasive threats as on growth with equity. Human security pays attention to individuals and communities, not just states. Human security is a concept that has emerged from efforts to devise new political strategies to ensure better protection of people.[71]

The United Nations Development Program (UNDP) initially launched the concept of human security as an "integrative" rather than a "defensive" concept in the *Human Development Report 1994*. This report identified seven interrelated dimensions of human security: economic security, food security, health security, environmental security, personal security, community security, and political security. The Commission on Human Security (CHS) further clarified the concept as "one that focuses on the individual and seeks protection from threats to human life, livelihood, and dignity, and the realization of full potential of each individual."[72] Furthermore, human security "addresses both conflict and developmental aspects including displacement, discrimination and persecution of vulnerable communities as well as insecurities related to poverty, health, education, gender disparities, and other types of inequality."[73]

The principle of human security is a very useful national security paradigm to address the root causes of violence and internal armed conflicts in the Philippines and thereby solve the insurgency problem. Because the process of state making and nation building in the Philippines is far from complete, the state-centric concept of security is therefore problematic when applied in the Philippine context. The concept of human security makes national security less problematic because the focus is the people and not the state.

The UNDP has proposed the human security framework as an alternative way of addressing the Mindanao problem.[74] The UNDP is also examining the roots of and current government responses to the Communist insurgency and Islamic secessionist movements in the Philippines within the frame of human security.[75] It is laudable to note that former National Security Adviser Roilo Golez, now a congressman, has introduced the concept of human security in one of his policy statements.[76] However, Golez applies the concept of human security in the context of regional security. Former President Fidel Ramos attempted to apply the concept of human security in the context of Philippine national security.[77] There is a need to translate this concept into a viable program of government.

## Conclusion

In theory, the Philippine government's definition of national security has become a comprehensive concept encompassing all dimensions: military, political, economic, sociocultural, and ecological. Its definition also attempts to be more people oriented by stressing the security needs of the people rather than the State.

In practice, however, national security in the Philippines caters more to the security of the State or regime security rather than the security of the people or human security. Its identification of threats to internal security and its concomitant strategy are still anchored on traditional perspectives and paradigms. The Philippine government continues to view insurgency as the major threat to national security.

Thinking outside the box, insurgency is the symptom and not the cause of insecurities in the Philippines. The insurgency problem in the country has deep root causes embedded in the identity dilemma of the Philippine nation–state and exacerbated by the politics of social exclusion and socioeconomic marginalization. The reason many Filipinos are mired in poverty and continue to suffer the multi-faceted consequences of backwardness and therefore ignite insurgency is that the Philippine state has lost its relative autonomy in insulating itself from the parochial interests of the dominant factions of the elite. Because the dominant elite captures the apparatuses of the state, the security of the elite has become the country's national security. The broad masses of the Filipino people have tremendous difficulties identifying with this brand of national security.

To make national security more reflective of the desires and aspirations of the Filipino people, there is an urgent need to strengthen the state's relative autonomy — a state that has the capability of resisting elite interests that run counter to societal needs, a state that has the capability to bring justice to the broad Filipino masses. As aptly stressed by former Defense Secretary Avelino Cruz, "the root cause of our insurgencies is injustice." The lack of justice, on the other hand, is the main cause of our country's current security problems. This message still holds water now and in the future.

## Endnotes

1. Barry Buzan, Ole Waever, and Jaap de Wilde, *Security: A New Framework of Analysis* (Boulder and London: Lynne Rienner Publishers, 1998).
2. Steve Smith, "The Contested Concept of Security," in Steve Smith and Amitav Acharya, *The Concept of Security Before and After September 11* (Singapore: Institute of Defence and Strategic Studies, May 2002), p. 1.

3. Muthiah Alagappa, "Rethinking Security: A Critical Review and Appraisal of the Debate," in his *Asian Security Practice: Material and Ideational Influences* (Stanford California: Stanford California Press, 1998), p. 29.

4. See Barry Buzan, "National Security and the Nature of the State," in *People, States and Fear: An Agenda for International Security Studies in the Post Cold War*, 2nd edition (London: Harvester Wheatsheaf, 1991), Chapter 2.

5. Alagappa, p. 30.

6. The most popular textbook on realism in the Philippines is Hans Morgenthau, *The Politics among Nations: The Struggle for Power and Peace* (New York: Alfred A. Knopft, Inc., 1948). For a classic book on realism, see Edward H. Carr, *The Twenty-Year's Crisis, 1919–1939: An Introduction to the Study of International Relations* (London: McMillan, 1939); and Edward Schwarzenberger, *Power Politics* (London: Cape Publishers, 1941).

7. Ralf Emmers, *Non-Traditional Security in the Asia–Pacific: The Dynamics of Securitization* (Singapore: Eastern Universities Press, 2004), p. 1.

8. Keith Krause and Michael Williams, "Broadening the Agenda of Security Studies: Politics and Methods," in *Mershon International Studies Review*, Vol. 40, No. 2 (October 1996), pp. 227–254.

9. Muthiah Alagappa, "Comprehensive Security: Interpretations in ASEAN Countries," in Robert Scalapino, Seizaburo Sato, Jusuf Wanandi, and Sung-joo Han (eds.), *Asian Security Issues: Regional and Global* (Berkeley: University of California Institute of East Asian Studies, 1988), pp. 50–78.

10. Alagappa, "Rethinking Security," p. 30.

11. Ibid.

12. Mohammed Ayoob, *The Third World Security Predicament: State Making, Regional Conflict and the International System* (Boulder: Lynne Rienner, 1995).

13. Brian L. Job (ed.), *The Insecurity Dilemma: National Security of Third World States* (Boulder: Lynne Rienner, 1992).

14. Keith Krause and Michael Williams (eds.), *Critical Security Studies* (Minneapolis: University of Minnesota Press, 1997).

15. Ken Booth, "Security and Emancipation" and "Security in Anarchy: Utopian Realism in Theory and Practice," in *International Affairs*, Vol. 67, No. 3 (1991), pp. 527–545. For an excellent summary, see Smith, p. 5.

16. Iris Marion Yong, *Justice and the Politics of Difference* (Princeton: Princeton University Press, 1990). Also see Drucilla Cornell, *Just Cause: Freedom, Identity, and Rights* (Lanham, MD: Rowman and Littlefield, 2000).

17. "Identity Politics," at: http://plato.stanford.edu/entries/identity-politics/ (accessed August 17, 2004).

18. Buzan, Waever, and de Wilde, p. 141.

19. Emmers, p. 2.

20. Buzan, Waever, and de Wilde, p. 142. Cited from Barry Buzan, Charles Jones, and Richard Little, *The Logic of Anarchy: Neorealism to Structural Realism* (New York: Columbia University Press, 1993), p. 35.

21. Ibid., p. 143.

22. Ibid. Also see Ernesto Laclau, *New Reflections on the Revolution of Our Time* (London: Verso, 1990).

23. Ibid., p. 23.

24. Maria Stern, "Politics of Identity," at: http://www.epd.uji.es/Comunes/Outlines/fall2004/stern.htm (accessed August 13, 2004).

25. For an elaborate discussion on the author's perspective of a weak state, see Rommel C. Banlaoi, "Globalization and Nation-Building in the Philippines: State Predicaments in Managing Society in the Midst of Diversity," in Yoichiro Sato (ed.), *Growth and Governance in Asia* (Honolulu: Asia–Pacific Center for Security Studies, 2004), pp. 203–214.

26. Buzan, Waever, and de Wilde, p. 141.

27. Ibid., p. 144.

28. Alan Collins, *Security and Southeast Asia: Domestic, Regional and Global Issues* (Singapore: Institute of Southeast Asia Studies, 2003), p. 64.

29. Ibid.

30. Buzan, Waever, and de Wilde, p. 120.

31. Ibid.

32. Collins, p. 24.

33. "Our National Security Strategy: A Reference Paper" (prepared by the Office of the National Security Adviser and the National Security Council Secretariat, September 1999).

34. Noel M. Morada and Christopher Collier, "The Philippines: States versus Society" in Muthiah Alagappa (ed.), *Asian Security Practice: Material and Ideational Influences* (Stanford California: Stanford California Press, 1998), p. 124.

35. Ibid.

36. Oscar L. Evangelista, *Building the National Community: Problems and Prospects and Other Historical Essays* (Quezon City: New Day Publishing, 2002), p. iii.

37. For an elaborate discussion on this topic, see Alexander P. Aguirre, "National Security: Concepts and Organization," in *National Security Review*, Vol. 18, No. 2 (2nd Semester 1998), pp. 18–23.

38. See Temario C. Rivera, *Landlords and Capitalists: Class, Family and State in Philippine Manufacturing.* (Quezon City: University of the Philippines Press, 1994).

39. Paul D. Hutchcroft, "The Politics of Privilege: Assessing the Impact of Rents, Corruption and Clientelism on Philippine Development," Institute for Popular Democracy Occasional Paper, No. 1 (February 1997).

40. Paul D. Huthcroft, *Booty Capitalism: The Politics of Banking in the Philippines* (Quezon City: Ateneo de Manila Press, 1998).

41. Aileen San Pablo Baviera, "Security Challenges of the Philippine Archipelago," *National Security Review*, Vol. 19, No. 2 (2nd Semester, 1999), pp. 1–12. This paper was first published in *Southeast Asian Affairs* (1998), pp. 213–221.

42. Soliman Santos, Jr., "Confronting Current Challenges on the Peace Front: Constraints and Opportunities" (Paper prepared for the conference "Waging Peace in the Philippines: Looking Back, Moving Forward" held in Ateneo de Manila University, December 10–12, 2002).

43. See Zachary Abuza, "Tentacles of Terror: Al-Qaeda's Southeast Asian Network," *Contemporary Southeast Asia*, Vol. 24, No. 3 (December 2002), pp. 427–465. Also see Rommel C. Banlaoi, *War in Terrorism in Southeast Asia* (Quezon City: Rex Book Store, 2004), also at: http://www.apan-info.net/terrorism/ banlaoiBook/index.htm.

44. For a detailed analysis, see International Crisis Group, *The Philippines: The Collapse of Peace in Mindanao*, Asia Briefing No. 83 (October 23, 2008).

45. For an excellent scholarly analysis of the origin and growth of the ASG, see Mark Turner, "Terrorism and Secession in the Southern Philippines: The Rise of the Abu Sayaff," *Contemporary Southeast Asia*, Vol. 17, No. 1 (June 1995), pp. 1–19.

46. For more detailed discussions on the ASG, see Rommel C. Banlaoi, *Al-Harakatul Islamiyah: Essays on the Abu Sayyaf Group* (Quezon City: Philippine Institute for Peace, Violence and Terrorism Research, 2008).

47. For a good perspective of the ASG problem, see Steven Rogers, "Beyond the Abu Sayyaf," *Foreign Affairs* (January/February 2004).

48. For a good analysis of the ASG threat, see Larry Niksch, "Abu Sayyaf: Target of Philippine–U.S. Anti-Terrorism Cooperation," *CRS Report for Congress* (January 25, 2002).

49. For ASG maritime terrorist capability, see Rommel C. Banlaoi, "Maritime Terrorism in Southeast Asia: The Abu Sayyaf Threat," *Naval War College Review*, Vol. 58, No. 4 (Autumn 2005), pp. 63–80; and Rommel C. Banlaoi, "The Abu Sayyaf Group: Threat of Maritime Piracy and Terrorism," in Lehr (ed.), *Violence at Sea: Piracy in the Age of Global Terrorism*, pp. 121–137.

50. Cabinet Oversight Committee on Internal Security, *National Internal Security Plan (NISP)*, Version 3. Restricted document. Quotations in this particular section come from this document, unless otherwise stated.

51. Marichu Villanueva, "Palace Announces RP-CPP Peace Talks Resume in Oslo, February 10–13," *The Philippine Star* (February 6, 2004), at: http://www.newsflash.org/2003/05/hl/hl019815.htm (accessed August 17, 2004).

52. Department of National Defense, *Defense Planning Guidance*, 2008–2013 (Quezon City: Department of National Defense, November 2006), p. 1.

53. The past practices of counterinsurgency in the Philippines have already been documented. See Alexander Aguirre and Ismael Villareal, *Readings on Counterinsurgency* (Quezon City: Pan Service Masters Consultants, Inc., 1987).

54. See for example John M. Collins, *Military Strategy: Principles, Practices, and Historical Perspectives* (Washington, DC: Brasseys, Inc., 2002). Chapter 16 of this book discusses counterinsurgency strategies of Clear-Hold-Consolidate-Develop.

55. See Walden Bello, *U.S.-Sponsored Low-Intensity Conflict in the Philippines* (San Francisco: Institute for Food & Development Policy, 1987).

56. Morada and Collier, p. 144.

57. Santos, p. 3.

58. Morada and Coller, p. 144.

59. "The National Peasant Situation: Philippines," at: http://www.bekkoame.ne.jp/_sukke/peasant4.htm (accessed August 18, 2004).

60. Ibid.

61. For some excellent studies on the Muslim problem, see T.J.S. George, *Revolt in Mindanao: The Rise of Islam in Philippine Politics* (New York, Melbourne, and Kuala Lumpur: Oxford University Press, 1980); Cesar A. Majul, *The Contemporary Muslim Movement in the Philippines* (Berkeley: Mizan Press, 1985); Peter Gowing, *Mosque and Moro: A Study of Muslims in the Philippines* (Manila: Federation of Christian Churches, 1964); and Cesar Majul, *Muslim in the Philippines* (Quezon City: University of the Philippines Press, 1973).

62. Andrew Tan, "The Indigenous Roots of Conflict in Southeast Asia: The Case of Mindanao," in Kumar Ramakrishna and See Seng Tan (eds.), *After Bali: The Threat of Terrorism in Southeast Asia* (Singapore: Institute of Defence and Strategic Studies, 2003), p. 98.

63. Orlando Quevedo, "The Root of Conflict in Mindanao," *MindaNews* (September 16, 2003).

64. See Djanicelle J. Berreveld, *Terrorism in the Philippines: The Bloody Trail of Abu Sayyaf, Bin Ladens East Asian Connection* (San Jose: Writers Club Press, 2001).

65. Catharin E. Dalpino, "Separatism and Terrorism in the Philippines: Distinctions and Options for U.S. Policy" (Testimony delivered before the Subcommittee on East Asia and the Pacific, House International Relations Committee of the U.S. Congress, June 10, 2003), p. 2.

66. Cited in Soliman Santos, Jr., *The Moro Islamic Challenge: Constitutional Rethinking for the Mindanao Peace Process* (Quezon City: University of the Philippines Press, 2001), p. 10.

67. For a critical analysis of this issue, see Kit Collier, "Dynamics of Muslim Separatism in the Philippines," in Damien Kingsburry (ed.), *Violence in Between: Conflict and Security in the Archipelagic Southeast Asia* (Singapore: Institute of Southeast Asian Studies, 2005), pp. 155–174.

68. For an excellent analysis of Philippine poverty, see Arsenio M. Balisacan, "Poverty in the Philippines: An Update and Reexamination," *Philippine Review of Economics*, Vol. 38, No. 1 (June 2001), pp. 15–52.

69. "Senator Legarda Decries Philippine Sovereign Debt Burden," at: http://deanjorgebo-cobo.blogspot.com/2003_05_06_DJB.html.

70. Catharin E. Dalpino, *Challenges for a Post-Election Philippines: Issues for U.S. Policy* (New York: Council on Foreign Relations Center for Preventive Action, May 11, 2004), p. 5.

71. For a brief description of the concept, see "The Concept of Human Security," at: http://www.eda.admin.ch/eda/e/home/foreign/humsec/Public/fshuse.html (accessed August 18, 2004).

72. For more elaboration see D. Mani, "Human Security: Concepts and Definitions," at: http://www.uncrd.or.jp/hs/doc/04a_10jun_mani_concept.pdf (accessed August 18, 2004).

73. Ibid.

74. Paul Oquist, "Mindanao and Beyond: Competing Policies, Protracted Peace Process and Human Security" (A 5th Assessment Mission Report of Multi-Donor Programme for Peace and Development in Mindanao, October 23, 2002).

75. "UNDP, HDN and NEDA Sign Project Document for 2004 Philippine Human Development Report on Peace, Human Security and Human Development" (July 5, 2004), at: http://www.undp.org.ph/news/readnews.asp?id=84 (accessed August 18, 2004).

76. Roilo Golez, "The Philippines and Regional Security in 2010," *National Security Review*, 40th Anniversary Issue (August 2003), pp. 15–22.

77. Fidel V. Ramos, "The Philippines in 2010: A Political Outlook," *National Security Review*, 40th Anniversary Issue (August 2003), pp. 23–36.

## Chapter 2

# Globalization and Nation-Building in the Philippines: State Predicaments in Managing Society in the Midst of Diversity after 9/11*

## Introduction

There is no doubt that globalization is one of the most powerful forces to have shaped the postwar era.[1] It is a force that has created a new world order, expanding the scale and speed of worldwide flows of capital, goods, services, people, ideas, and

* Revised and updated version of a paper originally published in Yoichiro Sato (ed.), *Growth and Governance in Asia* (Honolulu: Asia–Pacific Center for Security Studies, 2004), pp. 203–214. This paper was also presented to the conference "Growth and Governance in Asia," sponsored by the Asia–Pacific Center for Security Studies in Honolulu, Hawaii, on March 12–14, 2002.

27

even crimes across national borders, and increasing the complex interdependence of states and nonstate players.[2]

Everybody talks about globalization, yet there seems to be the absence of a single view on its impact on national and international security.[3] There is a view that globalization signals the demise of the nation–state and the rise of regional economies.[4] Others regard globalization as heralding the rise of a virtual state, undermining the traditional role played by the territorial state.[5]

Despite the advent of globalization, the state continues to be the most powerful player in global politics. The global campaign against terrorism in the aftermath of the September 11, 2001 attacks reaffirmed the centrality of state in the globalized world. While there may have been a proliferation of nonstate global players and the emergence of nontraditional global security issues that undermine the state's ability to fulfill its function of delivering services to the people, the state is still throwing its weight around and influencing the course of global events.

This chapter argues that the difficulties encountered by the Philippines in meeting the challenges of globalization stem from the nature of the Philippine state. The Philippines entered the global economic area with its domestic political economy unprepared. The Philippine state has failed to create the kind of fertile socioeconomic environment that would have prepared the country for global competition. The failure of the Philippine state to uplift the plight of the majority of its people also makes the country vulnerable to terrorist threats that undermine economic development.

## The Nature of the Philippine State

The Philippine state is not immune to the challenges of globalization. Like other states enjoying independence after World War II, the Philippine state is suffering the predicament of facing globalization while also undergoing the painful process of nation building in a highly diverse society. The twin problem of globalization and nation building intensifies the already gargantuan problems of the Philippine state in managing ethnic, religious, and socioeconomic diversities while building a common national identity. The security challenge posed by international terrorism compounds the dilemma of the Philippine state.

The state that developed after the granting of Philippine independence in 1946 may be described as both a premature and weak state. It is premature because the Philippine state was born before reaching the full term of statehood. That is, it became a state not through the development of a cohesive national consciousness but through the actions of its former colonial master, the United States. As a result, the state's legitimacy is contested in some regions of the country. The Philippine state's weakness, meanwhile, stems from its lack of relative autonomy from the parochial interests of dominant Filipino social classes, powerful political families and clans, influential landed elite, and wealthy Filipino capitalists.[6] The weakness of the Philippine state also produces and reproduces a contested notion of Philippine national security. As stated in Chapter 1, national security in developing countries usually means state security. Since most states in the developing world are weak states — meaning they are captives of the parochial interests of elite — state security means regime security, which is associated with the legitimacy of the regime in power. Filipino elite erroneously treats "regime security" or "regime legitimacy" as synonymous with national security.

The Philippine state is a premature and weak state because it lacks the following characteristics of a mature and strong state:

The ends and purposes of government have become settled and founded on a significant ideological consensus.

Most social groups (ethnic, religious, linguistic, and the like) have been successfully assimilated or have achieved protection, equality, or self-determination through autonomy, federalism, or other special devices.

Secessionism no longer constitutes a major goal of minorities. Territorial frontiers have become legitimized and sanctified through legal instruments.

Leaders are selected on the basis of a regular procedure, like elections. No group, family, clan, or sector can hold power permanently.

The military and policy organizations remain under effective civilian control.

The mores of governance preclude personal enrichment through various political activities.[7]

## Premature Philippine State

The Philippine state is a premature state because its claim for statehood is predominantly based on anticolonial sentiment rather on the natural bonds formed through common historical experience, consanguinity, and identification with a common language or a common religion.[8] The anticolonial sentiment in the Philippines was not even anchored on a popularly accepted notion of nationalism but rather on a limited or narrow elite conception articulated by 19th century Filipino thinkers initially spearheaded by Jose Rizal.[9] Anticolonial sentiments developed in the Philippines not as a result of a natural blossoming of "national consciousness" but as a result of overwhelming exasperation with the three centuries of oppression under the Spanish colonial administration and a half century of resentment under the American rule with a four-year colonial interception under the Japanese period.[10]

Another characteristic of a premature state is the question of legitimacy. The Philippine state is considered a legitimate state by virtue of international recognition and popular support. However, as in other premature states in the world, resistance groups such as local Communists, Muslim secessionists, and domestic terrorists are contesting the legitimacy of the Philippine state.

The premature nature of the Philippine state may also be attributed to the fact that it derives its legitimacy from the actions of its erstwhile colonial master, the United States. The Philippine state is a colonial creation supported by a minority of people constituting the elite, who in turn utilize the apparatuses of a weak state to get the needed "legitimacy" from the people through a defective electoral and party system.[11]

The Philippine state is a premature state because its identity is being challenged. The concept of a "Filipino national identity" is being contested by some Filipinos, especially those from the Muslim, Cordillera, and Cebu areas. Some Filipinos even identify themselves more with their regions or ethnic origins than with the "Filipino nation." The sense of Filipino regionalism seems to be greater than the sense of Filipino nationalism. One Filipino writer even laments:

> We are a paradox even to ourselves. The cliché question of identity, for instance, bedevils many of us, not because we are unsure of ourselves but because we cannot, to our own satisfaction, define ourselves.[12]

Before the colonial period, a Filipino identity never existed. Precolonial inhabitants of the archipelago called themselves *Ilocano, Bicolano, Cebuano, Tausug, Maranawan, Maguindanaons,* and so forth. The concept of "Filipino" came from the Spanish name "Felipe" in honor of King Philip. During the Spanish period, the use of "Filipino" was an elitist concept with racial connotations. It was used to describe the *Creoles,* Spaniards born in the Philippines. The natives were called *Indios* rather than *Filipinos.*[13] As a result of intermarriages between the *Creoles* and wealthy *Indios* and the emergence of Spanish and Chinese *mestizos,* the term *Filipino* eventually acquired a larger area of application in the 19th century.

Commemoration of the 100 years of the Philippine Revolution showed that the quest for Filipino nationalism and national identity still preoccupies many writers.[14] The Philippines remains a political community in search of national identity in an "imagined community."[15]

## A Weak State

The Philippine state is a weak state because its apparatuses have been captured or held by a family, clan, or prevailing group for the primary purpose of personal aggrandizement. The Philippine state continues to fail in insulating itself from the parochial interests of traditional families, clans, and groups that have dominated and benefited from Philippine politics.[16] These forces compete with the Philippine state in exercising effective control over its diverse population.[17]

As a result of the weakness of the Philippine state, "preferential access to state resources and state-conferred economic opportunities have traditionally been given to political elite, friends and relatives of the regime in control of the state power."[18] A weak Philippine state results in the "politics of privilege," a rent-seeking activity causing corruption and mismanagement of the Philippine political economy.[19] One scholar describes this as "booty capitalism," where private interests are pursued using public resources where the economic and political oligarchs use the apparatuses of the state.[20]

Compounding the situation is the paradoxical political setting in the Philippines where there is a structurally strong presidency operating in the context of a weak state. The Philippine presidency continues to be "the single most influential political position" in the country.[21]

There are two structural reasons for this. First, the Philippine president under a presidential system is the head of government. As the head of government, the Philippine president, like presidents in other systems, controls the bureaucracy as the chief administrator. As such, the Philippine president has tremendous control of the distribution and release of key personnel and material budgetary resources for the implementation of government programs nationwide.[22] If this system is combined with the "politics of clientelism" and with the "politics of privilege" in a weak Philippine state, the Philippine president becomes a "great patron" controlling the allocation of government resources in the form of various pork barrels.

Second, the Philippine president is also the head of state, which gives the president a very important symbolic function. Through its symbolic function, the Philippine president is the embodiment of state sovereignty. Thus, the Philippine president commands loyalty not only from the people but also from other political leaders. Combined with the patron–client characteristics of Philippine politics, the Philippine president has tremendous influence over legislation and legislators who prepare the national budget.[23] These make the Philippine president a very influential political figure in the country. A strong and influential presidency in a weak state opens a room for corruption aggravating the disparity of wealth in the Philippine society that creates socioeconomic, religious, and ethnic tensions.[24]

A premature and weak Philippine state has produced weak institutions of governance; thus, it is unable to manage the ethnic, religious, and socioeconomic diversities in its society. The advent of globalization and the global campaign against terrorism not only aggravate these diversities but also make the Philippine state and its institutions of governance even weaker for its failure to forge a national consensus necessary for nation building and socioeconomic development.

## Diversities and Tensions in Philippine Society

The Philippines is a highly diverse society. With an archipelago of more than 7,100 islands, its geographical setting has caused considerable fragmentation ethnically, religiously, and socioeconomically. Although there are some Filipino scholars arguing that the waters connecting these islands unite the Filipinos, these waters, however, only serve as channels of transportation facilitating interisland commerce and migration rather than transmitters of national unity and propagators of national consciousness. These waters even caused interisland conflicts due to ambiguous coastal boundaries and ineffective government policies. Aggravating the situation is the mountainous Philippine terrain making intraisland interaction even more problematic. The Philippines' physical geography has produced a highly diverse society, as indicated by the presence of at least five major languages spoken in the country with more or less 80 distinct ethnic dialects.

## Ethnic Diversity

Filipinos are products of mixed ethnicity composed of Malay, Chinese, and indigenous groups with Muslim, Spanish, and American influences. Of the three external influences, the impacts of the Americans are regarded to be the most pervasive and visible.[25] It is even argued that because of the great impact of the Americans on Philippine culture, Americans almost succeeded in replacing Filipino native cultures with theirs.[26] This prompted one American writer to describe Filipino culture as a "damage culture."[27] Filipino scholars, of course, vehemently denounce this.[28]

While the Malay group may dominate this ethnic mix, the most influential group is that of Chinese descent. The Filipino ethnic Chinese represent about 1.2 percent of the total Philippine population; more than half can be found in Metro Manila (primarily because the greater number of Chinese associations are in Metro Manila).[29] Most of the leading families in the Philippines controlling Philippine economy and politics have Chinese blood, including Jose Rizal, the Philippine national hero, and former President Corazon Cojuangco Aquino. Her cousin, Eduardo Cojuangco, Jr., once viewed as a crony of former President Ferdinand E. Marcos, chairs one of the biggest corporations in the Philippines — the San Miguel Corporation. Lucio Tan, identified as a crony of former President Joseph Estrada, is the wealthiest Filipino Chinese businessman, having owned the Philippine Airlines, the Asia Brewery, the Tanduay Distillery, and Fortune Tobacco Company.

The ethnic diversity of the Philippines is exemplified by the distribution of Filipino indigenous ethnic communities, which Filipinos call the *Lumads*. These indigenous groups are generally marginalized ones. The total number of indigenous ethnic communities in the country has not yet been accurately reported (partly due to their relative geographical isolation, making them inaccessible to census takers),[30] but the ethnic map of the Philippines identified at least 106 ethnic groups.[31] Most of these indigenous ethnic groups are found in the peripheral areas of the Philippines living in abject poverty and more often than not victims of government's developmental projects.[32]

## Religious Diversity

Although the dominant religion in the Philippines is Christianity (which is split into Roman Catholicism and Protestantism with its various denominations), the rise of Islam in the Philippines is a serious security concern not only because of the surge of Islamic fundamentalism being propagated by the minority but also because of the increasing confidence of Filipino Muslims in asserting their identity as a *Bangsamoro*, or *Moro* Nation. Some Muslim Filipinos refuse to call themselves Filipinos, viewing themselves more as members of the *Bangsamoro*. But the term *Moro* itself, like the concept of a Filipino, has alien roots. Spanish colonizers introduced the concept of *Moro* in the 16th century when they confused the Muslim people of Mindanao with *moors*.[33]

Were it not for the Spaniards who colonized the Philippines for 333 years using the Roman Catholic religion, the country would have been a Muslim state like its Southeast Asian neighbors.[34] As early as the 15th century, Islamic religion already existed in Sulu Archipelago in the southwest Philippines. By the mid-16th century, two sultanates had been established as far north as Manila.[35] Spaniards arrived in the Philippines in the midst of this wave of Islamic proselytism.[36]

Filipino Muslims are more active now in the politics of the Philippine nation–state.[37] They are more vocal because of the global and regional trends in Islamic resurgence.[38] The increase in "democratic space" as a result of the demise of authoritarian tendency in the Philippines is also enabling Muslim Filipinos to articulate their causes more boldly. The revolt in Mindanao is a function of the rise of Islam in Philippine politics.[39]

There are three major Muslim resistance groups, not to mention the various ethnic Muslim groupings such as the *Tausugs, Maguindanaons,* or *Maranawans*. These resistance groups called themselves Philippine Mujahideen.[40] All of them have once proclaimed a secessionist stand in their organizations' history because of socioeconomic and political motivations.[41]

The oldest resistant Muslim group is the *Moro* National Liberation Front (MNLF) founded by an ethnic Tausug leader, Nur Misuari. In 1974, the MNLF declared the establishment of the *Bangsamoro* Republic.[42] It has also received recognition from the Organization of the Islamic Conference as the "sole and legitimate representative" of the *Bangsamoro* people. The MNLF has since concluded peace talks with the Philippine government.[43] But the MNLF was split into three factions: the Anti-Nur Misuari MNLF faction, the Pro-Nur Misuari MNLF faction, and the MNLF Integrees. The Pro-Nur Misuari faction (otherwise known as the Misuari Breakaway Group or MBG) was alleged to be the main culprit in the Sulu massacre in 2002 that led to the arrest of Nur Misuari.

The second group is the *Moro* Islamic Liberation Front (MILF), which claims to be the vanguard of the Islamic movement in Mindanao. The late Hashim Salamat, supported by the ethnic Maguindanaons of Mindanao, founded the MILF in 1977 when he and his supporters split from the MNLF.[44] The MILF also has a splinter group, the Pentagon Group, now engaged in various criminal kidnapping and extortion activities. The Philippine government entered into peace talks with the MILF, but as of this writing there is an impasse in the peace talks because of the contested issue of ancestral domain.

The third group is the violent extremist Abu Sayyaf Group (ASG), which is believed to have an historical link with the al Qaeda network of Osama bin

Laden. The ASG aims to establish an Iranian-style Islamic State in the Southern Philippines.[45] Like the MNLF, the ASG was also factionalized[46] (see Chapter 3). According to various AFP (Armed Forces of the Philippines) reports, there were two major factions of the ASG operating independently in two major areas in the Southern Philippines: Basilan and Sulu. Khadafy Janjalani still heads the Basilan-based ASG. Galib Andang, otherwise known as Commander Robot, headed the Sulu-based ASG. But the Sulu group unexpectedly lost its leader with the capture of Commander Robot in December 2003. Commander Robot was eventually killed in a bloody jailbreak attempt on March 15, 2005.

Other AFP reports talked of another faction of ASG operating in Zamboanga City with Hadji Radzpal as the main leader. But Hadji Radzpal was also identified by other intelligence sources as one of the leaders of the Sulu-based faction of the ASG. Local leaders have denied the existence of an ASG faction in Zamboanga City.

The Basilan-based ASG was composed of 73 members as of 2002. These members were ASG hard-liners composed of 30 personal followers of Khadafy Janjalani, 30 personal followers of Isnilon Hapilon, and 13 followers of Abu Sabaya. The group of Hapilon was the main security arm of the Basilan-based ASG. The group of Abu Sabaya, on the other hand, joined the group of Khadafy Janjalani in running the daily planning and administrative affairs of the group. The Philippine military claimed that it killed Sabaya and two others in a naval encounter in June 2002. But Sabaya's body was never found, triggering speculations that he may still be alive despite the AFP's repeated pronouncements that Sabaya was among those who died and drowned in the waters of Sibuco Bay in Zamboanga del Norte.[47]

The Sulu-based ASG has become a loose organization of Muslim secessionist fighters loyal to the late Commander Robot. This faction of the ASG was responsible for the kidnapping of 21 tourists spending a vacation in a resort in Sipadan Island of Malaysia on April 23, 2000. The Basilan-based and Sulu-based factions of the ASG were also divided into different groups with their own leaders. As of 2002, the Basilan-based faction was composed of 10 armed groups and the Sulu-based faction was composed of 16 armed groups.

The ASG is the major government irritant in Mindanao because of its criminal activities such as kidnapping, extortion, and murder. It is listed as one of the international terrorists linked with al Qaeda. The Philippine government is presently implementing the policy of hot pursuit against the ASG.

## Socioeconomic Diversity

Pervasive poverty is the main national security problem of the Philippines.[48] According to the latest estimates of the National Statistics Office (NSO) released in 2006, approximately 24 out of 100 Filipino families did not earn enough money in 2003 to satisfy their basic food and nonfood requirements.[49] These figures indicate that a significant number of Filipino people are living below the minimum basic needs framework, which states that[50]:

> In order to sustain life, the family needs to be healthy, to eat the right kind of food, to drink safe water and to have good sanitation.
> To protect the family from any harm or danger, it needs to be sheltered in a peaceful and orderly environment and it should have livelihood that can support its family members to acquire their basic needs such as food, shelter, etc.
> To be able to attain the survival and security needs of the family, its members should be educated and be functionally literate in order to participate actively in any community development and to take care of its psycho-social needs.[51]

Filipinos were severely affected by the 1997 Asian financial crisis. In the latest survey, about 94% of the total Filipino families reported that they were affected by the financial crisis, whether they came from the lowest 40% or highest 60% income bracket. In response to the financial crisis, 1 in every 2 families in the lowest 40% changed their eating pattern, while 3 out of 10 families increased their working hours.[52] The 2008 global financial crisis also affected the Filipinos. According to the September 2008 study of IBON Foundation, the Philippines is vulnerable to the global economic crisis because of the country's chronic dependence on exports, foreign investment, and debt — including official development aid that ends up as foreign debt.[53]

## The Impact of Globalization on Nation-Building

The advent of globalization is compounding the already complicated problem of nation building in the Philippines. One reason is that globalization has not produced the same benefits for all ethnic and interest groups in the Philippine society. Combined with the lack of a strong and effective "safety net," globalization is exacerbating poverty and thereby intensifying ethnic, religious, and socioeconomic diversities. This constricts the capacity of the Philippine state to develop and to build the Filipino nation and to achieve economic development.

One product of this is the persistent separatist clamor of Filipino ethnic groups, particularly Muslim groups that feel they are being neglected in the process of globalization and they would be better off independent from the central Philippine government. Since the colonial times, Filipino Muslims have searched constantly for the kind of leadership that will transform their hopes and aspirations into economic and social reality.[54] Some Filipino Muslims who have become desperate with the situation have resorted to terrorist attacks to express their grievances.

Other interest groups have also expressed concern about the negative effects of globalization.[55] A study by the International Forum on Globalization found that globalization policies have contributed "to increased poverty, increased inequality between and within nations, increased hunger, increased corporate concentration, decreased social services and decreased power of labor vis-à-vis global corporations."[56]

Globalization has led to the widening of socioeconomic disparities in the Philippines as some social actors are given greater opportunities than others.[57] It has favored the more mobile, the more adaptable, and the globally scarce commodities and human skills as opposed to immobile, self-contained, and globally abundant ones. Traditional Philippine agriculture, for instance, has been unable to cope with globalization and, because of the relatively high price of Philippine agricultural products, "increasingly represents a drag on manufacturing and the more dynamic and globally tradable parts of the economy."[58]

There are countries where globalization has had positive effects on economy and politics. It has been noted that "effective adaptations to globalization are well under way in a number of developing countries."[59] As a result of globalization, some developing countries "have increased their share of trade in goods and services, and new technologies have created jobs and stimulated dynamic local economies."[60] Globalization is also said to have facilitated the spread of democratic governments in the developing countries and helped sustain "the legitimacy of those that have been created in recent years."[61] As a consequence of global integration brought by the process of globalization, improvements in the real incomes of those people in the developing economies can be expected.[62]

Globalization is not the root cause of the tensions in Philippine society. Poverty causes these tensions, and poverty is the result of weak institutions of governance. This weakness stems from the premature and weak nature of the Philippine state.

## Globalization and the Philippine State

If globalization has intensified socioeconomic divisions and conflicts, this is attributed to the inability of the Philippine state to implement policies preparing the country for global competitiveness. The Philippines finds it hard to cope with the globalization process because its weak institutions of governance have failed to create suitable socioeconomic and political conditions that will attract more capital and technology from both domestic and foreign sources necessary for economic growth. To overcome the challenges and reap the benefits of globalization, the weak and premature Philippine state needs to be reinvented through institutional reforms aimed at strengthening its institutions of governance and creating a suitable environment for growth.

## Reform of the Bureaucracy

The Philippines has a very inefficient bureaucracy, especially its revenue-generating agencies. The Philippine bureaucracy "has suffered from the limited technical skills and low morale of its personnel and has to live with recruitment rules and promotion procedures heavily tainted by patronage politics."[63] Under a premature and weak state, Philippine bureaucracy is marred by rampant corruption favoring the families and friends of the bureaucrats.[64]

Inefficient and corrupt bureaucracy intensifies the socioeconomic, religious, and ethnic tensions in the Philippines as it hampers the delivery of needed services to the people. It also leaves the Philippines unprepared to cope with the challenges of globalization.

Reforming the Philippine bureaucracy is a gargantuan task requiring a combination of a merit-based recruitment system and a clear-cut career incentives scheme that is able to attract and sustain the best and brightest into the civil service.[65] To reform the Philippine bureaucracy, the World Bank suggests the following measures:

> Limit the scope of patronage in public employment by depoliticizing the civil service and strictly regulating the use of casual and contractual workers.
>
> Decompress the government pay scale to provide competitive salaries up to senior levels.
>
> Strengthen performance evaluation, implement related awards and sanctions, and enhance meritocracy in appointments and promotions.[66]

## Electoral Reform

Philippine elections are characterized by irregularities, fraud, manipulation, vote buying, intimidation, and violence.[67] The prevalence of election fraud during the counting of ballots, the use or threat of force by political warlords to compel people to vote in their favor, and vote-buying practices among politicians are undermining the democratic process. Although the Philippines is among the few Asian countries with a long historical experience in electoral politics, Philippine elections are nothing more than overt expressions of competing personal interests and ambitions of party leaders who belong to dominant families, clans, landlords, and business groups.[68]

Despite the introduction of the Party-List Law to allow more room for sectoral representations in the House and to encourage small political parties to participate in local elections, marginalized sectors are still underrepresented because of patronage politics and the strong kinship system in the Philippines. Ironically, many "small parties" participating in the party-list system of election are "satellite" parties of traditional politicians.[69] Among the measures to reform Philippine elections are the following:

- Allow absentee voting.
- Computerize the election procedure and the counting of votes.
- Implement stiffer penalties for election offenses.
- Regulate campaign finance.
- Make electoral fraud a heinous crime under the law.

Chapter 7 discuses the nature of Philippine elections and its implications for national security.

## Political Party Reform

Philippine political parties are ideologically undifferentiated, except the underground Communist party. There is only one ideology guiding all electoral parties in the Philippines, the liberal ideology. As a result, Philippine political parties are highly personalistic rather than programmatic.

The most notable features of Philippine political parties are its minimal intraparty solidarity, endemic interparty switching, and similarity of all parties in terms of programs, organizations, and campaign strategies.[70] Filipino political party leaders are usually political patrons coming from the ranks of traditional politicians who are landlords, businessmen, and professional citizens coming from wealthy families and clans. These politically undifferentiated and oligarchic parties trigger party turncoatism and create politicians who are "political butterflies." Despite the constitutional mandate allowing a multiparty system in the Philippines, political parties in the Philippines, in general, are either administration parties or opposition parties.

As such, Philippine political parties are weak. Their weakness mirrors that of the Philippine state, which prevents the effective management of ethnic, religious, and socioeconomic tension in the country. Without a strong party system with a clear program of government, the Philippines will continue to be plagued with persistent national crises.

Since political parties are vital instruments in the articulation of demands and desires of the people and important vehicles to mobilize the people to achieve successful economic growth and effective governance, there is a move underway to reform and strengthen the Philippine party system. Suggested measures include the following:

- Increase party discipline by implementing the concept of "party whip" penalizing "political butterflies."
- Require political parties to build a reliable mass political base.
- Adopt measures to monitor continuity of party organization whose life span is not dependent on the life span of current leaders.
- Implement measures penalizing political parties showing incapability to have permanence in their organizational setups.

## Socioeconomic Reform

To bridge the gap between the few who are rich and the many who are poor, the Philippine government has formulated a series of medium-term development plans with socioeconomic reform packages. The Philippine government even accepts the view that successful economic growth and effective governance cannot be achieved without a strategy for socioeconomic reform. However, the weakness of the Philippine state is preventing it from implementing socioeconomic reform programs. Thus, implementation of socioeconomic reform programs is a function of institutional reform, which has been discussed above.

# Conclusion

The Philippine state is in the predicament of having to face globalization while also undergoing the painful process of nation building in a highly diverse society. The weakness of the Philippine state in facing these challenges is causing the pervasive poverty that results in ethnic, socioeconomic, and religious tensions. As aptly argued by Francis Fukuyama, a weak and incompetent state is the source of many problems in the developing world. These problems include local insurgency and domestic terrorism. State building is therefore one of the most important issues for the world community today.[71] To overcome the many governance problems in the Philippines, there is a need to strengthen the Philippine state and its institutions of governance through bureaucratic, electoral, party, and socioeconomic reforms.

# Endnotes

1. Jeffrey Frankel, "Globalization of the Economy," in Joseph Nye and John Donahue (eds.), *Governance in a Globalizing World* (Washington, DC: Brookings Institution Press, 2000), p. 45.
2. See Robert O. Keohane and Joseph S. Nye, Jr., "Globalization: What's New? What's Not? (And So What?)" *Foreign Policy*, No. 118 (Spring 2000), pp. 104–119. Also see their *Power and Interdependence: World Politics in Transition*, 3rd edition (New York: Longman, 2000); and *Transnational Relations and World Politics* (Cambridge: Harvard University Press, 1972).
3. Graham Allison, "The Impact of Globalization on National and International Security," in Joseph Nye and John Donahue (eds.), *Governance in a Globalizing World* (Washington, DC: Brookings Institution Press, 2000), pp. 72–85.
4. Kenichi Omae, *The End of Nation States and the Rise of Regional Economies* (New York: Free Press, 1995).
5. Richard Rosecrance, *The Rise of Virtual State: Wealth and Power in the Coming Century* (New York: Basic Books, 1999).
6. See Temario C. Rivera, *Landlords and Capitalists: Class, Family and State in Philippine Manufacturing* (Quezon City: University of the Philippines, 1994).

7. See K.J. Holsti, "War, Peace and the State of State," *International Political Science Review*, Vol. 16, No. 4 (1995), pp. 332–333.

8. Ibid., p. 327.

9. See Floro C. Quibuyen, *Rizal, American Hegemony and Philippine Nationalism: A Nation Aborted* (Quezon City: Ateneo de Manila Press, 1999). Also see Leon Ma. Guerrero, *The First Filipino: A Biography of Jose Rizal* (Quezon City: Guerrero Publishing, 1998); and John N. Shumacher, *The Making of a Nation: Essays on Nineteenth-Century Filipino Nationalism* (Quezon City: Ateneo de Manila Press, 1991).

10. See Onofre D. Corpuz, *The Roots of the Filipino Nation*, Vols. 1–2 (Quezon City: Aklahi Foundation, Inc., 1989).

11. Rommel C. Banlaoi and Clarita R. Carlos, *Political Parties in the Philippines: From 1900 to the Present* (Makati City: Konrad Adenauer Foundation, 1997). Also see Clarita R. Carlos and Rommel C. Banlaoi, *Elections in the Philippines: From Precolonial Period to the Present* (Makati City: Konrad Adenauer Foundation, 1997).

12. F. Sionil Jose, *We Filipinos: Our Moral Malaise, Our Heroic Heritage* (Manila: Solidaridad Publishing House, 1999), p. 2.

13. Renato Constantino, *The Making of a Filipino: A Story of Philippine Colonial Politics* (Quezon City: Foundation for Nationalist Studies, 1969), pp. 5–9.

14. Elmer Ordonez (ed.), *Nationalist Literature: A Centennial Forum* (Quezon City: University of the Philippines Press and the Philippine Writers Academy, 1995).

15. Benedict Anderson, *Imagined Communities: Reflections on the Origin and Spread of Nationalism* (London: Verso, 1983).

16. For excellent discussions on the role of families and clans in Philippine politics, see Dante C. Simbulan, *The Modern Principalia: The Historical Evolution of the Philippine Ruling Oligarchy* (Quezon City: University of the Philippines Press, 2005). Also see Bobby Tuazon (ed.), *Oligarchic Politics: Elections and Party-List System in the Philippines* (Quezon City: Center for People Empowerment and Governance, 2007); and Sheila Coronel, Yvonne Chua, Luz Rimban, and Booma Cruz, *The Rulemakers: How the Wealth and Well-Born Dominate Congress* (Quezon City: Philippine Center for Investigative Journalism, 2004).

17. The author's use of a weak state concept is heavily influenced by Joel Migdal, *Strong Societies and Weak States* (Princeton: Princeton University Press, 1988).

18. Franciso A. Magno, "Weak State, Ravage Forests: Political Constraints to Sustainable Upland Management in the Philippines," *Philippine Political Science Journal*, Nos. 33–36 (June 1991–December 1992), pp. 81–82.

19. Paul D. Hutchcroft, "The Politics of Privilege: Assessing the Impact of Rents, Corruption, and Clientelism on Philippine Development," *Institute for Popular Democracy Occasional Paper No. 1* (February 1997).

20 Paul D. Hutchroft, *Booty Capitalism: The Politics of Banking in the Philippines* (Quezon City: Ateneo de Manila Press, 1998).

21. Felipe B. Miranda, "Leadership and Political Stabilization in a Post-Aquino Philippines," *Philippine Political Science Journal*, Nos. 33–36 (June 1991–December 1992), p. 156.

22. Ibid.

23. See Olivia C. Caoili, *The Philippine Congress: Executive-Legislative Relations and the Restoration of Democracy*, *Philippine Political Science Journal*, Nos. 33–36 (June 1991–December 1992).

24. For an excellent account of corruption and governance in the Philippines, see Sheila Coronel (ed.), *Pork and Other Perks: Corruption and Governance in the Philippines* (Makati City and Quezon City: Philippine Center for Investigative Journalism, the Institute for Popular Democracy and the Evelio B. Javier Foundation, 1998).

25. F. Landa Jocano, *Filipino Prehistory: Rediscovering Precolonial Heritage* (Metro Manila: Punlad Research House, 2000), p. 37.

26. Ibid.

27. James Fallows, "A Damaged," *The Atlantic Monthly* (November 1987), pp. 49–58.

28. See Paz P. Mendez and F. Landa Jocano, *Culture and Nationhood: A Philosophy of Education for Filipinos* (Manila: Centro Escolar University Research and Development Center, 1991), pp. 1–6.

29. Teresita Ang See, "The Ethnic Chinese as Filipinos" in Leo Suryadinata (ed.), *Ethnic Chinese as Southeast Asians* (Singapore and London: Institute of Southeast Asian Studies, 1997), p. 174. For additional readings on Filipino ethnic Chinese, see Chinben See, "The Ethnic Chinese in the Philippines," in Leo Suryadinata (ed.), *The Ethnic Chinese in the ASEAN States: Bibliographical Essays* (Singapore and London: Institute of Southeast Asian Studies, 1989), pp. 203–220.

30. F. Landa Jocano, *Filipino Ethnic Indigenous Communities: Patterns, Variations, and Typologies* (Metro Manila: Punlad Research House, 1998), p. 21.

31. Ibid.

32. See F. Landa Jocano, *Problems and Methods in the Study of Philippine Indigenous Ethnic Cultures: A Preliminary Overview* (Quezon City: University of the Philippines Asian Center, 1994).

33. Peter Gowing, *Mosque and Moro: A Study of Muslims in the Philippines* (Manila: Federation of Christian Churches, 1964). Also see Cesar Majul, *Muslims in the Philippines* (Quezon City: University of the Philippines Press, 1973).

34. John Pelan, *The Hispanization of the Philippines* (Madison: University of Wisconsin Press, 1959).

35. David Wurfel, *Filipino Politics: Development and Decay* (Quezon City: Ateneo de Manila Press, 1988), p. 2.

36 Ibid. Also see Peter Gowing, ed., *Understanding Islam and Muslims in the Philippines* (Quezon City: New Day Publishers, 1988).

37. Patricio N. Abinales, "Mindanao in the Politics of the Philippine Nation-State: A Brief Sketch," *Philippine Political Science Journal*, Nos. 33–36 (June 1991–December 1992), pp. 120–141.

38. Mehol K. Sadain, *Global and Regional Trends in Islamic Resurgence: Their Implications on the Southern Philippines* (Pasay City: Foreign Service Institute, 1994).

39. See T.J.S. George, *Revolt in Mindanao: The Rise of Islam in Philippine Politics* (New York, Melbourne, Kuala Lumpur: Oxford University Press, 1980).

40. Alvaro Andaya, *Philippine Mujahideen, Mandirigma* (Manila: Published by the author, 1994).

41. See Samuel K. Tan, "The Socioeconomic Dimension of Moro Secessionism," *Mindanao Studies Reports*, No. 1 (1995). Also see his "The Moro Secessionist Movement in the Philippines," *Secessionist Movements in Comparative Perspectives* (London: International Center for Ethnic Studies, 1990).

42. Cesar A. Majul, *The Contemporary Muslim Movement in the Philippines* (Berkeley: Mizan Press, 1985).

43. See Abraham S. Iribani, "GRP-MNLF Peace Talks: 1992–1996" (MA Thesis: National Defense College of the Philippines, 2000).

44. See Margarita Cojuangco, "The Role of the MILF in the Mindanao Problem" (MA Thesis: National Defense College of the Philippines, 1988).

45. Jukpili M. Wadi, "Philippine Political Islam and the Emerging Fundamentalist Strand," in Carmencita C. Aguilar (ed.), *Cooperation and Conflict in Global Society* (Quezon City: International Federation of Social Science Organization, 1996).

46. For more details, see Rommel C. Banlaoi, "Leadership Dynamics in Terrorist Organizations in Southeast Asia: The Abu Sayyaf Case" in John T. Hanley, Kongdan Oh Hassig and Caroline F. Ziemski (eds.), *Proceedings of the International Symposium on the Dynamics and Structures of Terrorist Threats in Southeast Asia* (Alexandria, VA: Institute for Defense Analyses, 2005).

47. "Sabaya's Death Not the End of Abu Sayyaf, says Basilan Bishop," *MindaNews* (June 29, 2002), at: http://www.mindanews.com/2002/07/1st/nws29abu.html (accessed August 30, 2004). A very close friend of mine who was a member of the Special Warfare Group (SWAG) who did the actual operation against Abu Sabaya told me that Sabaya was indeed killed in the said battle.

48. For an excellent conceptual l and practical reading of Philippine poverty, see Arsenio M. Balisacan, "What Does It Take to Win the War against Poverty in the Philippines?" in Eduardo T. Gonzales (ed.), *Reconsidering the East Asian Economic Model: What's Ahead for the Philippines* (Pasig City: Development Academy of the Philippines, 1999), pp. 83–109. Also see Anna Marie A. Karaos, "Urban Governance and Poverty Alleviation in the Philippines," in Emma Porio (ed.), *Urban Governance and Poverty Alleviation in Southeast Asia: Trends and Prospects* (Quezon City: Ateneo de Manila University, 1997).

49. NSCO Web site, "FAQs on the Official Poverty Statistics of the Philippines," at: http://www.nscb.gov.ph/poverty/FAQs/default.asp.

50. NSO Web site, "Annual Poverty Indicators Survey" of the National Statistics Office, at: http://www.census.gov.ph/data/sectordata/ap98.html.

51. Ibid.

52. Ibid.

53. "Philippines Vulnrable to Global Financial Crisis: Ibon," at: http://www.pinoypress.net/2008/09/18/philippines-vulnerable-to-global-financial-crisis-ibon/.

54. See Romulo M. Espaldon, "Towards a National Muslim Development Policy" (undated manuscript). Espaldon was a Minister of Muslim Affairs and Ambassador to Saudi Arabia and Egypt.

55. For an excellent reference on this topic, see Perlita M. Frago, Sharon M. Quinsaat, and Verna Dinah Q. Viajar, *Philippine Civil Society and the Globalization Discourse* (Quezon City: Third World Studies Center, 2004).

56. Debi Barker and Jerry Mander (eds.), *Does Globalization Help the Poor? A Special Report* (San Francisco, California: International Forum on Globalization, 2002).

57. Emmanuel S. De Dios, "Between Nationalism and Globalization," in Filomena S. Sta. Ana III (ed.), *The State and the Market: Essays on a Socially Oriented Philippine Economy* (Quezon City: Action for Economic Reforms, 1998), p. 28.

58. Ibid.

59. Merilee S. Grindle, "Ready or Not: The Developing World and Globalization," in Joseph Nye and John Donahue (eds.), *Governance in a Globalizing World* (Washington, DC: Brookings Institution Press, 2000), p. 178.
60. Ibid.
61. Ibid.
62. Frankel, pp. 45–71.
63. Temario C. Rivera, "Democratic Governance and Late Industrialization," in Filomena S. Sta. Ana III (ed.), *The State and the Market: Essays on a Socially Oriented Philippine Economy* (Quezon City: Action for Economic Reforms, 1998), p. 257.
64. ·Alfred McCoy (ed.), *An Anarchy of Families: State and Families in the Philippines* (Madison: University of Wisconsin–Madison Center for Southeast Asian Studies, 1993).
65. Rivera (1998), p. 257.
66. See World Bank, "Combating Corruption in the Philippines," at: http://www.world-bank.org/eapsocial/library/corruption.htm.
67. See Luzviminda Tangcangco, *The Anatomy of Electoral Fraud* (Manila: MJAGM, 1992) and Ma. Aurora Catillo et. al., *Manipulated Elections* (Quezon City: University of the Philippines, 1985).
68. Renato S. Velasco, "Campaign Tactics in the 1987 Legislative Elections," in Renato Velasco and Sylvano Mahiwo (ed.), *The Philippine Legislature Reader* (Quezon City: Great Books Publishers, 1989), p.62.
69. See Soliman M. Santos, Jr., "The Philippine Tries the Party-List System: A Progressive Approach," and David Wurfel, "The Party-List Elections: Sectoral or National? Success or Failure?" both in *Kasarinlan: A Philippine Quarterly of Third World Studies*, Vol. 13, No. 2 (4th Quarter, 1997).
70. See Carl Lande, *Leaders, Factions and Parties: The Structure of Philippine Politics* (New Haven: Yale University Southeast Asian Studies Monograph Series No. 6, 1964).
71. Francis Fukuyama, *State-Building: Governance and World Order in the Twenty-First Century* (London: Profile Books Ltd., 2004).

## Chapter 3

# "Radical Muslim Terrorism" in the Philippines[*]

## Introduction

Though the problem of terrorism has become a very serious global security threat, it has deep domestic roots in the Philippines. The threat of international terrorism is inherently local in origin (see Chapter 4). There is even a view that al Qaeda, the most notorious network of radical Muslim terrorist organizations to date, will return to their local roots.[1] Thus, it is essential to consider the domestic milieu of the terrorist threat to fully grasp its complexities and nuances.

The Philippines is not spared from the threats posed by domestic terrorism. Linkages of domestic terrorist organizations in the Philippines with international terrorist organizations confound the virulence of these threats. The Philippine government even regards the local Communist insurgency as a very serious terrorist problem.

This chapter, however, focuses on terrorist threats in the Philippines emanating from radical Muslim groups. Although the problem of terrorism is not entirely a radical Muslim phenomenon, the lion's share of terrorist acts and the most devastating of them in recent years are said to have been perpetrated by radical Muslim organizations.[2] This chapter examines the following six radical Muslim

---

[*] Revised and updated version of a paper originally published in Andrew Tan, ed., *Handbook on Terrorism and Insurgency in Southeast Asia* (London: Edward Elgar Publishing, Limited, 2007), pp. 194–224.

organizations that have been reported to have committed acts of terrorism: the Nur Misuari Breakaway Group (MBG) of the *Moro* National Liberation Front (MNLF), the *Moro* Islamic Liberation Front (MILF), the Abu Sayyaf Group (ASG), the Rajah Solaiman Islamic Movement (RSIM), the Abu Sofia (AS) group, and the Al-Khobar Group (AKG). This chapter also includes a brief discussion on the concept of radical Muslim terrorism and on the historical context of the radicalization of selected Muslim organizations in the Philippines.

## What Is Radical Muslim Terrorism?

There is no clear-cut definition of radical Muslim terrorism. A definition of *radical Muslim* and *terrorism* is problematic. Existing literatures often use the term *Islamic radicalism* to refer to the strong wave of radical movements in the Muslim world. Muslim radicalism or Islamic radicalism is associated with many terms like *Islamic fundamentalism, Islamic revisionism, Islamic revivalism, Islamic activism, militant Islamism*, and *Islamic extremism*. All these terms have acquired pejorative or derogatory meanings in the Western world. These terms are loosely lumped within the broad universe of political Islam.[3] But even the terms *Muslim* and *Islamic* are conceptually ambiguous. They are often used interchangeably in discussions of Islam, though social and political scientists assert that there are important differences in the use of these terms.[4] The term *Muslim* refers to a religious and cultural reality, while *Islamic* denotes political intent. A RAND scholar simply states that a Muslim country is one in which the majority of its people are Muslims, while an Islamic state is one that bases the legitimacy of the government on Islam.[5]

The origin of Muslim radicalism is often attributed to the preaching of Muhammad ibn Abd-al Wahhab, a Muslim scholar who popularized an Islamic theology that would later be called "Wahhabism." Abd-al Wahhab teaches the "purification" of Islam based on Salafi faith. The word *Salafi* means "righteous ancestors of Muslims" in traditional Islamic scholarship. Salafism advocates a return to a *shari'a*-minded orthodoxy that aims to purify Islam from unwarranted accretions, heresies, and distortions, which Abd-al Wahhab avidly preaches. Thus, Wahhabism and Salafism are theologically connected. Wahhabism and Salafism are systems of belief that are said to have vigorously informed the "terrorist acts" of Osama bin Laden and other radical Muslim personalities. They fight for the *jihad*, seeking to re-create the Muslim *ummah* and *shari'a* to build an Islamic community worldwide.[6]

Wahabi or Salafi movements are found throughout the Muslim world.[7] After 9/11, Islamic movements and organizations adhering to Wahabism and Salafism, particularly those associated with al Qaeda, are labeled radical Muslim terrorists because of their vigorous involvements in a series of terrorist attacks, the largest of which was the 9/11 attacks on the United States. Radical Muslim terrorists are also those people or organizations committing acts of terror as a means to free themselves from the clutches of Western colonialism. The south Lebanon's Amal and Hizbullah, Khomeini's Revolutionary Guards of Iran, the Hamas of Palestine, and the Muslim Brotherhood of Egypt are among those organizations that have received the label of radical Muslim terrorism because of their "acts of terror" committed in the name of Islam to free them from foreign occupation.[8]

In other words, radical Muslim terrorism may be redundantly described as acts of terrorism committed by radical Muslim personalities or organizations. This label is contested because of the worn-out debate on the issue of what constitutes an "act of terrorism." Members of the international community have not yet developed a commonly accepted definition of terrorism. Moreover, some scholars are challenging the use of the term *radical Muslim* as an adjective to the concept of terrorism because people who are Christians, Buddhists, and Hindus can also undoubtedly commit said acts. Thus, the use of *radical Muslim terrorism* in this chapter is still subject to further contestation because of its many nuances. But for the purposes of this chapter, the six so-called radical Muslim terrorist groups mentioned previously that are considered threats to Philippine national security are covered.

## Brief Historical Background

To have a better understanding of the so-called rise of radical Muslim terrorism in the Philippines and its contemporary realities, it is imperative to discuss the subject in its proper historical perspective.

Islam arrived in Sulu in the last quarter of the 13th century. In 1450, the Sultanate of Sulu was established. Scholars trace Muslim radicalism or Muslim separatism in the Philippines to the mid-16th century when Spain colonized the Philippine islands in 1565.[9] Were it not for the Spanish colonial rule, which introduced Roman Catholicism in the archipelago, particularly in the major islands of Luzon and the Visayas, the Philippines would have been a Muslim state like its Southeast Asian neighbors.[10]

All Muslim radical groups in the Philippines, regardless of political persuasion and theological inclination, believe in the *Bangsamoro* struggle. The term *Bangsa* comes from the Malay word, which means nation. Spanish colonizers introduced the term *Moro* when they confused the Muslim people of Mindanao with the "moors" of Northern Africa.[11] Though the use of the term *Bangsamoro* to describe the national identity of Muslims in the Philippines is still contested; Muslim leaders regard the *Bangsamoro* struggle as the longest "national liberation movement" in the country, covering almost 400 years of violent resistance against Spanish, American, Japanese, and even Filipino rule.[12]

The first recorded military confrontation between Spaniards and the Muslims in the Philippines began as early as 1565, which ended in the Invasion of Brunei in 1578 and 1581.[13] During this confrontation, the Spaniards were said to have ably checked "the increasing Bornean political influence and commercial activities in Luzon and the Visayas by capturing the Bornean settlement in Manila in

1571."[14] Spanish colonial rule of the Philippines lasted from 1565 to 1898. But Spain established a strong and dominant Christian community in the entire archipelago, except many Muslim communities, which remained unconquered against the onslaught of Spanish colonialism.[15]

During the U.S. colonial rule of the Philippines (1901–1935), the Americans inherited the *Moro* problem.[16] The new colonial master recognized that the *Moro* areas had never come under effective Spanish rule. The Americans even kept the *Moros* out of the Philippine–American War from 1899 to 1901 by signing the Bates Agreement where the United States agreed to protect *Moros* from foreign intrusions and to respect the authorities of Sultans and other Muslim chiefs in Mindanao.[17] But the Americans saw the *Moros* from the very start as a minority to be integrated into the national life of the Philippines.[18] Although political integration took place during the American period with the establishment of a *Moro* Province, Muslims in the Philippines were continued to be seen as a religious and cultural minority, the long-term result of which was marginality, dissatisfaction, and, ultimately, rejection of the Philippine nation–state.[19]

Through *jihad*, *Moros* in the Philippines continued their resistance during the American occupation. Famous among Muslim resistance movements during the period were that of Datu Tunggul, Datu Camour, and Datu Ampuanagus in Lanao (1902–1903), Datu Ali in Cotabato (1903–1905), and Datu Panglima Hassan in Sulu (1903–1905). American response to these resistance movements resulted in the Lanao campaigns from 1899 to 1903, military operations against Datu Ali from 1903 to 1905, Bud Dajo Massacre in 1905, and the Bud Bagsak encounter in 1913, which is regarded as the last decisive fight of Muslims in the Philippines.[20] Additionally, there were organized disturbances in Kidapawan (1917), Lanao (1924, 1930–1934), and Jolo (1927).[21]

After decades of vigorous battle against the American forces, some *Moro* leaders realized their limitations to resist aggression and gradually accepted "the new situation which they were powerless to change and sought to make the best of it."[22] Moreover, the American military machine was so strong, leaving the Muslims "with no choice but to cooperate or collaborate."[23] To put an end to resistance, some Muslim leaders laid down their arms and resorted to peaceful means to pursue their cause during the Commonwealth Period.

During the Commonwealth Period (1935–1946), some *Moro* leaders participated in the 1935 National Assembly election. But only two Muslim leaders got their seats, prompting the Muslim groups to continue their fight for independence. But it was only the outbreak of the Pacific War in 1941 "that more or less blunted the Moro independence movement," which resulted in the Japanese invasion of the Philippines.[24] During the Japanese occupation, *Moros* joined anti-Japanese resistance groups. It has been argued that six months before U.S. forces led by General Douglas MacArthur landed in Leyte to retake the Philippines, "the Muslim territories in Mindanao were already free of the Japanese."[25] The end of World War II led to the total defeat of the Japanese Imperial Army and to the granting of Philippine independence.

When the United States granted the Philippines independence on July 4, 1946, the *Moro* communities were divided into two major groups: the integrationist or the assimilationist group, and the secessionist or liberationist group. The first group accepted Philippine sovereignty, while the other group believes that Mindanao belongs to a separate Islamic State that also deserves independence. Those who continue to defy the authority of the Christian-dominated Philippine government assert their separate identity as *Moros* and refuse to regard themselves as Filipinos, arguing as follows:

> The term Filipino can only refer to a segment of our people who bowed in submission to the might of Spain. Certainly, the Muslims do not fall under the category of Filipino. Being a historic people, the Muslims therefore cannot but reject the generalization that the word Filipino applies to them as well. Because when the word Filipino is applied to a segment of our people, the implication is that the word Filipino was derived or at least named in honor of King Felipe II … In so far as the Muslims are concerned, the application Filipino does not have any meaning to them.[26]

But the idea of *Morohood* is being challenged because the term *Moro* was the appellation applied to all the Muslim population of Southeast Asia by the Portuguese, who seized Malacca in 1511.[27] As stated earlier, Spain used the same label to describe Muslim inhabitants of the Philippine archipelago. Muslims in the Philippines have owned the term *Moro* to describe their collective identities.

Since the granting of Philippine independence, the government has been contending with *Moro* separatism. In 1951, some Muslims in the Philippines waged the Kamlong uprising, which lasted until 1955. In 1957, the Philippine government organized the Commission on National Integration (CNI) to provide scholarship to young Muslims and encourage the *Moros* to accept the authority of the government. The government also implemented a land reform program that encouraged Christians from the North to settle in Southern Philippines. By the 1960s, Southern Philippines "had been virtually taken over by a Christian majority except areas like Lanao, Cotabato, Basilan and Sulu."[28] Thus, the *Moro* "had become a minority in many parts of their traditional homeland, with many losing their land to the immigrant settlers through dubious legal transactions or outright confiscation."[29] From 76% in the 1900s, the population of Muslims in Mindanao declined to 20% in the 1990s. The massive influx of Christian Filipinos to Mindanao has terribly angered the *Moros*.

But the spark that strongly lit the Muslim rebellion was the Jabidah Massacre in March 1968. Otherwise known as the Corregidor Massacre, it took place in the Corregidor Island of the Philippines involving *Moro* army recruits being trained for Operation Merdek, a code name for the clandestine destabilization plan of the Armed Forces of the Philippines (AFP) aiming to infiltrate Sabah as part of the strategy of the Philippine government to strengthen its territorial claim. Allegedly, their trainers summarily executed between 28 and 64 *Moro* recruits undergoing military training.[30] Though it has been argued that the Jabidah Massacre was a myth,[31] the incident prompted Governor Udtog Matalam of Cotabato to form the Mindanao Independence Movement (MIM) declaring the establishment of an Islamic state in Mindanao.[32] But Matalam yielded to the request of the Philippine government to reconsider his cause. Other Muslim leaders who resent the continuing oppression of Muslims in the Philippines continue their resistance, leading to the establishment of the MNLF and other radical Muslim groups.

## The *Moro* National Liberation Front

There is no uniform account of the origin of the MNLF. A former MNLF spokesperson even stressed that *Moro* rebel leaders are still debating until today as to who really founded it.[33] Though Nur Misuari was the known founding chair of the MNLF, it is argued that the organization was conceptualized and organized by Abul Khayr Alonto and Jallaludin Santos, who were at that time active with the Mindanao Independence Movement (MIM) founded in 1969 as a reaction to the Jabidah Massacre. The MIM aimed for the establishment of an independent state covering many parts of Mindanao, Sulu, and Palawan. In the same year, other radical Muslim leaders formed the Union of Islamic Forces and Organization (UIFO) and *Anwar El Islam* to fight for *Moro* independence. The MIM and UIFO members reportedly underwent joint combat training in Malaysia that year.

The MNLF was officially established in 1972 as a national liberation movement of Muslims in the Philippines. Unlike other Muslim resistance groups in the Philippines, MNLF has a more secular ideology. The secular ideology of the MNLF is traced to the left-leaning ideology of Misuari, who became a member of a Marxist youth organization in the Philippines, the *Kabataang Makabayan* (KM), or the Nationalist Youth. Key members of KM organized the Communist Party of the Philippines (CPP), which has been waging an armed struggle against the Philippine government. The CPP also has Muslim membership.

Strictly speaking, the MNLF does not embrace Islamic fundamentalism but it religiously adheres to the concept of *Moro* nationalism. It aims for the establishment of a separate *Moro* nation in the Southern Philippines. Although the MNLF may not be strictly labeled as Islamic fundamentalist, it is arguably a radical Muslim resistance group advocating *jihad* to liberate the *Moro* people from the oppression of what it describes as Filipino colonialism of Imperial Manila.

In other words, the MNLF is a national liberation movement of radical, mostly secular-oriented Muslims in the Philippines. The Manifesto of the MNLF, released on April 28, 1974, states, "We, the five million oppressed *Bangsamoro* people, wishing to free ourselves from the terror, oppression and tyranny of Filipino colonialism which has caused us untold sufferings and miseries by criminality usurping our land, by threatening Islam through wholesale destruction and desecration of its places of worship and its Holy Book, and murdering our innocent brothers, sisters and folks in a genocidal campaign of terrifying magnitude hereby declares the establishment of the *Bangsamoro* Republic."[34] According to Misuari, the armed struggle of the MNLF "is a revolution for national salvation and human justice" based on *jihad*, which is the "path of struggle of Muslims, either in the moral, ethical, spiritual or political realm, to bring about a positive transformation of the inner self and the socio-economic and political order."[35]

Allegedly, the MNLF received support from Muslim backers in Libya and Malaysia. Its core members of 90 Muslim rebels were reportedly trained in Pulao Pangkor, Malaysia in 1969. The "Top 90" of the MNLF completed their military training in 1971. It was in 1972, after the declaration of martial law, when they elected Misuari as Chairman of the MNLF. Hashim Salamat, who would eventually organize the MILF, joined the second group of trainees in 1972. Salamat was elected chairman on foreign affairs and in 1974 acted as Vice Chairman of the MNLF. Salamat, however, never received confirmation by the MNLF central committee. In 1978, Salamat and his more Islamic followers broke from Misuari's secular leadership. In 1979, Salamat formed the short-lived *Bangsamoro* Liberation Organization (BMLO). But from 1978 to 1984, Salamat still used the name MNLF to describe his breakaway movement until it formed the MILF, which will be discussed further in the next section.

Meanwhile, MNLF members were divided over the issue of the appropriate form of struggle during its nascent stage: parliamentary or armed. To try the parliamentary means, Misuari initially participated in the 1971 Constitutional Convention Election for the province of Sulu.[36] Lacking political support, he lost the election. But when the *Ilaga*, a movement of local Christian politicians in Mindanao, was formed, the MNLF, through its military arm called the *Bangsamoro* Army, decided to wage an armed struggle to resist the atrocities of Christian leaders in Mindanao. The *Ilaga*, a term for rats, was responsible for strings of massacres against Muslims between 1970 and 1972. The *Ilaga* was also responsible for the burning of Muslim houses and mosques during those periods.

Furious by the atrocities committed against Muslims in the Philippines, the MNLF declared on March 18, 1974, the establishment of a *Bangsamoro* Republic in the Southern Philippines. The Organization of Islamic Conference (OIC) recognized the MNLF as the sole and legitimate representative of the *Bangsamoro* people. Under the auspices of the OIC, the MNLF and the Government of the Republic of the Philippines (GRP) held a peace talk in 1976 in Tripoli, Libya, to settle the Mindanao problem. This peace talk led to the signing of the Tripoli Agreement, which provided for *Moro* autonomy in the Southern Philippines and for a ceasefire. But after a lull in the fighting, the truce broke down in 1977. Until 1996, the MNLF engaged in armed confrontations with the AFP.

The National Memorial Institute for the Prevention of Terrorism (MIPT) has classified the MNLF as a terrorist organization.[37] Though the Philippine government has not officially labeled the MNLF as a terrorist organization, government forces claimed that the MNLF was responsible for series of urban terror bombings in Mindanao in 1975 that continued well into the 1980s.[38] Muslim radicals identified with the MNLF allegedly masterminded the throwing of grenades into movie theaters, parades, and public gatherings. But the MNLF leadership did not claim responsibility for any of these terror attacks. It was speculated that government agents were involved to discredit the MNLF.[39]

In 1986, the GRP and the MNLF held another round of peace talks to provide a just and lasting solution to the Mindanao problem, but the talks collapsed in May 1987. The MNLF reached a final peace agreement with the GRP in 1996, which led to the establishment of the Autonomous Region of Muslim Mindanao (ARMM). Misuari was chosen governor of the region and was made chairman of the Southern Philippines Council for Peace and Development (SPCPD). It was believed that by placing Misuari in charge of both institutions, "the peace settlement would gain wide recognition among the Muslim community and demonstrate to non-Muslims that autonomy can benefit all groups."[40] Other MNLF members were integrated into the AFP. In December 2004, at least 5,530 officers and enlisted personnel of the MNLF were integrated into the AFP in compliance with the 1996 Final Peace Agreement. The MNLF integrees have been assigned as regular and organic personnel of the 1st, 4th, and 6th Infantry Divisions, 53rd and 54th Engineer Brigades based in Mindanao.[41]

But issues of mismanagement and corruption bedeviled Misuari during his term as governor of ARMM and chairman of SPCPD. When he failed to seek reelection as ARMM governor, he threatened to resort to violence, which he carried out in Jolo in November 2001. Misuari organized what the AFP calls as the Misuari Breakaway Group (MBG) of the MNLF, which according to the military has resorted to terrorism. The MBG is presently drawing up support and sympathy for Misuari and conducting massive recruitment in Sulu, Basilan, Zamboanga City, and Sarangani. As of the last quarter of 2007, the MBG has the strength of 661 Muslim fighters loyal to Misuari (Figure 3.1). They operate largely in Sulu, Basilan, Zamboanga City, and Zamboanga del Norte of the Southern Philippines. Misuari was jailed in 2003 for an act of rebellion in Jolo town, which led to the death of 100 people. But Misuari posted bail in May 2008. According to Misuari, his group is the original MNLF. But MNLF members who respect the 1996 Peace Agreement stress that they constitute the mainstream MNLF. These factions of the MNLF pose a difficult challenge for Philippine national security policy.

The MBG/MNLF continues to operate in the Southern Philippines. The MBG was said to have forged alliances with the MILF and ASG to plant bombs, kidnap people, and commit murder and other acts of terrorism. According to an intelligence report, the MBG has intensified its alliance with ASG and the MILF "in the conduct of armed atrocities in pursuit of their common agenda."[42] ASG members even admit that they have connived with ASG fighters to conduct some of their operations. Ruland Ullah, a former ASG member and a state witness to the April 2000 Sipadan hostage crisis, said that ASG has hired MBG/MNLF fighters to

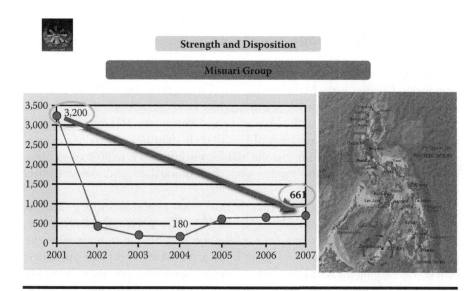

Figure 3.1 Strength of the Nur Misuari Breakaway Group. (From the Office of the Deputy Chief of Staff for Intelligence, April 2008.)

mount terrorist attacks. MNLF members have even acted as mercenaries of the ASG for an amount of at least $1,000. MNLF members allegedly provide sanctuaries for ASG members when the need arises.[43] They have also been sharing fighters to mount terrorist attacks not only in the Southern Philippines but also in Metro Manila.

On February 6, 2005, MBG forces simultaneously attacked four military posts in Sulu Province resulting in the death of 30 soldiers, the wounding of 80 others, and the evacuation of 35,000 villagers. Heavy fighting between the AFP and the MBG also broke out on February 24, 2005, as a result of the Philippine government's decision to mount heavy military operations against the MBG. The Philippine government has utilized the military service of MNLF integrees to fight not only the MBG but also the MILF.

## The *Moro* Islamic Liberation Front

The MILF was a breakaway faction of the MNLF. As stated previously, the late Hashim Salamat, known before as the Vice Chairman of the MNLF, founded the MILF in 1978. Though Salamat traced the origin of the MILF to 1962 when he founded the *Moro* Liberation Front (MLF) in Cairo, it was only in 1984 when he officially used the name MILF to describe his resistance group.[44] Unlike the MNLF, which is secular in orientation, the MILF is strictly Islamic or fundamentalist, to use the Western label. But Salamat argues, "There is no such thing as Islamic

Fundamentalism."[45] Though the MILF aims to establish a separate Islamic state in the Southern Philippines through *jihad*, Salamat contends, "Fundamentalism is alien to Islam."[46]

The MILF has a military arm called *Bangsamoro* Islamic Armed Forces (BIAF). As stated in Chapter 1, the MILF has personnel strength of almost 11,769 as of the last quarter of 2007. They operate in almost whole areas of the Southern Philippines, particularly in Maguindanao. But according to Salamat, the MILF has registered more than 70,000 participants from BIAF and more than 100,000 trained but not armed fighters. He even claims that the MILF constitutes 70% to 80% of all fighting forces in Mindanao with a modest navy, short of warships, and some members trained as fighter pilots.[47]

Though there were allegations that the MILF has established strong linkages with al Qaeda and Jemaah Islamiyah (JI), the Philippine government has not officially tagged the MILF as a terrorist organization in order not to undermine the peace talks, which as of this writing are in progress. Many Philippine politicians believe that tagging the MILF as a terrorist organization will cause the termination of the peace negotiations and the escalation of armed conflict in the Philippines. The MILF has renounced terrorism but persistently argued that it has a legitimate cause to wage armed struggle against the government to liberate the *Moros* from the bondage of Filipino colonialism.

But intelligence sources have established an MILF link with al Qaeda, which was traced to the Afghan war in the 1980s. Osama bin Laden reportedly instructed his brother-in-law Mohammed Jamal Khalifa to go to the Philippines in 1988 to recruit fighters. Salamat was reported to have sent 1,000 Filipino Muslim fighters in Afghanistan to undergo military training. Salamat saw the training of these Muslim fighters as vital to the strengthening of the MILF.

Khalifa left the Philippines in 1990, but returned to the country in 1991 to establish "a permanent al Qaeda network" to better support the MILF. Bin Laden believed that through the MILF, al Qaeda could establish permanent presence in the Philippines to serve as its base of terrorist operations in Southeast Asia.[48] Khalifa's front organization in the Philippines was believed to be the International Islamic Relief Organization (IIRO). It was a charitable organization registered in the Philippines at the Securities Exchange Commission on September 20, 1991. In the Securities Exchange Commission document, Khalifa was listed as the president and chairman of the board of trustees of the IIRO. One of the incorporators of IIRO was Jameela Yabo, a Filipina wife of Khalifa and sister of Abu Omar, who was then studying at the Mindanao State University. Khalifa used Yabo and Omar as conduits to penetrate Muslim Filipino communities through various charitable activities.

Aside from the IIRO, other charitable organizations that Khalifa allegedly used to fund his operations in the Philippines were the International Relations and Information Center, the Mercy International, the Benevolence International Corporation, and the Islamic Wisdom Worldwide.[49] While doing "charitable" activities in the Philippines, Khalifa reportedly used the Philippines as al Qaeda's base for other international terrorist operations, particularly in Southeast Asia. Through the IIRO and other Muslim relief groups, Khalifa reportedly channeled money to provide financial support to the MILF.

The MILF continues to deny its link with al Qaeda. But Al Haj Murad, the MILF Vice Chairman for Military Affairs, admitted in an interview held some-time in 1998 that bin Laden and Khalifa assisted the MILF cadres in Afghanistan. Salamat also acknowledged that bin Laden provided financial support to Muslim guerillas to build mosques and help poor Muslim communities.[50]

Based on various intelligence sources, the MILF was said to have also estab-lished linkage with JI, the so-called al Qaeda in Southeast Asia. Although MILF spokesperson Eid Kabalu said that the MILF–JI link is a recycled allegation and a black propaganda lodged against their organization, the International Crisis Group based in Brussels released a report describing this so-called link, stating, "While the MILF leadership continues to deny any ties, all evidence points to operational and training links. What is uncertain is whether top leaders are aware of the activ-ity and are unwilling to admit it."[51] The MILF even earmarked a training camp for JI, called Camp Hodeiba, set up in 1994.[52] JI reportedly used Camp Hodeiba to train MILF members in urban terrorism, particularly in bomb making. But some Muslim leaders and military officials claimed that JI members were the ones actu-ally receiving training from MILF fighters. According to a Muslim lawyer who has done research on the Mindanao problem, MILF members already received excel-lent training in the Middle East before the JI came in. Thus, "the MILF does not need training from JI, even in the area of bomb making. MILF is, in fact, training JI in some Muslim military camps in Southern Philippines."[53]

Aside from JI, intelligence reports also reveal that MILF has also forged a tac-tical alliance with the New People's Army (NPA), the armed group of the CPP. The Philippine government labels the CPP-NPA as a local Communist Terrorist Movement (CTM). Though the MILF says that it has no ties with the CTM, Salamat comments, "We feel that we have almost the same cause."[54] Salamat even underscores, "Since we have the same enemy and we face the same problem, then our religious beliefs cannot prevent us from having alliances even with the so-called godless people."[55]

In 2002, the MILF and CTM reportedly held a joint two-month "Special Explosives and Sniper Course" training at an NPA camp Sariaya, Quezon, of Southern Luzon. The training reportedly started on November 16, 2002, and was supposed to have ended in December 2002. Due to skirmishes between the CTM and AFP forces, the training was extended up to February 2003. In March 2003, the Southern Mindanao Regional Community of the NPA reportedly dispatched around 30 armed personnel to Davao Oriental to sup-port MILF forces fighting the government. The Far South Mindanao Region Command of the NPA also directed its front committees to support MILF forces in Sarangani. Joint elements of CPP-NPA and MILF are also operating in Misamis Oriental. According to an intelligence report, "The NPA is expected to stage more joint offensives with the MILF in areas where both parties exert political and military influence."[56]

The MILF has also reportedly established links with the ASG, the most notorious radical Muslim terrorist group in the Philippines. Though the MILF continues to deny any links with the ASG, Salamat once said, "The MILF shares a common goal with the Abu Sayyaf Group: to establish an independent Islamic State."[57] The MILF leadership even regards Abdurajak Janjalani as a *Moro* martyr.[58]

Recent intelligence sources reveal that ASG and MILF members share fighters in their operations. A confession of a captured ASG member states that "sometimes the MILF would plant a roadside bomb against soldiers and the Abu Sayyaf would shoot the soldiers wounded in the blast."[59] MILF and ASG members also conduct joint training with JI operatives, particularly in the area of bomb making. The Intelligence Service of the Armed Forces of the Philippines states, "During explosives training, JI teaches the MILF or ASG skills in the making of bombs with cell phones, in the identification of the different types of explosives and paraphernalia like TNT, black powder, PETN [pentaerythritol tetranitrate], ammonium nitrate, C4, detonating cords, and detonators."[60]

## The Abu Sayyaf Group

Because of the spate of kidnap-for-ransom activities it has perpetrated, the ASG became an international sensation. But it remains to be the least understood radical Muslim terrorist group in the Philippines. Many scholars and journalists mistranslated ASG to mean "bearer of the sword."[61] But ASG really means in Arabic, "father of the swordsman."[62]

There is no uniform view of the ASG. The United States has listed the ASG in its list of Foreign Terrorist Organizations, while the United Nations has designated it as one of the three terrorist organizations in Southeast Asia along with al Qaeda and the JI.[63] Some regard the ASG as part of the international fundamentalist movement, linked to Osama bin Laden, which aims to establish an independent Islamic state in the Philippines.[64] Others see the ASG as the agent provocateur of the Philippine military and the Central Intelligence Agency, while the Philippine government continues to condemn the ASG as a mere bandit gang that aims to amass funds through kidnap for ransom, extortion, and other criminal activities.[65] But its members and sympathizers claim that the ASG represents the legitimate desire of all Muslim resistant groups in the Philippines aiming to establish a separate Islamic state.

There is also no uniform account of the origin of the ASG. It has a very nebulous beginning.[66] Existing literatures regard Abdurajak Abubakar Janjalani as the founder of ASG. But many works have failed to discuss the real intention of Janjalani when he organized the group. To elaborate his real motive in establishing the ASG amid various speculations about the nature and objectives of the organization, Janjalani issued an undated public proclamation, presumably written between 1993 and 1994, which aptly stressed what he called the "Four Basic Truths" about the ASG, to wit:

1. It is not to create another faction in the Muslim struggle that is against the teaching of Islam, especially the Koran, but to serve as a bridge and balance between the MILF and MNLF whose revolutionary roles and leadership cannot be ignored or usurped.
2. Its ultimate goal is the establishment of a purely Islamic government whose "nature, meaning, emblem and objective" are basic to peace.
3. Its advocacy of war is necessity for as long as there exist oppression, injustice, capricious ambitions and arbitrary claims imposed on the Muslims.
4. It believes that "war disturbs peace only for the attainment of the true and real objective of humanity — the establishment of justice and righteousness for all under the law of the noble Quran and the purified sunnah."[67]

Despite the nebulous origin of the ASG, the military establishment believed that in 1990, Janjalani formed the Mujahideed Commando Freedom Fighters (MCFF) to wage *jihad* against the Philippine government for the establishment of an independent Islamic state in the Southern Philippines. The Philippine military regarded the MCFF as the forerunner of the ASG. When the MCFF attracted some "hard core" followers in Basilan, Zulu, Tawi-Tawi, and Zamboanga, it was later called the ASG.

But according to Noor Muog, one of the key leaders of the ASG now working for the Philippine government, the MCFF was a misnomer. The forerunner of the ASG was the *Jamaa Tableegh*, an Islamic propagation group established in Basilan in the early 1980s by Abdurajak Janjalani. This group conducted seminars, symposia, and small-group discussions to propagate Islam. It was also through this group where Abdurajak delivered some of his Islamic discourses. Because of charismatic lectures of Abdurajak, the *Jamaa Tableegh* received popularity not only in Basilan but also in Zamboanga and Jolo.[68] The involvement of some of its followers in antigovernment rallies prompted the military to put the group under surveillance. Key followers of *Jamaa Tableegh* formed the nucleus of the ASG, which Abdurajak Janjalani initially called *Al-Harakatul Al-Islmiyah* (AHAI) or the Islamic Movement. The AHAI drew material and financial support from the extremist element in Iran, through the Hezbollah; in Pakistan, through the Jamaat-Islami and Hizbul-Mujahideen; in Afghanistan, through Hizb-Islami; in Egypt, through Al Gamaa-Al-Islamiya; in Algeria, through Islamic Liberation Front; and in Libya, through the International Harakatul Al-Islamia.

The ASG reportedly established link with the al Qaeda in the 1990s. It was said that Janjalani befriended bin Laden while in Peshawar, Pakistan. [69] Janjalani also became a very close friend of Ramzi Yousef, who reportedly planned in the

Philippines the *Bojinka* plots, believed to be the worst terrorist plots in the country. The *Bojinka* plots aimed to bomb 11 U.S. jetliners and assassinate Pope John Paul II, who visited Manila in 1995. During his travel to the Philippines via Malaysia, Yousef reportedly stayed in Basilan and trained around 20 ASG fighters. The Philippine National Police (PNP) narrates that as of September 1994, Yousefhas had a fully established terrorist cell in the Philippines.

The ASG was also reported to have established links with JI. Among JI personalities, Al Ghozi became the most sensational terrorist figure in the Philippines, having been identified as the major suspect in a series of bombings in the country. Known as "Mike the bomb maker," Al Ghozi was known to be Hambali's most trusted Indonesian colleague and became a student of Bashir in the 1980s. Al Ghozi used a lot of aliases while in the Philippines. Police authorities arrested him on charges of illegal possession of explosives just three hours prior to his scheduled flight to Bangkok on January 15, 2002. During the investigation, Al Ghozi admitted the following:

- That he first entered the Philippines in 1996 via Manado, Indonesia, to conduct "area study/familiarization" and to establish contacts within the MILF, particularly in Camp Abubakar. He left the Philippines in January 1997 but returned in March 1998 using the name of Edris Anwar Rodin to visit various places in Mindanao. After six months, he returned to Indonesia.
- That in March 1999, he visited Mindanao and went back to Indonesia after three months. In October 2000, he went to the Philippines again. In January 2001, he applied for another Philippine passport using the name Randy Andam Alih. While in the Philippines, he was allegedly given instructions by Hambali to procure explosives at Cebu. After this trip, he proceeded to Malaysia.
- That in November 2001, he went back to the Philippines via Singapore and stayed in Cebu to buy more explosives. He proceeded to General Santos City to acquire a storage room with the help of a certain Malagat.
- That he was the "Freedom Fighter" who called up a local newspaper office and claimed responsibility for the December 30, 2000, bombings that killed 20 people and wounded 100 others.[71]

In July 2003, Al Ghozi escaped from his prison cell in Manila. But through intensified manhunt and joint military–police operations, he was killed in a shootout in Mindanao on October 12, 2003, a date coinciding with the first-year anniversary of the 2002 Bali bombing. Intelligence sources reveal that the number of JI members in the Philippines collaborating with ASG was placed at 33 as of December 2004. The Philippine National Police Intelligence Group (PNP-IG) estimates a higher figure when it reports that the number of JI operatives in the Philippines may be placed at 60 as of April 2005.[71] These JI operatives continue to exploit local Muslim secessionist rebels in the Philippines by sharing their demolition skills.[72]

In connection with the 2005 Valentine's Day bombings, two Indonesians and a Malaysian allegedly belonging to the JI were arrested by intelligence operatives in Zamboanga City on February 23, 2005. But the arrest of Rohmat, alias "Zaki," on March 16, 2005, gave more substantial information about the recent JI-ASG linkages. Zaki, an Indonesian national, confessed to several crimes involving the ASG since 2000, including training members to make bombs in JI-run camps.[73] Known as the "ASG bomb trainer," Zaki admitted that he trained ASG members in bomb making, particularly the use of mobile phones as detonating devices and the use of toothpaste as bomb paraphernalia.[74] He also admitted to having coordinated the 2005 Valentine's Day bombings, which resulted in the brutal death of 10 people and the serious wounding of at least 150 others.

Contrary to the public opinion and some media reports, the ASG is not a homogenous organization. The ASG is a highly factionalized group of radical Muslim terrorist groups in the Philippines. The death of Abdurajak Janjalani on December 18, 1998, aggravated the factionalization of the ASG. Although remaining ASG leaders appointed Khadafy Janjalani, his younger brother, as successor, the young Janjalani did not have the ideological zeal and leadership charisma of his older brother. At present, the ASG has two major factions operating autonomously in Basilan and Sulu provinces of Mindanao. Khadafy Janjalani heads the Basilan faction. Galib Andang (aka Commander Robot), on the other hand, headed the Sulu faction until March 16, 2005, when he met his untimely death during a failed jailbreak attempt. Though the military identifies one faction operating in Zamboanga City, other sources say that this faction belongs to the Sulu-based ASG. Interestingly, the Basilan and Sulu factions of the ASG are also factionalized. As of 2002, the Basilan-based faction was composed of 10 armed groups and the Sulu-based faction was composed of 16 armed groups. Table 3.1 shows the Basilan-based groups of the ASG. Table 3.2, on the other hand, shows the Sulu-based groups of the ASG.

These tables show that the ASG is a very loose coalition of many groups of radical Muslim terrorist leaders commanding their own loyal followers in the Southern Philippines. These groups have mixed objectives from Islamic fundamentalism to mere banditry. Not all groups are truly committed to the idea of a separate Islamic State in the Southern Philippines, though there is no doubt that some groups are really committed to the cause. Some Muslim bandit groups in the Southern Philippines want to be associated with the ASG for prestige, political expediency, and economic gains. It has been reported recently, however, that the younger Janjalani is reviving the radical Islamist agenda of the ASG.

As discussed in Chapter 1, the ASG strength was reduced to 383 combatants as of the last quarter of 2007, a sharp decline from its peak of more than 1,000 combatants in the early 1990s. Though the ASG strength increased to around 400 in the first quarter of 2009, it is still a small organization compared with the NPA and MILF. Despite its small number, the ASG can still wreak huge terrorist havoc because of its enormous ability to solicit strong local support from Muslim relatives, friends, classmates, and neighbors of ASG fighters. Moreover, the ASG continues

**Table 3.1   Basilan-Based Faction of the ASG**

| Name of Group | Known Leaders of the Group |
|---|---|
| Ampul Group | Mauran Ampu or Abu Mauran |
| Apting Group | Abu Apting |
| Danggatil Group | Moto Danggantil or Mata Danggatil |
| Hapilon Group | Sahiron Hapilon |
| Isnilon Group | Isnilon Hapilon |
| Jainuddin Group | Nadjalin Jainuddin |
| Janjalani Group | Hector Janjalani or Abu Abral |
| Kaw Jaljalis Group | Kalaw Jaljalis or Boy Granada |
| Salagin Group | Abu Salagin |
| Masiraji Sali Group | Hamsiraji Sali |

*Source:* Armed Forces of the Philippines, Office of the Deputy Chief of Staff for Operations, J3 (2002).

to have effective alliances with rogue factions of the MNLF, MILF, and some JI personalities operating in the Philippines.

A police intelligence report reveals that ASG has forged alliances with MBG members or gunmen loyal to jailed MNLF leader Nur Misuari.[75] Captured ASG members even admitted during police interrogation that they hired some MBG followers or rogue members of the MNLF to mount some piracy and terrorist attacks in Mindanao. MNLF members acted as mercenaries of the ASG for an amount of $1,000 each and provided sanctuaries for ASG members during hot military pursuits.

As stated earlier, ASG and MILF members have also shared fighters in some of their major operations. But some scholars still believe that the ASG and the MILF are unaligned organizations despite similar aims and comparable origins.[76] Intelligence reports, however, reveal that MILF and ASG members have been receiving joint training with JI operatives, particularly in the area of bomb making. JI-ASG-MILF linkage, therefore, remains intact and operational. The PNP-IG estimates that the number of JI operatives in the Philippines may be placed at around 50 as of December 2007. These JI operatives continue to exploit local Muslim secessionist rebels in the Philippines by sharing their demolition skills.

The ASG, as discussed in Chapter 1, has also developed a capability to wage maritime terrorism. In fact, waging maritime terrorism is inherent in the capability of the ASG. Most ASG members and followers belong to Muslim families and communities of fishermen with a century-old seafaring tradition. Because ASG

### Table 3.2   Sulu-Based Faction of the ASG

| Name of Group | Known Leaders of the Group |
| --- | --- |
| Robot Group | Galib Andang or Cmdr Robot |
| Amil Group | Julius Aminulla Amil |
| Asiri Group | Basiri Asiri |
| Badja Group | Datu Panglima Badja |
| Bauddin Group | Salapuddin Bauddin |
| Hayudini Group | Nidzmi Hayudinni or Cmdr Takulong |
| Hadji Radzpal Group | Hadji Radzpal or Abu Rayhan |
| Irijani Group | Mudjahid Irijani |
| Jamal Group | Yahiya Jamal or Abu Alvarez |
| Kalim Group | Pati Kalim |
| Landi Group | Kumander Landi |
| Mali Group | Sulaiman Mali |
| Saabdula Group | Nadzmi Saabulla or Cmdr Global |
| Sahiron Group | Radullah Sahiron |
| Sali Group | Hesseim Sali |
| Shariff Group | Wahid Shariff |

*Source:* Armed Forces of the Philippines, Office of the Deputy Chief of Staff for Operations, J3 (2002).

members live in the waters of Basilan, Sulu, and Tawi-Tawi, they have gained tremendous familiarity with the maritime environment. Most Muslim Filipinos living in coastal communities are known deep-sea divers. ASG members' deep knowledge of the maritime domain also gives them ample capability to conduct piracy and wage maritime terrorist attacks.

Because of its embedded seaborne abilities, ASG's first known terrorist attack was maritime in nature when on August 24, 1991, it bombed the *M/V Doulous*, a Christian missionary ship and a European floating library docked at the Zamboanga port. In August 1993, the ASG abducted Mr. Ricardo Tong, a prominent shipyard owner in Zamboanga City. The abduction of Mr. Tong demonstrated that during its infancy stage, the prime target of the ASG was the maritime sector.

The ASG proved its maritime terrorist capability when it waged another attack on April 23, 2000, when it kidnapped some 21 tourists, including 10 foreigners, from a Malaysian beach resort in Sipadan. On May 22, 2001, ASG guerrillas raided the luxurious Pearl Farm beach resort on Samal Island of Mindanao. This incident resulted in the killing of two resort workers and the wounding of three others. Though no hostages were taken during this attack, the Samal raid demonstrated anew the willingness of ASG to pursue maritime targets.

On May 28, 2001, the ASG waged another maritime terror when it abducted 3 American citizens and 17 Filipinos spending a vacation at the Dos Palmas resort in Palawan. Thus far, the Dos Palmas incident was the most notorious and the most sensationalized attack of the ASG. The incident received international coverage because several of the victims were murdered and beheaded, including an American citizen.

Because American hostages were involved, the U.S. military sent army operation forces to the Philippines to train AFP forces in counterterrorism. The U.S. Pacific Command even extended US$2 million assistance to the Philippines from its regional security assistance program as a result of the Dos Palmas incident. But when the lives of the two American hostages were put in danger, the U.S. Army special operations forces changed the scope of their mission in the Philippines by facilitating the rescue of the American citizens. During a rescue operation mounted by the AFP in 2002, two victims, including an American missionary, Martin Burnham, were killed. His wife, Gracia Burnham, the well-known survivor of the kidnap incident, wrote a memoir of her captivity at the hands of the ASG.[77]

The most gruesome maritime terrorist attack of the ASG was the February 27, 2004, burning of *MV Superferry 14*, a commercial vessel carrying 899 passengers. The ASG claimed responsibility for the explosion and stressed that the incident was a "just revenge" of the group for the "brutal murder" of *Bangsamoro* people amid the "on-going violence" in Mindanao. The burning of the *MV Superferry 14* was carried out through the assistance of another radical Muslim terrorist group in the Philippines, the Rajah Solaiman Islamic Movement (RSIM).

## Rajah Solaiman Islamic Movement

Some writers have traced the origin of the RSIM to the Balik Islam (Return to Islam) movement.[78] While founding members of the RSIM have indeed associated themselves with the Balik Islam, it is careless to associate Balik Islam with RSIM — it is like associating Islam with terrorism. Started in the 1970s, Balik Islam is a legitimate organization of at least 200,000 Christian converts to Islamic faith. Followers prefer to be called *reverts* based on the belief that Islam was the original religion of the Philippines. The RSIM, organized only in 2001, represents a very minuscule fraction of reverts.

Though Ahmad Santos (Hilarion del Rosario Santos III) was the known RSIM commander, the group was founded with the leading role of Sheik Omar Lavilla (Rueben Lavilla). With the arrest of Santos on October 26, 2005, Lavilla is believed to be running the daily operation of the RSIM to date. Lavilla has called RSIM members "Urban Mujahideens."

During his interrogation, Santos admitted to having organized a group of 20 radical Muslim reverts in 2001 to undergo "*jihad* trainings" in a camp in Anda, Pangasinan, of Central Luzon. Santos and Lavilla originally called this group *Haraka* or *Harakat*, which literally means "the movement." General Rodolfo "Boogie" Mendoza, the father of counterterrorism investigation in the Philippines, says that "the name Rajah Solaiman Movement was initially suggested by Ahmad Santos as a joke but it was eventually adopted." The RSIM was used in honor of the first Muslim ruler of Manila. RSIM aims for the Islamization of the entire Philippines.

The RSIM was estimated to have a membership of 50 to 100 "hard core activists."[79] If we define "hard core activists" to mean individuals who have the intent and capability to wage terrorism, RSIM membership is not more than 30 members. The AFP identifies only 25 active members of the RSIM as of April 2008. These active members are reported to have been conducting recruitment drives in Luzon and in the Visayas. Though small at present, the RSIM draws its strength from its alleged continuing collaboration with likeminded terrorist groups like the ASG, JI, and al Qaeda.

The RSIM has established ties with the ASG. At the time of his arrest in October 2005, Santos served as the Chief of the ASG Media Bureau. Prior to that, ASG leader Khadafy Janjalani reportedly gave the RSIM the equivalent of about US$200,000 for its initial operational activities in Manila, which included the recruitment and conversion of Christians to Islam, then sent them for terrorist training.[80] The RSIM collaborated with the ASG in the 2004 *MV Superferry 14* bombing and the 2005 Valentines Day bombings, which were reportedly planned as suicide missions.[81] The RSIM has allegedly formed its own armed wing called Khalid Trinidad Army, a small group of terrorists named after Khalid Trinidad, an RSIM member himself. Police operatives killed Trinidad in an encounter on May 1, 2002.

The RSIM was also reported to have established links with JI. Santos confessed that he collaborated with Omar Patek, one of the key suspects in the 2002 Bali bombings, while hiding in Mindanao in early 2004. Patek allegedly gave the RSIM an amount of P250,000 (US$5,000) to be used in the foiled Ermita Plot. Ermita is a place in Manila frequented by foreign tourists. Santos admitted to having used this money to conduct surveillance operations in Ermita and to rent a house in Quezon City where he hid 600 kilos of explosive materials discovered by police and military authorities on March 23, 2005.

During its embryonic stage, the RSIM reportedly established links with al Qaeda. Santos confessed that the RSIM "aided in training and giving shelter to the terrorists responsible in the September 11 terrorist attack." General Mendoza's paper on the RSIM states, "The Al Qaeda pilots got their first training in Angeles City, Pampanga…But before leaving for the United States, the pilots were said to have gone to the RSIM training camp established by Ahmad Santos in their family property in Barangay Mal-Ong, Anda, Pangasinan."

The PNP regarded the International Information Center, a Muslim center based in Quiapo, Manila, as a front of the RSIM. The Philippine Association of Muslimah Darul Eeman, Inc., was also reported to be a front of ASG to recruit Metro Manila–based Islam converts into its fold.[82] The following Balik Islam groups have also aroused official curiosity: Al Maarif Education Center (Baguio City), Da'rul Hijra Foundation, Inc. (Makati City), and Islamic Learning Center (Pangasinan). Police authorities said that the RSIM is the newest terrorist threat facing the Philippines today.[83] Though the RSIM may be the smallest among the radical Muslim terrorist groups operating in the Philippines, it has trained some suicide bombers to become "martyrs of Islamic faith." Santos admitted during police interrogation to have trained potential suicide bombers from the ranks of RSIM hard core *jihadists*.[84] Santos confessed that he started the training of suicide bombers as early as February 2002. Trainees were indoctrinated on the belief that "the greatest sacrifice is giving one's life for Allah and Islam." After a month of training, five RSIM members reportedly took the *Shaheed* (martyrdom pledge) to undergo a suicide mission scheduled in May 2002. This mission allegedly aimed to assassinate President Gloria Macapagal Arroyo (PGMA) with the use of a "truck bomb." But the raid of RSIM hideouts in Central Luzon that year halted the mission. The raid resulted in the death of one and the arrest of four potential suicide bombers. The raid also indicated the strong resolve of the Philippine law enforcement authorities to clamp down on terrorists.

In April 2004, the RSIM revived the mission after seven different potential suicide bombers took another *Shaheed*.[85] But the mission was preempted as a result of the series of counterterrorism operations conducted during May and June 2004. Out of the seven potential suicide bombers, two were arrested and another two were reportedly declared "inactive" because of intensified intelligence operations of the Philippine government. But the remaining three potential suicide bombers remain allegedly at large as of this writing.

The RSIM has also penetrated some legitimate Balik Islam organizations to radicalize some of their members. Though Islam is undoubtedly a religion of peace, RSIM's radical interpretation of Islam makes the group an instrument of political violence. The Office of Muslim Affairs (OMA) has reported that more than 110,000 Filipinos have converted to Islam as of the first quarter of 2005. But another source states that Balik Islam comprises nearly 200,000 of the more than 6.6 million local Muslim community in the Philippines.[86] Records also show that Balik Islam is now the seventh biggest group of the 13 local Muslim tribes.[87] As of January 2003, at least 33 mosques in Metro Manila have been constructed, 29 in Northern Luzon, 15 in Central Luzon, 56 in Southern Luzon, and 38 in the Visayas. Because of this trend, Islam is becoming the fastest growing religion in the Philippines. It has also been reported that at least 20,000 Balik Islam, live in traditionally Catholic Luzon. According to General Mendoza, "The spread of Islam is not necessarily the problem; it's the spread of the radical interpretation of Islam."[88] OMA Chief Zamzamin Amaptuan commented that converts are heavily prone to indoctrination to the "deviant" interpretation of Islam because they are more aggressive and so engrossed in a faith that they recently accepted.[89] Amaptuan feared, "In some way, this aggressiveness can be converted to something else," like terrorism. Amaptuan also reported that OMA has accredited 78 Muslim organizations in the Philippines. According to him, most of these organizations listed *da'wah*, or propagation, as their primary objective.[90] The practice of *da'wah* has triggered police suspicion because of the allegation that this practice is being used as a front of RSIM "for terrorist operations, or at least as an avenue for laundering money used to finance training and the acquisition of weapons, ammunition and bomb-making paraphernalia."[91] RSM's alleged link with ASG has created further suspicions that Muslim converts are being used for urban terrorism.

As stated earlier, the blasting of the *Superferry 14* on February 27, 2004, has been described as the handiwork of ASG-RSIM conspiracy. Redento Cain Dellosa, an RSIM member, confessed that he deliberately planted a bomb on *Superferry 14*. The ASG even claimed responsibility for the explosion and stressed that the incident was a "just revenge" of the group for the "brutal murder" of *Bangsamoro* people amid the "on-going violence" in Mindanao. ASG Chief Khadafy Janjalani strongly warned that the "best action of ASG was yet to come."

Though the Philippine government initially denied the involvement of ASG and RSIM in the incident, the Marine Board Inquiry in charge of investigating the *Superferry 14* incident confirmed that the ASG indeed masterminded the explosion with the assistance of RSIM. In the telephone radio interview pertaining to the *Superferry 14* incident, ASG spokesperson Abu Soliaman even taunted the Philippine government by saying, "Still doubtful about our capabilities? Good. Just wait and see. We will bring the war that you impose on us to your lands and seas, homes and streets. We will multiply the pain and suffering that you have inflicted on our people."[92]

The RSIM, upon instruction of ASG, allegedly masterminded the three simultaneous bombings in Makati City, General Santos City, and Davao City on the eve of Valentines Day celebration in 2005. These bombings resulted in the death of seven people and the wounding of at least 150 others. RSIM reportedly assisted the ASG in the bombing that occurred in Makati City. The RSIM had also planned to mount another terrorist attack on the eve of the 2005 Holy Week celebration. But military intelligence operatives foiled this plan when they arrested RSIM member Tyrone Dave Santos (alias Daud Santos) in a raid conducted in an alleged RSIM building in Quezon City for carrying 10 sacks of explosive materials. These explosives were intended to be used during the Lenten season to bomb soft targets in Metro Manila in retaliation to the killing of ASG members during the aborted jailbreak in March 2005. The Philippine police charged Daud Santos for illegal possession of explosive devices, but he was released after posting P200,000 (US$4,000) bail. The Philippines does not have a law on terrorism, and illegal possession of explosives is a "bailable" offense under the existing Philippine criminal law.

Interestingly, Daud Santos, tagged by police authorities as an ASG member, is a brother of RSIM founder Ahmed Santos. RSIM links with ASG, therefore, run in the family. In fact, Amina Lim Dungon, one of the wives of ASG spokesman Abu Sulaiman, is the sister of Lorraine Lim Dungon, who is one of the three wives of RSIM leader Ahmed Santos. ASG leader Khadafy Janjalani's wife, Zainad Lim Dungon, is a sister of Amina and Lorraine. These make Sulaiman, Santos, and Janjalani not only "brothers-in-arms" but also brothers-in-law. Some International Islamic Center (ICC) officers are also kin to Fi-Sabillilah and RSIM leaders.[93] According to a chief police superintendent, "If you make an extended family tree of top Islamic radicals, you will come out with something like a tightly woven spider's web."[94]

This view is shared by another top police officer who argues that that ties between ASG and RSIM and even MILF and MNLF "are more personal than ideological" because "there are blood ties, and they have an experience of strife with government."[95] General Florencio D. Fianza, the president's special envoy on transnational crime, says that ASG, RSIM and even MILF and MNLF help each other to carry out terrorist activities.[96] But Fianza contends that though they help each other, they also have their own share of infightings and turf wars.

## Abu Sofia Group

Another small but loosely labeled radical Muslim terrorist group in the Philippines was the Abu Sofia (AS) group. Military sources described the AS as a breakaway faction of the MILF engaged in banditry and kidnap-for-ransom activities. Bebis Binago, a brother of a local MILF commander, headed the said bandit group.[97] There were reports indicating that AS had established links with the ASG in terms of providing shelter to fugitive members and conducting kidnap-for-ransom activities.

Though AS did not have a veneer of ideology attached to it, its alleged links with the ASG and MILF, however, prompted police authorities to subsume it under the terrorist threat.[98] The group was suspected for its involvement in the bombings of shopping malls in central Mindanao in 2002 and 2003. The group was also reported to having given refuge to top ASG leaders, particularly Khadafy Janjalani and Isnilon Hapilon. But the death of Binago on January 6, 2004, in a military encounter has led to the hibernation of the AS Group.

Alo Binago, brother of the slain leader Bebis Binago, revived the group when he headed the kidnapping of a South Korean national in early 2006. But Alo Binago, along with two other members, was arrested on July 28, 2006, in Maguindanao province. According to the joint PNP-AFP Anti-Terror Task Force based in Sultan Kudarat, the three members of the AS Group were plotting more bombings and kidnapping activities and had been meeting with radical Muslim terrorists in

Mindanao prior to their arrest.[99] Law enforcement authorities believe that some members of the AS Group are still active and continue to have links with the ASG and the MILF.[100]

## Al-Khobar Group

The latest Muslim terrorist group operating mainly in the Davao del Sur, Saranggani, South Cotabato, and North Cotabato areas is the Al-Khobar Group (AKG). Though the Philippine military considers this group as a mere extortion gang, its link with Muslim personalities associated with the NPA, ASG, and MILF opens the possibility that the AKG may mutate into a radical Muslim terrorist group. According to Musali Calo, arrested member of the AKG, the group was organized by Zabide Abdul, alias Commander Beds of the MILF.[101] The Philippine military identified the AKG as responsible for a series of bus bombings in Mindanao, particularly in Koronadal City, Tacurong City, and Kidapawan City.

## Conclusion

Muslim radicalism in the Philippines has deep historical, economic, social, and political roots. But among the radical Muslim groups in the Philippines, only the ASG and the RSIM have officially been tagged as terrorist organizations by the government. Though the MNLF-MBG and the MILF have not been officially labeled as terrorist organizations, the police and military establishments have reported their "acts of terrorism" as warranting the label. But the Philippine government is cautious in labeling the MNLF as a terrorist organization because of the 1996 peace agreement. The government also faces difficulties in labeling the MILF as a terrorist organization because of the ongoing peace talks. But all groups discussed in this chapter are called Muslim radicals, except AS, which is considered by the Philippine government as a mere bandit group.

The label "radical Muslim terrorism" to describe Muslim separatist groups in the Philippines remains hotly contested. There are reports, however, of "terrorist acts" committed by these groups, prompting the police and military establishments to describe all armed groups fighting the government in Mindanao as Southern Philippine terrorist groups.[102]

Though the idea that "one man's terrorist is another man's freedom fighter" is vigorously abused and a worn-out description, all so-called radical Muslim terrorist groups in the Philippines, except AS, believe that their followers are freedom fighters. Those who died in the fight were even called martyrs by *Moros*. In fact, a former Congressman from Davao Oriental stressed that contrary to media and military reports, many people in Mindanao "consider the MNLF and MILF as allies and not enemies," arguing further that "the MNLF and MILF are one with us in our aspirations for an independent Mindanao."[103]

There is no doubt, however, that some activities of so-called radical Muslim groups have sown tremendous fear, wrecked havoc, and cost the lives of many innocent civilians. These activities may constitute acts of terrorism. But the absence of a commonly accepted definition of terrorism and the pejorative meanings attached to radical Muslims make the term "radical Muslim terrorism" a continuing subject of tremendous contestation not only in the Philippines but also in its Southeast Asian neighbors.

# Endnotes

1. For a complete copy of the article, please access *BigNews Network* (November 10, 2004), at: http://feeds.bignewsnetwork.com/redir.php?jid=855f4c0dfb7e7357&cat=c 08dd24cec417021 (accessed November 10, 2004).

2. Sameul Bar, "The Religious Sources of Islamic Terrorism," *Policy Review*, No. 125 (June and July 2004.)

3. See Nazih Ayubi, *Political Islam: Religion and Politics in the Arab World* (New York: Routledge, 1991).

4. Angel Rabasa et al., *The Muslim World after 9/11* (Santa Monica, CA: RAND Corporation, 2004), p. 5.

5. Ibid.

6. Ibid. See also GlobalSecurity.org, "Salafi Islam," at: http://www.globalsecurity.org/ military/intro/islam-salafi.htm.

7. Ibid., p. 15. Also see Maududi, Sayyid Abul A'la, *A Short History of the Revivalist Movement in Islam*, (Lahore: Islamic Publication Ltd., 1991).

8. Juan Cole, "Foreign Occupation Has Produced Radical Muslim Terrorism" (March 2005), at: http://www.juancole.com/2005/03/foreign-occupation-has-produced.html.

9. Andrew Tan, "Southeast Asia as the Second Front in the War against Terrorism: Evaluating the Threat and Responses," *Terrorism and Political Violence*, Vol. 15, No. 2 (2003), p. 115.

10. John Pelan, *The Hispanization of the Philippines* (Madison: University of Wisconsin Press, 1959).

11. See Peter Gowing, *Mosque and Moro: A Study of Muslims in the Philippines* (Manila: Federation of Christian Churches, 1964).

12. Samuel K. Tan, "History of the Mindanao Problem," in Amina Rasul (ed.), *The Road to Peace and Reconciliation: Muslim Perspective on the Mindanao Conflict* (Makati City: Asian Institute of Management, 2003), p. 4.

13. Cear Majul, *Muslims in the Philippines* (Quezon City: University of the Philippines Press, 1973), p. 108.

14. Ibid.

15. Samuel K. Tan, "History of the Mindanao Problem," p. 5.

16. For an excellent account of Muslims in the Philippines during the American colonial rule, see Peter G. Gowing, *Mandate in Moroland: The American Government of Muslim Filipinos, 1899–1920* (Quezon City: New Day Publishers, 1983).

17. W.K. Che Man, *Muslim Separatism: The Moros of Southern Philippines and the Malays of Southern Thailand* (Manila: Ateneo de Manila Press, 1990), p. 47.

18. Dona J. Amoroso, "Inheriting the *Moro* Problem: Muslim Authority and Colonial Rule in British Malaya and the Philippines," in Julian Go and Anne L. Foster (eds.), *The American Colonial State in the Philippines: Global Perspectives* (Manila: Anvil Publishing, 2005), p. 142.

19. Ibid., p. 143.

20. Samuel K. Tan, *Internationalization of the Bangsamoro Struggle* (Quezon City: University of the Philippines Center for Integrative and Development Studies, 1995), p. 27.

21. Ibid. p. 28.

22. Che Man, *Muslim Separatism: The Moros of Southern Philippines and the Malays of Southern Thailand*, p. 55.

23. Samuel K. Tan, *The Filipino Muslim Armed Struggle, 1900–1972* (Manila: Filipinas Foundation, Inc., 1977), p. 57.

24. Tan, *Internationalization of the Bangsamoro Struggle*, p. 28.

25. Robert Maulana Alonto, "Four Centuries of Jihad Underpinning the Bangsamoro Muslims' Struggle for Freedom" (1999), at: http://www.muslimedia.com/archives/sea99/phil-jihad.

26. Alunan Glang, *Muslim Secession or Integration?* (Quezon City: R.P. Garcia, 1969), p. 21. Also cited in Che Man, *Muslim Separatism: The Moros of Southern Philippines and the Malays of Southern Thailand*, pp. 55–56.

27. Thomas M. McKenna, *Muslim Rulers and Rebels: Everyday Politics and Armed Separatism in the Southern Philippines* (Manila: Anvil Publishing, 1998).

28. Majul, *Muslims in the Philippines,* p. 29.

29. Andrew Tan, "The Indigenous Roots of Conflict in Southeast Asia: The Case of Mindanao," in Kumar Ramakrishna and Tan See Seng (eds.), *After Bali: The Threat of Terrorism in Southeast Asia* (Singapore: World Scientific Publishing/Institute of Defence and Strategic Studies, 2003), p. 99.

30. "Jabidah Massacre," at: http://www.moroinfo.com/hist8.html. Also see Marites D Vitug and Glenda M. Gloria, *Under the Crescent Moon: Rebellion in Mindanao* (Quezon City: Ateneo Center for Social Policy and Public Affairs and Institute for Popular Democracy, 2000), pp. 2–25.

31. Arnold M. Azurin, "The Jabidah Massacre Myth," in his *Beyond the Cult of Dissidence in Southern Philippines and Wartorn Zones in the Global Village* (Quezon City: University of the Philippines Center for Integrative and Development Studies, 1996), pp. 93–103.

32. Majul, *Muslims in the Philippines,* p. 30.

33. Abraham S. Iribani, *GRP-MNLF Peace Talks, 1992–1996: Issues and Challenges* (Quezon City: National Defense College of the Philippines, 2000), p. 99.

34. *The Manifesto of the Moro National Liberation Front* (April 28, 1974).

35. Nur Misuari, *MNLF Guidelines for Political Cadres and Military Commanders,* n.p. (Bangsa Moro Research Center of the *Moro* National Liberation Front, 1984), pp. 6–7.

36. Iribani, *GRP-MNLF Peace Talks, 1992–1996: Issues and Challenges,* p. 100.

37. See MIPT Terrorism Knowledge Base, "*Moro* National Liberation Front," at: http://www.tkb.org/Group.jsp?groupID=202.

38. McKenna, Muslim Rulers and Rebels: Everyday Politics and Armed Separatism in the Southern Philippines, p. 181.

39. Ibid., p. 324.

40. Jacques Bertrand, "Peace and Conflict in the Southern Philippines: Why the 1996 Peace Agreement Is Fragile?" *Pacific Affairs*, Vol. 73, No. 1 (Spring 2000), p. 42.

41. "DND cites gains in campaign vs CPP-NPA, Abu Sayyaf, other criminal elements" (January 3, 2005), at: http://www.news.ops.gov.ph/archives2005/jan03.htm.

42. Office of the Chief of Staff for Intelligence Updates on the Activities of the ASG and the MBG (Quezon City: General Headquarters of the Armed Forces of the Philippines 2002).

43. Jomar Canlas, "State Witness Bares MNLF, MILF Links with Abu Sayyaf," *The Manila Times* (March 28, 2005).

44. Hashim Salamat, *Referendum: Peaceful, Civilized, Diplomatic and Democratic Means of Solving the Mindanao Conflict* (Camp Abubakre As-Siddique: Agency for Youth Affairs-MILF, 2002), p. 30.

45. Ibid., p. 32.

46. Ibid. See also Salamat Hashim, *The Bangsamoro Mujahid: His Objectives and Responsibilities* (Mindanao: Bangsamoro Publications, 1984).

47. Ibid. See also Salamat Hashim, *The Bangsamoro People's Struggle against Oppression and Colonialism* (Camp Abubakre As-Siddique: Agency for Youth Affairs-MILF, 2001).

48. Zachary Abuza, *Militant Islam in Southeast Asia: Crucible of Terror* (Boulder, Colorado: Lynne Rienner Publishers, Inc., 2003), p. 91.

49. Rohan Gunaratna, *Inside Al Qaeda: Global Network of Terror* (New Delhi: Roli Books, 2002), p. 182.

50. Ibid., p. 185.

51. International Crisis Group, "Southern Philippine Backgrounder: Terrorism and the Peace Process" *ICG Asia Report*, No. 8 (July 13, 2004), p. i.

52. Maria A. Ressa, *Seeds of Terror: An Eyewitness Account of Al-Qaeda's Newest Center of Operations in Southeast Asia* (New York: Free Press, 2003), p. 7.

53. Conversation with a Muslim lawyer who is providing consulting services for the ARMM and other Muslim organizations in the Philippines.

54. Salamat, *Referendum: Peaceful, Civilized, Diplomatic and Democratic Means of Solving the Mindanao Conflict* (2002), p. 34.

55. Salamat, *Referendum: Peaceful, Civilized, Diplomatic and Democratic Means of Solving the Mindanao Conflict* (2002), p. 34.

56. Office of the Assistant Secretary for Plans and Programs, "CPP-NPA-MILF Tactical Alliance," in *Moro Islamic Liberation Front Reference Folder* (Quezon City: Department of National Defense, 2004).

57. Salamat, *Referendum: Peaceful, Civilized, Diplomatic and Democratic Means of Solving the Mindanao Conflict* (2002), p. 46.

58. Ibid., p. 57.

59. Rommel Banlaoi, "Leadership Dynamics in Terrorist Organizations in Southeast Asia: The Abu Sayyaf Case" (Paper presented to the international symposium *The Dynamics and Structures of Terrorist Threats in Southeast Asia,* organized by the Institute of Defense Analyses in cooperation with the Southeast Asia Regional Center for Counter-Terrorism and the U.S. Pacific Command held at Palace of Golden Horses Hotel, Kuala Lumpur, Malaysia, April 18–20, 2005). Also in John T. Hanley, Kongdan Oh Hassig, and Caroline F. Ziemke (eds.), *Proceedings of the International Symposium on the Dynamics and Structures of Terrorist Threats in Southeast Asia* (Alexandria, VA: Institute for Defense Analyses, 2005).

60. A paper obtained from the Intelligence Service of the Armed Forces of the Philippines on March 29, 2005.

61. See, for example, Turbiville, Jr., pp. 38–47.

62. Jose Torres Jr., *Into the Mountain: Hostages by the Abu Sayyaf* (Quezon City: Claretian Publications, 2003), p. 35.

63. Carl Thayer, "Leadership Dynamics in Terrorist Organizations in Southeast Asia" (Paper presented to the international symposium, The Dynamics and Structures of Terrorist Threats in Southeast Asia, organized by the Institute of Defense Analyses in cooperation with the Southeast Asia Regional Center for Counter-Terrorism and the U.S. Pacific Command held at Palace of Golden Horses Hotel, Kuala Lumpur, Malaysia, on April 18–20, 2005).

64. See Eusaquito P. Manalo, Philippine Response to Terrorism: The Abu Sayyaf Group (MA Thesis: Naval Post Graduate School, Monterey, California, December 2004).

65. Ibid.

66. Glenda Gloria, "Bearer of the Sword: The Abu Sayyaf Has Nebulous Beginnings and Incoherent Aims," *Mindanao Updates* (June 6, 2000).

67. Quoted in Samuel K. Tan, *Internationalization of the Bangsamoro Struggle* (Quezon City: University of the Philippines Center for Integrative and Development Studies, 2003), revised edition, p. 96.

68. Abu Hamdie, "The Abu Sayyaf Group" (undated and unpublished manuscript).

69. See Zachary Abuza, "Tentacles of Terror: Al Qaeda's Southeast Asian Linkages," (Paper presented in the conference *Transnational Violence and Seams of Lawlessness in the Asia–Pacific: Linkages to Global Terrorism*, held at the Asia–Pacific Center for Security Studies, Honolulu, Hawaii, February 12–21, 2002), p. 6. Also published in *Contemporary Southeast Asia*, Vol. 24, No. 2 (December 2002), pp. 427–466.

70. Ibid.

71. Interview with Police Chief Superintendent Ismael R. Rafanan, Director of the Philippine National Police Intelligence Group, held at Camp Crame, Quezon City, on April 1, 2005.

72. Alcuin Papa, "Military: JI Members Still Training Locals," *Philippine Daily Inquirer* (January 18, 2005).

73. "Alleged bombs expert for Jemaah Islamiyah regional network arrested in Philippine," *Channel News Asia*, at: http://www.channelnewsasia.com/stories/southeastasia/view/138779/1/.html (accessed April 12, 2005).

74. Interview with General Marlu Quevedo, Chief of the Intelligence Service of the Armed Forces of the Philippines, held at Camp General Emilio Aguinaldo, Quezon City, on March 29, 2005.

75. Jim Gomez, "Filipino Terror Group's Reach Grown Nationally," Associated Press (March 8, 2005).

76. Charles Donnely, "Terrorism in the Southern Philippines: Contextualizing the Abu Sayyaf Group as an Islamist Secessionist Organization" (Paper presented to the 15th Biennial Conference of the Asian Studies Association of Australia held in Canberra, June 2–July 29, 2004), p. 4.

77. Gracia Burnham and Dean Merrill, *In the Presence of My Enemies* (Wheaton, IL: Tyndale House Publishers, 2003).

78. See Peter Chalk, "Christian Converts and Islamic Terrorism in the Philippines," *Terrorism Monitor*, Vol. 4, Issue 8 (April 20, 2006). Also see International Crisis Group, "Philippines Terrorism: The Role of Militant Islamic Converts," *Asia Report*, No. 110 (December 19, 2005).

79. Chalk, "Christian Converts and Islamic Terrorism in the Philippines."

80. "Summary of Report on Rajah Solaiman Movement" (April 12, 2004).

81. Philippine National Police, "Fact Sheet on the Rajah Solaiman Movement."

82. A paper obtained from the National Intelligence Coordinating Agency, March 1, 2005.

83. Joe Cochrane, "Filipino Authorities Say the Newest Threat to the Country Is a Shadowy Terror Group Made Up of Radical Muslim Converts," *Newsweek International Edition* (May 17, 2004), at: http://msnbc.msn.com/id/4933472/ (accessed on August 28, 2004).

84. Philippine National Police, "Executive Summary: Update on the Arrest of Hilarion Santos" (October 28, 2005).

85. Philippine National Police, "Executive Summary: Update on the Arrest of Hilarion Santos."

86. Villaviray, Johnna "When Christians Embrace Islam," *Manila Times* (November 17, 2003), at: http://www.manilatimes.net/others/special/2003/nov/17/2003117spel.html. Also see the same article at http://www.geocities.com/WestHollywood/Park/ 6443/ Philappines/mtl.html (accessed June 23, 2005).

87. Ibid.

88. Ibid.

89. Ibid.

90. Ibid.

91. Ibid.

92. Marco Garrido, "After Madrid, Manila?" *Asia Times* (April 24, 2004), at: http://www.atimes.com/atimes/Southeast_Asia/FD24Ae01.html (accessed August 28, 2004).

93. Inday Espina-Varona, "Brothers in Arms," *Philippine Graphics*, Vol. 15. No. 38 (February 28, 2005), p. 24.

94. Ibid.

95. Ibid., p. 25.

96. Interview with General Florencio D. Fianza of the Office of the Special Envoy on Transnational Crime on April 1, 2005.

97. Stephen Ulph, "Philippine Terror War Goes On Despite Peace Talks," *Jamestown Foundation Terrorism Focus,* Vol. 2, No. 3 (Febuary 3, 2005), p. 3.

98. Amina Rasul-Bernardo, "Ethnic Conflict, Peace and Development: A Philippine Case Study," Paper presented at the CSID 6th Annual Conference, Washington, DC (April 22–23, 2005), at: http://www.islam-democracy.org/documents/[df/6th_ Annual_Conference-AminaRasulBernardo.pdf (accessed June 23, 2005) p. 1.

99. Agence France Press, "Three Muslim Extremists Captured in Maguindanao," *ABS-CBN News* (July 29, 2006).

100. A phone interview with military official in Cotabato City (July 30, 2006).

101. For a news account, see Malu Cadelina Manar, "Al Khobar Leader Is MILF Commander: Arrested Bomber," *Sun Star* (February 27, 2008), at: http://www.sunstar.com.ph/static/ net/2008/02/27/al.khobar.leader.is.milf.commander.arrested.bomber.html.

102. Marites D. Vitug, and Glenda M. Gloria, *Under the Crescent Moon: Rebellion in Mindanao*, p. 229.
103. Gico Dayanghirang, "Federal Republic of Mindanao," e-mail message sent on June 30, 2005.

# Chapter 4

# Local Government Response against Terrorist Threats in the Philippines: Issues and Prospects*

## Introduction

Although the global campaign against terrorism took place in the aftermath of the September 11 terrorist attacks on the United States, the Philippine campaign against international terrorism preceded 9/11. As early as 1985, the Philippines already felt the specter of international terrorism when notorious leaders of the Muslim secessionist movement in the Southern Philippines reportedly established linkages with "foreign terrorist groups" like the Abu Nidal Organization (ANO) and the Liberation Tigers of Tamil Eelam (LTTE).[1] On December 2, 1987, Philippine national police operatives discovered an ANO cell in Manila leading to the arrest of five so-called Palestinian terrorists with Jordanian passports. On

* Revised version of a paper originally published in Colin Durkop (ed.), *Security Management in Asian Cities* (Singapore: Konrad Adenauer Foundation, 2005), pp. 29–54. This chapter was also presented to the 12th International Conference of the East and Southeast Asia Network for Highly Performing Local Governments organized by the Konrad Adenauer Foundation and the Local Government Development Foundation, Rendezvous Hotel, Singapore on December 2–3, 2004.

May 19, 1995, combined police and military forces arrested nine LTTE members including its infamous leader *Selvarajah Balasingan*.[2]

But the United States and other major powers did not pay serious attention to the threat of terrorism in the Philippines because it was viewed as only "local" in scope. The United States even regarded terrorist threats in Southeast Asia as posing no clear and present danger to international security because the region only had a total of 186 international terrorist incidents from 1984 to 1996. This figure was low compared with 2,703 attacks in Western Europe, 1,621 attacks in Latin America, 1,392 attacks in West Asia, and 362 attacks in Africa.[3]

After 9/11, however, the United States radically altered its perceptions of Southeast Asian terrorism when its intelligence agencies unearthed various evidences linking terrorist groups in Southeast Asia with Osama bin Laden's al Qaeda Group.[4] The United States now views Southeast Asia as the major breeding ground for terrorism that has the capability to wreak havoc not only against America but also against substitute targets in Asia. In the war on terrorism in Southeast Asia,[5] the United States declared the Philippines as a major front-line state because of the confirmed linkages of its local terrorist groups with global terrorist network.[6]

Linkages of Filipino terrorists with international terrorists began when bin Laden established the al Qaeda Group in 1988 to wage international *jihad* in Afghanistan.[7] Bin Laden reportedly directed Mohammad Jamal Khalifa, his brother-in-law, to go to the Southern Philippines and recruit Filipino Muslim fighters for the Afghan war. *Moro* Islamic Liberation Front (MILF) leader Hashim Salamat deployed a thousand Filipino Muslim fighters to Afghanistan to undergo military training. Salamat regarded this training vital to strengthening the military capability of the MILF, a splinter and more radical group of the *Moro* National Liberation Front (MNLF). Khalifa left the Philippines in 1990 but returned to the country a year after to establish a permanent al Qaeda network in the Philippines through the Abu Sayyaf Group (ASG).[8]

At present, the ASG is the most nefarious locally based terrorist organization in the Philippines with verified international linkages with al Qaeda and its Southeast Asian network, the Jemaah Islamiyah (JI).[9] Though the MILF has also been reported to have established strong linkages with al Qaeda and JI,[10] the ASG caught greater international media attention because of its series of kidnapping activities, the most sensationalized of which was the Dos Palmas incident in March 2001.[11] Because of the growing terrorist threats posed by ASG, the Philippine government launched the Philippine Strategy to Combat Terrorism shortly after the 9/11 event.

This chapter examines the local government aspect of the Philippines' antiterrorism strategy and describes the role of local government units (LGUs) in responding to the threat of terrorism in the Philippines. This chapter also identifies issues and prospects of this antiterrorism strategy and examines its implications for good local governance in the Philippines.

# Terrorism in the Philippines: A Local Government Menace

The threat of international terrorism is inherently local in origin. Though terrorist operations are now global in scope, LGUs have always been the major arena of terrorist activities and the main victims of terrorist atrocities. It has been reported that al Qaeda will begin to disintegrate within a couple of years because its various factions will start to squabble and militants will return to their "local roots."[12] Professor Michael Clarke, a British academic, even argues that "terrorism will go back to being about more local issues."[13] Thus, a decisive local response is also an indispensable component of the struggle against international terrorism.

In the Philippines, the burning of Jolo town by Islamic militants on February 7, 1974, was a classic example of terrorist attacks on LGUs. The attack on the town of Ipil, Zamboanga del Sur, in April 1995, the Mindanao bombings in October 2002, and the Davao bombing in March 2004 were just some of the many terrorist attacks on Philippine LGUs. According to the Department of National Defense, the Ipil incident was the "most destructive single act of terrorism" thus far conducted by the ASG. The attack resulted in the death of 68 persons, the wounding of 114 others, and the destruction of P500 million worth of properties. The ASG, the most notorious terrorist group in the Philippines, started as a local terrorist organization based in Basilan of the Southern Philippines.[14]

Though ASG's main area of operation is far-flung LGUs in the Southern Philippines, it also operates in various Philippine cities. It has attracted some secret followers in Manila — the Philippine capital. The Rajah Solaiman Islamic Movement is the major Muslim organization in Manila known to have established links with ASG. The group is named after Rajah Solaiman, the last king of Manila before the Spanish conquest in the 1500s. Most of its members are Muslim converts. Like the ASG, converts claim they want to remake the country into an Islamic state.[15]

# Philippine Strategy to Combat Terrorism

To demonstrate the Philippine government's strong resolve to combat terrorism at the national and local levels, it formed the Inter-Agency Task Force against International Terrorism on September 24, 2001, under the direct supervision of the Office of the President. This Inter-Agency Task Force aimed to coordinate intelligence operations and to facilitate the identification and neutralization of suspected terrorist cells located in remote LGUs in the Philippines. To freeze the financial assets of international terrorists, the Philippine Congress passed the Anti-Money Laundering Act on September 29, 2001. President Arroyo also announced on October 12, 2001, its 14-pillar approach to combat terrorism (see Box 4.1).

## BOX 4.1    14 PILLARS TO COMBAT TERRORISM IN THE PHILIPPINES

- Designates Cabinet Oversight Committee on Internal Security as the lead antiterrorism body.
- Seeks to undertake and consolidate intelligence projects.
- Calls on the armed forces and the Philippine National Police to address terrorist violence.
- Holds accountable all public and private organizations abetting terrorism.
- Seeks regional consensus and cooperation especially with Indonesia and Malaysia in the war against terrorism.
- Anticipates legal issues and concerns.
- Pursues Christian-Muslim dialogue and seeks to promote ecumenism.
- Calls for greater vigilance and concrete measures against all possible terrorist supplies, materials, and finances.
- Mobilizes disaster coordination efforts in the event of catastrophic attack.
- Secures critical infrastructure.
- Protects overseas workers and seeks their immediate transfer if needed.
- Seeks the integration of the global terrorist threat in the AFP/PNP modernization program.
- Asks for media responsibility.
- Seeks to address the socioeconomic and political roots of perceived fanaticism.

On the basis of the 14 pillars to combat terrorism, the Philippine government also issued General Order No. 2 on May 9, 2002, directing the Armed Forces of the Philippines and the Philippine National Police to prevent and suppress acts of terrorism and lawless violence in affected localities in Mindanao. Together with General Order No. 2, the Philippine government issued on the same day the Memorandum Order No. 61 to provide measures in quelling the acts of terrorism in "terrorist-infected" LGUs in the Southern Philippines.

Through the Operation Center of the Cabinet Oversight Committee on Internal Security (COCIS)[16] the Philippine government formulated the National Plan to Address Terrorism and its Consequences as Annex K to the National Internal Security Plan (NISP). The Philippine government approved the NISP on November 26, 2001, through Memorandum Order 44. The COCIS was tasked to implement the national antiterrorism plan by involving all national government agencies, LGUs, and the private sectors in the campaign (see Figure 4.1).

But the Philippine government abolished the COCIS in October 2004. The task of managing and implementing the antiterrorism plan was then transferred to Anti-Terrorism Task Force (ATTF), which was originally formed on March 24, 2004, under the COCIS. The ATTF is now operating under the Office of the President. The ATTF aimed to establish an extensive antiterrorism information system and accelerate intelligence fusion among all intelligence units in the Philippines in the identification of terrorism personalities, cells, groups, and organizations in various LGUs (see Figure 4.2). It also aimed to conduct an extensive information drive at both national and local levels "to prepare the public and all stakeholders to get involved in the national anti-terrorism campaign."[17]

With the creation of ATTF, the Philippine government adopts the 16-point counterterrorism program to operationalize the 14-point antiterrorism policy of the national government (see Box 4.2). Although the ATTF organizational structure involves a local government unit, this unit does not have a clear organizational structure of its own. The ATTF does not even have a counterpart structure at the local level. But the ATTF operationalizes its local government section through the local Peace and Order Councils.

## Local Government Response to Combat Terrorism

To better appreciate the Philippine local government response against terrorism, it is imperative to describe the nature of Philippine LGUs, which are divided into the following categories:

*Region* — A subnational administrative unit comprised of several provinces having more or less homogenous characteristics, such as ethnic origin of inhabitants, dialect spoken, agricultural produce, and so forth.

*Province* — The largest unit in the political structure of the Philippines. It consists, in varying numbers, of municipalities and in some cases component cities. Its functions and duties in relation to its component cities and municipalities are generally coordinative and supervisory.

*City* — There are three classes of cities in the Philippines: the highly urbanized; the independent component cities, which are independent of the province; and the component cities, which are part of the provinces where they are located and subject to their administrative supervision.

*Municipality* — A political corporate body endowed with the facilities of a municipal corporation, exercised by and through the municipal government in conformity with law. It is a subsidiary of the province, which consists of a number of barangays within its territorial boundaries, one of which is the seat of government found at the town proper (*poblacion*).

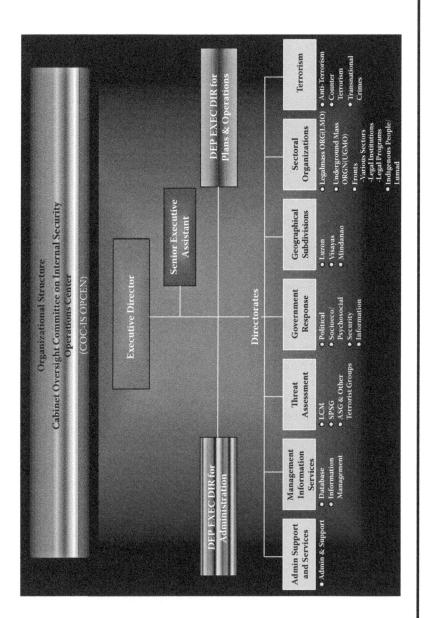

**Figure 4.1** Organizational structure of the defunct Cabinet Oversight Committee on Internal Security. (From the Operation Center, Cabinet Oversight Committee on Internal Security, July 2004.)

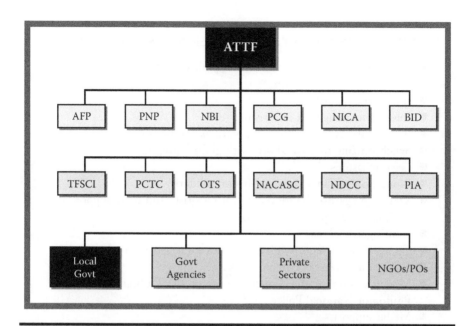

**Figure 4.2 Organizational structure of the Anti-Terrorism Task Force. (From the Anti-Terrorism Task Force Accomplishment Report, June 2004.)**

*Barangay (Village)* — The smallest political unit into which cities and municipalities in the Philippines are divided. It is the basic unit of the Philippine political system. It consists of less than 1,000 inhabitants residing within the territorial limits of a city or municipality and administered by a set of elective officials, headed by a barangay chairman (punong barangay).[18]

Speaking at an antiterrorism command conference in Cebu City on March 27, 2003, President Arroyo urged all local government executives from provincial to village levels to help in the prevention, intervention, and containment of all terrorist acts. She also directed the Department of Interior and Local Government (DILG) to pass a circular describing the role and participation of Philippine LGUs in the government's antiterrorism campaign. As part of its mandate to build the capacity of local governments in combating transnational crime, the Philippine Center on Transnational Crime even conducted some crisis management simulation exercises for LGUs.[19]

Because terrorism is not only a national security problem but also a serious local peace and order problem, local government sectors in the Philippines joined the national government in the campaign against terrorism.

In November 2002, the League of Municipalities of the Philippines (LMP) passed a resolution condemning terrorism in the strongest terms. Presently composed of 1,500 member municipalities, LMP regards terrorism as "a serious threat

**BOX 4.2   16-POINT COUNTER-TERRORISM PROGRAM**

■ Supervision and implementation of policies and actions of the government against terrorism.
■ Intelligence coordination.
■ Internal focus against terrorism.
■ Accountability and private corporations and personalities.
■ Synchronizing internal efforts with global outlook.
■ Legal measures.
■ Promotion of Christian and Muslim solidarity.
■ Vigilance against the movement of terrorists and their supporters, equipment, weapons, and funds.
■ Contingency plans.
■ Comprehensive security plans for critical infrastructures.
■ Support for overseas Filipino workers.
■ Modernization of the Armed Forces of the Philippines and the Philippine National Police.
■ Media support.
■ Political, social, and economic measures.
■ Ensuring the accountability of local and national government in cleaning the government of terrorist and criminal coddlers.
■ Strengthening the peace process.

*Source:* Anti-Terrorism Task Force Accomplishment Report, June, 2004.

to the security and well-being not only of the Filipino people but also of the whole civilized world."[20] It urged all municipalities in the Philippines to adopt a unified course of action to fight terrorism and criminality by

■ Activating the Peace and Order Council;
■ Creating a local intelligence-gathering network; and,
■ Establishing other strategies and mechanisms to fight the menace, including provisions for funds.

The LMP also established a closer partnership with a defense establishment in order to implement its antiterrorism plan at the municipal level. During its major island conferences and general assemblies, LMP involved various defense officials in its programs and activities in order to increase the awareness of municipal chief executives on terrorism and counterterrorism.

The League of Cities of the Philippines (LCP) also joined the fight against terrorism when it expressed its unwavering support on the passage of antiterrorism bill. It even supported the passage of the controversial national identification system and vowed to acquire modern equipment such as metal detectors and to train bomb-sniffing dogs that would be utilized against terrorist threats.[21] The LCP is presently composed of 116 member cities.

The League of Provinces of the Philippines (LPP), on the other hand, asked the national government for the timely release of internal revenue allotment to LGUs in order to finance its drive against terrorism. But President Arroyo urged Philippine provinces to take the initiative in raising their own funds.[22] The LPP comprises 79 member provinces to date.

To fight terrorism at the grassroots level, the *Liga ng mga Barangay sa Pilipinas* (LBP, or League of Philippine Villages) also launched its antiterrorism campaign when it forged a closer partnership with the ATTF. On June 8, 2004, the league and the ATTF published advocacy material, *Gabay ng Barangay Laban sa Terorismo* (Villages Guide against Terrorism), to increase local government awareness about the gravity of terrorist threats. This advocacy material contains fundamental discussions on the definition of terrorism and how to respond to terrorist threats at the village level. The league adopts what it calls "4A's to Fight Terrorism": Awareness, Alertness, Action, and Advocacy.[23] The league is composed of more than 42,700 members.

Though various local government associations in the Philippines have expressed their support of the antiterrorism campaign to the national government, they have not yet developed their own capabilities to fight the menace. Beyond making motherhood statements, leagues of local governments do not have the money and technical expertise to wage their own battle against terrorism. Their primarily role is to assist the national government in the antiterrorism advocacy and awareness campaigns.

Also LGUs do not have the wherewithal to fight terrorism without national government support. They do not have their own operational capability to respond to these threats. They heavily rely on police and military forces deployed at the local levels.

But there are mechanisms where local governments can participate in the fight against terrorism. The ATTF, for example, has been implementing the national antiterrorism plan at various local levels through the DILG and by directly engaging the participation of LGUs and other local government associations (LGAs), like the LMP, LCP, LPP, and LBP. Policy and military operatives also "share" intelligence information with local leaders through different local Peace and Order Councils.

Another mechanism where police and military officials coordinate with local chief executives in the campaign against terrorism is the Area Coordinating Center (ACC) of the COCIS. The ACC is a security and peace and order "facility or office" established at the local levels "as a proactive, reactive and post conflict mechanism to address various concerns at regional and local levels of governance and solve problems of coordination and response" to internal security threats like terrorism.[24] Anchored on the principle that peace and development are two sides of the same coin, the ACC supplements and coordinates the functions of the Local

Development Councils and Local Peace and Order Councils in the promotion of internal security (see Figure 4.3). The ACC is organized in a province, a city, a municipality, and a barangay (village) "to provide a venue and serve as point of contact or nerve center for coordination and integration efforts of various stakeholders" (see Figures 4.4 and 4.5).

Complementary with the ACC is the National Plan to Address Terrorism and Its Consequences (NPTC), formulated by the Directorate on Terrorism of the defunct COCIS. The NPTC operationalizes the 14 Pillars of Policy and Action against Terrorism at the national and local levels through the ATTF. The NPTC also prescribes the national framework, strategies, and operational concepts to address terrorism; and it also undertakes measures at the local level "to protect the people, restore government services, and provide emergency relief to individuals or organizations affected as the results or effects of terrorism."[25] More importantly, the NPTC prescribes concepts, policies, strategies, and procedures in addressing terrorist-based crises and their consequences through the integration of crisis management and consequence management.[26]

At the local level, crisis management committees are constituted at the various Peace and Order Councils from the region to the village levels (see Figure 4.6).

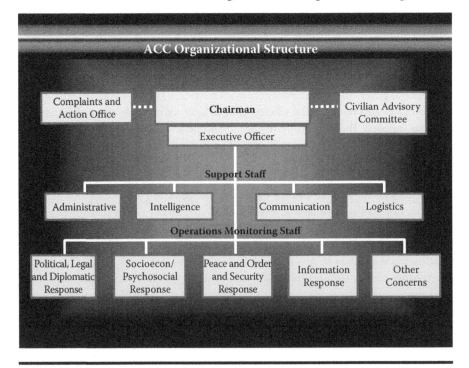

**Figure 4.3  Organizational structure of the Area Coordination Center. (From the Operation Center, Cabinet Oversight Committee on Internal Security, July 2004.)**

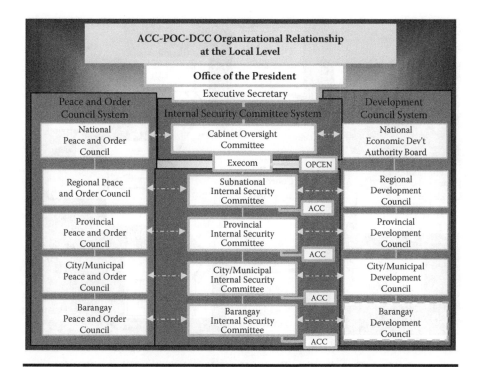

**Figure 4.4  ACC-POC-DCC organizational relationship at the local level. (From the Operation Center, Cabinet Oversight Committee on Internal Security, July 2004.)**

Consequence management committees, on the other hand, are constituted at the various local disaster coordinating councils (DCCs) (see Figure 4.7). The ACC coordinates the functions of the local Peace and Order Council (POC) and the local DCC in the fight against terrorism and other threats to internal security.

The NPTC, therefore, provides proactive, reactive, and even postconflict response to terrorist threats. But it also recognizes that "certain political, socio-economic and psychological conditions in the country serve as spawning ground of violence and terrorism." Thus, the NPTC aims to address these conditions through a comprehensive approach. This comprehensive approach includes the waging of "war against poverty as it wages war against terrorism."[27] An integral component of the antipoverty strategy of the NPTC is the implementation of a poverty-reduction program of the government through the *Kapit-Bisig Laban sa Kahirapan* (KALAHI, Joining Hands to Fight Poverty) program.

The KALAHI program is the government's overarching program for a "focused, accelerated, convergent, expanded and strategic effort to reduce poverty" in the Philippines to address the root causes of insurgency and terrorism. The National Anti-Poverty Commission, chaired by no less than the President of the Philippine Republic, supervises the implementation of the KALAHI Program.

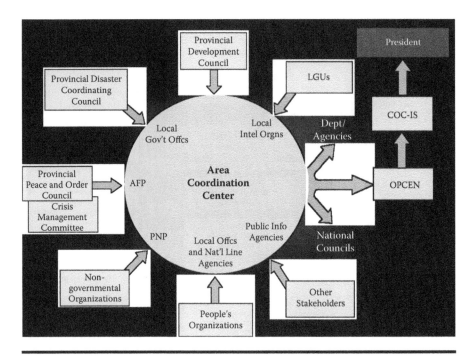

**Figure 4.5** **Area Coordination Center Operational relationships with other sectors. (From the Operation Center, Cabinet Oversight Committee on Internal Security, July 2004.)**

Philippine LGUs are tasked to implement this poverty reduction program at the grassroots level. The KALAHI poverty reduction programs at the local government levels are being integrated in local development plans through

Training of Local Poverty Reduction Action Officers with the DILG in poverty diagnosis, targeting, planning, and monitoring at the provincial, municipal, and barangay levels; and,

Testing and modeling of local poverty reduction planning project implementation and monitoring, with the help of training and guidebooks that will be disseminated to LGUs of KALAHI municipalities and barangays.

The COCIS was originally tasked to integrate the KALAHI program in the implementation of the NPTC at the local level. The abolition of COCIS, however, has put the operation of ACC and NPTC on uncertain ground.

The ATTF was the main agency of the national government in charge of implementing the national antiterrorism plan of the Philippine government at the local level by coordinating with the DILG and the local government sector. Through the concerted efforts of police and military institutions and with the cooperation

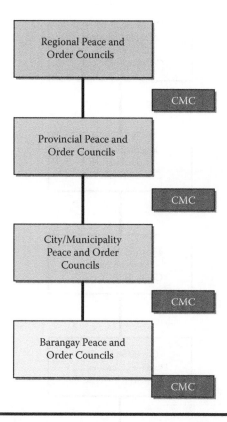

**Figure 4.6  Crisis Management Committees (CMC) at the local levels. (From the Primer on the National Plan to Address Terrorism and Its Consequences, 2002.)**

of concerned LGUs, the ATTF was able to arrest, capture, and neutralize various terrorist personalities in the Philippines.[28] With the passage of the Human Security Act in 2007, the ATTF has been replaced by the Anti-Terrorism Council.

## Issues and Prospects for Good Local Governance

From the foregoing, the Philippines has some exemplary practices to share in the fight against terrorist threats. The Philippine government has formulated a national plan against terrorism involving various LGUs and LGAs. The ATTF, the antiterrorism "superbody" in the Philippines, is structured to involve the participation of local government in the campaign against terrorism. The ATTF is also mandated to ensure that all existing local mechanisms (local peace and order councils, local disaster coordinating councils, local poverty reduction offices, and so forth) are integrated in the implementation of antiterrorism strategy of the government that addresses both the short-term and long-term threats of terrorism.

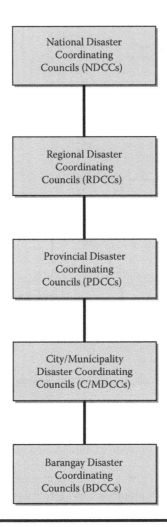

**Figure 4.7  Consequence Management Committees at the local levels: Disaster Coordinating Council system. (From the Primer on the National Plan to Address Terrorism and Its Consequences, 2002.)**

While local governments have already been recognized as part and parcel of the national government antiterrorism strategy, most LGUs in the Philippines still have a very limited operational capability to confront terrorism. Most LGUs have a very weak emergency response system to respond to terrorist attacks. Although the National Disaster Coordinating Council (NDCC) has released a manual for local government on contingency planning for complex emergencies, which includes terrorist attacks,[29] there has been no existing institutionalized command and control system that is recognized or known to all responding emergency and disaster mitigation units at the local levels.[30]

Shortly after the 9/11 terrorist attacks, Secretary Angelo Reyes, former NDCC Chairman, aptly commented that there was no clear chain-of-command structure, particularly in the National Capital Region in the event of massive terrorist attacks in the capital city. Reyes even lamented that LGUs and the national government have a serious problem in their communication system to deal with terrorism-related disasters. He said that there was no universal communication network or frequency where all responding teams could switch on to automatically in times of emergency caused by terrorist attacks.[31] This situation, unfortunately, persists. Furthermore, only few LGUs have fully established their DCCs to face the consequences of terrorist attacks. According to NDCC, there are only 1,381 DCCs established at the local levels nationwide out of least 43,600 LGUs from regional to barangay levels.[32] Out of 79 provinces, only 15 province DCCs have been established. Out of 115 cities, only 41 city DCCs have been established. Out of 1,500 municipalities, only 384 municipality DCCs have been established; and out of at least 42,000 barangays, only 941 have been established. These figures reflect the limited consequence management capability of LGUs in responding to terrorist threats.

Another major issue is the existence of various local councils in the Philippines whose functions are enormously overlapping. As stated earlier, the Philippines has the following local councils: POC, the Development Council, the ACC, and the proposed Local Critical Infrastructure Protection Council. Though the ACC aims to coordinate the functions of these councils, the ACC is facing the difficult problem of institution building due to the abolition of COCIS.

Thus, LGUs continue to be strongly vulnerable to terrorist attacks. In Philippine cities alone, the Department of National Defense and DILG identified at least 273 vital installations in Metro Manila as potential terrorist targets. These are the Malacanang Palace, power plants, the mass transit system, television and communication facilities, and foreign embassies. They also identified at least 57 privately owned facilities, like the oil depots, that were vulnerable targets of terrorism. At least 358 buildings in Makati City were described as potential targets of terrorist groups.[33] It fact, it has been argued that "City officials will have to realize that terrorism thrives best in urban centers where the opportunities of terrorist targets are great and detection of terrorist cells and organizations much more difficult."[34]

The proposed National Critical Infrastructure Protection Plan prepared by the Task Force for the Security of Critical Infrastructure also identifies the following sectors as vulnerable to terrorist attacks: water sector, food and agriculture sector, health sector, emergency response services sector, government sector, energy sector, transportation sector, banking and finance sector, information and communication sector, and strategic commercial centers sector.[35]

To prevent terrorist attacks from happening, there is a need to enhance the capability of the intelligence community operating at the local levels by utilizing the already established POCs. In fact, the POCs can serve as the operational arm of the ACC and the proposed Local Critical Infrastructure Protection Council.

Compared with other local councils, POCs already have a longer life span. They only need further institutionalization to fully implement their mandated functions.

It is also imperative to train local leaders, through the POCs, on how to coordinate with intelligence and law enforcement agencies to gather information in preempting terrorist attacks on vulnerable LGUs. Without coordination, law enforcement agencies will not know what information to collect, "and analysts, therefore will not have the necessary pieces to assemble or forecast a composite of impending threats."[36]

Philippine military officials, however, have admitted that the Philippines has a very weak intelligence network, particularly at the local level. Although the Philippine government issued Administrative Order No. 68 on April 8, 2003, to strengthen the National Intelligence Coordinating Agency, the government's intelligence capability remains weak at both the national and local levels. Former Armed Forces chief of staff General Narciso Abaya candidly acknowledged that the nonsharing of intelligence information by military spy units deployed in various LGUs in the Philippines is hampering the government's antiterrorism campaign.[37] Abaya said that a culture exists among intelligence units in the Philippines to withhold vital intelligence information from other groups and stressed that "I think we have to improve on our intelligence. The trend now is not the need to know but the need to share. That is the emerging trend among intelligence units all over the world."[38] He further lamented, "Sometimes, our intelligence units zealously keep to themselves intelligence information which, if fused with the information of other intelligence units, would give a more comprehensive picture of the enemy."[39] These problems identified by Abaya still persist.

There was also a serious allegation that the military and provincial governments are coddling some terrorists connected with ASG. Based on the report of the International Peace Mission that went to Basilan on March 23–27, 2002, it was found that there were "consistent credible reports that the military and the provincial government are coddling the Abu Sayyaf."[40] Thus, the Peace Mission finds that a military solution to the ASG threat "will not work to solve the problem."[41]

As early as 1994, in fact, there were allegations that some local police and fake police officers were involved in the ASG attempt to smuggle firearms in Zamboanga City from Manila and Iloilo on board the vessel *MV Princess of the Pacific*. But the police and the military authorities stressed that connivance with ASG "is not being tolerated" and contended that those found guilty of this misdemeanor will be punished accordingly.

To win the war on terrorism, addressing its root causes at the local level is imperative. Poverty and injustices are roots that attract people to resort to terrorism. The KALAHI program is an important initiative of the government to address the root causes of terrorism. But the poverty reduction program of the government will not succeed unless it implements the principle of accountability and transparency in governance. All government efforts will be wasted unless the government really promotes transparent and accountable governance at both the national and local levels. Good governance is the most effective weapon against terrorism.

There is also need to overcome the dichotomized thinking that addressing terrorist threats is a concern of police and military establishments and not civilian bureaucracy. As stated earlier, the National Plan to Address Terrorism and Its Consequences and the National Internal Security Plan assert that the war on terrorism has to be fought holistically.

To surmount the terrorist threats and other threats to Philippine internal security, the Arroyo government, as discussed in Chapter 1, adopted the Strategy of Holistic Approach (SHA) as the grand strategy to overcome insurgency and terrorism problems in the Philippines (see Figure 1.2 in Chapter 1) The SHA consists of four major components (see Box 4.3):

1. Political/Legal/Diplomatic
2. Socioeconomic/Psychosocial
3. Peace and Order/Security
4. Information[42]

What is needed is to develop the capacities of local government on how to implement the SHA at the local level because combating the threat of terrorism also requires the long-term commitment and determination of the local political leadership.

Finally, terrorist threats in the Philippines have a global dimension. Terrorist threats in one country also create threats in other countries. Thus, fighting terrorism will not only require the long-term commitment and determination of the local and national political leadership, it also requires bilateral (see Chapters 8 through 10), regional, and international cooperation of all states (see Chapter 15). Its participation in the global campaign against terrorism and Association of Southest Asian Nations (ASEAN) cooperation to combat terrorism provides the Philippines the proper arena to fight terrorism at the global and regional fronts.

# Conclusion

The Philippine government has provided various mechanisms to actively involve local governments in the fight against terrorism. Through the cooperation of local governments, the military, and police, antiterrorist operatives were able to identify, arrest, and neutralize terrorist leaders and members operating in various LGUs in the Philippines. The arrest and neutralization of terrorists have prevented the occurrence of some terrorist attacks that could have brought catastrophic effects on the Philippines. Due to the weakness of the Philippine intelligence system and enforcement agencies, the Philippines remains vulnerable to terrorist attacks. When terrorist attacks occur, local governments are the first victims.

## BOX 4.3 COMPONENTS OF THE STRATEGY OF HOLISTIC APPROACH

The political/legal/diplomatic component of the SHA pushes for "political reforms and institutional development to strengthen democratic institutions and empower the citizenry to pursue personal and community growth." This component aims to develop and propagate Philippine democracy to "confront the communist ideology" and the Islamic fundamentalist ideology. The cornerstone of this particular component is the peace process based on the "Six Paths to Peace" formula:

- Pursuit of social, economic, and political reforms.
- Consensus-building and empowerment for peace.
- Peaceful, negotiated settlement with the different rebel groups.
- Programs for reconciliation, reintegration, and rehabilitation.
- Conflict management and protection of civilians caught in armed conflict.
- Building and nurturing a climate conducive to peace.

The socioeconomic/psychosocial component of the SHA, on the other hand, aims to alleviate poverty in the country through the acceleration of development programs of the Philippine government. This component also aims to develop and strengthen "a spirit of nationhood among the people, which includes developing national character/identity without losing cultural integrity."

The peace and order/security component aims "to protect the people from the insurgents and provide a secure environment for national development." More importantly, this component has the specific goal of denying the insurgents "access to their most important resource — popular support."

Finally, the information component is the integrating component in the SHA. It "refers to the overall effort to advocate peace, promote public confidence in government and support government efforts to overcome insurgency and terrorism through tri-media and interpersonal approaches."

*Source:* Operation Center, Cabinet Committee on Internal Security, July 2004.

Preventing acts of terrorism cannot be solved through military solution alone. A more comprehensive solution that addresses the root of terrorism is imperative. Poverty and injustices are major roots of terrorism in the Philippines. Unless poverty is alleviated and justice is observed at the local levels, the Philippines will continue to face the vicious cycle of terrorist threats. As stressed by one analyst, there is a need to mitigate the success of terrorism with "the politics of truth and justice."[43]

Though the Arroyo government adopted the SHA as the grand strategy to overcome insurgency problems and terrorist threats in the Philippines, the success of SHA depends on the effectiveness of the Philippine government in winning the hearts and minds of the people at various local levels suffering poverty and injustices. One important way of doing this is to transform the quality of local governance in the Philippines to be more transparent, accountable, responsive, and participatory (see Chapter 6).

# Endnotes

1. Department of National Defense, *The Philippine Campaign against Terrorism* (Quezon City: Department of National Defense, 2002), p. 3.
2. Ibid.
3. Mohammed Jahwar Hassan, "Terrorism: Southeast Asia's Response," *PacNet Newsletter* (January 4, 2002), at: http://www.csis.org/pacfor/pac0201.htm (accessed on October 26, 2004).
4. Reyco Huang, "Al Qaeda in Southeast Asia: Evidence and Response," *CDI Terrorism Project* (February 8, 2002). Also at: http://www.cdi.org/terrorism/sea-pr.cfm (accessed October 26, 2004).
5. For the author's detailed discussion on the war on terrorism in Southeast Asia, see Rommel C. Banlaoi, *War on Terrorism in Southeast Asia* (Quezon City: Rex Publishers, 2004). As a supplementary material, see Maria Ressa, *Seeds of Terror: An Eyewitness Account of Al-Qaeda's Newest Center of Operations in Southeast Asia* (New York: Free Press, 2003).
6. For a more detailed discussion on this topic, see Rommel C. Banlaoi, "The Role of Philippine–American Relations in the Global Campaign against Terrorism: Implications for Regional Security," *Contemporary Southeast Asia*, Vol. 24, No. 2 (August 2002), pp. 294–312. Also see Rommel C. Banlaoi, "Philippine-American Security Relations and the War on Terrorism in Southeast Asia," in Wang Xingsheng (ed.), *International Relations of the Asia–Pacific after 9/11 and China's Accession to WTO* (Guangzhou: Zhongshan University Institute of Southeast Asian Studies, 2003), pp. 80–95.
7. For a critical appraisal of these linkages, see Clive Williams M.G., "The Question of Links between Al Qaeda and Southeast Asia," in Kumar Ramakrishna and see Seng Tan (eds.), *After Bali: The Threat of Terrorism in Southeast Asia* (Singapore: Institute of Defence and Strategic Studies, 2003), pp. 83–96.

8. Zachary Abuza, "Tentacles of Terror: Al Qaeda's Southeast Asian Linkages" (Paper presented at the conference "Transnational Violence and Seams of Lawlessness in the Asia–Pacific: Linkages to Global Terrorism," held at the Asia–Pacific Center for Security Studies, Honolulu, Hawaii, on February 12, 2002), p. 6.

9. Ibid. Also see Office of the Deputy Chief of Staff for Operations, J3, *Knowing the Terrorists: The Abu Sayyaf Study* (Quezon City: Headquarters of the Armed Forces of the Philippines, n.d.); and Office of the Assistant to the Chief of Staff for Intelligence, *Field Handout: Doctrinal Extract for the Abu Sayyaf Group* (Headquarters of the Philippine Marine Corps, January 21, 2002).

10. For a recent study on MILF/JI/al Qaeda linkages, see International Crisis Group, "Southern Philippines Backgrounder: Terrorism and the Peace Process," *ICG Asia Report*, No. 80 (July 13, 2004). Also at: http://www.icg.org/home/index.cfm?id=2863&l=1 (accessed October 20, 2004).

11. For a victim's point of view of the Dos Palmas incident, see Gracia Burnham and Dean Merrill, *In the Presence of My Enemies* (Wheaton, Illinois: Tyndale House Publishers, Inc., 2003). Also see Djanicelle J. Berreveld, *Terrorism in the Philippines: The Bloody Trail of Abu Sayyaf, Bin Laden's East Asian Connection* (San Jose: Writers Club Press, 2001).

12. Michael Holden, "Al Qaeda 'To Disintegrate' in 2 Years — U.K. Adviser," *BigNews Network* (November 10, 2004), at: http://feeds.bignewsnetwork.com/redir.php?jid=85 5f4c0dfb7e7357&cat=c08dd24cec417021 (accessed November 10, 2004).

13. Ibid.

14. For an insightful analysis on the evolution of ASG, see Rohan Gunaratna, "The Evolution and Tactics of the Abu Sayyaf Group," *Janes Intelligence Review* (July 2001). For a very excellent historical analysis, see Graham H. Turbiville, Jr., "Bearer of the Sword," *Military Review* (March/April 2002), pp. 38–47.

15. Joe Cochrane, "Filipino Authorities Say the Newest Threat to the Country Is a Shadowy Terror Group Made Up of Radical Muslim Converts," *Newsweek International Edition* (May 17, 2004), at: http://msnbc.msn.com/id/4933472/ (accessed August 28, 2004).

16. The Philippine government formed the Cabinet Oversight Committee on International Security on June 19, 2001 through Executive Order No. 21. It is chaired by the Executive Secretary with the Secretary of National Defense as Vice-Chair.

17. Inter-Agency Anti-Terrorism Task Force, "Government Response to Terrorism" (undated).

18. National Statistics Coordination Board, "Concepts and Definitions: Local Government Units," at: http://www.nscb.gov.ph/activestats/psgc/articles/con_lgu.asp (accessed April 20, 2004).

19. Philippine Center on Transnational Crimes, "Terrorism and Counter-Terrorism in the Philippines: A Philippine Perspective," at: http://www.pctc.gov.ph/edocs/updates/tandctia.htm (accessed October 29, 2004).

20. League of Municipalities of the Philippines, Resolution Number 001-2002 (November 12–14, 2002).

21. "Mayors Vow to Lead Fight vs Terrorism, Support National ID System," *Philippine Star* (October 22, 2002).

22. Jayme Arroyo, "Local Gov't Officials Use 10-10-10 to Clamor for Release of IRA," *Cuberdyaryo,* at: http://www.cyberdyaryo.com/features/f2001_1023_03.htm (accessed October 26, 2004).

23. Liga ng mga Barangay sa Pilipinas (League of Philippine Villages), *Gabay ng Barangay Laban sa Terorismo (Villages Guide against Terrorism)* (June 8, 2004).
24. Operation Center, "Primer on Area Coordination Center: Local Government Level" (Quezon City: Cabinet Oversight Committee on Internal Security, Version 3 undated).
25. Directorate on Terrorism, *Primer on the National Plan to Address Terrorism and Its Consequences* (Quezon City: Operation Center of the Cabinet Oversight Committee on Internal Security, 2002), p. 6.
26. Ibid., p. 7.
27. Ibid., p. 11.
28. Inter-Agency Anti-Terrorism Task Force, "Accomplishment Report" (March–June 2004).
29. National Disaster Coordinating Council, *Contingency Planning for Emergencies: A Manual for Local Government Units* (Quezon City: National Disaster Coordinating Council and UN Refugee Agency, May 2003).
30. Manny Mogato, "Reyes Cites Serious Flaws in RPs Disaster Preparedness," *Cyberdyaryo* (September 19, 2001), at: http://www.cyberdyaryo.com/features/f2001_0919_0.1.htm (accessed October 26, 2004).
31. Ibid.
32. See National Disaster Coordinating Council, "Organized/Reorganized Disaster Coordinating Councils," at: http://www.ndcc.gov.ph/dcs.html (accessed October 28, 2004).
33.. Mogato, op. cit.
34. Gaudioso C. Sosmena, Jr., "Philippine Cities: Its Vulnerability to Terrorism," *National Security Review*, Vol. XX, No. 2 (June 2002), p. 65.
35. Task Force for the Security of Critical Infrastructure, *National Critical Infrastructure Protection Plan, 2004–2010* (Manila: Cabinet Oversight Committee on Internal Security, July 2004).
36. Randy Borum, "Counter-Terrorism Training Post 9/11" in *The Changing Face of Terrorism*, Rohan Gunaratna (ed.), (Singapore: Eastern Universities Press, 2004), p. 67.
37. Karl B. Kaufman, "Weak Intel Blamed on Overzealous Spy Units," *The Manila Times* (March 26, 2004), at: http://www.manilrtimes.net/national/2004/mar/26/yehey/top_stories/20040326top6.html (accessed August 30, 2004).
38. Ibid.
39. Ibid.
40. For a complete copy of the report, see *Basilan: The Next Afghanistan?* (Report of the International Peace Mission to Basilan, Philippines, March 23–27, 2002), at: http://www.bwf.org/pamayanan/peacemission.html (accessed August 30, 2004).
41. Ibid.
42. Cabinet Oversight Committee on Internal Security, *National Internal Security Plan (NISP)*, Version 3. RESTRICTED document. Quotations in this particular section come from this document, unless otherwise stated (2004).
43. Chaiwat Satha-Anand, "Mitigating the Success of Terrorism with the Politics of Truth and Justice," in Uwe Johannen, Alan Smith, and James Gomez (eds.), *September 11 Political Freedom: Asian Perspectives 911* (Singapore: Select Publishing, 2003), pp. 30–45.

## Chapter 5

# The Military and Democracy in the Philippines in the Age of Terror: Toward Democratic Control of the Armed Forces of the Philippines*

## Introduction

When the Philippine government successfully thwarted the mutiny of at least 300 junior officers and soldiers of the Armed Forces of the Philippines (AFP) on July 27, 2003, at Oakwood Premier Ayala Center in Makati City, President Gloria Macapagal Arroyo described the moment as a great "triumph for democracy." To prevent the military from intervening and staging another coup, President Arroyo

---

* Revised and updated version of a paper delivered at the seminar sponsored by the Hans Seidel Foundation and organized by the Foundation for Communication Initiatives held in Makati City on October 27, 2003.

directed the Secretary of National Defense "to institutionalize a course on coup d'etat, conspiracies, operations and consequences in all military schools."[1]

This chapter argues that the threat of military intervention in Philippine politics may be attributed not only to the quality of education and training of military officers, but also to the failure of the Philippine government to exercise democratic control of its armed forces. While the Philippine Constitution of 1987 requires the military to be subordinated to the civilian control, this paper contends that a mere civilian control does not prevent military intervention in a democratizing state. This chapter argues that a democratic control of the Philippine armed forces is an option to effectively contain the military and to prevent military abuse as it currently wages war against terrorist threats.

## Framework for Analyzing Military Interventionism: Toward Democratic Control of the Armed Forces

There are various explanations on why the military intervenes in politics. Samuel Huntington says that the major factor that draws the soldier into the political arena "is not his own strength but rather the weakness of the political system."[2] This runs counter to the idea of Morris Janowitz, who argues that military intervenes in politics because of the superior quality of its organization and the shared values of the officer corps.[3]

Samuel E. Finer, on the other hand, regards the sociocultural environment as the key factor for military intervention. Finer contends that a low level of political culture is likely to result in military intervention.[4] Finer also says that military intervention is the product of both the ability and the disposition of soldiers to intervene.

According to Peter Calvert and Susan Calvert, there are push and pull factors of military intervention. Push factors include the ambitions of individual officers, factional disaffection, and institutional activity said or believed to be in the national interests.[5] Pull factors, on the other hand, include the association of the armed forces with military victories, a general perception of a lack of cohesion, discipline, or stability in society, and a specific perception by the armed forces of threats to the military institution or to the officer class, or to the dignity or security of the nation.[6]

Calvert and Calvert also describe the "contagion theory of military intervention," stating that coups in neighboring states contribute to the will of soldiers to intervene. They also talk about the "habituation theory of military intervention," stating that coups are encouraged by the tradition of past coups.[7] This is related with a theory of "internal contagion" of B.C. Smith, stating that once military intervention has occurred, there is likely to be another coup. According to Smith, "A country with no experience of *coup d'etat* is less likely to have one than a country where one has already taken place."[8]

Calvert and Calvert also regard intervention as a defense mechanism of the military establishment to maintain its institutional interests in the midst of contending civilian interests.[9] Military leaders also justify intervention to provide substitute structure for weak and divided civilian government.[10] Lucian Pye has, in fact, articulated this perspective when he points out that in the midst of political instability, the military represents "the only effectively organized element capable of competing for political power and formulating public policy."[11]

The country's level of economic development also encourages military intervention. In their examination of military intervention of sub-Saharan Africa, McGowan and Johnson observe that "the lower the economic growth and level of industrial employment, the higher the incidence of military intervention in politics."[12] There is also a class dimension of military intervention. The idea of praetorianism occurs "when the middle class is too weak to defend democratic civilian institutions."[13] This view is consistent with the perspective of Huntington, who argues that "in societies that are too underdeveloped to have produced a middle class the military will be a radical force" (trying to abolish feudalism, but when a middle class has developed, the military will side with it as a conservative force.)[14]

External factors also encourage military intervention. The involvement by a foreign power has been identified as crucial in the decision of the military to stage a *coup d'etat*.[15] Smith observes that the influence of foreign support in the form of clandestine military, security, and intelligence agencies (like the Central Intelligence Agency [CIA]) have "been critical in a number of Third World *coups*."[16] External dimension of military intervention is also related with the contagion theory of Calvert and Calvert, described earlier.

But the crucial issue at hand is how to prevent military intervention in politics.

Huntington provides the classic prescription to prevent the military from intervening in politics. He recommends the promotion of military professionalism and maximization of objective civilian control of the armed forces. But according to Robin Luckham, the concept of civilian control has already been considered irrelevant by the "widespread continuation of authoritarian politics by democratic means."[17] According to this view, there is a strong possibility to have a civilian control that is not democratic. Thus, Luckham advances the idea of democratic control based on the recognition that civilian governments are not necessarily democratic and that the most effective way to contain the military is through the democratic process.

Luckham underscores that preventing the military from intervening and reintervening does not rest solely upon military establishments. He contends that much of the answer about military intervention in politics lies beyond military establishments themselves. He enumerates the following as important variables in preventing military intervention: democratic institutions that function effectively and remain legitimate, in an active civil society in which social and political forces remain strong enough to deter military intervention, in economies that grow and redistribute resources so as to minimize discontent and conflict, and in an international environment that supports democratic institutions.[18] In other words, democratic control is a crucial element in preventing military intervention in politics.

According to Andrew Cottey et al., the idea of democratic control of the armed forces involves three distinct but interrelated issues.[19]

First is the extent to and ways in which civilian government regulates the influence of the armed forces in *domestic politics*. This is based on the assumption that the military establishment should be prevented from participating in domestic politics and should be trained to remain the apolitical servant of the democratic government.[20]

Second is the control of *defense policy*. This is based on the idea that the "definition and development of defense policy should be under the control of democratic, civilian authorities and that the military should confine itself to implementing decisions made by those authorities."[21]

Third is the extent and ways in which the military influences a state's *foreign policy*. This is based on the principle that the state's foreign policy, especially on matters requiring the deployment and use of military force, must be under the control of the democratic civilian institutions.[22]

Apparently, the democratic control of the armed forces is a highly normative and prescriptive concept. In fact, Luckham regards democratic control "as a contested process, not as a fixed attribute of existing democracies."[23] This is because democracy itself is a highly contested concept.

But the democratic control of the armed forces views democracy as more than the military returning to their barracks. It also means "civilians taking responsibility for governing through the formal institutions which make up the political system and through social institutions which allow individuals to express their concerns."[24] One important mechanism in which individuals can democratically express their concerns is participation in elections. Luckham even regards election as the main criterion for the presence of democracy.[25] He underscores that the past two or three decades have seen a dramatic decline in the political role of the military because elections have replaced coups as the mechanisms for regime succession and elite circulation.

## A Brief History of the Philippine Military

There is no uniform history of the Philippine military. One historian traces the history of the Philippine military to the precolonial period when the inhabitants of what we now call the Philippines organized different armed forces for different barangays (villages) for purposes of protection.[26] Another historian regards the Battle of Mactan of 1521 as the most celebrated episode in the military history of the Philippines in the precolonial period, as it featured the military victory of Lapu-Lapu against the forces of Ferdinand Magellan.[27] But the AFP traces its origin to the Tejeros Convention of 1897. The official history of the AFP is as follows:

> The origin of the ARMED FORCES OF THE PHILIPPINES (AFP) could be traced to the Tejeros Convention in 1897 — where the

revolutionary government of General Emilio Aguinaldo created the Philippine Army under Captain General Artemio Ricarte. This Army was the offshoot of the Revolutionary Forces, which took arms against the Spanish Government from August 30, 1896 up to December 10, 1898 when the treaty of Paris was entered into by the United States of America and Spain. The same Army engaged the Americans during the hostilities between the Philippines and the United States which began on the night of February 4, 1899 and lasted up to September 25, 1903 — when the last of Filipino Generals, General Simeon Ola surrendered to the Americans. After the Filipino-American war, the country's armed forces organized through the promulgation of the National Defense Act in 1935 which created the Philippine Army, with the off-shore patrol and Army Air Corps as its major components. The Philippine Constabulary, was then existing under the Department of Interior.[28]

Some scholars trace the origin of the Philippine military to the 1935 National Defense Act.[29] Others trace it to granting of Philippine independence in 1945, when the United States tasked the Philippine government to organize its own armed forces. Official records show, however, that on December 23, 1950, the AFP was founded, with four major services: Philippine Army, Philippine Air Force, Philippine Navy, and the Philippine Constabulary. The Philippine Constabulary, now called the Philippine National Police, was transferred to the Department of Interior and Local Government. At present, the AFP has three major services with five unified commands and twelve wide-support and separate units. The AFP describes itself "as the Philippines' guardian of democracy."[30]

## Military Intervention in Philippine Domestic Politics

In theory, a professional military is expected to disengage itself from domestic politics and to remain apolitical. A state with a functioning democratic control of its armed forces prevents the military from intervening in domestic politics. Since its creation, however, the Philippine military has been part and parcel of Philippine domestic politics. Richard Kessler, an avid observant of Philippine politics, has commented that the Philippine military "has been employed in Philippine society not to ensure peace and justice but to protect the privileged position of the ruling elite."[31]

The military played a vital role in the electoral victory of President Manuel Roxas in 1946 and was active in the 1949 electoral success of President Elpidio Quirino.[32] During the 1951 Philippine elections, the Commission on Elections (COMELEC) deputized the AFP to guard the polls.[33] The AFP assumed a very important political role when President Ramon Magsaysay, who served as the secretary of Philippine national defense, employed a great number of military officers to civilian posts. Within one year after his assumption into office, Magsaysay appointed more than 122 officers to civilian positions, which included several cabinet posts.[34] Under the Magsaysay administration, the AFP was involved in many nonfighting missions, called "civic actions," for purposes of political propaganda and counterinsurgency operations. These missions included infrastructure projects (road building, irrigation, artesian well digging, construction of schools and community centers, and the like), food production, medical services, and even legal assistance to rural people in order to successfully win their hearts and minds.[35]

The role of the military in Philippine domestic politics became more influential during the administration of President Ferdinand E. Marcos, particularly during the entire martial law period. The military became the primary basis of Marcos's political power. Marcos also organized the Civilian Home Defense Force (CHDF) to support AFP's role not only in counterinsurgency operations but also in suppressing oppositions against Marcos's "constitutional" authoritarian rule in the rural areas, particularly in Mindanao. Under the Marcos Administration, the AFP grew tremendously in number and took many inherently civilian functions. Military officers took control of many civilian offices like the Bureau of Telecommunications, Bureau of Posts, Philippine Ports Authority, and National Computer Center.[36] Military officers also seized for "unpaid loans" the privately owned Jacinto Iron & Steel Sheets Corporation and 14 other Jacinto family businesses.[37] Men in uniform also got important positions in many government-owned-and-controlled corporations.

Marcos justified the role of the military to perform inherently civilian functions in the name of development and modernization.[38] Because of the expanded political role of the military under martial law, several generals proudly admitted that "martial law had given the AFP new confidence in its own ability to run the government."[39] Thus, the AFP has received an image of being the "republic of the armed forces of the Philippines."

Marcos's authoritarian regime only met its final demise when the disgruntled factions of the Philippine military headed by Fidel Ramos, his own chief of the national police force, and Juan Ponce Enrile, his own minister of defense, supported a People Power uprising in EDSA in 1986. According to Felipe Miranda of the University of the Philippines, "The military's already significant political role became more crucial as it played a pivotal role in the 1986 overthrow of Marcos."[40]

As a result of the military-backed popular uprising, Marcos left the country to have an exile in Hawaii until he died. The People Power installed Corazon C. Aquino, wife of Benigno Aquino, who was the arch political contender of Marcos, as the President of the Philippines. It was during the administration of President Aquino when democracy was said to have been "restored" in the Philippines.

Despite the so-called restoration of Philippine democracy, the military continued to play a significant role in Philippine domestic politics.[41] Although President Aquino ordered the military to "return to their barracks,"[42] forcibly retired overstaying generals of the AFP, and replaced military officers occupying civilian posts, the military remained influential in the realm of Philippine politics. There is even a view that the EDSA uprising brought the Philippine military to the fore as a power broker.[43]

Though the Aquino government attempted to assert civilian control by reorienting the AFP toward the acceptance of the civilian supremacy over the military, some discontented factions of the AFP still mounted eight different coup attempts against her government, one of which was headed by former Colonel Gregorio Honasan, who became a Philippine senator and was allegedly involved in the 2003 Oakwood mutiny.[44] This indicated that some military leaders, particularly those from the Reform the Armed Forces Movement (RAM), found it difficult to submit themselves to civilian control.[45] The series of coups against the Aquino government also undermined the consolidation of civilian control of the military.[46]

To protect the Aquino Administration from further military assaults, retired generals were given important civilian posts as a reward for their "loyalty" to the constituted civilian authorities. One excellent example is the appointment of retired General Rafael Ileto as the secretary of national defense. The former AFP Chief of Staff Ramos, who would later succeed President Aquino during the 1992 presidential election, succeeded Ileto as the secretary of national defense.

During the Ramos Administration, the military continued to perform important nonmilitary responsibilities. Filipino soldiers were even trained to perform duties and operations "other than war." Ramos offered a general amnesty to military officers involved in the past coups. Some of these officers, who opted to retire, got important civilian positions in the Ramos government as presidential advisers or consultants on national security concerns. Other officers found their fortune in the Philippine Congress either as senators or congressmen after retirement. Some got cabinet positions as heads of departments.

Unlike his immediate predecessor, Ramos never experienced coup attempts in his Administration. As a former chief of the Philippine Constabulary and Integrated National Police during the Marcos Administration and former AFP Chief of Staff and secretary of national defense under the Arroyo Administration, Ramos was able to establish control of the military during his presidential term. But his ability to control the military was not based on the strength of the civilian institutions but on the ability of Ramos to demand obedience from his former subordinates in the military. Ramos even boosted the morale of the Philippine military by approving the AFP Modernization Program to adjust to the situation unleashed by the withdrawal of American military troops in 1991.[47]

The trend of recruiting retired military officers to occupy civilian positions in the government continued during the administration of President Joseph Estrada. Although Estrada appointed former Senator Orlando Mercado as the civilian head of the Department of National Defense (DND) during his term, retired generals still dominated undersecretary positions. Estrada also appointed several retired military officers to various civilian posts.

The Philippine military intervened again in politics when it withdrew its support from the Estrada Administration in 2001. Mercado and General Angelo Reyes, Estrada's own AFP Chief of Staff, rallied against him in EDSA at the height of what Filipino historians would call People Power II. Initially initiated by civil society movements protesting against Estrada for his alleged plunder of the Philippine economy, the People Power II (also known as EDSA II) led to the downfall of his administration. Estrada's own vice president, Gloria Macapagal Arroyo, succeeded him after a week-long popular protest.

Like her predecessors, Arroyo relied on the political support of the military to protect her administration from opposition leaders coming from both the civilian and military sectors. Upon assumption into office, she appointed Eduardo Ermita as acting secretary of national defense. Ermita was a retired general, a former congressman, and an influential leader of her coalition party. When Reyes retired from the military service as Chief of Staff of the AFP shortly after EDSA II, Arroyo immediately appointed him as the new secretary of national defense.

It was during the Arroyo Administration when a rogue faction of the AFP staged a mutiny at Oakwood Premier Ayala Center. The mutineers clarified that they did not attempt to grab power. They just wanted to air their grievances against the alleged rampant graft and corruption in the AFP. Among their complaints were the alleged irregularities in the procurement system in the AFP, favoritism within the ranks, the alleged involvement of some military officers in terror bombings in Mindanao, and the alleged selling of firearms to insurgents by some AFP officers. Although the mutiny did not aim to capture state power, their actions demonstrated an apparent intervention in politics. The Oakwood mutiny revealed the weakness of the civilian authority to assert democratic control of its own armed forces.

Because of alleged pressures from active and retired generals, Reyes was forced to resign in the aftermath of the Oakwood mutiny in August 2003. Reyes's resignation also happened in the midst of several coup rumors surrounding the Arroyo Administration. After Reyes's resignation, President Arroyo proclaimed herself concurrent Secretary of National Defense, making her the first woman civilian head of the defense establishment. During her stint as defense secretary, Arroyo ordered the restructuring of the defense establishment and emphasized civilian authority in the chain of command. After the restructuring, Arroyo appointed Ermita as the new Secretary of National Defense in October 2003.

Despite the restructuring of the DND organization under Arroyo, retired military officers continue to dominate the leadership in the defense establishment. The study made by the Philippine Center for Investigative Journalism observes that since the restoration of Philippine democracy in 1986, four sectors in the civilian government have been identified as having hosted a significant number of military appointees. These are DND, Department of Transportation and Communications, the Bureau of Customs, and government-owned corporations and special economic zones.[48] According to Glenda Gloria of the Philippine Center for Investigative Journalism:

- Of the 21 defense secretaries since 1941, more than half — 11 — had served in the Philippine military. Of these 11, 6 got their military training from the United States, either at West Point, at Fort Leavenworth, or as a member of the United States Armed Forces for the Far East (USAFFE). At least 26 military officers have been assigned to the DND since Marcos fell from power in 1986.
- In addition, at least 26 retired and active-duty military officers have been assigned to the Department of Transportation and Communications (DOTC) since 1986. The department is one of the government's top revenue-generating sectors. Under the Arroyo and Ramos governments, military officers headed the Land Transportation Office, which is in charge of issuing driver's licenses and car registrations and is the government's fifth biggest revenue earner.
- There are many military appointees in government-owned-and-controlled corporations (GOCCs) as well as in special economic zones (free ports) that were established following the liberalization of the economy after the 1986 People Power revolution. Board memberships in GOCCs are considered patronage posts, given the huge allowances that board members receive (a high of P100,000 a month in the case of the Social Security System, for example).
- Under the Ramos, Estrada, and Arroyo administrations, at least 37 military officers occupied posts in GOCCs and special economic zones.
- The Bureau of Customs, too, which is the government's biggest revenue-generating agency, has had its shares of military appointees — nine under the Aquino, Ramos, Estrada, and Arroyo administrations.[49]

Under the Arroyo administration, former chiefs-of-staff received civilian portfolios immediately after retirement. Former AFP Chief of Staff Roy Cimatu was appointed Ambassador-at-Large for Overseas Filipino Workers; former Chief of Staff Dionisio Santiago got the position of Director of the Bureau of Correction, and former Defense Secretary Reyes got a job as Ambassador-at-Large for Counterterrorism and later Chief of the National Anti-Kidnapping Task Force.

In short, military officers remain active in Philippine domestic politics after their retirement. Civilian political leaders continue to rely on the military for political support, indicating the weakness of the Philippine civilian institution. Military leaders continue to provide security blankets for Filipino politicians assuming leadership in a political system with fragile democracy.

## The Role of the Military in Philippine Defense Policy

The idea of democratic control of the military states that the definition and development of defense policy should be the prerogative of civilian leaders and that only the military implements decisions of civilian authorities.

In the Philippines, the military defines and develops the country's defense policy.[50] Although the AFP Strategic Planning Document states that policy guidance "should ideally be provided by civilian authorities at the highest level," in reality, the military gives policy guidance to civilian authorities on defense matters.[51] The only published defense policy paper of the Philippines was, in fact, conceptualized and authored not by civilian thinkers but by junior military officers assigned at the DND.[52]

In 2001, a civilian defense official organized a group of civilian thinkers in the DND to publish a defense white paper articulating a defense policy of the Philippines from a civilian perspective. But retired generals occupying vital positions in the DND rejected the 2001 draft. Another draft was produced in 2002 involving civilian consultants of the DND. But it suffered the same fate because of a strong reservation of retired and active military officials. In 2003, the DND commissioned some civilian academics to produce a new draft of Philippine defense white paper. But the draft never received approval because defense and military officials in the DND could not put their minds together.

Military officers and assistants remain very influential in defense-related matters. Policy pronouncements, speeches, and press releases of the president and the secretary of national defense on national defense matters were products of "completed-staff-work" not of civilian employees but of military assistants. In the DND itself, military assistants are the ones handling most of the policy-related work of the department. Most civilian employees in the DND only perform routine and administrative functions. Based on the 1998 human resource management audit conducted by former Chairman of the Civil Service Commission Patricia Santo Tomas, now Secretary of the Department of Labor and Employment, 22% of the civilian personnel at the Office of the Secretary of National Defense is doing administrative work while more than 80% of its total human resource complement is performing clerical and technical support functions.[53] Military assistants numbering around 300 military officers and enlisted personnel are still performing many substantive and policy-oriented functions of the DND.[54]

Thus, many substantive functions of the DND will be derailed if military assistants will be required to go back to their mother units. In the graduate thesis made by Ma. Anthonette C. Velasco, a former assistant secretary for personnel of the DND, it says that "the pull-out of uniformed personnel from the DND proper led to the notable organizational dysfunctions such as lack of quality staff work, ambiguities in the reporting system, overlapping lines of supervision and accountability, and the lack of career advancement opportunities for civilian employees."[55]

The ongoing National Defense Review (NDR), which ironically was conceived in 2001 not by a civilian leader but a retired general occupying a very vital civilian post in the DND, has already recognized this problem.[56] The NDR Project Teams aim to really empower civilian leadership in the DND. Unfortunately, the NDR initiative is not taking off as expected because it challenges the status quo. The NDR, if pushed through, will be an important step in transforming Philippine defense toward a genuine democratic control of the armed forces. Complementing the NDR is the implementation of Philippine Defense Reform, which will be discussed in the next chapter of this volume.

# The Role of the Military in Philippine Foreign Policy

In the area of Philippine foreign policy, civilian authorities have asserted effective control. The defense and military establishments recognize the authority of civilian leaders in the pursuance of Philippine foreign policy. This may be attributed to the reality that most military leaders have been trained to perform functions pertaining to internal security more than on external defense.

Like many armed forces of the developing world, Philippine armed forces are paying more attention to internal security matters than on the issue of external defense. The Philippines has a National Internal Security Plan but no external defense plan. The Philippines has, in fact, been relying on the external security umbrella of the United States. This eroded not only the external defense capability of the Philippines but also its wherewithal to think strategically on external defense matters.

Its weak external defense capability is one of the major sources of gripes and demoralization in the Philippine armed forces. The Philippine military laments the reality that the AFP is one of the few armed forces in Asia with no external defense capability and with no modern weapons to defend its territory. One observer commented, "Philippine defense capabilities have been a perennial joke within ASEAN. Lacking modern air and naval forces, the islands have been rife with smuggling, piracy, and fishery poaching."[57] According to Dr. Renato de Castro of De La Salle University in Manila, "Not only was the AFP inferior to its ASEAN counterparts in equipment, but it also found itself ill-equipped to contain a number of domestic security threats."[58] The late Capt. Rene Jarque, then of the Office of Special Studies of the AFP, also observed:

> The reliance on the United States' defense support coupled with successive insurgency problems eroded our external defense capability, not only in terms of equipment but also in the equally important aspects of personnel and resource management, doctrine and training. The general orientation of the armed forces, manifested in the mindset of many officers and soldiers, has become insular and shortsighted. In addition, we were not able to develop a strong tradition of strategic thought and

planning that today, many officers exhibit an inability or unwilling-ness to think strategically. Likewise, the entire defense establishment is beginning to suffer the consequences of past decisions and actions that were driven by political whims and disjointed policies in response to short-term contingencies.[59]

Although the AFP attempted to implement its modernization program, intense bureaucratic politics between civilian and military leaders prevented the program from taking off.[60] This was aggravated by the onslaught of the 1997 Asian financial crisis, which delayed the implementation of force modernization programs in many Southeast Asian countries.[61]

The implementation of the AFP modernization program could have prepared the Philippine military to perform its external defense missions. Due to the rising prob-lem of Communist insurgency and Muslim secessionism, the AFP concentrated on internal security operations working in tandem with the Philippine National Police.

Although civilian leaders have effective control of Philippine foreign policy, this does not mean, however, that civilian leaders have established democratic control of the armed forces on external defense matters. This phenomenon is only reflective of the fact that external defense has been neglected in the Philippine military. But in the area of defense diplomacy, military officers continue to prevail upon civilian employees in the DND. Junior military officers serving as military assistants in the DND are the ones calling the shots in the area of defense diplomacy. Civilian employees play only a minor role in defense diplomacy, and this role is purely administrative. Philippine defense diplomacy (particularly with the United States, Australia, Japan, China, Malaysia, and Indonesia) is being shaped and managed not by civilian officers of the DND but by military officers at the headquarters of the AFP. On matters of deployment of military troops for peacekeeping purposes, the military establishment continues to prevail upon the DND.

## Conclusion

While the Philippine Constitution requires civilian supremacy over the military, the Philippine armed forces continue to play an important role in Philippine politics. The role the Philippine military plays in domestic politics provides them several opportunities to intervene, not to mention the capability of the military institution and the disposition of other military leaders to intervene. The military continues to play a dominant role in defense policy, which should have been con-trolled by civilian authorities. Although the Philippine military has no major role in the pursuance of Philippine foreign policy, which at present is under effective civilian control, the armed forces continue to prevail upon civilian employees on matters of defense diplomacy, especially in the deployment of military troops for peacekeeping purposes.

Using our framework for analysis, the Philippine government has not established an effective democratic control of its armed forces. This lack of effective democratic control makes the Philippines vulnerable to military intervention. The prevailing economic and political conditions in the Philippines also encourage the military to intervene in Philippine politics.

To prevent the military from intervening, there is a need to assert a democratic control of the armed forces. This requires not only the empowerment of civilian institutions but also the implementation of a nationwide security sector reform. This kind of reform upholds the principle of accountable and transparent management of national security institutions, which include the military. Chapter 6 discusses the state of security sector governance in the Philippines and examines policy issues and challenges in security sector reform.

# Endnotes

1. President Gloria Macapagal Arroyo, "Foundation Speech" (delivered at the National Defense College of the Philippines on the occasion of the 40th NDCP Foundation Day on August 12, 2003).
2. Samuel P. Huntington, *The Soldier and the State: The Theory and Politics of Civil Military Relations* (Cambridge and London: The Belknap Press of Harvard University Press, 1957).
3. Morris Janowitz, *The Military in the Political Development of New Nations* (Chicago: University of Chicago Press, 1964). Also see his *The New Military: Changing Patterns of Organization* (New York: Russell Sage Foundation, 1964). Also cited in Paul Cammack, David Pool, and William Tordoff, "The Military," in their *Third World Politics: A Comparative Introduction*, 2nd edition (London: McMillan, 1993), p. 133.
4. Samuel E. Finer, *The Man on Horseback: The Role of the Military in Politics* (Baltimore: Penguin Books, 1976). Also cited in Cammack, Pool, and Tordoff, *Third World Politics*, p. 133.
5. Peter Calvert and Susan Calvert, "The Armed Forces and Politics" in their *Politics and Society in the Third World*, 2nd edition (London and New York: Longman, 2001), p. 168.
6. Ibid.
7. Ibid.
8. B.C. Smith, "Military Intervention in Politics," in his *Understanding Third World Politics: Theories of Political Change and Development* (London: MacMillan Palgrave, 2003), p. 184.
9. Calvert and Calvert, "The Armed Forces and Politics," p. 170.
10. Ibid., p. 174.
11. Lucian Pye, *Aspect of Political Development* (Boston: Little, Brown and Company, 1966), p. 283.
12. P. McGowan and T. Johnson, "African Military Coups d'etat and Underdevelopment: A Quantitative Historical Analysis," *The Journal of Modern African Studies*, 22 (1984), pp. 633–666. Also cited in Smith, "Military Intervention in Politics," p. 184.
13. Ibid.

14. Ibid., p. 181.

15. Ibid., p. 189.

16. Ibid.

17. Robin Luckham, "Democratic Strategies for Security in Transition and Conflict," in Gawin Cawthra and Robin Luckham (eds.), *Governing Insecurity: Democratic Control of Military and Security Establishments in Transitional Democracies* (London and New York: Zed Books, 2003), p. 15.

18. Robin Luckham, "Democracy and the Military: An Epitaph for Frankenstein's Monster," *Democratization*, Vol. 3, No. 2 (Summer 1996), p. 11.

19. Andrew Cottey, Timothy Edmunds, and Anthony Forster, "Democratic Control of the Armed Forces in Central and Eastern Europe: A Framework for Understanding Civil Military Relations," *Economic and Social Research Council Working Paper*, No. 1 (September 1999), p. 4.

20. Ibid.

21. Ibid., p. 5.

22. Ibid.

23. Luckham, "Democratic Strategies for Security in Transition and Conflict," p. 15.

24. Tricia Jhun and Enrique Pumar, "Civil-Military Relations in Latin America: Lessons Learned" (Rapporteur's report of presentations at the May 4–6, 1995, conference), at http://www.american.edu/academics.depts/sis/democracyla/rapprt.htm, p. 4.

25. Luckham, "Democratic Strategies for Security," p. 11.

26. Cesar Pobre, *History of he Armed Forces of the Filipino People* (Quezon City: New Day Publishers, 2000), pp. 1–4.

27. Uldarico S. Baclagon, *Military History of the Philippines* (Manila: St. Mary's Publishing, 1975).

28. Armed Forces of the Philippines, "History," at http://www.armedforces.mil.ph/history.html (2003).

29. See for example Richard J. Kessler, "Development and the Military: Role of the Philippine Military in Development" in J. Soedjati Djiwandono and Yong Mun Cheong (eds.), *Soldiers and Stability in Southeast Asia* (Singapore: Institute of Southeast Asian Studies, 1988), p. 215.

30. Armed Forces of the Philippines, "About Us," at http://www.afp.mil.ph/ (2003).

31. Kessler, "Development and the Military: Role of the Philippine Military in Development" (1988), p. 214.

32. David G. Timberman, *A Changeless Land: Continuity and Change in Philippine Politics* (Singapore: Institute of Southeast Asian Studies, 1991), p. 45.

33. Ibid.

34. Kessler, "Development and the Military: Role of the Philippine Military in Development" (1988), p. 218.

35. Felipe B. Miranda and Ruben F. Ciron, "Development and the Military in the Philippines: Military Perceptions in a Time of Continuing Crisis," in J. Soedjati Djiwandono and Yong Mun Cheong (eds.), *Soldiers and Stability in Southeast Asia* (Singapore: Institute of Southeast Asian Studies, 1988), p. 173. Also cited in Ibid.

36. David Wurfel, *Filipino Politics: Development and Decay* (Quezon City: Ateneo de Manila Press, 1988), p. 143.

37. Ibid.

38. See Miranda and Ciron, "Development and the Military in the Philippines," p. 165. Also see Armando Gatmaitan and Gregorio C. de Castro, "Notes on the Role of the Military in Socio-Economic Development," *Philippine Journal of Public Administration* (July 1968).

39. See Harold Maynard, "A Comparison of Military Elite Role Perceptions in Indonesia and the Philippines" (Unpublished dissertation, American University, 1976), p. 535. Also cited in Ibid., p. 144.

40. Felipe Miranda, "Leadership and Political Stabilization in a Post-Aquino Philippines," *Philippine Political Science Journal*, Nos. 33–36 (June 1991–December 1992), p. 158.

41. For a detailed account of the Philippine military after EDSA, see Criselda Yabes, *The Boys from the Barracks: The Philippine Military after EDSA* (Metro Manila: Anvil Publishing, Inc., 1991).

42. Edmundo Garcia and Evelyn Lucero Gutierrez, eds., *Back to the Barracks: The Military in Democratic Transition* (Quezon City: National Institute for Policy Studies, 1992).

43. Yabes, *The Boys from the Barracks*, p. vii.

44. Raymond Jose G. Quilop, "Civil-Military Relations: An Overview of the Philippine Experience," at: www.apan-info.net/partners/uploads/ AFP-OSS-CMR%20for%20 Kasarinlan.pdf (2002).

45. Ibid.

46. Ibid.

47. Renato Cruz de Castro, "Adjusting to the Post-U.S. Bases Era: The Ordeal of the Philippine Military's Modernization Program," *Armed Forces and Society*, Vol. 26, No. 1 (Fall 1999), pp. 110–137.

48. Philippine Center for Investigative Journalism, "Out of the Barracks," *Excerpt: The Investigative Reporting Magazine*, Vol. IX, No. 2 (April–June 2003), p. 1. Also see Glenda Gloria, *We Were Soldiers: Military Men in Politics and the Bureaucracy* (Makati City: Friedrich Ebert Stiftung, 2002).

49. Ibid.

50. See Col. Cristolito P. Balaoing, "Defense Planning: Challenges for the Philippines," *Philippine Military Digest*, Vol. IV, No. 1 (January–March 1999), pp. 22–54.

51. Office of the Chief of Staff for Plans and Programs (J5), *AFP Strategic Planning: AFP Manual 5–1* (Quezon City: Armed Forces of the Philippines, 1984). This document is classified "RESTRICTED."

52. Department of National Defense, *In Defense of the Philippines: 1998 Defense Policy Paper* (Quezon City: Department of National Defense, 1998).

53. Patricia Santo Tomas, "Managing Human Resource: The Case of the Department of National Defense" (Unpublished report submitted to the Secretary of National Defense on September 17, 1998).

54. Ma. Anthonette C. Velasco and Angelito M. Villanueva, "Reinventing the Office of the Secretary of National Defense" (MA Thesis: National Defense College of the Philippines, 2000), p. 9.

55. Ibid., p. 10.

56. Department of National Defense, *National Defense Review I — Core Programs* (Quezon City: Department of National Defense, 2001).

57. Sheldon W. Simon, "Evolving Roles for the Military in the Asia–Pacific" (Paper presented in the Asia–Pacific Center for Security Studies, Honolulu, Hawaii, on March 28–30, 2000). Also see his "The Many Faces of Asian Security: Beyond 2000" (Paper presented in the conference held at the Arizona State University in April 2000).
58. De Castro, "Adjusting to the Post-U.S. Bases Era" (Fall 1999), p. 120.
59. Jose Rene N. Jarque, *A Conceptual Framework for the Defense of the Philippines: A Working Paper* (Quezon City: Office of Strategic and Special Studies of the Armed Forces of the Philippines, 1996), pp. 1–2.
60. Renato de Castro, "The Military and Philippine Democratization: A Case Study of the Government's 1995 Decision to Modernize the Armed Forces of the Philippines," in Felipe B. Miranda (ed.), *Democratization: Philippine Perspectives* (Quezon City: University of the Philippines Press, 1997), pp. 241–280.
61. Carlyle A. Thayer, "Force Modernization in Southeast Asia and Its Implications for the Security of the Asia–Pacific" (Paper delivered at the National Defense College of the Philippines on September 20, 2000).

*Chapter 6*

# Security Sector Governance in the Philippines: A Policy Challenge in the Age of Terrorism*

## Introduction

Among countries in Southeast Asia, the Philippines has the reputation of being the first independent democracy in Asia. But the democratic governance of its security sector remains problematic because of a strong influence of the military in various security-related activities, particularly in addressing political unrest, internal armed conflicts, and terrorist threats.[1]

The 1987 Philippine Constitution provides an overarching legal framework that defines the functions of the security sector under a democratic and republican state where "civilian authority is, at all times, supreme over the military." This assumes

---

* Revised and updated version of a paper originally entitled "Security Sector Governance in the Philippines," presented to the international workshop "Challenges of Security Sector Governance," organized by the Friedrich-Ebert-Stiftung (FES), Institute of Defence and Strategic Studies (IDSS), and Geneva Centre for the Democratic Control of the Armed Forces (DCAF) at Hotel Plaza Parkroyal, Singapore, February 14–15, 2006.

that the Armed Forces of the Philippines (AFP) is accountable to the democratically elected civilian government. Yet, the same constitution urges the AFP to be "the protector of the people and the State," which creates an ambiguous role of the military amid political crises facing the civilian leadership. Some analysts argue that this constitutional provision can provide the AFP a passport to "intervene" in domestic politics and assert its "constitutional duty" to step in when the civilian government is deemed to have lost its legitimacy.[2] This constitutional provision is also said to have made it easier for some elements of the Philippine military to take over the government "on the pretext of protecting the people and the state."[3] The AFP even admits that a misuse of this provision can attract some of its officers to pursue military adventurism and inflame the "messianic complex" of some soldiers.[4]

Allegations of widespread corruption in the civilian and military bureaucracy,[5] weak electoral and party systems,[6] mass poverty and economic difficulties,[7] indecisive civilian leadership,[8] and fragile constitutional democracy[9] are some of the major issues that are said to have increased the propensity of the Philippine military to intervene in civilian political affairs.[10] The continued appointment to the civilian bureaucracy of retired military and police officers and the continuing involvement of men-in-uniforms in nontraditional security roles are also viewed to have blurred the professional lines between civilian and military functions, which results in the further weakening of civilian institutions[11] and the continuing politicization of the military.[12] Confluences of these issues enormously affect the strengthening of democratic governance of the Philippine security sector.

This chapter aims to take stock of pertinent issues affecting security sector governance in the Philippines and to provide a descriptive analysis of the factors impinging on the good governance of the Philippine security sector.

## The Security Sector in the Philippines

From a traditional and narrow perspective, the Philippine security sector refers primarily to the AFP that is tasked to protect the state against internal and external security threats. As of January 2007, the AFP had a total of 113,000 personnel, with the Philippine Army having the biggest number with 65,000 personnel, followed by the Philippine Navy with 35,000 personnel, and the Philippine Air Force with 15,000 personnel.[13] But to view the AFP as the main security sector is utterly misleading because it is only based on a limited definition of security.[14] This limited definition is apparently anchored on the realist school where the concept of security is viewed in pure military sense.[15] Other scholars have challenged this limited definition of national security arguing that security has become a broad concept that goes beyond its military dimension.[16] Security is a comprehensive concept that includes economic, political, sociocultural, environmental and human security.[17] Thus, there is also a broader concept of the security sector, which "is taken to mean all those organizations which have the authority to use, or order the use of force, or threat of force, to protect the state and its citizens, as well as those civil structures that are responsible from their management and oversight."[18] Given this view, there are three pillars of the Philippine security sector:

1. Groups with a mandate to wield the instruments of violence — military, paramilitary, and police forces.
2. Institutions with a role in managing and monitoring the security sector — civilian ministries, parliaments, and nongovernmental organizations.
3. Bodies responsible for guaranteeing the rule of law — the judiciary, the penal system, and human rights ombudsmen, and, where these bodies are particularly weak, the international community.[19]

Aside from the AFP, therefore, the Philippine security sector includes but is not limited to the following:

■ The AFP and its various intelligence services, including the Civilian Armed Forces Geographic Units (CAFGUS)
■ The Philippine National Police (PNP) and its various intelligence services
■ The Philippine Coast Guard and its intelligence services
■ The Intelligence and Enforcement Group of the Bureau of Customs
■ Local Peace and Order Watchers or the *Barangay Tanod* (Village Watchers as well as Metropolitan Manila Development Authority Traffic Enforcers)
■ The Office of the President and its various departments, like the Department of National Defense (DND), the Department of Interior and Local Government (DILG), the Department of Foreign Affairs (DFA), the Department of Trade and Industry, the Department of Finance, and the Department of Budget and Management, the National Security Council (NSC), and the National Intelligence Coordinating Agency (NICA)
■ Independent commissions like the Commission on Human Rights (CHR), the National Police Commission, and the Philippine Anti-Graft Commission (PAGC), the Commission on Audit, the Commission on Appointment, and the Philippine Commission for Good Government (PCGG)
■ The Supreme Court of the Philippines, the Office of the Ombudsman, and the *Sandigang Bayan*
■ The Philippine Senate and the Philippine House of Representatives, particularly their committees on defense, security, peace and order, foreign affairs, and legislative oversight
■ Civil society organizations like strategic think tanks, human rights organizations, and other governance watch groups

The National Security Council (NSC) is the lead agency of the national government mandated to address the multifaceted national security concerns of the Philippines.

Its principal function is to coordinate the formulation of policies relating to or with implications for Philippine national security. But its major activities, so far, have been largely confined to making key decisions on high-impact external and internal security issues confronting the country. The major external security concern of the Philippines is the South China Sea Disputes.[20] Its major internal security issues, on the other hand, are local communism, Muslim secessionism, and domestic terrorism posed by the New People's Army (NPA), *Moro* Islamic Liberation Front (MILF), and the Abu Sayyaf Group (ASG), respectively.[21]

The main document that defines the present juridical personality of the NSC is the Executive Order No. 115 dated December 24, 1986. This document states that the NSC is responsible to perform the following duties:

- To advise the President with respect to the integration of domestic, foreign, military, political, economic, social, and educational policies relating to the national security so as to enable all concerned ministries, departments, and agencies of the government to meet more effectively, problems and matters involving the national security;
- To evaluate and analyze all information, events, and incidents in terms of the risks they pose or implications upon and/or threats to the overall security and stability of the nation, for the purpose of recommending to the President appropriate responses thereto and/or action thereon;
- To formulate and coordinate the implementation of policies on matters of common interest to the various ministries, departments, and agencies of the government concerned with the national security, and to make recommendations to the President in connection therewith;
- To insure that policies adopted by the NSC on national security are effectively and efficiently implemented; and,
- To make such recommendations and/or render such other reports as the President may from time to time direct.[22]

The NSC does not conduct its own regular meeting to address those threats. The president usually convenes NSC meetings on an *ad hoc* basis depending on the present national crises situation. So far, President Gloria Macapagal Arroyo held nine meetings of the NSC from 2001 to 2004, compared with only four meetings during the time of President Joseph Estrada (1998–2001), seven meetings during the time of President Fidel Ramos (1992–1998), and three meetings during the time of President Corazon Aquino (1986–1992).[23] President Ferdinand Marcos held the most meetings — 33 — from 1972 to 1986. After the restoration of Philippine democracy in 1986, President Aquino reorganized the NSC to be a democratic collegial body that includes pertinent security players in the Philippines. In 1987, the NSC comprised the following members:

- President
- Vice President
- Executive Secretary
- Secretary of Foreign Affairs
- Secretary of National Defense
- Secretary of Justice
- Secretary of Labor and Employment
- Secretary of Local Government
- National Security Director
- AFP Chief of Staff
- "Such other government officials and private citizens as the President may designate from time to time"[24]

Since then, however, the membership of the NSC has undergone some changes to accommodate the widening scope of the security sector and the broadening concept of security. In the aftermath of the September 11, 2001, terrorist attacks, President Arroyo expanded the membership of the NSC pursuant to Executive Order No. 34 dated September 17, 2001. The NSC now includes the following members:

- President as Chairman
- Vice President
- Senate President
- Speaker of the House of Representatives
- Senate President Pro-Tempore
- Deputy Speakers of the House for Luzon, Visayas, and Mindanao
- Majority Floor Leader of the Senate
- Majority Floor Leader of the House
- Minority Floor Leader of the Senate
- Minority Floor Leader of the House
- Chairman, Senate Committee on Foreign Relations
- Chairman, Senate Committee on National Defense and Security
- Chairman, Senate Committee on Public Order and Safety
- Chairman, House Committee on Foreign Relations
- Chairman, House Committee on National Defense and Security Chairman, House Committee on Public Order and Safety
- Executive Secretary
- National Security Director General as Secretary
- Secretary of Foreign Affairs
- Secretary of National Defense
- Secretary of Justice

- Secretary of Interior and Local Government
- Secretary of Labor and Employment
- Presidential Spokesperson
- Head, Presidential Legislative Liaison Office
- Presidential Legal Counsel
- Past Presidents of the Philippines and other government officials and private citizens whom the President may designate from time to time

Though the above NSC membership shows the inclusion of many relevant players in the Philippine security sector accommodating both elected and duly appointed civil authorities from both the executive and legislative branches of the government, the NSC does not include judicial authorities and special oversight bodies like the CHR, the Office of the Ombudsman, the PCGG, and the PAGC. It is also noticeable that the AFP Chief of Staff is not included in the NSC membership, which is meant to stress the supremacy of civilian authorities over the military. Ironically, retired military officers are usually appointed to assume the post of the NSC Secretary General acting concurrently as the National Security Adviser (NSA), with the exception of the current NSA, Norberto Gonzales, who was recruited from the civil society. The present head of the NICA who provides intelligence support to the NSC also comes from the military sector.

The NSC membership allows private citizens to be represented in the council and encourages the civil society to be involved in NSC discussions. But confidentiality over "national security concerns" prevents civil society from really participating. This situation creates a dilemma of balancing transparency and secrecy over issues of national security. Attempting to ensure the participation of various players of the Philippine security sector in addressing the country's internal security problems, the Philippine government formed the Cabinet Oversight Committee on Internal Security (COCIS) on June 19, 2001, through Executive Order No. 2, as amended by Executive Order No. 138 issued on October 21, 2002. It was chaired by the executive secretary, with the secretary of national defense as vice chair. The main task of the COCIS was to implement the government's National Internal Security Plan (NISP) by involving all national government agencies, local government units, and the private sectors in the internal security campaign.

One notable feature of the NISP is the inclusion of a poverty-reduction program in the counterinsurgency campaign through close coordination with the National Anti-Poverty Commission that is tasked to implement the *Kapit-Bisig Laban sa Kahirapan* (KALAHI) program, a poverty alleviation strategy of the Philippine government. Among the strategies of KALAHI are asset reform, human development services, employment and livelihood opportunities, and convergence mechanism. The convergence principle calls for the active participation of national government agencies with local government units, nongovernmental organizations, private sector organizations, academic communities, and local communities in the antipoverty campaign.

But some progressive sectors of the Philippine society are criticizing the implementation of the NISP for a adopting a Strategy of Holistic Approach (SHA), which is directed primarily against local communism and Muslim secessionism rather than the total well-being of the Filipino people.[25] Despite the claim of being holistic, the NISP's operational methodology of Clear-Hold-Consolidate-Develop, later called Clear-Hold-Defend-Develop, is said to be a predominantly military approach based on counterinsurgency doctrine developed by American scholars.[26] The NISP itself admits that this counterinsurgency approach was effective in dismantling the *Partido Komunista ng Pilipinas* in the 1950s during the time of President Magsaysay. Edward Lansdale of the Central Intelligence Agency (CIA) assisted Magsaysay in the implementation of this counterinsurgency approach.[27]

President Arroyo abolished the COCIS on September 7, 2004, and created the National Security Council Cabinet Group (NSCCG) pursuant to Presidential Administrative Order No. 104. The NSCCG comprises the following members:

- National Security Adviser
- Secretary of Interior and Local Government
- Secretary of National Defense
- Secretary of Justice
- Secretary of Foreign Affairs
- Presidential Adviser on the Peace Process
- Presidential Adviser on Constituency Affairs
- Chair of the Mindanao Economic Development Council

But this particular order does not provide any detailed functions of the NSCCG. It only states that the group "shall meet upon call of the President who shall preside at all meetings."[28] To encourage the participation of various agencies of the national and local governments in addressing terrorist threats besetting the Philippines, the government formed the Anti-Terrorism Task Force (ATTF) on March 24, 2004, originally placed under the defunct COCIS. Currently under the Office of the President, the ATTF aims to conduct an extensive information drive at both national and local levels "to prepare the public and all stakeholders to get involved in the national anti-terrorism campaign."[29] It is noteworthy that the ATTF not only encourages the involvement of national and local government agencies, but it also urges members of the civil society in the government's drive against terrorism. Some members of the civil society, however, are critical of the activities of the ATTF for alleged human rights abuses committed by the military in the antiterrorism campaign.[30]

All security players in the Philippines are subject to the oversight functions of the Philippine Congress, which has the power to allocate budget, confirm appointments of officials, and call for legislative inquiry in aid of legislation.[31] The Commission on Audit, on the other hand, ensures the financial accountability of the security sector.[32] To investigate mismanagement, fraud, and corruption in the security sector, there is the Office of the Ombudsman that acts as a "watchdog" to monitor the "general and specific performance of government officials and employees."[33] The Office of the Ombudsman aims to protect the people from abuse and misuse of governmental power, which includes military power, for personal aggrandizement.[34] The Philippines also has the Commission on Human Rights (CHR), which oversees the functions of the security sector in the area of human rights promotion and protection.[35] The CHR issues certification for military and police officials prior to promotion. Civilian officials head all these bodies. Furthermore, the Philippines promotes free press that provides investigative reports on the state of the Philippine security sector.

In other words, the Philippines has very impressive and exemplary legal and formal mechanisms that strongly promote the good governance of the security sector. In practice, however, the Philippine government is facing difficulties in the democratic management of the security sector because of the historical, social, cultural, political, and cultural contexts in which pertinent players find themselves.

## The State of Security Sector Governance

As a relatively young democratic republic with weak institutions of governance in a diverse society beset by internal armed challenges and other nontraditional security threats, the Philippines is arguably suffering from a weak governance of the security sector. In the past, the Philippines had one of the better-governed security players in Asia. It adopted a constitution in 1935 upholding the principle of supremacy of civilian authority over the military by putting the armed forces under the supreme control and supervision of an elected civilian president serving as their commander-in-chief.[36] The 1935 Constitution also empowered the Philippine Congress to exercise oversight functions of the military establishment through budgetary allocation and confirmation of military appointments and promotion.[37] The 1935 Constitution, therefore, provided a sound legal policy framework for the development of a corps of professional Filipino soldiers inspired by the "professionalization" of the military of its erstwhile colonial master, the United States.

When the United States restored Philippine independence in 1946, the Philippines became one of best-equipped and well-trained professional soldiers in Asia.[38] On June 30, 1946, the United States turned over a total of 36,800 armed forces to the Philippine government, composed of 33,000 army, 2,000 air force, and 1,800 naval force equipped with previously used American army weapons and supplies.[39] During the administration of President Manuel Roxas (1946–1948), the Philippine government signed the Military Assistance Agreement in March 1947. With U.S. military assistance and support, the AFP then became one of the finest armed forces in Asia. During this period, the AFP was seen as a professional force because "it was essentially apolitical, subordinate to civilian authority, and capable of performing its duties efficiently."[40] It was also viewed that during this time, "the

AFP was completely subordinated to the civilian political authority. The President, being the Commander-in-Chief, enjoyed considerable control powers over the military. Congress fully used its authority to allocate funds and confirm senior military promotions."[41]

The Philippines and the United States also signed the Military Bases Agreement (MBA) in 1947, which provided the Philippines an efficient external defense capability under the auspices of the United States. Because the United States provided a strong external defense support to the Philippines, the AFP concentrated on defending the state against internal threats posed initially by local Communist insurgency and later by Muslim separatist insurgency. A theory of civil–military relations states that when military professionals perform a lot of domestic functions, they become politicized and may be tempted to intervene in civilian political affairs.[42] The decision to divert military resources away from its inherent external war-fighting roles to domestic activities can also lead to the politicization of the armed forces, weakening of democratic institutions, and waning of legitimacy of civilian officials.[43]

Involvement of the military in domestic security affairs became more pronounced during the administration of President Ramon Magsaysay (1953–1957), who earlier served as the secretary of national defense during the administration of President Elpidio Quirino (1948–1953). With the assistance of Lieutenant Colonel Edward Lansdale of the Joint U.S. Military Advisory Group, the AFP during the Magsaysay administration embarked on a vigorous military campaign against local Communist insurgency posed by the Huks. In support of the government's counter-insurgency operations, the AFP also performed various civic duties like infrastructure activities, medical missions, and legal services to citizens in the countryside. Magsaysay even appointed at least 122 military officers to civilian posts, which encouraged the military to assert an active role in civilian political affairs.[44]

The administration of President Carlos Garcia (1957–1961) reinforced the role of the military in civilian matters when he enunciated the Socio-Economic Program, which strongly urged the AFP to perform socioeconomic development functions. It was only during the administration of President Diosdado Macapagal (1961–1965) that the government required the AFP to return to their barracks. Macapagal even ordered the passage of a code of conduct for the AFP, upholding the "supremacy of civil authorities."[45] But long years of military involvement in domestic politics failed to transform the political orientation of the AFP.

The military role in domestic politics became more apparent when President Ferdinand Marcos (1965–1986) declared that socioeconomic development was an integral function of the armed forces. Marcos emphasized, "It would be culpable negligence on our part if the peaceful uses of military forces were not availed of to the fullest extent possible in our continuing program of economic development."[46] The declaration of martial law in 1972 arguably led to the rapid strengthening of the military role in domestic politics. Though Marcos still upheld civilian control, there was the concomitant weakening of democratic control of the AFP because of his authoritarian leadership. Marcos abolished the 1935 Constitution and replaced it with his own constitution in 1973. Under the 1973 Constitution, Marcos asserted his own brand of governance called "constitutional authoritarianism" to justify his dictatorial rule with the military as the primary basis of his power.[47]

Except for Marcos, there was no civilian oversight institution that regulated the behavior of the military during the entire martial law period because Marcos abolished the Philippine Congress that functioned as the national legislature from 1946 to 1972.[48] Though the 1973 Constitution mandated the creation of an Interim National Assembly to perform legislative functions, it was, however, never convened. Marcos amended the 1973 Constitution to replace the Interim National Assembly with an interim *Batasang Pambansa,* or interim national legislature. But elections to the interim *Batasang Pambansa* were not held. Instead, Marcos created in 1976 a *Batasang Bayan,* whose members were all Marcos appointees, to function as the national legislature. But the *Batasang Bayan* functioned more as a consultative body rather than as a legislative and oversight body.[49] Thus, there was no legislative institution to oversee the activities of the military. It was only in 1978 when members of the *Batasang Pambansa* were elected to perform legislative functions. But the *Batasang Pambansa* functioned more as a rubber stamp of Marcos until 1986. Even the Philippine Judiciary lost its independence because from 1972 to 1986 the military became the most important institution of governance of Marcos administration. Political parties were even marginalized because Marcos ensured one-party dominance through his *Kilusang Bagong Lipunan,* or New Society Movement. Marcos also suppressed the media and the right to free press.

Though Marcos was a civilian leader asserting supreme authority over the military, democratic control was apparently gone astray. Under Marcos's authoritarian regime, the AFP arrogated upon itself the power of governance by taking various civilian functions. Military officers took control of many civilian offices and received vital positions in many government-owned-and-controlled corporations.[50] Rather than curbing the power of the military, Marcos expanded the role of the military to maintain his position in an authoritarian regime.[51]

Marcos justified the role of the military to perform inherently civilian functions to promote development,[52] prompting some military officials to declare, "martial law had given the AFP new confidence in its own ability to run the government."[53] He used the intelligence services of the police and the military to monitor and suppress both the legal opposition and the local Communist insurgency that aimed to topple his authoritarian regime.[54] Marcos also utilized patronage politics to demand loyalty of both the military and civilian leaders. He overextended the retiring of generals loyal to him and marginalized those officers critical of his policy. Because of overextension of officers loyal to Marcos, there was slow attrition at the top with concomitant slow promotion from below. During the Marcos administration, the AFP lost its professionalism leading to the rapid demoralization of some ranks, particularly of junior officers. This led to the formation of the Reform the Armed Forces Movement (RAM) in 1982 by middle-level officers of the AFP headed by then Colonel Gregorio "Gringo" Honasan, a military aide of then Defense Minister Juan Ponce Enrile.

The principle objective of RAM was to restore the "pre-martial law profession-alism" of the AFP. Composed mostly of graduates from the Philippine Military Academy, RAM, as its name suggests, advocated for military reforms in the AFP. Most of its members viewed themselves as protectors of the people against corrupt, abusive, and incompetent civilian leaders. Some of its leaders embraced a more populist and sometimes leftist ideology. It was only in 1985 that RAM received greater support from other AFP officers who provided military backing for the 1986 popular uprising.[55] Called People Power, this military-backed popular upris-ing restored the pre-martial law democracy in 1986, led to the demise of Marcos's authoritarian regime, and installed President Corazon Aquino (1986–1992).

The Aquino government passed the 1987 Constitution mandating the creation of an independent judiciary, a bicameral parliament, and some constitutional com-missions that have oversight functions of the security forces. As stated earlier, the 1987 Constitution promotes the civilian democratic control of the AFP. But some disgruntled elements of the AFP found it very cumbersome to submit themselves to civilian control, having been socialized in a political environment where the military is viewed as "the savior of the people."[56] The AFP, therefore, continued to play a significant role in Philippine domestic politics[57] despite repeated orders to "return to their barracks" after the democratic restoration.[58] Though the Aquino administration forcibly retired overstaying generals of the AFP and replaced mili-tary officers occupying civilian posts, the military remained influential in the realm of Philippine politics, particularly as a power broker.[59] Like Marcos, Aquino also used patronage politics to lure the support of the military. During democratic tran-sition, retired generals were even given important civilian posts as a reward to their "loyalty" to the duly constituted civilian authorities.

The Aquino government attempted to assert civilian control, reorienting the AFP toward the acceptance of the civilian supremacy over the military by reorga-nizing the military and police establishments to assume a new role in a restored democracy. Aquino delineated the functions of the military and the police through the 1987 Constitution, which states that the Philippine government must have a police organization that is "national in scope and civilian in character."[60] She also signed Executive Order No. 247 on July 24, 1987, to abolish Marcos's National Intelligence Security Authority and the Civil Intelligence and Security Agency and replaced them with the NICA headed by a director general who was supposed to be recruited from the civilian sector. But retired generals were appointed to the NICA post. NICA was mandated to be "the focal point for the direction, coordination and integration of government activities involving intelligence, and the prepara-tion of intelligence estimates of local and foreign situations for the formulation of national policies by the President."[61]

In short, Aquino implemented vigorous reforms of security institutions in the Philippines for them to play a new role in a restored democracy. But her reform efforts did not prevent rogue factions of the AFP from mounting eight coup attempts against her government, which undermined the consolidation of civilian control of the military.[62] These coup attempts included the following:

1. The February 1986 coup attempt
2. The July 1986 Manila Hotel mutiny
3. The November 1986 "God Save the Queen" plot
4. The January 1987 GMA-7 incident
5. The April 1987 "Black Saturday" incident
6. The July 1987 takeover plot of the Manila International Airport
7. The August 1987 coup attempt
8. The December 1989 coup attempt[63]

To conduct a fact-finding investigation of the 1989 coup attempt, Aquino created a commission headed by Hilario G. Davide. Based on the result of the investigation, the Davide Commission enumerated the following causes of coups in the Philippines:

- Failure of the government to deliver basic services especially in the rural areas.
- Graft and corruption.
- Too much politics and grandstanding of politicians, and unfair criticism, even humiliation, at the hands of politicians.
- Bureaucratic efficiency, which exacerbates the alienation and poverty of the people.
- Poor and nonresponsive military leadership which is manifested by a *tayo-tayo* system [clique system], factionalism, and inadequate financial and logistical support for the soldier in the field.
- Lack of genuine reconciliation.
- Uneven treatment of human rights violations committed by the military and the CPP–NPA (Communist Party of the Philippines–New People's Army).
- Absence of good government.
- Softness on the CPP-NPA and left-leaning elements,
- Failure of the civilian leadership to effectively address economic problems.[64]

In 1990, Aquino made a landmark decision when she signed Republic Act 6965 creating the PNP as part of her government's public safety reform. This act mandates that "the police force shall be organized, trained and equipped primarily for the performance of police functions" and that "its national scope and civilian character shall be paramount." It also specifies that "no element of the police force shall be military nor shall any position thereof be occupied by active members of the Armed Forces of the Philippines."[65] More importantly, the PNP was placed under the control of the DILG in order to civilianize the police force. But during the Aquino administration, the civilianization of the police force was not actually achieved because graduates of the Philippine Military Academy continued to occupy vital positions in the PNP hierarchy. This revealed the dependence of the PNP on the military for police leadership. Thus, concerns were raised that "predominant values imbibed by certain members of the PNP in their former military setting could be carried over to the present national police organization."[66]

During the administration of President Fidel Ramos (1992–1998), some military and police officers continued to perform important nonmilitary and nonpolice responsibilities either as cabinet members, presidential advisers, or consultants on national security and public safety concerns. Filipino soldiers were even trained to perform duties and operations "other than war."[67] Ramos even offered a general amnesty to military officers involved in the past coups. Other officers found their fortune in the Philippine Congress either as senators or congressmen after retirement. Notably, the Ramos government never experienced a single coup attempt.

Ramos was able to establish control of the military and the police during his full presidential term. But his ability to control the military and the police was not based on the strength of the civilian institutions but on the ability of Ramos to demand obedience from his former subordinates in the military. Prior to becoming president, Ramos served as chief of the Philippine Constabulary-Integrated National Police during the Marcos Administration and the AFP during the Aquino Administration. When Ramos assumed the presidency, he attempted to boost the morale of the Philippine military by passing Republic Act No. 7898, otherwise known as the AFP Modernization Law, on February 23, 1995. This Act approved the AFP Modernization Program as a response to the situation unleashed by the withdrawal of American military troops in 1991.[68] He even ordered the AFP to concentrate on external defense and the PNP to focus on internal security to professionalize the two organizations. In 1998, Ramos signed Republic Act No. 8551, otherwise known as the "Philippine National Police Reform and Reorganization Act of 1998" for the PNP to concentrate on peace and order concerns. But the poor implementation of the AFP Modernization Program further demoralized the Filipino soldier, creating some restiveness within their ranks. In fact, "excessive civilian control" is being blamed for the poor implementation of the AFP Modernization Program.[69] Inadequate resources, poor pay, and limited capacity building created some grievances in the military. To contain the military and get the loyalty of the soldiers, Ramos lured officers by giving them important positions in the government.

The trend of recruiting retired military officers to occupy civilian positions in the government continued during the short-lived administration of President Joseph Estrada (1998–2001). A study made by Glenda Gloria indicates that since 1986, military officers continue to be appointed to civilian positions in the bureaucracy.[70] Although Estrada appointed former Senator Orlando Mercado as the civilian head of the DND, retired generals still dominated several undersecretary positions.

Like his predecessors, Estrada appointed several retired military officers to various civilian posts.[71] Estrada also gave the military "new" roles such as environmental protection, disaster management, antidrug campaigns, anticorruption campaigns, and other nation-building tasks.[72] With these "new" roles, the Philippine military intervened again in domestic politics when it withdrew its support from the Estrada Administration in 2001 at the height of the impeachment process against the president for alleged plunder of the Philippine economy.[73] Then Vice President Gloria Macapagal Arroyo succeeded him after a weeklong popular protest now called People Power II.

Arroyo also relied on the political support of the military to protect her administration from opposition leaders sponsoring some destabilization activities. Immediately upon assumption into office, she appointed retired general Eduardo Ermita as acting secretary of national defense. When then AFP Chief of Staff Angelo Reyes retired from the military service shortly after the People Power II, Arroyo immediately appointed him as the new defense chief. Reyes issued Department Circular Number 02 on May 26, 2003, to fine-tune the organization and functions of the DND to make it more responsive to the present situation. But the fine-tuning of the DND organization did not materialize due to inevitable leadership changes in the defense establishment after the July 2003 Oakwood Mutiny.

Two years after President Arroyo assumed office, a restive faction of the AFP staged a mutiny at Oakwood Premier Ayala Center on July 23, 2003. Though the mutineers clarified that they did not attempt to grab power and only wanted to air their grievances against the alleged rampant graft and corruption in the AFP, their actions were seen in the literature as an apparent military intervention in politics. Among their complaints included the alleged irregularities in the procurement system in the AFP, favoritism within the ranks, alleged involvement of some military officers in terror bombings in Mindanao, and reported selling of firearms to insurgents by some AFP officers.[74] The Oakwood Mutiny disclosed the weakness of the civilian authority to assert democratic control of its own armed forces.

To investigate and evaluate "all the facts and circumstances surrounding the [military] rebellion, its roots, and the provocations that inspired it," Arroyo signed the Presidential Administrative No. 78 dated July 20, 2003, creating the Fact Finding Commission headed by Retired Supreme Court Justice Florentino P. Feliciano. The Feliciano Commission found that the grievances of Oakwood mutineers "are not unique to the military but rather reflect insistent demands for reforms made by practically all sectors" of the Philippine society.[75] Among the root causes of military rebellion identified by the Feliciano Commission are the following:

■ The politicization of the military amid the erosion of civilian political institutions that had oversight powers over the military, particularly during and since the imposition of martial law, is a cause of military adventurism.

- Failure on the part of the government to enforce the law deprives the law of its power to deter, particularly among those who had engaged in previous coup plots against the government but who were granted unconditional amnesty in 1995 without prior punishment.
- The key role of the AFP in the campaigns against Communist insurgency and *Moro* secessionism creates civilian government dependence upon the military.
- Enlistment by civilian persons, including politicians, of military support for their personal and political ambitions contributes to military politicization and adventurism.[76]

In the aftermath of the Oakwood mutiny, Reyes was forced to resign in August 2003 as the secretary of national defense. President Arroyo designated herself as the concurrent secretary of national defense, which made her the first woman civilian head of the defense establishment. During her stint as defense secretary, Arroyo ordered the restructuring of the defense and military establishment and emphasized civilian authority in the chain of command. Despite the restructuring effort, retired military officers continue to shape the policy direction of the defense and military establishment. To address this issue, Arroyo also formed the Office of the Presidential Adviser for the Implementation of the Recommendations of the Feliciano Commission headed by a University of the Philippines professor, Carolina Hernandez, who is also a known expert on civil-military relations. Among its major recommendations are the appointment of a civilian secretary of national defense, return of the National Intelligence Coordinating Agency (NICA) to its original mandate, observance of the military's political neutrality, and effective institutionalization of a grievance mechanism in the AFP.

To reform the intelligence service of the national government, Arroyo called for the holding of the "National Intelligence Summit" in 2002. But the government failed to realize the objectives of the summit because of the disagreements of many stakeholders. Instead, Arroyo issued Administrative Order No. 68 on April 8, 2003, to strengthen NICA. But prior to his retirement, former AFP Chief of Staff Narciso Abaya candidly acknowledged that the nonsharing of intelligence information by military spy units was hampering the government's internal security campaign.[77] Abaya said that a culture exists among intelligence units in the Philippines to withhold vital intelligence information from other groups and stressed, "I think we have to improve on our intelligence. The trend now is not the need to know but the need to share. That is the emerging trend among intelligence units all over the world."[78] He further lamented, "Sometimes, our intelligence units zealously keep to themselves intelligence information which, if fused with the information of other intelligence units, would give a more comprehensive picture of the enemy [of the state]."[79]

To really professionalize the Philippine military, the Arroyo government embarked on Philippine Defense Reform (PDR). The PDR aims to provide a "framework for introducing a comprehensive, institutional, structural and systemic reform package at the strategic level for the defense and military establishment."[80] It was a product of the Joint Defense Assessment (JDA) conducted by American and Filipino defense and military officials in 2001 and 2003. The PDR originally aimed to pursue 10 key areas of reforms, which include among others the implementation of a strategy-driven, multiyear defense planning system and improvement of personnel management systems.

Upon the recommendation of the Feliciano Commission, Arroyo appointed a civilian secretary of national defense, her chief legal adviser, Avelino Cruz, Jr., who is presently tasked to implement the PDR. To carry out this task, the DND created the undersecretary for PDR in the person of retired Major General Ernesto Carolina. According to Undersecretary Carolina, the PDR is a transformation program that essentially aims to reengineer systems, retool personnel, and improve competence of the DND. The PDR is presently pursuing the following fourfold goals:

1. To provide the overall framework to link the implementation of the recommendations of the JDA and other AFP reform measures.
2. To improve institutional and individual core competencies in the AFP.
3. To implement a realistic defense capability program to address current and emerging threats.
4. To broaden defense and security relationships with key allies.[81]

The implementation of PDR provides many opportunities for the improvement of the democratic governance of the security sector because it is a vital component of security sector reform. But there are larger issues that pose tremendous challenges to security sector governance in the Philippines, which can undermine the PDR. These challenges will be discussed in the next section.

# Challenges of Security Sector Governance in the Age of Terrorism

As a democratic and republican state, the Philippines has excellent legal mechanisms that promote the democratic governance of the security sector. In practice, however, the Philippines has to face various governance issues that have implications for effective security sector governance.[82] The Asian Development Bank (ADB) argues that most problems confronting the Philippines may be attributed to the lack or absence of good governance, which includes the governance of the security sector.[83]

One major challenge facing security sector governance in the Philippines is the limited capacity of the civilian bureaucracy to exercise effective control and management of the security sector, particularly the military and the police and their respective intelligence services. Though the Philippine bureaucracy upholds various democratic principles necessary for the promotion of good governance in the security sector,[84] it lacks the capacity to effectively govern the security sector because of rampant bureaucratic corruption and limited competence of civil service personnel.[85]

An ADB study showed that the Philippines ranked second to Bangladesh among 102 countries in terms of bureaucratic corruption in 2003.[86] The Hong Kong–based Political and Economic Risk Consultancy Ltd. ranked the Philippines as Number 2 of the 10 most corrupt countries in Asia in 2005. Even the AFP is tainted with strong allegations of graft and corruption, particularly in the logistic and procurement system.[87] The plunder case against Major General Carlos Garcia illustrated the type of corruption happening in the military.[88] Though corruption in the Philippine military is just a drop in the big bucket compared to the corruption in the civilian sector, bureaucratic corruption arguably results in the weakness of the general public administration and the public service system in country. The weakness of civilian bureaucracy makes it vulnerable to the influence of the military. Samuel Huntington even argues that the major factor that draws the soldier into the political arena is the weakness of the civilian bureaucratic system.[89]

To curb graft and corruption and improve the civil service system in the Philippines, the Arroyo government embarked on some antigraft and corruption reform initiatives. It enacted the Government Procurement Reform Act, or RA 9184, that aims to redefine the procedures and processes in government purchasing. The Act was expected to result in enhanced transparency, competitiveness, and accountability in procurement.[90] It also supported the formation of the Inter-Agency Anti-Graft Coordinating Council and the Coalition against Corruption/Transparency and Accountability Network to help in the conduct of lifestyle checks of government and military officials.[91]

But the Philippine bureaucracy continues to suffer "from the limited technical skills and low morale of its personnel and has to live with recruitment rules and promotion procedures heavily tainted by patronage politics."[92] Though the Philippines has many talented people that can improve the Philippine bureaucracy, many Filipino professionals prefer to work abroad in search of a greener pasture. In a report released by the Department of Labor and Employment, Filipinos seek employment overseas due to higher pay and better benefits, not because there are few jobs in the Philippines.[93] Thus, only few talented people prefer to work in the Philippine civil service. This situation is confounded by the habit of civilian leaders to appoint retired military officers to civilian posts, particularly those posts with national security duties like defense, police, prisons, intelligence, customs, immigrations, ports authority, aviation authority, investigation bureaus, and the like. This habit blurs the division of professional responsibility between civilian and military officials and undermines the principle of supremacy of civilian authorities over the military. Adding insult to injury is the fact that even the current chief executive does not have a full control of the intelligence services of the state. This was indicated by the "Hello Garci" wiretapped tape controversy that has recently disturbed the present government.[94]

To strengthen and reform the Philippine bureaucracy and improve public service delivery, the Arroyo government embarked on the rationalization of the functions and agencies of the Executive Branch. Arroyo signed Executive Order 366 on October 4, 2004, directing all agencies of the national government to conduct a strategic review of their operations and organizations for purposes of focusing government efforts and resources on its vital/core services; improving the quality and efficiency of government services delivery by eliminating/minimizing overlaps and duplication; and improving agency performance through the rationalization of service delivery and support systems and organization structure and staffing.[95] It is still premature to assess the rationalization program of the Philippine government. But there is a strong call from the academe to involve nongovernmental organizations, private sector organizations, and the larger civil society in the strengthening of Philippine bureaucracy.[96]

Aside from the weakness of civilian bureaucracy, another challenge of security sector governance in the Philippines is the issue of legislative control and oversight. An important oversight power of the legislature is the power of investigation that requires military and civilian officials to appear before Congress in order to answer queries in aid of legislation. But members of the Philippine Congress are being criticized for using their power only for grandstanding and to get back at those who earned their displeasure.[97] It has also been observed "that serious attention to undertaking legislative oversight activities has been lacking because of low political returns, lack of expertise of members and staff member support to conduct oversight activities, and inadequate data and information to support oversight activities."[98] A University of the Philippines professor argues, "While civilian oversight institutions had been restored by the 1987 Constitution, these institutions remained weak and largely uninformed about defense and security issues. Politicians tend to exercise these powers irresponsibly and many continue to enlist the support of officers and soldiers in their personal and political agenda."[99] Moreover, the Philippine Congress has been tainted with many allegations of graft and corruption that exacerbate its credibility dilemma.[100]

Judicial control of the security sector is also a major challenge. If the Philippine legislature is suffering from a credibility dilemma, the Philippine judiciary is agonizing from an integrity crisis because of allegations that judges can be bought and cannot be trusted.[101] Rampant delay in the disposition of court cases at all levels has already been documented. As of June 2004, it was reported that there were 837,436 pending cases in various Philippine courts.[102] This situation is aggravated by the judiciary's lack of independence because the Supreme Court and other lower courts failed to insulate themselves from interferences of politicians and high-rank-ing public officials.[103] To address many problems confronting the Philippine judi-cial system, the Philippine judiciary is implementing the Judicial Reform Support Project that aims to support an accessible judicial system in order to foster public trust and confidence.[104] The project particularly aims to:

- Improve case adjudication and access to justice through the implementation of modern case management techniques, planning and tools, and the upgrad-ing of information and communication systems. Case management reform will include electronically integrating court processes, enabling analysis of cases, and case management performance of the courts.
- Enhance institutional integrity by (1) strengthening the Code of Ethics for justices, judges, lawyers and court personnel; (2) strengthening the moni-toring of the conduct, operations and performance of judges, lawyers, and court personnel; (3) implementing the computerized Judicial Performance Management System within the pilot model courts and higher courts of the judiciary; and, (4) implementing a gender-sensitive Human Resources and Development Master Plan for nonjudicial personnel, strengthening the over-all capacities of the Philippine Judicial Academy as well.
- Strengthen institutional capacity through the implementation of a decen-tralized administration model for the judiciary; installing comprehensive, computer-based financial and administrative systems; developing model inte-grated court facilities; and strengthening policy, research, and development capabilities, including the establishment of an electronic judicial library.
- Assist in strengthening support for the reform process, ensuring that judges and other stakeholders are able to participate in the development and imple-mentation of key reform activities.[105]

The Philippine electoral system also poses a major challenge to security sector gov-ernance in the Philippines. In theory, election is a democratic process by which the country's political leaders are chosen by and made accountable to the people. But the Philippine electoral system is tainted by irregularities.[106] The military and the police forces are also said to have participated in election irregularities.[107] In fact, the result of the 2004 elections is highly contested because of alleged massive frauds and violence.[108]

The weakness of the electoral system is aggravated by a weak political party system. Political parties in the Philippines are formed as a matter of convenience and political expediency rather than a tool of democratic governance.[109] This situation widens the "democratic deficit" in the country.[110] A weak party and electoral system increases the propensity of the military to stage a coup as an "alternative" mechanism for regime succession and elite circulation. But a strong party and electoral system, however, can replace a military coup as instrument of leadership succession.[111]

A weak electoral and party system reveals the fragility of existing democracy in the Philippines. Thus, there is a strong call for electoral reforms in the Philippines to strengthen democracy even in its minimalist expression. To pursue electoral reforms, the Philippine government is considering the following recommendations of former Chief Justice Hilarion Davide, who was appointed by the President as the presidential adviser for electoral reforms:

- Fix the term of office of members of the House of Representatives and provincial, city, and municipal elective officials to four years.
- De-synchronize elections and hold, as a consequence, national and local elections on different dates.
- Ban the appointment of elective local officials and members of the House of Representatives to any public office during the term for which they were elected.
- Ban the appointment of senators to any public office within three years from their election for a particular term.
- Prohibit political dynasties (clear definition of which should already be made instead of definition being left to Congress) and provide harsh sanctions for violations.
- Prohibit elective officials from changing their party affiliation during the term for which they were elected and provide harsh sanctions for violations.
- Adopt certain electoral reforms proposed by the Consultative Commission as follows:
  - Develop the party system.
  - Develop two major political parties.
  - Provide financial assistance to the political parties on the basis of their share of the votes cast.
  - Prohibit financial contributions from foreign governments.[112]

There is also a lack of transparency in the security sector. The Philippines does not have a published national security white paper to inform the public of the government security policy and predicaments. Though the NSC attempted in 1999 to produce a white paper, it was never approved nor did it receive serious public scrutiny.[113] In 1998, the DND released its so-called defense white paper,[114] but this white paper was also never circulated to the wider public for debate and discussions. Only few officials of the security sector obtained a copy of this so-called defense white paper. The 1998 defense white paper has already been made available on the Internet for public viewing,[115] but the DND Web site does not have a link to this document as of this writing, indicating a lack of interest on the subject.[116] The DND attempted to produce a defense white paper in 2002 and 2003, but all drafts never received approval because defense and military officials had a hard time putting their minds together. Thus, the civil society has a narrow understanding of the government's defense and security perspectives because of a lack of transparency documents on defense and military issues. Among Southeast Asian countries, the Philippines is one of the few that has not produced its defense or security white paper.

Accountability of officials is also a major challenge confronting good governance of the security sector. There is a general failure to make erring officials in the security sector accountable for their mistakes and lapses in judgments, particularly those who have participated in coups and military rebellions as well as those who have committed graft and corruption. This reinforces a sense of impunity among some military officers and public officials.[117] In fact, this problem is one of the major observations of the Feliciano Commission, which urges the Philippine government to enforce the law against violators. The Feliciano Commission contends that erring officers, troops, and civilian partners "must be treated in accordance with law to control and reverse the culture of impunity."[118]

Finally, one very important challenge of security sector governance in the Philippines was the question of legitimacy of the chief executive. President Arroyo battled with bitter allegations of election irregularities committed in 2004. The "Hello Garci" tape controversy put the legitimacy of the Arroyo government under a cloud of doubt. A theory of civil-military relations in developing countries contends that when the legitimacy of civilian government is low, military intervention occurs more frequently.[119] In the midst of a legitimacy crisis, the Arroyo administration heavily relied on the loyalty of the armed forces. This situation indicates the weakness of the civilian leadership to effectively govern the security sector.

## Conclusion and Policy Recommendations

Though existing legal mechanisms uphold the supremacy of civilian authorities over the military, this principle is being undermined by the continuing appointment of retired military officers to inherently civilian posts. Civilian authorities, on the other hand, continue to rely on the political support of the military for the stability of the civilian government. Thus, the governance of the Philippine security sector is problematic because of the limited capacity of the civilian government and other challenges mentioned in the previous sections of this chapter.

To overcome these challenges, it is imperative for the Philippine government to really pursue a comprehensive security sector reform (SSR). Though the Philippine government is already implementing the Philippine Defense Reform (PDR), this initiative is incomplete because it is only confined to defense and military sectors. The primordial aim of SSR is to go beyond defense and military reforms. It aims to transform the wider security institutions so that they play an effective, legitimate, and democratically accountable role in providing external and internal security for their citizens.[120] Reform of the security sector requires broader and more comprehensive consultation with the goal of strengthening civilian control and oversight, professionalization of the security forces with concomitant demilitarization and peace building, and more importantly, the strengthening of the rule of law.[121]

One step for conducting an SSR is for the chief executive to initiate the holding of a Security Sector Summit with the participation of all members of the security sector described in this chapter. The Philippine government's experiences in holding economic and political summits can provide useful lessons for the holding of Security Sector Summit, which can set the agenda and direction of SSR.

Because the Philippines is facing internal armed challenges posed by local Communist insurgency, Muslim separatism, and radical Muslim terrorism affecting the good governance of the security sector, the Philippine government has to address the structural causes of internal armed conflicts, insurgency, terrorism, and political unrest. Thus, comprehensive structural reforms are imperative for SSR. Structural reforms shall include the following:

- Improving the country's distribution of wealth. This entails a serious implementation of economic reforms that aim to address the interconnecting problems of poverty and unemployment. Though there are various causes of internal armed conflicts and terrorism in the Philippines, poverty and unemployment have been identified as some of the major causes.
- Strengthening political representation. This requires the reform of the country's electoral and party systems. The legitimacy of civilian authorities remains vulnerable to various political challenges because results of elections are often contested. Political parties, on the other hand, are facing enormous difficulties in truly representing the will and interests of the people because of the lack of concrete party programs. Philippine political parties are highly personalistic rather than programmatic in orientation. A weak electoral and party system distorts the main essence of representative democracy in the Philippines.

There is also a need to pursue reform of Philippine institutions to strengthen democratic governance of the security sector. The three branches of the Philippine government have to undergo the following reforms:

*Strengthening Philippine bureaucracy* — The rationalization of the functions and agencies of the Executive Branch under Executive Order 366 is in the right premise as it intends to make government "do the right things in the best way within affordable levels and in the most accountable manner."[122] But to sustain this reform effort, there is a need to really strengthen the Philippine civil service system by building a professional and motivated workforce with a new work culture "that emphasizes a strong client orientation and excellence, integrity, and management that is knowledge based."[123]

*Enhancing legislative oversight* — An Asian Development Bank (ADB) study underscores that as the principal policymaking branch of government, "the Legislature performs a crucial role in the pursuit of good governance. Laws create the legal and institutional frameworks through which transparency, accountability, participation, and predictability of rules and regulations can be ensured in government."[124] Moreover, the legislature performs oversight functions of the security sector. But the Philippine legislative system lacks the capacity to perform this oversight function.

*Improving administration of justice* — To establish judicial control of the security sector, there is a need to strengthen the country's civilian justice system through the enhancement of judicial integrity and competence. The lack of justice is often cited as one of the major causes of political unrest, internal armed conflicts, and military intervention in the Philippines.

Aside from structural and bureaucratic reforms, there is also a need to encourage "public control" of the security sector and accommodate external support for SSR, to wit:

*Encouraging "public control" of the security sector* — Because the military continues to shape the agenda of the Philippine security sector, much information on national security issues remains restricted, confidential, or secret. Only propaganda information on national security is made available to the public. Confidentiality and secrecy of information fail to nurture an informed national debate on multifaceted security issues facing the Philippines, particularly those pertaining to internal armed conflicts. Though the Philippines has a vibrant civil society, its ability to exercise democratic governance of the security sector is constrained by its lack of understanding of defense and military issues and concerns. Most members of the Philippine civil society, in fact, have a pejorative view of the military establishment due to the historical baggage of martial law and the human rights abuses committed by some soldiers. This situation widens the cleavage between the public and the military sector.

*Accommodating external support for SSR* — Some literatures have already demonstrated the vital role of the international community in SSR.[125] External support must therefore be encouraged in the reform process. The PDR is an excellent example of a reform process with the external assistance of the United States. But the reform process must be extended to the wider security sector and to more external partners like Australia, Canada, China, and the European Union.

The foregoing discussions have illustrated the complexity of security sector governance in the Philippines. It is therefore imperative for the Philippines to implement a serious reform of its security sector in order to improve the country's security sector governance. Good governance of the security sector is an effective weapon against military rebellion, insurgency, and terrorism.

# Endnotes

1. For a good assessment of the situation, see V. Selochan, "The Military and Fragile Democracy of the Philippines," in R.J. May and V. Selochan (eds.), *The Military and Democracy in Asia and the Pacific* (Canberra: Australian National University, 2004), document available at: http://epress.anu.edu.au/mdap/mobile_devices/ch04.html.

2. See for example Carolina C. Hernandez, "Institutional Responses to Armed Conflict: The Armed Forces of the Philippines" (Background paper submitted to the Human Development Network Foundation, Inc., for the Philippine Human Development Report 2005); R.J. Intengan, *The Armed Forces of the Philippines: Defender of the Nation, Guardian of Democracy, and the Servant of the People* (Quezon City: Center for Strategic Studies, 2005); and Felipe Miranda, "Leadership and Political Stabilization in a Post-Aquino Philippines," *Philippine Political Science Journal*, Nos. 33–36, (June 1991–December 1992), pp. 142–222.

3. J. Malaya, "Proposed Amendments to the 1987 Philippine Constitution," in A. Nachura and J. Malaya (eds.), *Liberal Views on Constitutional Reform* (Manila: National Institute for Policy Studies, 2003), p. 130.

4. Armed Forces of the Philippines. *Information Kit in Response to Standing Issues* (Quezon City: AFP Headquarters, 2005). Also see V. Cabreza, "Messianic complex in military academy backed," *Philippine Daily Inquirer*, August 4, 2003.

5. See for example Sheila Coronel (ed.), *Pork and Other Perks: Corruption and Governance in the Philippines* (Quezon City: Philippine Center for Investigative Journalism, Evelio B. Javier Foundation and Institute for Popular Democracy, 1988).

6. See for example Edna Co, Jorge Tigno, Melissa Lao, and M. Sayo, *Philippine Democracy Assessment: Free and Fair Elections and the Democratic Role of Political Parties* (Manila and Quezon City: Friedrich-Ebert-Stiftung and National College of Public Administration and Governance, 2005); Rommel Banlaoi and Clarita Carlos, *Political Parties in the Philippines: From 1900 to the Present* (Makati City: Konrad Adenauer Foundation, 1996); Clarita Carlos and Rommel Banlaoi, *Elections in the Philippines: From 1900 to the Present* (Makati City: Konrad Adenauer Foundation, 1996).

7. See for example Walden Bello, *The Anti-Development State: The Political Economy of Permanent Crisis in the Philippines* (Quezon City: Department of Sociology, University of the Philippines and Focus on the Global South, 2004).

8. See for example Felipe Miranda, "Leadership and Political Stabilization in Post-Aquino Philippines," *Philippine Political Science Journal*, Nos. 33–36 (June 1991–December 1992), pp. 142–222.

9. Selochan, "The Military and Fragile Democracy of the Philippines" op.cit.

10. Francisco Nemenzo et al., *Blueprint for a Viable Philippines: Highlights, Analysis and Recommendations*, document available at: http://www.yonip.com/main/articles/archive06.html (2006).

11. Glenda Gloria, *We Were Soldiers: Military Men in Politics and the Bureaucracy* (Quezon City: Friedrich-Ebert-Stiftung, 2003), p. 34.

12. For a detailed discussion, see Felipe Miranda, *The Politicization of the Military* (Quezon City: University of the Philippines Center for Integrative and Development Studies, 1992).

13. Armed Forces of the Philippines, Office of the Deputy Chief of Staff for Personnel, January 2007.

14. See Barry Buzan, "National Security and the Nature of the State" in his *People, States and Fear: An Agenda for International Security Studies in the Post Cold War*, 2nd edition (London: Harvester Wheatsheaf, 1991), Chapter 2.
15. The most popular textbook on realism in the Philippines is Hans Morgenthau, *The Politics among Nations: The Struggle for Power and Peace* (New York: Alfred A. Knopft, Inc., 1948). For a classic book on realism, see E.H. Carr, *The Twenty-Year's Crisis, 1919–1939: An Introduction to the Study of International Relations* (London: McMillan, 1939) and E. Schwarzenberger, *Power Politics* (London: Cape Publishers, 1941).
16. K. Krause and M. Williams, "Broadening the Agenda of Security Studies: Politics and Methods," *Mershon International Studies Review*, Vol. 40, No. 2 (October 1996), pp. 227–254.
17. See Muthiah Alagappa, "Rethinking Security: A Critical Review and Appraisal of the Debate," M. Alagappa (ed.), *Asian Security Practice: Material and Ideational Influences* (Stanford California: Stanford California Press, 1998).
18. International Alert, *Towards a Better Practice Framework in Security Sector Reform: Broadening the Debate* (Amsterdam: Netherlands Institute of International Relations "Clingendael," 2002).
19. Ibid. Also see H. Dylan, *A Review of the Security Sector Reform* (London: The Conflict, Security and Development Group, Center for Defense Studies, King's College London, 1999), p. 29.
20. See for example Rommel Banlaoi, "The ASEAN Regional Forum and the Management of Conflicts in the South China Sea," in James Chin and Nicholas Thomas (eds.), *China–ASEAN: Changing Political and Strategic Ties* (Hong Kong: Centre of Asian Studies, the University of Hong Kong, 2005), pp. 181–209; Aileen Baviera, *Bilateral Confidence Building with China in Relation to the South China Sea Disputes: A Philippine Perspective* (Ontario, Canada: Department of Foreign Affairs and International Trade, 2001); Ian Storey, "Creeping Assertiveness: China, the Philippines and the South China Sea Dispute," *Contemporary Southeast Asia*, Vol. 21, No. 1 (April 1999); D. Dzurek, *The Spratly Islands Disputes* (Durham: International Boundaries Research Uni, 1996); Chen Jie, "China's Spratly Policy: With Special Reference to the Philippines and Malaysia," *Asian Survey*, Vol. 34, No. 10 (October 1994).
21. For an official perspective, see "Our National Security Strategy: A Reference Paper" (Prepared by the Office of the National Security Adviser and the National Security Council Secretariat, September 1999) and *In Defense of the Philippines: 1998 Defense Policy Paper* (Quezon City: Office of the Secretary of National Defense, 1998). For a scholarly analysis, see Noel Morada and C. Collier, "The Philippines: States Versus Society," in M. Alagappa (ed.), *Asian Security Practice: Material and Ideational Influences* (Stanford, California: Stanford California Press, 1998), pp. 549–578; and Aileen Baviera, "Security Challenges of the Philippine Archipelago," *Southeast Asian Affairs 1998* (Singapore: Institute of Southeast Asian Studies, 1998), pp. 213–221.
22. Executive Order No. 115, "Reorganizing the National Security Council and Defining Its Membership, Function, and Authority and for other Purposes" (December 24, 1986). Document available at: http://www.lawphil.net/executive/execord/eo1986/ eo_115_1986.html.
23. Alexander Aguirre, "The Bureaucratic Politics of National Security Council System in the Philippines" (Lecture delivered at the National Defense College of the Philippines on January 27, 2005).
24. Ibid., Section 1.

25. P. Oquist, "Mindanao and Beyond: Competing Policies, Protracted Peace Process and Human Security" (A 5th Assessment Mission Report of Multi-Donor Programme for Peace and Development in Mindanao, October 23, 2002).

26. See for example J.M. Collins, *Military Strategy: Principles, Practices, and Historical Perspectives* (Washington, DC: Brasseys, Inc., 2002). Chapter 16 of this book discusses counterinsurgency strategies of Clear-Hold-Consolidate-Develop.

27. See Walden Bello, *U.S.-Sponsored Low-Intensity Conflict in the Philippines* (San Francisco: Institute for Food & Development Policy, 1987).

28. Administrative Order No. 104, "Providing for Cabinet Groups to Enable the Government to Address Major Concerns in the Implementation of the Administration's 10-Point Agenda" (September 7, 2004), Section 2. Document available at: http://www.ops.gov.ph/records/ao_no104.htm.

29. Inter-Agency Anti-Terrorism Task Force, "Government Response to Terrorism" (undated).

30. See Ibon Foundation, Inc., *A New Wave of State Terror in the Philippines* (Manila: Ibon Books, 2005). Also see Maris Diokno, "State-Civil Society Dynamics on the Anti-Terrorism Bill," Marlon Wui and Glenda Lopez (eds.), *State Civil-Society: Relations in Policy-Making* (Quezon City: Third World Studies Center, 1997), pp. 147–178.

31. For the official Web site of the Philippine Senate, see: http://www.senate.gov.ph/Default.htm. For Philippine House of Representatives, see: http://www.congress.gov.ph/.

32. For more information about the Commission on Audit, please visit its official Web site at: http://www.coa.gov.ph/.

33. For more information about the Office of the Ombudsman, please visit its official Web site at: http://www.ombudsman.gov.ph/Index.php?pagename=Home&tag.

34. Ibid.

35. For more information about the Commission on Human Rights, please visit its official Web site at: http://www.chr.gov.ph/.

36. Hernandez, op. cit., p. 1.

37. Ibid.

38. For historical background, see *A History: the Ministry of National Defense, 40th Anniversary* (Quezon City: Ministry of National Defense, undated).

39. The Davide Fact-Finding Commission, *The Final Report of the Fact-Finding Commission* (Makati: Bookmark, 1990), p. 29.

40. R.J. Kessler, "Development and the Military: Role of the Philippine Military in Development," in J.S. Djiwandono and Y.M. Cheong (eds.), *Soldiers and Stability in Southeast Asia* (Singapore: Institute of Southeast Asian Studies, 1988), p. 217.

41. The Davide Fact-Finding Commission, *The Final Report of the Fact-Finding Commission*, op. cit., p. 30.

42. See M. Rasmussen, "The Military Role in Internal Defense and Security: Some Problems," *The Center for Civil-Military Relations Occasional Paper*, No. 6 (Monterey, California: Naval Postgraduate School, October 1999), p. 1. Also see A. Stepan (ed.), *Authoritarian Brazil: Origins, Policies and Future* (New Haven and London: Yale University Press, 1973).

43. Ibid., p. 2.

44. Kessler, "Development and the Military: Role of the Philippine Military in Development," op. cit., p. 218.

45. Ibid. Also see H. Waynard, "A Comparison of Military Elite Role Perceptions in Indonesia and the Philippines" (Ph.D. Dissertation: American University, 1976), p. 366.
46. Ferdinand Marcos, "State of the Nation Address" (January 22, 1968).
47. David Wurfel, *Filipino Politics: Development and Decay* (Quezon City: Ateneo de Manila Press, 1988), p. 114.
48. Manuel Caoili, "The Philippine Congress and the Political Order," *Philippine Journal of Political Administration*, Vol. 30, No. 1 (January 1986), pp. 1–35.
49. Olivia Caoili, "The Batasang Pambansa: Continuity in the Philippine Legislative System," *Philippine Journal of Political Administration*, Vol. 30, No. 1 (January 1986), pp. 36–59.
50. Wurfel, *Filipino Politics: Development and Decay*, op. cit., p. 143.
51. Carolina Hernandez, "Restoring Democratic Civilian Control Over the Philippine Military: Challenges and Prospects," *Journal of International Cooperation Studies* (Fall 2002).
52. See Felipe Miranda and Ruben Ciron, "Development and the Military in the Philippines," J.S. Djiwandono and Y.M. Cheong (eds.), *Soldiers and Stability in Southeast Asia* (Singapore: Institute of Southeast Asian Studies, 1988), p. 165. Also see Armando Gatmaitan and Gregorio C. de Castro, "Notes on the Role of the Military in Socio-Economic Development," *Philippine Journal of Public Administration* (July 1968).
53. See H. Maynard, "A Comparison of Military Elite Role Perceptions in Indonesia and the Philippines" (Unpublished dissertation, American University, 1976), p. 535. Also cited in Ibid., p. 144.
54. For a good account, see Alfred McCoy, *Closer Than Brothers: Manhood at the Philippine Military Academy* (Manila: Anvil Publishing, 1999); Wurfel, *Filipino Politics: Development and Decay*, op. cit., Chapter 5.
55. Ibid, Chapter 7.
56. Maynard, "A Comparison of Military Elite Role Perceptions in Indonesia and the Philippines" (1967), op. cit.
57. For a detailed account of the Philippine military after EDSA, see C. Yabes, *The Boys from the Barracks: The Philippine Military after EDSA* (Metro Manila: Anvil Publishing, Inc., 1991).
58. Ed Garcia and Eric Gutierrez (eds.), *Back to the Barracks: The Military in Democratic Transition* (Quezon City: National Institute for Policy Studies, 1992).
59. Yabes, *The Boys from the Barracks*, op. cit., p. vii.
60. The 1987 Philippine Constitution, Article XVI, Section 6.
61. Executive Order No. 246, "Providing for the Creation of the National Intelligence Coordinating Agency and for other Purposes" (July 24, 1987).
62. Yabes, *The Boys from the Barracks*, op. cit., p. vii.
63. The Davide Fact-Finding Commission, *The Final Report of the Fact-Finding Commission* (1990), op. cit., p. 118.
64. Ibid., pp. 470–471.
65. Republic Act 6965, otherwise known as "The Department of Interior and Local Government Act of 1990."
66. R. Cuaderno, "Towards Developing a Civilian Culture in the Philippine Police Service," *Public Safety Review*, Vol. 1, No. 1 (September 2000), p. 223.

67. For an excellent historical analysis, see Cesar Pobre, *History of the Armed Forces of the Filipino People* (Quezon City: New Day Publishers, 2000).

68. Renado de Castro, "Adjusting to the Post-U.S. Bases Era: The Ordeal of the Philippine Military's Modernization Program," *Armed Forces and Society*, Vol. 26, No. 1 (Fall 1999), pp. 110–137.

69. Renado de Castro, "The Dilemma between Democratic Control versus Military Reforms: The Case of the AFP Modernization Program, 1991–2004," *Journal of Security Sector Management* (March 2005). Document available at: http://www.jofssm. org/issues/jofssm_sp_03_asia_decastro.pdf.

70. Gloria, *We Were Soldiers*, op. cit.

71. Ibid.

72. For more discussions on the topic, see C.R. Carlos, "New Roles of the Military: Perspectives from the Philippines" (Paper presented during the 5th ARF Meeting of Heads of Defense Universities/Colleges/Institutions held on August 27–31, 2001 in Tokyo, Japan). Document available at: http://www.nids.go.jp/english/exchange/arf/ pdf/philippines_paper.pdf.

73. See Amado Doronilla (ed.), *In between Fires: Fifteen Perspectives on the Estrada Crisis* (Pasig City: Anvil Publishing, 2001), and A. Laquian and E. Laquian, *The Erap Tragedy: Tales from the Snake Pit* (Pasig City: Anvil Publishing, 2002).

74. These grievances are also articulated in Trillanes Paper. See A. Trillanes, "A Study on Corruption in Philippine Navy" (October 2001). Document available at: http:// www.pcij.org/HotSeat/trillanes.html. Trillanes is one of the leaders of the Oakwood mutineers.

75. *The Report of the Fact-Finding Commission* (October 17, 2003), p. 33.

76. Ibid., pp. 39–40.

77. Karl B. Kaufman, "Weak Intel Blamed on Overzealous Spy Units," *The Manila Times* (March 26, 2004), at: http://www.manilatimes.net/national/2004/mar/26/yehey/top_ stories/20040326top6.html (accessed on August 30, 2004).

78. Ibid.

79. Ibid.

80. Department of National Defense, *The Philippine Defense Reform Program* (2003). Document available at: http://www.dnd.gov.ph/DNDWEBPAGE_files/html/pdrpage. htm.

81. Department of National Defense, *Philippine Defense Reform: Information Briefing* (Quezon City: Office of the Undersecretary for Philippine Defense Reform, December 2005). The author is grateful to Undersecretary Ernesto Carolina for providing this briefing.

82. For more discussion, see Rommel C. Banlaoi, "Identity Politics and National Security in the Philippines," *Pilipinas: A Journal of Philippine Studies*, Nos. 42–43 (2005).

83. Asian Development Bank, *The Philippines: Country Governance Assessment* (Manila: Asian Development Bank Manila Office, 2005). Document also available at: www.adb. org/Documents/Reports/CGA/pga-feb-2005.pdf.

84. Ledivina Carino, *Bureaucracy for Democracy* (Quezon City: College of Public Administration, University of the Philippines, 1992).

85. Sheila Coronel (ed.), *Pork and other Perks: Corruption and Governance in the Philippines* (Quezon City: Philippine Center for Investigative Journalism, the Evelio B. Javier Foundation, and the Institute for Popular Democracy, 1998).

86. D. Dumlao, "RP No. 2 on corruption list ADB survey covered over 700 firms in 2003," *Philippine Daily Inquirer*, January 20, 2005 at: http://news.inq7.net/nation/index.php?index=1&story_id=24830.
87. For an excellent study, see M. Mariano et.al., *The Power of Reform in the AFP LogCom: A True Story, The Struggle Continues* (Quezon City: HHP Cooperative Development, Inc., 1992).
88. Alex Pabico, "Ex-AFP Comptroller Guilty of Corruption" (December 2, 2005). Document available at: http://www.pcij.org/blog/?p=512.
89. Samuel Huntington, *The Soldier and the State: The Theory and Politics of Civil Military Relations* (Cambridge and London: The Balknap Press of Harvard University Press, 1957).
90. For more information, see *The 2005 Accomplishments of the Arroyo Administration*. Document available at: http://www.news.ops.gov.ph/accomplishments2005.htm.
91. Ibid.
92. Temario Rivera, "Democratic Governance and Late Industrialization," Sta. Ana III, F.S. (ed.), *The State and the Market: Essays on Socially Oriented Philippine Economy* (Quezon City: Action for Economic Reforms, 1998), p. 257.
93. "Enough Jobs But No Taker Says DOLE," *Philippine Star*, February 15, 2005.
94. The "Hello Garci" tape controversy refers to the alleged telephone conversation between President Arroyo and COMELEC Commissioner at the height of the May 2004 elections. For more stories about the controversy, see "Tale of the Tape" at: http://www.time.com/time/asia/2005/phil_arroyo/phil_tape.html.
95. Executive Order No. 366, "Directing a Strategic Review of the Operations and Organizations of the Executive Branch and Providing Options and Incentives for Government Employees Who May Be Affected by the Rationalization of the Functions and Agencies of the Executive Branch," October 4, 2004. Available at: http://www.ops.gov.ph/records/eo_no366.htm.
96. For detailed discussion, see The Diliman Governance Forum, "Reinventing/Reengineering & Reorganizing the Bureaucracy in the Philippines: Why We Should Be More Hopeful," held at NCPAG Assembly Hall, UP Diliman, September 15, 2004. Highlights of the proceedings available at: http://www.upd.edu.ph/~ncpag/dgf/archives/highlights091504.html.
97. Asian Development Bank, *The Philippines: Country Governance Assessment*, p. 55.
98. Ibid.
99. Hernandez, "Institutional Responses to Armed Conflict: The Armed Forces of the Philippines," op. cit., p. 2.
100. Coronel (ed.), *Pork and Other Perks*, op. cit., pp. 32–55.
101. Asian Development Bank, *The Philippines: Country Governance Assessment*, op. cit., p. 97. Also see A.G.M. La Vina and D.M. Arroyo, *The Public Verdict on the Performance of the Judiciary* (Makati City: Transparent Accountable Government, 1993).
102. Ibid., p. 100.
103. Ibid.
104. For more information, see "Judicial Reform Support Project." Document available at: http://www.projectmaps-worldbank.org.ph/Projects1-JRSP.htm.
105. Ibid.
106. Carlos, and Banlaoi, *Elections in the Philippines*, op. cit.
107. Gloria, "Split Loyalties," *Newsbreak* (June 21, 2004), p. 25.

108. Rommel Banlaoi, "2004 Philippine Election: Thinking Outside the Ballot Box?" *Asian Affairs*, No. 22 (2004), pp. 31–47.
109. E. Co et. al., *Philippine Democracy Assessment,* op. cit.
110. See Paul Hutchcroft and Joel Rocamora, "Strong Demands and Weak Institutions: The Origins and Evolution of the Democratic Deficit in the Philippines," *Journal of East Asian Studies*, Vol. 3 (2003), pp. 259–292.
111. G. Cawthra and R. Luckham, (eds.), *Governing Insecurity: Democratic Control of Military and Security Establishments in Transitional Democracies* (London and New York: Zed Books, 2003), p. 7.
112. Official Web site of the Republic of the Philippines, "Davide's recommendations on electoral reforms will be seriously considered – PGMA," April 10, 2006. Document available at: http://www.gov.ph/news/?i=14895.
113. "Our National Security Strategy: A Reference Paper" (Prepared by the Office of the National Security Adviser and the National Security Council Secretariat, September 1999).
114. *In Defense of the Philippines: 1998 Defense Policy Paper* (Quezon City: Office of the Secretary of National Defense, 1998).
115. Document available at: http://www.resdal.org.ar/Archivo/d000006b.htm.
116. See DND Web site at: http://www.dnd.gov.ph/.
117. C.G. Hernandez, "Institutional Responses to Armed Conflict: The Armed Forces of the Philippines," op. cit., p. 2.
118. *The Report of the Fact-Finding Commission*, op. cit., p. 43.
119. J. Doorn, "The Military and the Crisis of Legitimacy," G. Harries-Jenkins and J.V. Doorn, (eds.), *The Military and the Crisis of Legitimacy* (London: Sage Publications, 1976), p. 28.
120. International Alert, *Toward a Better Practice Framework in Security Sector Reform*, op. cit., p. 1.
121. Ibid.
122. Karina Constantino-David, "Current Efforts on Reinventing/Reengineering & Reorganizing the Bureaucracy" (Paper presented to the Diliman Governance Forum, "Reinventing/Reengineering & Reorganizing the Bureaucracy in the Philippines: Why We Should Be More Hopeful" held at NCPAG Assembly Hall, UP Diliman, September 15, 2004), pp. 1–5.
123. Asian Development Bank, *The Philippines: Country Governance Assessment*, op. cit., p. 35.
124. Ibid, p. ix.
125. See T. Winkler, The Reform and Democratic Control of the Security Sector and International Order (Geneva: Geneva Center for Democratic Control of the Armed Forces, 2002); G. Kummel, Why Engage in Security Sector Reform Abroad: International Norms, External Democratization and the Role of DCAF (Geneva: Geneva Center for Democratic Control of the Armed Forces, 2002).

## Chapter 7

# Philippine Elections and National Security after 9/11: Thinking Outside the Ballot Box?*

## Introduction

Although the Philippines has the longest history of democratic elections in Southeast Asia,[1] the conduct of the May 10, 2004, elections revealed the archaic characteristic of the Philippine electoral system. Despite earlier attempts to computerize the counting procedure to modernize the electoral process, paper ballots were counted manually. From voters' registration to the canvassing of ballots, the whole electoral exercise was no different from previous elections — personality-oriented and surrounded by traditional issues of frauds, irregularities, and violence.[2] Because of the failure of the Philippine government to implement a genuine electoral reform after the May 2004 and May 2007 elections, the conduct of the 2010 elections and beyond is bound to repeat the terrible mistakes of the past.

This chapter examines the role of elections in advancing Philippine national security. It focuses on the May 2004 election as a case study to demonstrate how

* Revised and updated version of a paper originally entitled "2004 Philippines Elections: Thinking Outside the Ballot Box?" published in *Asian Affairs*, No. 22 (2004), pp. 31–47.

the infirmities of the current electoral system in the Philippines can undermine Philippine security.

The political exercise in May 2004 saw the reelection of President Gloria Macapagal Arroyo, who declared the recently concluded elections as "generally peaceful and orderly." But opposition groups led by action-star-turned-politician Fernando Poe, Jr., contested the results of the elections because of alleged massive frauds and violence. Tampering and switching of ballots, vote shaving, and vote buying were reported to have prevailed during the elections. At least 202 people (including 29 candidates) were reportedly killed in election-related violence, the highest number of election fatalities thus far in Philippine electoral history.[3]

Because of frauds and violence, foreign observers expressed serious concerns about the future of Philippine democracy — the first-ever established in Asia after World War II. Foreign observers even found the May 2004 elections as "too violent, messy and absurd."[4] Although Foreign Affairs Secretary Delia Alberts said that other foreign observers noticed "the improvements" in Philippine elections,[5] local analysts described the May 2004 elections as "the worst ever" since the Philippines became a republic.[6] This situation is causing cynicism in some people and encouraging other forces to "think outside the ballot box" and explore other ways of political succession to bring Philippine politics "back to health."[7]

The sad state of the Philippine electoral system has become a national security concern because of reported violence, fraud, and anomalies. Though the Philippine government initiated a series of policy reforms in the aftermath of the September 11, 2001 terrorist attacks to improve the country's economy and political system, the electoral process continues to suffer from structural infirmities and systemic defects.

Like in the past, no genuine program-based political parties contested for official posts. All so-called political parties that participated in the May 2004 elections were merely coalitions of factions of the political elite organized largely for electoral purposes. These electoral coalitions were largely based on personalities rather than ideologies. No substantial political issues were debated during the whole campaign period, defeating the whole purpose of the electoral exercise. Candidates concentrated instead on character assassination of rival candidates rather than on intelligent discourses of pertinent national security issues. Because of the lack of overarching principles that can strongly bind allegiance of party members, Philippine "political parties" are characterized by constantly shifting loyalties to prominent elite personalities, not to issues or programs of government.[8] Thus, campaign activities were like a series of entertainment shows featuring politicians singing and dancing rather than debating on how to surmount the serious socioeconomic problems besetting the country. The practice prevailed in the 2007 Philippine elections because of the absence of a comprehensive electoral reform.

# The Socioeconomic and Security Contexts of Philippine Elections

The Philippines held the May 2004 elections in the context of a lingering socioeconomic crisis and growing security threats. From being the most dynamic economy in Asia in the 1950s, the Philippines has become one of "the sick men" of Asia. The poverty situation is worsening, with over 40% of the Philippine population living below the poverty threshold or poverty line.[9] The National Statistics Coordination Board (NSCB) defines the poverty line "as the minimum income required to meet the food requirements and other nonfood basic needs." Based on the latest NSCB record, the annual per capita poverty threshold was estimated at P11,906 (around US$200) in 2002, a 2.5% increase over the 2000 threshold of P11,620. With this threshold, according to NSCB, a family of five members should have a monthly income of P4,961 (around US$90) to meet its food and nonfood basic needs. With an average inflation rate of 4.5% forecast by the Philippine Central Bank in 2004 and the seemingly unstoppable oil price hike as a result of instabilities in the world market, the face of Philippine poverty is expected to worsen. Though many candidates raised the rhetoric of poverty in their campaigns, nobody presented a clear program of action on how to reduce, if not to eradicate, the scourge of poverty in the country.

The Philippines just suffered from a chronic budget deficit in 2004 when it held the May 2004 elections. It posted a budget deficit of P64.7 billion for the first four months of the year. The ballooning Philippine foreign debt aggravates the budget crisis. According to the Freedom from Debt Coalition (FDC), a cause-oriented organization, Philippine total debt has reached an alarming figure of US$96 billion, including both public and private borrowings, foreign and domestic.[10] More than 31% of the 2004 national budget was earmarked to debt servicing. Economists project that a rise in foreign interest rates would make repayment even more cumbersome and such scenario "would thrust the Philippines into a financial crisis of Argentinean proportions."[11] Though the debt problem poses a clear and present danger to the Philippine economy, presidential candidates during the 2004 elections only paid lip service to the issue. A nuisance presidential aspirant, however, became the butt of a joke when he promised to personally pay all the foreign debt of the Philippine republic.

The Philippines also had to confront internal security threats posed by the New Peoples' Army (NPA), the Abu Sayyaf Group (ASG), and the *Moro* Islamic Liberation Front (MILF).

When the Philippines held the May 2004 elections, the NPA strength was placed at 9,208. Based on the 2006 Third Quarter Threat Assessment of the Armed Forces of the Philippines (AFP), the government has achieved a "significant" feat against local communist insurgency. From its strength of around 8,500 NPA combatants in 2005, NPA strength was reduced to around 7,260 in 2006. But according to the Department of National Defense (DND), the NPA remains capable of organizing the masses and establishing organs of political power at the grassroots through infiltration, coercion, and intimidation. Intelligence sources even state that the NPA has the capability to undertake selective terrorist actions and guerrilla operations against high-impact targets to create an atmosphere of instability and hopelessness in the countryside, the hotbed of Communist insurgency. Police sources also state that the NPA can conduct agitation-propaganda by exploiting popular issues to provoke the populace and distort public perception. The NPA also has a strategy of riding on the peace and electoral processes to consolidate its forces and expand its areas of influence. It is very sad to note that during the campaign period, candidates did not discuss thoroughly the NPA problem. The NPA issue was only mentioned during the elections because of its "permit-to-campaign" scheme in its controlled areas to raise funds. The NPA problem has been festering in the country for more than three decades.

Another equally disturbing internal security concern of the Philippine government is the terrorist threat posed by the ASG.[12] During the May 2004 elections, the ASG strength was estimated to be more than 500 members. Like the NPA problem, the ASG was not the subject of serious discourse during the campaign. Recently, it has been reported that ASG members have built capabilities to wage maritime terrorist attacks in Southern Mindanao, particularly in the Island of Solo and Tawi-Tawi.

The military and defense establishments reported that the MILF strength was placed at around 12,000 during the May 2004 elections. The reported linkage of MILF elements with the Jemaah Islamiyah (JI), an al Qaeda–linked terrorist organization, is also a major source of internal security concern.[13] However, the MILF problem was one of the most neglected topics during the May 2004 elections.

## Face, Phase, and Pace of Philippine Elections

In theory, election is a democratic process by which the country's political leaders are chosen by the people. Election makes political leaders accountable to the people they have sworn to serve. In the Philippines, however, the real face of the election merely serves as occasion for intraelite competition. Elections are nothing but overt expressions of competing interests of the Filipino elite rather than venues of contending programs of government. To use Joseph Schumpeter's jargon, Philippine elections are an apparent display of narrow "competitive elitism" legitimizing elite dominance of Philippine politics.

Though election, in theory, allows people to participate in the democratic process, in reality, Filipino voters participate in the election for the same reason they go to cockfights, boxing matches, basketball games, festivals, and beauty contests.[14] Election season is a like a big sports or concert season — highly entertaining. This explains the large number of crowds during campaigns, because they provide opportunities for people (voters and nonvoters alike) to see candidates and other celebrities live, up-close, and in person. Indeed, electoral politics in the Philippines is like show business — it is a big "show" and a big "business."

It is a big "show" partly because of entertainment. Elections have also become a mere facade of democracy. In the Philippines, political parties are not the real mobilizing organizations but the politician's electoral machinery and network of relatives, friends, political associates, and allies.[15]

It is a big business because of the money involved during the campaign. President Arroyo alone reported that she spent P333 million (US$6 million) for her campaign expenses, not to mention the total campaign expenses of her party, the amount of which has not been disclosed to date. But former Solicitor General Frank Chavez said that Arroyo spent as much as P1 billion to P2 billion in private campaign contributions on top of government funds.[16]

The Philippines observes five major sequential election phases: voter registration, voting, counting, canvassing, and proclamation. As early as August 2003, the Commission on Elections (COMELEC), the independent constitutional body tasked to run all elections in the Philippines, already campaigned for the system of continuing registration as mandated by Republic Act 8189, or "The Voters' Registration Act of 1996." Official records of the COMELEC indicate a total of 43,536,028 registered voters for the May 10, 2004, elections, representing almost 50% of the total Philippine population.[17] Around 65% actually cast their ballots.

The COMELEC and the Department of Foreign Affairs (DFA) also campaigned for the registration of all Filipino citizens working abroad as mandated by Republic Act 9189, otherwise known as "The Overseas Absentee Voting Act of 2003." But out of the total 1.7 million potential absentee Filipino voters, the DFA's Overseas Absentee Voting Secretariat reported only 350,029 absentee registrants. The secretariat also reported that 44% or 152,264 absentee registrants were from the Middle East and African region, 43% or 150,995 from the Asia–Pacific region, 10% or 35,007 from Europe, and 3% or 11,762 from the Americas.[18] In the first-ever overseas absentee voting conducted in Philippine election history, 65% cast their ballots, which according to the secretariat was "very good." But compared with the total number of potential absentee Filipino voters, the turnout was low, indicating the failure of the COMELEC to convince as many to participate in the May 2004 elections.

The overall voting process encountered several problems. Thousands of voters were disenfranchised all over the country, representing 5% to 10% of all registered voters. Names of those disenfranchised were not on the voters list. Guillermo Luz, Secretary-General of the National Citizen's Movement for Free Elections, lamented that the election day brought a "considerable amount of confusion" because of the incorrect voters list. Ironically, there were also names of people who had died since the last election but were still in the COMELEC-revalidated and certified valid list.[19] This raised speculations that some unscrupulous parties could have voted using the names of the dead.[20] Aggravating the situation were reports stating that "indelible" inks used during the elections were not really indelible. This caused concerns of what Filipinos called "flying voters" — voters that "fly" from one precinct to another to cast multiple votes to distort election outcomes in favor of certain candidates.

Many of the 300,000 election precincts nationwide did not start the voting on time because of the failure of election officials to deliver the required ballots and other election paraphernalia. Other precincts also postponed the election because of election failure. There were also reports of power interruptions in some areas causing further delays in the voting and even in the counting processes. Past elections saw the snatching and switching of ballot boxes after suspicious electric power outages. These prompted COMELEC Chairman Benjamin Abalos to lament during the election day that "not everything materialized as we have envisioned." This revealed that the COMELEC was utterly ill prepared to perform its functions during the May 2004 elections.

If voting was slow, the counting and the canvassing phases were the slowest. The commission was snail-paced in the canvassing of ballots. COMELEC officials took almost a month before they could proclaim the 12 senators, more than two weeks to proclaim party-list and district representatives, and at least a week to proclaim local officials. Some proclamations were even protested because of alleged cheating and irregularity. Most protest cases are pending in the electoral tribunal.

In the presidential race, the Joint Congressional Committee tasked to canvass the votes proclaimed Arroyo as the winner. The final tally had Arroyo with 12,905,808 votes and Poe with 11,782,232 — a difference of 1,123,576 votes. Three other candidates were well behind. Opposition leaders, however, are still complaining of massive and systematic cheating like vote paddling, vote shaving, and ballot snatching. The opposition claimed that Arroyo's camp manipulated the May 2004 elections to win another term in office.

Computerization or automation of elections could have prevented the issue of massive fraud and widespread cheating. It could also have made the voting easier and the counting faster. The automation project, mandated by Republic Act 8436 enacted in 1997, aimed to install at least one counting machine in every municipality and city to facilitate the counting of results within 24 to 48 hours. But the Philippine Supreme Court nullified the automation project because of irregularities in the bidding procedure and anomalies in the contract. The country spent P1.3 billion for the mothballed automation project. The nullification of the automation project painted a bad image of the COMELEC prior to the election day.

## The Rise of Celebrity Politics

The May 10, 2004, election was the fourth presidential election since the so-called restoration of Philippine democracy in 1986. The next presidential election will be held in 2010. Five candidates vied for the presidency in 2004: the reelectionist Arroyo; the action star Poe; former Chief of the Philippine National Police, now

Senator Panfilo M. Lacson; former Senator and former Education Secretary, Raul S. Roco, and born-again televangelist Eduardo C. Villanueva. Among these candidates, only Arroyo and Poe were the two leading presidential aspirants.

Arroyo, daughter of former President Diosdado Macapagal, ran under the banner of K4 — a loose coalition of pro-administration parties. K4 stands for *Koalisyon ng Katapatan at Karanasan para sa Kinabukasan* (Coalition of Honesty and Experience for the Future), the acronym of which was patterned after the famous Taiwan male pop singing group F4. This choice of acronym was reflective of celebrity politics in the Philippines to attract the greatest number of voters. In fact, two of the 12 senatorial candidates of K4 were active celebrities — action stars Lito Lapid and Ramon Revilla, who were officially proclaimed as senators by the COMELEC. Opposition senatorial candidate Jinggoy Estrada, another action star and a son of the former president, also won the race. This brought a total of three action stars in the Philippine Senate, the upper legislative chamber and the breeding ground for future presidents.

The rise of celebrity politics affirms that Philippine elections are nothing more than popularity contests. Philippine elections are not contests of principled ideas but contests of personalities. Even during the selection of candidates, administration and opposition parties sacrificed the rigor of leadership tests in favor of tapping celebrities who can rake in votes. Though President Arroyo claimed that she campaigned on the basis of programs rather than personalities, she also took advantage of celebrity politics. Arroyo supporters sponsored the "Gloria Macapagal Arroyo look-alike talent show" at the height of election campaigns. Arroyo even attended the concert of Philippine superstar Nora Aunor during the election period to shore up her popularity. Fans claimed that Aunor and Arroyo were look-alikes. Aunor also supported Arroyo at the height of the EDSA 2 uprising in 2001, which led to the ousting of former President Joseph Estrada, a multi-award-winning action superstar of Philippine movies.

Arroyo's bid for reelection was marred by various controversies. She announced in late 2002 that she would not seek another term. But she changed her mind when the presidential campaign began in October 2003. Critics regarded her change of mind as an indication of her ability to break her promises. But among the presidential candidates, Arroyo had the strongest competitive advantage because of her access to government resources and machinery. She was even accused of using public funds during the campaign period. Her strength can also be attributed to her administration's achievement in reinvigorating the once ailing Philippine security alliance. The Arroyo government supported the American-led global war on terrorism, which led to the destruction of the Taliban regime in Afghanistan. The Arroyo government also joined the "coalition of the willing" in the American-led war against Saddam Hussein's regime in Iraq. It was during the Arroyo administration when the United States designated the Philippines as a major non-North American Treaty Organization (NATO) ally.

The Arroyo administration's close relations with the Bush Administration enhanced her political profile and made her the likely choice of the United States in the Philippine presidential race. As one writer opines, "The Philippines is the real decision maker in the present Philippine electoral process; no one has been able to ascend to Malacanang, and stay there, without its blessings."[21] In fact, a COMELEC official prematurely announced, amid the Congress debate over canvassing issues, that President Arroyo won in the May 10th presidential election. Based on the leaks filtered out, Arroyo won her seat by winning 12,554,127 votes, or 39.5%, and Poe garnered 11,493,345 votes, or 36.6%. This figure almost perfectly predicted the official canvassing result done by the Philippine Congress. Although COMELEC Chairman Abalos denied leaking the said information, he disclosed that he had voted for Arroyo during the election and admitted making his own tally of the votes for president and vice president. This raised concerns from the opposition that the Office of the President was "conditioning the mind" of the people to cover the alleged plan to rig the election outcome.[22]

But Arroyo's spokesperson Ignacio Bunye said that the leaking of results was intentional to balance the rumors of the opposition that Poe won the election. Although Bunye said that the information was not the official election result, because the Congress had yet to proclaim the winner, he argued that "if we didn't reveal the true condition, the public might think that what the United Opposition coalition said was true" — that Poe had won the election.

Poe's popularity was undeniably high. His supporters continue to believe that Poe won the election. A very close friend of former President Estrada, Poe had a huge fan base that could bring him to the Malacanang Palace — the seat of presidential power. Because personality matters in Philippine elections, his complete inexperience in politics posed no obstacle. Since Philippine elections are excellent examples of popularity contests, Poe's "box-office appeal" was the main source of his strength in the ballot box. Poe had never entered politics before, except during election campaigns of Estrada. He has never been a member of any political party.

Lacking a political party of his own, the opposition created a political party for him, the *Koalisyon ng Nagkakaisang Pilipino* (KNP, Coalition of United Filipino) for purposes of the presidential election. The brainchild of KNP was former Senate President Edgardo Angara, leader of *Laban ng Demokratikong Pilipino* (LDP, Fight of Democratic Filipino), which was the largest opposition party during the Arroyo Administration. Angara earlier ran for president but lost. Angara's LDP was split during the May 2004 elections because of the contested issue of standard bearer. Senator Lacson, an LDP member, expected to be endorsed by the party as the opposition bet in the presidential race. But Angara handpicked Poe, a non-LDP member, for president. This created disarray in the opposition, leading Angara to establish KNP to rally behind Poe. Lacson, on the other hand, pursued his presidential ambition under the banner of the divided and fragile LDP.

KNP, as an electoral coalition, can die anytime after election because of the lack of party principle. Moreover, the life span of electoral coalition also depends on election period. Like other political parties in the Philippines that participated in the national elections, KNP was a mere electoral coalition of the opposition elite. It did not have clear ideology. Though his main campaign rhetoric was "the unity of the Filipino people," KNP had no coherent program of government to make this happen. Poe was the KNP's standard bearer because of one major criterion — he was a very popular action star who could attract the votes of the masses. Because of his popularity, his political rivals questioned his citizenship to disqualify him from the race. But the Court affirmed Poe as a "natural-born Filipino." To Poe's utter dismay, the Philippine Congress announced that he lost the presidential race.

## The Party List Alternative

If mainstream Philippine political parties are personality-based, there are minor parties that are based on coherent political agenda. These minor parties participate in the party list election, an electoral system of proportional representation in which electorates vote among parties rather than among candidates. Votes are given to parties in proportion to the number of votes they get.

The Philippine party list system is mandated by Republic Act 7941 enacted into law in 1995 as a response to the urgent call of some progressive sectors to establish "new politics" in the Philippines. The party list system reflects the move of progressive sectors "towards program-based politics focused on competent parties with comprehensive programs rather than on personalities."[23] This system gives hopes to the Philippine political system suffering rapid political decay.

The Philippines first tried the party list system in the 1998 elections "to enable Filipino citizens belonging to marginalized and underrepresented sectors, organizations and parties" to become members of the House of Representatives, the lower chamber in Philippine legislature.[24] In the Philippines, electorates have to cast two votes for their congressional representatives: one for a district representative and another one for a party list representative. In the House of Representatives, 26% of the 260 seats are reserved for party list. Every 2% of total party list votes cast gets a seat in the House, with a maximum of three seats.

In the May 2004 elections, the COMELEC proclaimed 23 party list representatives. Three seats went to *Bayan Muna* (Nation First), Association of Philippine Electric Cooperatives, and *Akbayan* (Citizens Action Party). Two seats went to *Buhay Hayaan Yumabong* (Let Life to Prosper), and *Anakpawis* (Sweat's Child). The Citizen's Battle Against Corruption (Cibac), *Gabriela* (A Women's Party), *Partido ng Manggagawa* (Labor Party), *Butil* (Seed) Farmers Party, Alliance of Volunteer Educators, Veterans Freedom Party, Coop-Nattco, *An Waray* (The Waray), *Anak Mindanao* (Son of Mindanao) and *Alagad* (Follower) won one seat each.

National Security Adviser Roberto Gonzales branded some of these parties as fronts of the Communist Party of the Philippines (CPP) and the NPA. Gonzales declared the CPP/NPA as the single biggest threat to Philippine national security.

Through the National Internal Security Plan (NISP), the AFP and the Philippine National Police (PNP) have intensified their tactical operations against the NPA. Gonzales claimed that the CPP/NPA fielded political candidates in the election using the cover of party lists in order to use government money to fund the growth of the communist movement.[25] But the concerned party lists (like *Bayan Muna*, *Akbayan*, and *Anak Pawis*) assailed the allegation. *Bayan Muna* representative Satur Ocampo, who became a spokesperson of the CPP, denied the charges, arguing that "I decided not to go back to the underground. And I opted to explore all the possibilities in the legal, democratic movement that is recognized and being encouraged." But a study showed that the local communist movement deliberately participates in the national, local and party list elections as part of its political programs under a united front work.[26]

Nonetheless, the holding of party list elections revealed the optimism of legal left-leaning organizations to wage structural reforms in the Philippines through the parliamentary means. The growing number of party-list representatives after the May 2004 elections was a landmark in Philippine electoral history. Party lists are challenging the landscape of the elite-dominated House of Representatives. Analysts contend that the strengthening and expansion of the Philippine party list system can break the old elitist parties of prominent personalities. According to Joel Rocamora of the Philippine Institute for Popular Democracy, the Philippine party list system can "lessen the intensity of personal and clan contests that are the main source of violence and money politics" in the country.[27]

## The Role of the Church

There are forces in Philippine politics that are already exasperated with the electoral system. The conservative Catholic Church has already expressed utter dismay. Losing patience in the snail-pace canvassing of votes for president and vice president, Manila Archbishop Gaudencio Rosales underscored that he no longer believes in Philippine electoral politics "particularly on the way Filipino politicians practiced it."[28] The Archbishop also said that the greatest destructive element that ever visited the country in the last 58 years is Philippine politics.[29]

This kind of statement was a clear indication of growing remorse of people regarding the current state of Philippine politics, particularly if the remorse came from the own mouth of the Church. The Philippine Catholic Church played a pivotal role in the People Power of 1986 and 2001. The Church's ability to mobilize a huge number of people for legal mass actions can make and can change the course of Philippine history. The Church is also one of the most powerful power brokers in the Philippines that has the ability to make and break kings.

Archbishop Rosales already began making a history when the Church organized a movement, the *Pondong Pinoy* (Filipino Fund), to take the people "beyond the politics of money, power, class, greed and family ambitions that has held the country captive for many generations."[30] The *Pondong Pinoy* movement also aimed to bank on a massive catechetical program in preparation for the concrete act by individuals and families of setting aside 25 centavos of their money that can be offered during mass or even in schools and other institutions.[31]

## Rumors of Military Intervention

Some disgruntled elements of the Philippine armed forces have also expressed concerns about the quality of Philippine electoral politics. A week before the election day, the drumbeat of coup rumors and black propaganda became so loud that it prompted President Arroyo to issue a statement urging all members of the military to stay out of politics. Like the Catholic Church, the Philippine military played a pivotal role in the 1986 and 2001 People Power. In a democratic system, the military is expected to be an "apolitical" sector of the society. Mainstream theories of civil-military relations uphold the principle of civilian supremacy over the military.

This principle, however, is problematic in the Philippines. While the Philippine military respects the civilian authority, some officers find it hard to accept that civilians are supreme. Compared with many civilian bureaucracies, the military finds the armed forces more disciplined, more organized, and more systematic. The concept of "civilian supremacy" gives some officers the notion that the military is "inferior" compared with civilians. Because of the perceived weakness of the civilian bureaucracy, some officers began questioning the bureaucracy they were being asked to protect. This situation encourages the Philippine military to intervene in politics. Randy David, a sociology professor and a famous columnist, explains why the Filipino soldiers have become politicized:

> It was Marcos who first brought the military into the sphere of our nation's political life. During martial law, regional commanders exercised greater political power than governors. Marcos cultivated the personal loyalty of generals, making sure that no one in the military would dare plot against his regime. He gathered information on his generals, and showered those who blindly obeyed his orders with enormous benefits. Civilian authority, in the person of Marcos, no doubt remained supreme during those years, but it destroyed the military's professional ethos.[32]

During the May 2004 election period, the Philippine intelligence uncovered a twin-plot of military and civilian personalities against the Arroyo Administration. The first plot, dubbed as *Oplan Aklas Bayan* (Operation Resistance of the Nation), was allegedly a rightist-leftist plot to wage massive protests against election fraud and to destabilize the Arroyo government. Rebel soldiers whose aim was to capture the seat of power in order to install a military junta allegedly organized the second plot, *Oplan Andres* (Operation Andres, named after a plebian revolutionary leader). The rebel soldiers involved in the July 2003 Oakwood Mutiny in Makati City allegedly developed the *Oplan Andres*, which according to the armed forces was still an active and live plot. This plot planned to establish a Philippine military junta to be led allegedly by Senator Gringo Honasan, a retired military colonel involved in a series of coup attempts during the administration of former President Corazon Aquino in the mid-1980s. The plot presumed that Poe would win the election but would soon be toppled by a junta.[33] Honasan, however, denied the said plot. He even declared earlier that he would support President Arroyo's platform to promote "vigorous implementation of programs for peace, unification, reconciliation and development."[34]

The spread of coup rumors before and after the May 2004 elections demonstrated the fragile state of Philippine democracy. Though members of the armed forces are prevented from joining political parties to promote their political convictions, they still possess the coercive apparatus of the State that can be used to grab political power. Because of the infirmities of the existing electoral system and the weaknesses of the present party system in the country, soldiers are forced to think outside the ballot box and explore other extraconstitutional means of leadership succession. The 1987 Philippine Constitution states that the AFP is the protector of the people and the state. This constitutionally mandated function drives some elements of the AFP to intervene.

## Conclusion

The May 2004 elections have been dogged by bitter allegations of mass fraud, cheating, violence, coup rumors, destabilization plots and other irregularities.[35] Because of alleged fraud and manipulation, Poe filed a protest case before the Supreme Court election tribunal. Anticipating mass protests by Poe's followers, Philippine security forces were on red alert to quell possible unrest and mob rule. In fact, forces of the Philippine National Police used water cannons to disperse some 1,500 Poe supporters who tried to march on the presidential palace on June 18, 2004, to protest the alleged election fraud. A powerful bomb was also found near a Department of Interior and Local Government building, while another explosive device was found at the canteen of the Department of National Defense in Camp Aguinaldo military headquarters on June 20, 2004. Arroyo analysts said that these bomb threats were part of the destabilization plots of the opposition. Considering that the bomb threats occurred in two major government offices in charge of public safety and national defense, these revealed the vulnerability of the Arroyo government.

The May 2004 elections also took place amid socioeconomic tensions and internal security threats. But the May 2004 elections did not seriously tackle vital issues confronting the country because candidates focused on personalities rather than issues of governance. This is very disturbing because elections should be a venue to debate on contending programs of government. This has also indicated that the Philippines continues to be a very fragile democracy in Asia. If this kind of situation persists, the Philippines will continue to face the vicious cycle of poverty, mismanagement, and political decay.

# Endnotes

1. For a study of elections in Southeast Asia, see Dieter Nohlen, Florian Grotz, and Christof Hartmann (eds.), *Elections in Asia and the Pacific: A Data Handbook*, Vol. II "Southeast Asia, East Asia and the South Pacific" (Oxford: Oxford University Press, 2001). For a chapter on the Philippines, see Christof Hartmann, Grahan Hassal, and Soliman Santos, Jr., "The Philippines," pp. 185–238.

2. For excellent materials, see Luzviminda Tangcangco, *The Anatomy of Electoral Fraud* (Manila: MJAGM, 1992), and Ma. Aurora Catillo et al., *Manipulated Elections* (Quezon City: University of the Philippines, 1985).

3. Neal H. Cruz, "And they call the polls 'peaceful'?" *Philippine Daily Inquirer* (May 14, 2004). For a detailed history of Philippine elections, see Clarita R. Carlos and Rommel C. Banlaoi, *Elections in the Philippines: From Pre-Colonial Period to the Present* (Makati City: Konrad Adenauer Foundation, 1996).

4. "Foreign observers find Philippine election too violent, messy and absurd," *BBC Monitoring Asia–Pacific* (May 13, 2004). This article can also be accessed at: http://proquest.umi.com/pqdweb?index=6&did=000000636299641&SrchMode=1&sid=1&Fmt=3&VInst=PROD&VType=PQD&RQT=309&VName=PQD&TS=1086843940&clientId=8975.

5. Blancha S. Rivera, "Poll violence shocks international observers," *Philippine Daily Inquirer* (May 13, 2004).

6. Isagani Cruz, "Shallow elections," *Philippine Daily Inquirer* (May 15, 2004).

7. The title of this article is inspired by another article. See Todd A. Eisenstadt, "Thinking Outside the (Ballot) Box: Informal Electoral Institutions and Mexico's Political Opening," *Latin American Politics and Society* (Spring 2003), pp. 25–55.

8. For classic materials on Philippine political parties and elections, see Dapen Liang, *Philippine Parties and Politics: A Historical Study of National Experience in Democracy* (San Francisco: The Gladstone Company, 1970), and Carl Lande, *Leaders, Factions and Parties: The Structure of Philippine Politics* (New Haven, CT: Yale University Southeast Asian Studies, 1964).

9. For an excellent analysis of Philippine poverty, see Arsenio M. Balisacan, "Poverty in the Philippines: An Update and Reexamination," *Philippine Review of Economics*, Vol. 38, No. 1 (June 2001), pp. 15–52.

10. "Senator Legarda Decries Philippine Sovereign Debt Burden" at: http://deanjorge bocobo.blogspot.com/2003_05_06_DJB.html (2003).

11. Catharin E. Dalpino, *Challenges for a Post-Election Philippines: Issues for U.S. Policy* (New York: Council on Foreign Relations Center for Preventive Action, May 11, 2004), p. 5.

12. For an excellent material, see Djanicelle J. Berreveld, *Terrorism in the Philippines: The Bloody Trail of Abu Sayyaf, Bin Laden's East Asian Connection* (San Jose: Writers Club Press, 2001). Also see Rommel C. Banlaoi, *Al-Harakatul Islamiyah: Essays on the Abu Sayyaf Group* (Quezon City: Philippine Institute for Political Violence and Terrorism Research, 2007).

13. See Zachary Abuza, "Tentacles of Terror: Al-Qaeda's Southeast Asian Network," *Contemporary Southeast Asia*, Vol. 24, No. 3 (December 2002), pp. 427–465. Also see Rommel C. Banlaoi, *The War on Terrorism in Southeast Asia* (Quezon City: Strategic and Integrative Studies Center, 2003) also at: http://www.apan-info.net/terrorism/banlaoiBook/index.htm.

14. Joel Rocamora, "Formal Democracy and Its Alternatives in the Philippines: Parties, Elections and Social Movements" (Paper presented at the conference Democracy and Civil Society in Asia: The Emerging Opportunities and Challenges, Queens University, Kingston, Ontario, Canada, August 19–21, 2000).

15. Rocamora, p. 10. Also see Randolph David, "Re-Democratization in the Wake of the 1986 People Power Revolution: Errors and Dilemmas" (undated manuscript).

16. "GMA Poll Expenses: Whopping P333-M, Still Way Below Limit" *Philippine Star* (June 11, 2004) at: http://www.newsflash.org/2004/02/hl/hl100482.htm.

17. See Commission on Elections at: http://www.comelec.gov.ph/.

18. Carina Roncesvalles, "Absentee Voting for 2004 to Suffer from Birth Pains" *Business World* (October 23, 2003).

19. "Irregularities in Philippine elections" at: http://ip-o.org/Philippine_elections_monitoring.htm (May 10, 2004).

20. Ibid.

21. Alexander Martin Remollino, "Philippine Elections: Under the Watch of Uncle Sam," *People's Media Center Reports*, Vol. 3, No. 2 (May 2, 2004). Posted by Bulatlat.com at: http://qc.indymedia.org/news/2004/05/478.php.

22. Nikko Dizon, "Comelec Leak Outrageous," *The Philippine Star* (May 26, 2004).

23. For an excellent brief and succinct overview of the system, see "The Party List System in the Philippines" at: http://www.cpcabrisbane.org/Kasama/2003/V17n3/PartyList.htm.

24. For detailed discussions, see Soliman M. Santos, Jr., "The Philippines Tries the Party-List System (A Progressive Approach), *Kasarinlan: A Philippine Quarterly of Third World Studies*, Vol. 13, No. 2 (4th Quarter, 1997), pp. 5–18.

25. Maria Ressa, "Communist Rebels 'Biggest Threat'" *CNN International Edition* (May 5, 2004) at: http://www.cnn.com/2004/WORLD/asiapcf/05/05/philippines.poll.violence/.

26. Rodolfo B. Mendoza, Jr., *CPP/NPA/NDF Electoral Struggle* (Quezon City: Philippine National Police, 2004), pp. 1–15.

27. Quoted by Annie Ruth C. Sabangan, "Elite Democracy Puts RP in Crisis," *The Manila Times* (February 3, 2004), p. 1.

28. Leslie Ann G. Aquino, "Rosales Airs Dismay over Local Politics," *Manila Bulletin* (June 11, 2004).

29. Ibid.

30. Ibid.

31. Ibid.

32. Randy David, "Why Have Our Soldiers Become Politicized?" *Philippine Daily Inquirer* (August 2, 2003).

33. Alcuin Papa and Christian Esguerra, "AFP says rightist, leftist plot has twin," *Philippine Daily Inquirer* (May 27, 2004).
34. Carlito Pablo, Cynthia Balana, and Christine Avendano, "Honasan Backs GMA Platform, but Senator Insists He's Still for FPJ," *Philippine Daily Inquirer* (May 4, 2004).
35. Nikko Dizon, "Comelec Leak Outrageous," *The Philippine Star* (May 26, 2004).

# BILATERAL
# SECURITY ISSUES

*Chapter 8*

# The Role of Philippine–American Relations in the Global Campaign against Terrorism: Implications for Regional Security*

## Introduction

When the United States called for global support to combat terrorism in the light of the 9/11 attacks, the Philippines immediately responded by quickly granting the United States flight rights for its military aircraft.[1] The Philippines also offered Clark Air Field and Subic Bay Naval Base for use by the International Coalition against Terrorism as transit points or staging areas for troops fighting terrorism in Afghanistan. Philippine President Gloria Macapagal Arroyo even expressed a willingness to deploy Philippine troops to Afghanistan, contingent upon approval by the Philippine Congress.

American officials have praised the Philippine government's support in the global campaign against terrorism and have described the Philippine initiative as

* This chapter is taken from *Contemporary Southeast Asia*, Vol. 24, No. 2 (August 2002), pp. 294–312. Reproduced here with the kind permission of the publisher, Institute of Southeast Asian Studies, Singapore (http://bookshop.iseas.edu.sg).

"outstanding." The Americans even commended President Arroyo for being "very quick to speak up, very quick to take action" to help the United States fight international terrorists.[2] In his twenty-minute speech during the six-month anniversary of 9/11, President George W. Bush singled out President Arroyo for "courageously opposing the threat of terror."[3] President Arroyo was the only head of state mentioned by President Bush in this speech. To recognize Philippine support in combating terrorism, the Bush Administration promised President Arroyo that the United States would give the Philippines US $92.3 million in military equipment to bolster not only its ability to counter terrorism but also to increase its wherewithal to fight local insurgents.[4]

This exchange of mutual support is a landmark in Philippine–American relations as it revives the once-ailing security alliance between the two countries. When the Americans closed their bases in the Philippines as a result of the termination of the Military Bases Agreement (MBA) in 1991, Philippine–American relations hit their lowest point, with the security relationship being practically moribund.

President Arroyo's full support for the U.S.-led war on terrorism and strong commitment to the United States in combating the terrorist network in Southeast Asia reinvigorated Philippine–American ties. This prompted one American security analyst to describe the Philippines as an American "front-line state in the war on terrorism."[5] What are the implications of reinvigorated Philippine–American relations for regional security? This chapter will examine the role of Philippine–American relations in the global campaign against terrorism and its implications for the security of Southeast Asia.

## A Historical Background to Relations

Philippine relations with the United States have played an important role in the security of not only Southeast Asia but also the entire Asia–Pacific region. Those relations began as early as 1898 when Filipino and American troops collaborated against Spain, which had been the colonial master of the Philippines for 333 years. Then President Emilio Aguinaldo responded to the request of Commodore George Dewey to provide Filipino assistance against a "common enemy." Dewey provided arms and supplies to Filipino forces while Aguinaldo sent manpower to fight Spanish forces.[6]

In the aftermath of the Spanish-American War, a vanquished Spain ceded the Philippines to the Americans in the Treaty of Paris. That treaty became the basis of American rule in the Philippines. With the Treaty of Paris, the United States established colonial control of the Philippines based on the American perception that the Philippines was an important strategic outpost in the Asia–Pacific.[7] Even then, U.S. President William McKinley viewed the Philippines as a strategic country with strong potential in servicing the commercial and naval needs of the United States.[8] American businessmen also saw the Philippines as a strategic gateway to the rich markets of Asia, and a hub for American trading activity in the Asia–Pacific region.

## The Philippines as a Strategic American Colony: 1898–1935

From 1898 to 1935, the Philippines became an important strategic colony of the United States. The Philippines served as a vital instrument of American policy toward Asia and the Pacific. At that time, the United States was looking for new opportunities and lands, driven by its need for raw materials to feed its industries and to serve as markets for its goods. The Payne-Aldrich Tariff Act of 1909 was the American legal instrument to promote *free trade* in the Philippines, until 1934 when the Tydings-McDuffie Act reimposed the quota system.[9]

During the American colonial period, there were moves among the Filipino elite to legally seek Philippine independence in the U.S. Congress.[10] Some of the Filipino elite went to the United States on independence missions until the U.S. Congress passed the Hare-Hawes-Cutting Act on January 17, 1933.[11] The law provided for a 10-year commonwealth government in the Philippines. It also allowed the establishment of U.S. naval, air, and other military reservations in the country.

However, Manuel L. Quezon opposed the law and sought in the United States the passing of the Tydings-McDuffie Law, which was essentially no different from the Hare-Hawes-Cutting Law. As a result of the Tydings-McDuffie Law, the Philippines, with the blessings of the United States, established the Commonwealth Government of the Philippines on November 15, 1935, with Quezon as President. The Commonwealth provided the Philippines a 10-year transition period before the assumption of full independence in 1945.

## America in the Philippine Defense System

With the commonwealth government, the Philippines passed Commonwealth Act No. 1, otherwise known as the National Defense Act of the Philippines. This Act mandated the setting up of a Philippine defense system supported by a citizens' army consisting of a regular force of around 10,000 personnel and a reserve force of about 400,000 personnel. It also intended to establish a Philippine Navy and an Army Air Corps. The Americans played an influential role in this defense system when Quezon conferred on General Douglas MacArthur, the retired Chief of Staff of the U.S. Army, the title of Field Marshall of the Philippine Army.

With the establishment of U.S. military reservations in the Philippines, and with the active involvement of MacArthur in the Philippine defense system, the Philippines became a prime target for Japanese aerial bombardments right from the start of World War II.[12] Quezon attempted to secure from the United States full Philippine independence and to declare the Philippines a neutral state to prevent Japanese attacks, but to no avail.

## The Japanese Colonial Rule

The Japanese established a puppet government in the Philippines on January 3, 1942, when the Japanese commander in chief officially declared the end of U.S. colonial rule in the Philippines.[13] Quezon evacuated to the United States where he established a commonwealth government in exile.

Filipino radicals opposed the Japanese colonial rule of the Philippines. Filipino resistance groups like the *Hukbalahap* (*Hukbo ng Bayan Laban SA Hapon*, Filipino Resistance Army against Japan) and the *Partido Komunista ng Pilipinas* (Philippine Communist Party) spearheaded a national liberation movement against the Japanese Imperial Forces.[14] Through the combined forces of the *Hukbalahap* and the U.S. Armed Forces in the Far East headed by General MacArthur, the Japanese Imperial Forces were finally subdued, resulting in the liberation of the Philippines. The United States claimed to have granted Philippine independence on July 4, 1945, a date coinciding with the anniversary of American independence.

## The Philippine Independence

The Philippines has the worldwide distinction of being the first country to gain independence and form a U.S.-style democratic government in Southeast Asia. This American-style democracy was the strong glue that was said to have bound Philippine–American relations after World War II. Since then, the main bulk of Philippine diplomatic history was the history of Philippine–American relations.

Philippine bilateral relations with the United States overwhelmingly guided Manila's foreign relations after World War II.[15] Philippine diplomatic history was "one of American action and of Philippine reaction."[16] Even then President Manuel Roxas, during his inauguration speech as President of the Third Philippine Republic, asserted that his conviction was to "subscribe irretrievably" to the U.S. foreign policy and to commit "to the cause and international program of the United States of America."[17]

## The "Unequal" Treaties

On July 4, 1946, the Philippine government signed two important agreements with the United States that legally defined the parameters of Philippine–American relations: the 1946 Philippine–American Treaty on General Relations and the 1946 Philippine–American Trade Act. Eight months later, the Philippine government signed the Philippine–American MBA on March 14, 1947, which the Philippine Senate ratified on March 26, 1947. The Philippine–American Assistance Pact, on the other hand, was signed on March 21, 1947.

These agreements served American economic and security interests in the Asia-Pacific region. For example, the MBA supported the U.S. Seventh Fleet, which used Subic Naval Base in Olongapo. The Thirteenth U.S. Air Force was posted at Clark Air Field in Pampanga. These U.S. bases became instrumental to American strategy during the Korean and Vietnam Wars. When the United States withdrew from Vietnam, American bases in the Philippines served as the only U.S. overseas bases, which underpinned America's forward defense strategy in Asia and the Pacific. Filipinos resisted these agreements because they were negotiated at the time when the Philippines lay prostrate from the heavy devastation of World War II.[18]

## The Idea of Collective Defense

To provide "collective defense" to both countries, the Philippines and the United States signed the Mutual Defense Treaty (MDT) on August 30, 1951. It was signed at the time when the Philippines was saddled with postwar reconstruction concerns. The Treaty recognizes that "an armed attack in the Pacific Area on either of the Parties would be dangerous to its own peace and safety and declares that it would act to meet the common dangers in accordance with its constitutional processes."[19] Nationalist Senator Claro M. Recto opposed the MDT, arguing that it did not contain any provision for automatic retaliation from the United States. Moreover, Recto underscored the fact that the Treaty was vague and did not amount to any commitment at all. He urged for an automatic retaliatory formula similar to that of the North Atlantic Treaty Organization (NATO).[20]

## The Bases Pull Out and the Fading of Philippine–American Relations

From 1946 to 1992, the issue that predominantly shaped Philippine–American relations was the U.S. military bases.[21] When the Philippine Senate rejected the proposed Philippine–American Treaty of Friendship, Cooperation and Security in 1991, the Americans withdrew their forces from the Philippines.[22] The proposed Treaty could have extended the stay of U.S. forces in the country. In 1992, the United States withdrew its last remaining troops from the Philippines. As a result of the U.S. withdrawal, the "once-strong" and "once-special" Philippine–American relationship has been essentially moribund.[23] Since the U.S. bases had long been regarded as the "linchpin of a partnership built around a network of bilateral and multilateral arrangements between the Philippines and the U.S.," the security relationship between the two countries was said to have been left on uncertain ground.[24]

The only legal framework guiding Philippine–American security relations in the postbases period is the 1951 MDT. After the U.S. withdrawal, both countries have repeatedly reaffirmed the MDT to be the anchor of their security relationship. However, they were unable to fashion a new and mutually acceptable defense relationship until 1999, when the Philippine Senate ratified the Philippine–American Visiting Forces Agreement (VFA).[25]

## The Visiting Forces Agreement (VFA) Ratification

The two countries signed the VFA in the midst of various security uncertainties in the Asia–Pacific. The Philippines signed the VFA primarily to deter the perceived Chinese aggression in the South China Sea. The weak conditions of the Armed Forces of the Philippines (AFP) and the lack of Philippine wherewithal to respond to transnational security concerns in the region also convinced Manila to ratify the VFA. The ratification of the VFA is believed to have renewed but not necessarily revived Philippine–American security relations. The VFA provides the legal framework for the two countries to resume the joint military exercises. It also lays down rules governing the conduct of American troops while on Philippine soil. The VFA is said to have provided substance to the MDT, reminding both countries of their "special relations."

# The War on Terrorism and the Reinvigoration of Philippine–American Relations

Since the VFA ratification, the Philippines and the United States have been conducting joint military exercises under the series called "Balikatan." The present war on terrorism reinforces the conduct of Balikatan, with an added dimension of antiterrorism. The Balikatan 2002-1 exercises reinvigorated the once dormant Philippine–American alliance,[26] and relations have recently been described as at their peak because of the exercises. There are at least three justifications for the reinvigoration of Philippine–American relations:

1. The Philippines has active militant Muslim groups, particularly the Abu Sayyaf Group (ASG) and the *Moro* Islamic Liberation Front (MILF), believed to have a link with the al Qaeda Group of Osama bin Laden.
2. The Philippines has an MDT with the United States, making the Philippines a reliable American ally in its antiterrorist campaign.
3. The Philippines has a VFA with the United States, which justifies the presence of American troops on Philippine soil.

## The Moro Islamic Liberation Front — The Al Qaeda Link

With the existence of the MILF and the ASG, the Philippines reportedly became one of al Qaeda's operational hubs. The MILF link with al Qaeda can be traced to the Soviet invasion of Afghanistan. When bin Laden established al Qaeda in 1988 to wage an international *jihad* (holy war) in Afghanistan, he reportedly directed Mohammad Jamal Khalifa, his brother-in-law, to go to the Philippines and recruit Filipino Muslim fighters for the Afghan War. The MILF, through the leadership of Hashim Salamat, was reported to have sent 1,000 Filipino Muslim fighters to Afghanistan to undergo military training. Salamat saw the training of these Muslim fighters as vital to the strengthening of the MILF as the splinter group of the *Moro* National Liberation Front (MNLF) headed by Nur Misuari, who later became the governor of the Autonomous Region of Muslim Mindanao and is presently incarcerated for an alleged of rebellion. Khalifa left the Philippines in 1990 but returned to the country in 1991 to "establish a permanent Al Qaeda network."[27]

Khalifa's front organization in the Philippines was believed to be the Islamic International Relief Organization (IIRO). It was a charitable organization registered on September 20, 1991, in the Philippines at the Securities Exchange Commission (SEC). In the SEC document, Khalifa was listed as the president and chairman of the board of trustees of the IIRO.[28] One of the incorporators of IIRO was Jameela Yabo, a Filipina wife of Khalifa and sister of Abu Omar, who was then studying at the Mindanao State University. Khalifa used Yabo and Omar as conduits to penetrate Muslim Filipino communities through various charitable activities in the Philippines. While doing "charitable" activities in the Philippines, Khalifa reportedly used the Philippines as al Qaeda's base for other international terrorist operations.[29]

Through the IIRO and other Muslim relief groups, Khalifa reportedly channeled money to provide financial support to the MILF. Al Haj Murad, the MILF Vice Chairman for Military Affairs, even admitted in an interview held sometime in 1998 that bin Laden and Khalifa helped and assisted the MILF cadres in Afghanistan.[30]

## The Abu Sayyaf Group — The Al Qaeda Link

Apart from the MILF, the ASG is believed to have an established link with al Qaeda. The ASG founder, Ustadz Abdurajak Janjalani, was reported to have befriended bin Laden while in Peshawar, Pakistan. Janjalani also became a very close friend of Ramzi Yousef, who was described to have planned in the Philippines the *Bojinka* plots, believed to be the worst terrorist plots in the country. The *Bojinka* plots aimed to bomb 11 U.S. jetliners and assassinate Pope John Paul II, who visited Manila in 1995.[31]

During his trip to the Philippines via Malaysia, Yousef reportedly stayed in Basilan and trained about 20 ASG fighters. The Philippine National Police revealed that by September 1994, Yousef had fully established a cell of terrorists in the Philippines. Among the members of this cell were the following:[32]

> *Wali Khan Amin Shah* — A "Pakistani–Afghan" national reported to be a very close associate of Yousef. Wali Khan had extensive travels to the Philippines, Malaysia, Hong Kong, and Thailand using seven passports with different

names but bearing the same picture. He was believed to have been the overall financial manager of the Yousef cell.

*Abdul Hakim Ali Hasmid Murad* — A Pakistani national reported to have arrived in the Philippines between November 1990 and February 1991. In December 1994, he came again to the Philippines to participate in the *Bojinka* plots aimed to assassinate the Pope. He was trained in bomb making and flying commercial aircraft. He was arrested in 1995 was convicted for the 1993 World Trade Center bombing in the United States.

*Abu Omar* — A Filipino national who became the brother-in-law of Khalifa. Omar reportedly used a charitable organization as a front organization to channel money and to fund the terrorist activities of the local Muslim militants.

*Munir Ibrahim* — Reported to be a wealthy Saudi Arabian from Jeddah who came to the Philippines to support terrorist activities in the country.

*Salem Ali/Sheik Mohammad* — Claimed to be a plywood exporter who befriended Rose Mosquera, a bargirl in Quezon City, who opened a bank account for him at the Far East Bank at the SM Megamall. Salem Ali was said to have also supported terrorist activities in the Philippines.

*Mohammed Sadiq Odeh* — Reported to have participated in various terrorist operations in the Philippines in the early 1990s and was convicted for his participation in the 1988 U.S. embassy bombings in Kenya.

## The Mutual Defense Treaty and the Philippine–American Response to Terrorism

The 9/11 terrorist attacks and the presence of homegrown terrorists in the Philippines with historic and financial links to al Qaeda prompted the Philippines to maximize its relations with the United States to combat terrorism. To demonstrate the Philippine commitment to the existing Philippine–American security alliance, as mandated by the MDT, the Philippine Government was the first in Asia to declare full support to the U.S.-led International Coalition against Terrorism. The Philippines offered Clark and Subic for use by the International Coalition as transit points or staging areas for troops fighting in Afghanistan, and expressed a willingness to deploy Philippine troops if requested by the international community, subject to the approval of the Philippine Congress. Through the MDT, the Philippines allied itself with the United States against terrorism.

To also express the Philippine Government's strong resolve in combating terrorism, Manila formed the Inter-Agency Task Force against International Terrorism on September 24, 2001. The purpose of this Task Force was to coordinate intelligence operations and facilitate the identification and neutralization of suspected terrorist cells in the Philippines. To freeze the financial assets of international terrorists, the Philippines passed the Anti-Money Laundering Act on September 29, 2001.

President Arroyo also announced a 14-pillar approach to combat terrorism (see Box 4.1 in Chapter 4 for the complete list).

With the 14-pillar approach to combat terrorism, the Philippines welcomed the presence of American troops to conduct joint military exercises. President Arroyo facilitated U.S. military involvement in the Philippines for the following purposes:

- To maintain and secure future cooperative engagement activities with the United States.
- To enhance domestic security through improved military capabilities.
- To gain American assistance in the war against the country's Muslim separatists.[33]

During the 50th anniversary (2001) of the signing of the MDT, the United States promised to assist the Philippines in acquiring new military equipment that will include a C-130 transport plane, eight Huey helicopters, a naval patrol boat and 30,000 M-16 rifles plus ammunition.[34] The United States has, in fact, been sending its military advisers to assist the Philippine military in antiterrorist training and strategy.

## The VFA, Republic of the Philippines (RP)–U.S. Balikatan 2002-1 Exercises and the War on Terrorism

The VFA provides the legal justification for conducting the Balikatan 2002-1 exercises. Balikatan (the word literally means *shoulder-to-shoulder*) is based primarily on the MDT, requiring the two countries to conduct joint military exercises to develop their capacity to resist aggression and combat common adversaries.

Filipino and American forces had been conducting these exercises even before the 9/11 attacks. Since 1981, Balikatan has been held almost annually, until 1996 when it was suspended because of questions regarding the legality of U.S. forces visiting the country for purposes of joint training. The signing of the VFA in 1999 saw the resumption of Balikatan. The Balikatan 2002-1 exercises focused on counterterrorism. They were launched in February 2002 and have four specific objectives:

1. To improve the interoperability of Philippine and U.S. forces against terrorism.
2. To enhance the combat capability of the Philippine Southern Command, or Southcom, infantry battalions based in Mindanao.
3. To ensure quality in intelligence processing.
4. To upgrade Philippine–U.S. capability to wage effective civil, military, and psychological operations.[35]

Balikatan 2002-1 exercises are also being guided by the following terms of reference:

- The exercises are to advise, assist, and train the Philippine military relative to Philippine efforts against the ASG, which will be conducted in Basilan and in Zamboanga. Related support activities are to be conducted in Cebu.
- They are to be carried out and completed within a period of six months with the participation of 660 U.S. personnel and 3,800 Philippine troops.
- Only 160 U.S. troops organized in 12-man Special Forces Teams shall be deployed with the Armed Forces of the Philippines field commanders.
- U.S. troops would not engage in combat operations, without prejudice to their right to self-defense.[36]

The United States is training Filipino soldiers within the framework of the *Balikatan* exercises not only to eliminate indigenous terrorists linked to Osama bin Laden but also "to prevent the Philippines from becoming a haven of future terror groups."[37] Philippine National Security Adviser Roilo Golez said, "The Basilan training could serve as a model for training by U.S. forces of troops in Yemen and Georgia, which Bush indicated could also be future havens [for] terror groups."[38]

The U.S. Department of Defense views the *Balikatan* exercises as designed to improve the Philippine-U.S. combined planning, combat readiness, and interoperability.[39] The training is also intended to enhance Philippine–American security relations and to "demonstrate U.S. resolve to support the Philippines against external aggression and state-sponsored terrorism."[40] In 2001, according to Admiral Dennis Blair, then commander in chief of the U.S. Pacific Command, America's "largest military operation against terrorism [outside of Afghanistan]" was in the Philippines, where a U.S. Joint Task Force was providing training, some equipment, intelligence support, and advisers to the AFP.[41] The most notable feature of Balikatan 2002-1 is the revitalization of Philippine–U.S. security alliance after almost a 10-year hiatus in the two countries' bilateral security ties.[42]

## Implications for Regional Security

Because of the previous role that the Philippines had played in U.S. Southeast Asian security policy, the reinvigoration of Philippine–American defense ties has implications for regional security because of the following perceptions:

- Through the Philippine–American Balikatan 2002-1 joint military exercises, the American presence has been significantly reestablished not only in the Philippines but also in Southeast Asia.
- Reinvigorated Philippine–American relations enhance the American network of strategic bilateral alliances in the Asia–Pacific. When tied together, this network of alliances could be useful as a counterweight against any potential aggressor in the region.

■ The American military presence in the Philippines deters terrorism not only in Southeast Asia but also in other countries that are suspicious of the U.S. regional presence.

## A Regional Coalition against Terrorism

The reinvigoration of Philippine–American relations has enhanced U.S. strategic alliances in Southeast Asia. This is part of Washington's plan to strengthen relations with countries sharing common regional interests. To consolidate regional efforts in combating terrorism in Southeast Asia, the United States has proposed to link its military exercises with the Philippines in the context of the U.S.-initiated Exercise Team Challenge. The Exercise Team Challenge is a multinational military exercise involving major American friends and allies in Asia, such as Australia, Singapore, and Thailand.[43] In fact, the Philippine Government has already initiated a regional coalition against terrorism with the member-states of the Association of Southeast Asian Nations (ASEAN). The Philippines, Malaysia, and Indonesia commenced the formation of this regional coalition by signing on May 7, 2002, the Trilateral Agreement on Exchange of Information and Establishment of Communication Procedures as a regional counterterrorism measure. The agreement is part of Southeast Asia's battle against regional militant groups through the mutual exchange of information. The United States has welcomed the agreement because it is designed as a deterrent against potential terrorist threats and other transnational crimes in Southeast Asia.

Thailand, Singapore, and Brunei have shown interest in this regional coalition.[44] In March 2002, Thailand, another U.S. ally in Southeast Asia, hosted the planning conference of the Southeast Asia Cooperation against Terrorism (SEA-CAT) exercise. Attended by participating navies from Indonesia, Malaysia, the Philippines, Singapore, and the United States, SEA-CAT was the first of its kind. Its purpose was to establish a regional coordination infrastructure for information-sharing and exchange, supporting a multinational response to combat terrorism.

## The China Factor

There are fears in Beijing that the U.S. military presence in the Philippines is not merely for the purposes of dealing with terrorists but is also directed at China. The Texas-based think tank Strategic Forecasting Inc. (STRATFOR) has said that the United States is using the global war on terror to spread its forces in Asia and increase its influence in a region that is steadily coming under China's shadow.[45] Some American security analysts have viewed China as a power with the potential of being an American strategic adversary in the Asia-Pacific region.[46] Although 9/11 had a positive impact on U.S.–China relations, having increased contacts between Beijing and Washington, at the strategic level the United States still considers China a threat.[47]

China welcomes the U.S. role in maintaining a generally stable security environment in Asia. However, Beijing is critical of the U.S. military presence in the region, in general, and in the Philippines, in particular, because of the perception that it is intended to "constrict" Chinese activities in the region, specifically related to the South China Sea.[48] In its 2000 Defense white paper, China had already expressed alarm at the United States strengthening its military presence and bilateral alliances in the region.[49]

The aftermath of 9/11 and the heightened American presence in the Philippines have unleashed some repercussions on China's strategic posture in Southeast Asia. After 9/11, China reportedly changed its security calculus and was forced to reevaluate its geopolitical position vis-à-vis its relations with the United States and with other claimant states to the Spratly Islands in the South China Sea.[50] However, General Richard Myers, Chairman of the U.S. Joint Chiefs of Staff, has emphasized that the target of the increased U.S. military presence in Southeast Asia is terrorism and not China.[51] He said that Balikatan 2002-1 is "not an issue about China" but an issue "about our presence in the region to promote stability and... good commerce."[52]

The Philippine Government has also paid attention to the sensitivities of China vis-à-vis the revitalization of Philippine–American relations. The Philippines does not want its relations with China to be affected by the reinvigorated Philippine–American ties. To demonstrate the Philippines' strong resolve to establish constructive cooperative relations with China, Manila is engaging Beijing in the war on terrorism through the Asia–Pacific Economic Cooperation (APEC) forum, the ASEAN+3 mechanism, and through the ASEAN Regional Forum.

## The Taiwan Issue and the Bases Factor

Another regional implication of reinvigorated Philippine–American relations is the perception that the U.S. presence in the Philippines is part of a strategic package to defend Taiwan. The RAND Corporation revealed a study arguing that the United States has established a plan to set up a small base in Zamboanga as part of the "defense of Taiwan." RAND argues, "As far as the Philippines is concerned, the strategy would entail expanding cooperation with the Philippines to support Taiwan if need be."[53] RAND has even identified Zamboanga International Airport as a place to establish a small American base because it "is fairly well suited to fighter operations, with runway dimensions significantly larger than a minimal base and parking space for two or three squadrons of aircraft types."[54] The former American military facilities at Clark have also been identified as a very good location because of "ample parking space for at least a wing of fighter size aircraft and runway dimensions adequate for the majority of USAF aircraft, including heavy bombers and strategic air-lifters."[55]

The U.S. Department of Defense Quadrennial Defense Review (QDR) of September 2001 has reaffirmed this idea. Given all the changes in the international security environment and the Department's new strategic approach to defense issues and concerns, the QDR states that the U.S. global military posture will be reoriented to "develop a basing system that provides greater flexibility for U.S. forces in critical areas of the world, placing emphasis on additional bases and stations beyond Western Europe and Northeast Asia."[56] In the absence of a permanent basing system, the QDR states that the U.S. global military posture be reoriented to "provide temporary access to facilities in foreign countries that enable U.S. forces to conduct training and exercises."[57]

China has expressed some concern at the presence of U.S. forces in the Philippines and its link with the issue of Taiwan. However, Admiral Dennis Blair has stressed that U.S. forces in the Philippines "certainly will not be there in permanent bases."[58] To assuage the fear of some nations about the idea of permanent basing arrangements with the Philippines, Blair stressed: "We [the Americans] will be in temporary bases [only] working with our Philippine allies."[59] The Philippine Government has also underscored that it would "never allow the establishment of foreign military bases in the country," arguing that to do so would violate the 1987 Philippine Constitution.[60] The Philippine Government, however, is amenable to the possibility of an American presence in the country on a temporary basis for purposes of advancing common security interests in Southeast Asia.

## Conclusion

The campaign against global terrorism has reinvigorated Philippine–American security relations. As a result of ongoing Philippine–U.S. joint military exercises against terrorism, bilateral security relations are now at their peak. The Philippines' reinvigorated relationship with the United States has implications for regional security because of the traditional role this relationship has played in the management of peace and stability in Southeast Asia. The Philippines welcomes the United States because of the recognition of their existing alliance, as provided for by the MDT. Moreover, the interests of the Philippines and the United States have converged on the issue of terrorism, justifying the reinvigoration of their alliance. Both have the specific objective of crushing the ASG and other terrorist groups in Southeast Asia.

What will happen when and if the ASG is destroyed? Will the reinvigorated Philippine–American relations continue? When the campaign against terrorism is over, what will then be the course of Philippine–American relations? How will this affect Philippine–China relations?

It can be argued that the reinvigoration of Philippine–American relations would not prevent the Philippines from enhancing its relations with China. Although the Philippines has a dispute with China over territory in the South China Sea, it is not an issue that will be unbridgeable between the two countries. If the war on terrorism has provided the glue that has bound the Philippines and the United States, the South China Sea might well serve as the sea that links, rather than divides, the Philippines and China.

# Endnotes

1. Transcript: Assistant Secretary Kelly's "Dialogue" Broadcast November 16, 2001 (U.S. official praises Philippine antiterrorism efforts), at: http://U.S.info.state.gov/regional/ea/easec/philip.htm.
2. Ibid.
3. Jennie L. Ilustre, "Bush Cites Macapagal Guts in War vs. Terror," *Philippine Daily Inquirer*, at: http://www.inq7.net/nat/2002/mar/13/nat_4-1.htm.
4. Steven Mufson, "U.S. to Aid Philippines' Terrorism War: Bush Promises Military Equipment, Help in Freezing Inrugents' Assets," *Washington Post* (November 20, 2002), at: http://www.washingtonpost.com/ac2/wp-dyn?pagename=article&node=&contentId=A61478-2001Nov20&notFound=true.
5. Angel M. Rabasa, "Southeast Asia After 9/11: Regional Trends and U.S. Interests" (Testimony presented to the Subcommittee on East Asia and the Pacific House of Representatives Committee on International Relations, December 12, 2001).
6. See Shulan O Primavera, "The Politico-Military Dimension of the Post-EDSA RP–U.S. Relations: An Assessment" (MA Thesis: National Defense College of the Philippines, 1990), p. 52.
7. For more discussion, see Bonifacio S. Salamanca, "The Beginning of Filipino–American Relations, 1901–1921," *American Historical Collection Bulletin*, Vol. III, No. 3 (October 1975).
8. For an excellent discussion on this topic, see Patricia Ann Paez, *The Bases Factor: Realpolitik of RP–U.S. Relations* (Manila: Center for Strategic and International Studies of the Philippines, 1985), Chapter 1.
9. Teodoro Agoncillo, *History of the Filipino People*, 8th edition (Garotech Publishing: Quezon City, 1990), p. 311.
10. See Bonifacio Salamanca, *The Filipino Reaction to American Rule, 1901–1913* (Connecticut: The Shoe String Press, 1968).
11. For detailed discussion, see Daniel R. Williams, *The Odyssey of the Philippine Commission* (Chicago: A.C. McClurg, 1913).
12. Paez, op. cit., p. 5.
13. For a detailed discussion of Japanese rule of the Philippines, see Teodoro A. Agoncillo, *The Fateful Years: Japan's Adventure in the Philippines, 1941–1945*, 2 Vols. (Quezon City: R.P. Garcia Publishing Company, 1965). Also see Claro M. Recto, *Three Years of Enemy Occupation: The Issue of Political Collaboration in the Philippines* (Manila: People's Publishers, 1946).
14. For detailed discussion about the Huk, see William J. Pomeroy, *The Forest: A Personal Record of the Huk Guerilla Struggle in the Philippines* (New York: International Publishers, 1963); Uldarico S. Baclagon, *Lessons from the Huk Campaign in the Philippines* (Manila, 1960). For detailed discussion about Philippine communism, see Alfredo Saulo, *Communism in the Philippines: An Introduction,* Revised edition (Quezon City: Ateneo De Manila Press, 1990).

15. Frederick Kintanar, "Disengaging Foreign Policy from Strategic Military Alliance," *Diliman Review*, Vol. 34, No. 3 (1986), p. 9.

16. Milton Walter Meyer, *Diplomatic History of the Philippine Republic* (Honolulu: University of Hawaii Press, 1965), p. 4.

17. See Jose Ingles, *Philippine Foreign Policy* (Manila: Lyceum of the Philippines Press, 1983), p. 18.

18. See letter of Brig. Gen. Cesar De Leon Go, then President of the National Defense College of the Philippines, to Undersecretary of National Defense Feliciano M. Gacis, Jr. on RP-U.S. Security Relations, October 7, 1992.

19. See Article IV of the Mutual Defense Treaty.

20. Primavera, p. 89.

21. See Enrique Voltaire Garcia III, *U.S. Military Bases in the Philippines: Impact on Philippine–American Relations* (Chicago: University of Chicago Press, 1967); and Eduardo Z. Romualdez, *A Question of Sovereignty: The Military Bases and Philippine–American Relations, 1944–1979* (Manila, 1980).

22. For a detailed discussion on the Senate vote, see Senate of the Philippines, *The Bases of Their Decision: How the Senators Voted on the Treaty of Friendship, Cooperation and Security between the Government of the Republic of the Philippines and the Government of the United States of America* (Manila: The Legislative Publications Staff Secretariat, 1991).

23. See Richard D. Fisher, Jr., "Rebuilding the U.S.–Philippine Alliance," *The Heritage Foundation Backgrounder*, No. 1255 (February 22, 1999).

24. See Hermann Joseph S. Kraft and Renato C. De Castro, *U.S. Military Presence in Southeast Asia: Forward Deployment in the Post Bases Era* (Manila: Foreign Service Institute Center for International Relations and Strategic Studies, 1994), p. 1.

25. For detailed discussion on how the Senate voted, see The Philippine Senate, *The Visiting Forces Agreement: The Senate Decision* (Pasay City: The Philippine Senate Publications Staff, 1999).

26. Paolo Pasicolan, "Strengthening the U.S.–Philippine Alliance for Fighting Terrorism," *Heritage Foundation Executive Memorandum*, No. 815 (May 13, 2002).

27. Zachary Abuza, "Tentacles of Terror: Al Qaeda's Southeast Asian Linkages" (Paper presented at the conference "Transnational Violence and Seams of Lawlessness in the Asia–Pacific: Linkages to Global Terrorism" held at the Asia–Pacific Center for Security Studies, Honolulu, Hawaii on February 12–21, 2002), p. 6. Abuza claimed to have obtained this information from the Philippine Department of National Defense in the manuscript entitled "The Philippine Campaign against Terrorism" (2001).

28. Ibid. Also see Christine Herrera. "Gemma Linked to Bin Laden Group Funding Sayyaf, MILF," *Philippine Daily Inquirer* (August 10, 2002).

29. Ibid., p. 8.

30. Ibid. Also see *Philippine Daily Inquirer* (August 9, 2000).

31. Ibid.

32. Based in Ibid. Also see Philippine National Police, *After Intelligence Operations Report* (February 27, 1995), and Ma. Concepcion B. Clamor, "Terrorism and Southeast Asia: A Philippine Perspective" (Paper presented at the conference "Transnational Violence and Seams of Lawlessness in the Asia–Pacific: Linkages to Global Terrorism" held at the Asia–Pacific Center for Security Studies, Honolulu, Hawaii, on February 12–21, 2002).

33. Virtual Information Center, "Special Press Summary: U.S. Operations in the Philippines" (March 13, 2002), at: http://www.apan-info.net/frameset.htm.

34. Ibid.

35. Ibid.

36. Ibid.

37. See "Future Terror Havens Target Of Balikatan," *The Manila Bulletin*, at: http://www.mb.com.ph/news.php?art=7753&sect=12&fname=MT0203127753f.txt.

38. Ibid.

39. Linda D. Kozaryn, "Attacks Continue in Afghanistan; Philippines Training Under Way," at: http://www.defenselink.mil/news/Apr2002/n04242002_200204243.html.

40. Ibid.

41. Admiral Dennis Blair, "The Campaign against International Terrorism in the Asia–Pacific Region" (Remarks made to the Asia Society Hong Kong Center on April 18, 2002).

42. See Renato de Castro, "The Philippine–U.S. Alliance from 1990–2002: A Case Study of the Natural Cycle of Alliance" (Inaugural Lecture of the Dr. Aurelio Calderon Professorial Chair of Philippine–American Relations, delivered at De La Salle University, May 6, 2002).

43. "RAND Study Reveals U.S. Wants to Set Up Military Base in Philippines" (March 13, 2002), at: http://www.apan-info.net/frameset.htm.

44. Ambassador Albert del Rosario, "A Progress Report on the Philippines: The Balikatan Exercises, the Abu Sayyaf, and Al-Qaeda," Heritage Lectures, No. 738 (March 27, 2002). Also at: http://www.heritage.org/library/lecture/hl738.html.

45. Strategic Forecasting, Inc., "Philippines: U.S. Exercises May Lead to Regional Base," at: http://www.stratfor.com/country.php?ID=99.

46. Graham T. Allison and Robert Blackwill, America's National Interests (A Report from the Commission on America's National Interests, 2000), p. 24.

47. Yu Bin, "United States–China Relations and Regional Security after September 11," Issues and Insights, No. 2-02 (Honolulu: Pacific Forum CSIS, April 2002).

48. See Xu Ximbo, "U.S. Security Policy in Asia: Implications for China–U.S. Relations," *Contemporary Southeast Asia*, Vol. 22, No. 3 (December 2000), p. 486.

49. "White Paper: China's National Defense in 2000," October 16, 2000. For an Internet version, access: http://www.ceip.org.

50. Dan Ewing, "China's Changing Security Calculus," *Korea Herald* (January 21, 2002). Also at: http://www.nixoncenter.org/publications/articles/011602China.htm.

51. "Terrorism, Not China, Target of U.S. Military Presence: Myers," *Philippine Daily Inquirer* (April 28, 2002), p. 1. Also at: http://www.inq7.net/nat/2002/apr/28/nat_21.htm.

52. Ibid.

53. "RAND Study Reveals U.S. Wants to Set Up Military Base in Philippines" (March 13, 2002), at: http://www.apan-info.net/frameset.htm.

54. Ibid.

55. Ibid.

56. U.S. Department of Defense, Quadrennial Defense Review Report (Washington, DC: Department of Defense, September 30, 2001), p. 26.

57. Ibid.

58. Transcript: Admiral Blair Outlines Fight against Philippine Terrorists (Interview with NHK Television in Tokyo, February 5, 2002) at: http://U.S.info.state.gov/regional/ ea/easec/blairnhk.htm.

59. Ibid.

60. Official press statement of Malacanang in Daxim L. Lucas, Felipe F. Salvosa II, and Rey Luis Banagudos, "U.S. Bases Nixed, But Balikatan Extension Still Hangs," *Businessworld* (April 29, 2002).

## Chapter 9

# Philippines–China Defense and Military Cooperation: Problems and Prospects in the Post-9/11 Era*

## Introduction

Pursuant to Article 2 of the Memorandum of Understanding (MOU) on Defense Cooperation signed in November 2004 by the Philippine Department of National Defense (DND) and the Chinese Ministry of National Defense, the two countries conducted the First Philippines–China Defense and Security Dialogue (PCDSD) in Camp General Emilio Aguinaldo, Quezon City, on May 22–25, 2005.

The holding of the said dialogue is a milestone in Philippines–China relations as both countries finally cover the hitherto neglected aspect of their bilateral ties. The Armed Forces of the Philippines (AFP) called the occurring of the dialogue

---

* Revised and updated version of a paper presented to the International Conference on the 30 Years of Philippines–China Relations, "Charting New Directions in a Changing Global Environment," organized by the Philippine Association for Chinese Studies (PACS) on October 22, 2005 at Crowne Plaza Galleria Manila, Ortigas Center. Reproduced here with the kind permission of PACS through Dr. Aileen Baviera. Also published as a monograph entitled *Defense and Military Cooperation between the Philippines and China: Broadening Bilateral Ties in the Post-9/11 Era* (Taipei: Center for the Advancement of Policy Studies, June 2007).

"the first time" in the entire diplomatic history of Philippines–China relations. The People's Liberation Army (PLA), on the other hand, described the holding of the event as "first, frank, and fruitful" to increase the level of exchanges of their defense officials and military officers and to intensify their cooperation on defense and military security issues in order to make their bilateral relations relevant and responsive to the needs of the 21st century.

This chapter aims to analyze the current situation and future trends of Philippines–China defense and military cooperation. It aims to identify some problems confronting this type of cooperation and describes some prospects for broader bilateral defense and military cooperation. Although both countries are optimistic about the future direction of their defense ties, this chapter argues that this type of cooperation is arduous to sustain and very difficult to operationalize in the context of a Philippine–American security alliance and in the midst of growing strategic competition between China and the United States. Moreover, there are still sovereignty issues that remain unsettled between the countries, and these can obstruct pursuance of their defense cooperation. But there are nontraditional security issues where both countries' national interests converge that can provide the Philippines and China many opportunities to intensify their defense and military cooperation.

## Background on Philippines–China Defense and Military Cooperation

### Moment of Amity, 1945–1949

When the United States granted Philippine independence in 1946, the very first Treaty of Amity that the Philippines ever entered into was with the Republic of China (ROC), called Nationalist China at that time by the Philippine government. Concluding a treaty of friendship with ROC was a high diplomatic priority of then President Manuel Rojas.[1] ROC, on the other hand, was one of the first countries to recognize the Philippines as an independent republic in the aftermath of World War II.

With the signing of Philippine–China Treaty of Amity, the Philippine Government established its Consulates General Office in Amoy and Shanghai in 1947. To strengthen Philippine–ROC diplomatic ties, the Philippines opened a legation in Nanking in March 1948.[2] The Philippines and ROC had very close military relations because of their strong security relations with the United States. ROC's War College even inspired the establishment of the National Defense College of the Philippines (NDCP) in 1963.[3]

## Era of Hostility, 1949–1974

The Philippine diplomatic relations with ROC were short-lived because of domestic political changes in China. When Mao Tse-tung proclaimed the People's Republic of China (PRC) in 1949, the Philippines closed its legation in Nanking, established a liaison office in Guangzhou, and in 1950 finally transferred to Taipei.

Because of ideological differences, the Philippines' defense and military relations with the PRC, then called Communist China by the Philippine government, became very adversarial. The Philippine government declared the PRC as a serious security threat because of its alleged support to the Local Communist Movement. The Cultural Revolution in China inspired the formation of the Maoist-inspired Communist Party of the Philippines (CPP) and its military arm, the New People's Army (NPA), which until now has been pursuing the Maoist military strategy of encircling the center from the countryside through a protracted people's war.[4] During the Korean War in the 1950s, Filipino and Chinese armed forces fought on opposite sides.[5] The Philippine military even suspected the ethnic Chinese community in the country as a "fifth column." The presence of ethnic Chinese caused a severe paranoia among non-Communist states in Southeast Asia during the height of the cold war.[6]

In the 1950s, China only had military cooperation with Communist nations and to insurgent movements in Southeast Asia, particularly in Cambodia, Indonesia, Malaysia, Myanmar, the Philippines, and Thailand.[7] China's strongest military cooperation was with the former Soviet Union, which provided Beijing substantial technical and financial assistance to modernize the PLA. China also entered into a defense treaty with North Korea in 1961 and provided military and financial assistance to Vietnam until 1978. At the height of the Vietnam War, the Philippines and China fought again at the opposite sides.

## Normalization Period, 1975–1995

When Beijing experienced strategic, territorial, and ideological differences with the former Soviet Union, China explored the establishment of relations with the United States, which led eventually to the normalization of U.S.–PRC diplomatic relations in the 1970s. The Philippines followed suit with the opening of Philippines–China diplomatic relations on June 9, 1975. Since then, Philippine–China diplomatic relations have become one of the most important bilateral relations of the Philippines with foreign countries. Both countries entered into various bilateral cooperation agreements covering wide-ranging areas like trade and investment; tourism and air services; cultural, scientific and technical cooperation; agricultural cooperation; avoidance of double taxation; and postal parcel agreement.

Though both countries have dynamic relations in economic, cultural, and diplomatic areas, exploration of bilateral defense cooperation only began in the mid-1990s. Although China began developing military contacts with Europe and the

United States in the late 1970s,[8] contacts between the armed forces of the Philippines and China were almost absent, except during very limited visits of defense and military officials. The end of the cold war and the changing sociocultural interactions between China and other Southeast Asian countries in the 1990s[9] have, however, prompted the Philippines and China to explore bilateral cooperation in defense and military areas. They started their defense cooperation by building greater trust and confidence through increased high-level exchange of visits of officials from both countries' defense and military establishments.

## Troubled Relations, 1995–2000

The Philippines explored the possibility of building defense ties with China after the termination of the Philippine–American Military Bases Agreement in 1991. Engaging China was an option, though a quite reluctant one, to broaden Manila's strategic choice in the postbases era. However, the Mischief Reef incident in 1995 created a diplomatic crisis between the two countries. This held in abeyance all talks of possible defense cooperation between them. The incident has terribly angered the Philippine military because of the suspicion that the Mischief Reef incident was the handiwork of the PLA. As retaliation, the Philippine Navy destroyed Chinese markers around some other reefs and captured 60 "fishermen" from Chinese trawlers.[10] Former President Fidel Ramos, who earlier served as the AFP chief of staff and secretary of national defense, urged the Philippine military to shift from an internal counterinsurgency campaign to an external defense operation.[11] The General Headquarters of the AFP issued the Rules of Engagement for External Threat on May 22, 1997.

The Mischief Reef issue also encouraged the AFP to strongly push for the passage of the AFP Modernization Law to increase its capability to defend its national territory against external threats.[12] The immediate passage of the force modernization law was no doubt influenced by the Mischief Reef controversy in the South China Sea.[13] The Philippines even solicited the support of the members of the ASEAN Regional Forum to condemn China and sponsored the drafting of a Regional Code of Conduct in the South China Sea to prohibit the building of any structures on the disputed islands.[14] But China objected to the "internationalization" of the South China Sea disputes and opposed the effort to pass a code of conduct. China considered the South China Sea disputes a bilateral concern.

To address their existing bilateral differences over territorial disputes, the Philippines and China signed the Joint Statement on PRC–RP (Republic of the Philippines) Consultations on the South China Sea and on other areas of cooperation in August 1995. This statement revived their interests to pursue defense and military cooperation, though still marred with mutual suspicions. But to express China's desire to establish closer defense and military friendship with the Philippines, General Xiong Gungkai, PLA vice chief of general staff, visited Manila in May 1996. During this visit, both countries exchanged cordial views on regional and national security concerns. They also explored the possibility of exchanging their respective defense attachés to overcome their lingering suspicions of each other. The exchange of defense attachés started their initial defense cooperation, which they regarded as an opportune time to elevate their bilateral relations to a higher plane.

Aiming to sustain their optimism for the prospects of defense cooperation, then Philippine Defense Secretary Renato De Villa visited Beijing on July 29, 1996. During this visit, the Philippines and China signed the Agreement on the Establishment of the Offices of the Defense and Armed Forces Attaché. It was in this agreement that the Philippines and China strongly recognized the importance of their bilateral relations. They even expressed their interest to strengthen their defense cooperation beyond the exchange of defense attachés. As a warm gesture, therefore, China extended a military loan assistance of US$3 million to the Philippine government, which translated into delivery of 40 military dump trucks to the engineering brigade of the AFP. The Philippines actually received the 40 dump trucks in May 1998.

With the signing of the Agreement on the exchange of defense attaché, the Philippines and China also decided to conduct bilateral intelligence exchange to intensify their military-to-military contacts. They launched their first Intelligence Exchange (INTELEX) in March 1998. Their fifth INTELEX was held in April 2000, but it has not been followed through since. Both countries claimed that this bilateral undertaking not only facilitated the development of friendly relations and cooperative ties between the two countries' armed forces, but it also contributed to the overall confidence-building measures in their bilateral relations.

China made a follow-up visit in September 1996 when PLA Chief Fu Quangyou went to Manila to demonstrate China's sincerity to strengthen military-to-military contacts between the two countries. In February 1997, Defense Minister Chi Haotian visited the Philippines to promote cordial relations between the countries' defense establishments.

But the PRC's strategic intention was put to doubt when the Philippines discovered that China fortified its structures in the Mischief Reef in 1999. This irked the Philippines, considering that both had already made an understanding in 1995 to halt any construction activities on the disputed island. Former Defense Secretary Orlando Mercado described the incident as an indication of China's "creeping invasion" of Philippine territory.[15] China explained that the said structure was a mere "fishermen's shelter" to be used during adverse weather. But the 1999 structure looked like a military garrison with heliport, satellite radio, and missile frigates spotted nearby.[16]

Also in 1999, the Philippine Navy chased and collided with a Chinese fishing boat in the Scarborough Shoal, sinking the Chinese vessel. The Scarborough Shoal is a large atoll in the eastern South China Sea about 122 nautical miles off Luzon. Like the Mischief Reef, the Philippines and China both claim the island.

The Scarborough Shoal is within the 200-mile exclusive economic zone of the Philippines as defined by the United Nations Convention on the Law of the Sea.[17]

The Mischief Reef and Scarborough issues unleashed enormous domestic anxieties and left indelible ink of distrust in Philippine military thinking toward China. This promoted the Headquarters of the Philippine Navy to issue on June 30, 1999, the Rules of Engagement (ROE) in the Conduct of Naval Operations at the Kalayaan Island Group (KIG) to enforce Philippine sovereignty in the KIG. The AFP even repaired the runway on the Philippine-controlled Pag-Asa (Thitu) Island of the KIG to efficiently facilitate access of military planes and helicopters in the area. The AFP also intensified the activities of the western command of the Philippine Navy to protect not only Philippine national security but also the security and stability of Southeast Asia. The Philippine Navy stepped up its patrols in the South China Sea and continually blasted territorial markers that Chinese forces had set up in various other features of the contested islands. The Philippine Navy and the Philippine Coast Guard also intensified their coordinated campaign against illegal fishermen in the Philippines' Exclusive Economic Zone and arrested several Chinese fishermen poaching on Philippine territorial waters.

## Sustaining Friendship, Enhancing Cooperation, 2000 and Beyond?

Despite territorial controversies, the Philippines and China signed the Joint Statement on the Framework of Bilateral Cooperation in the Twenty-First Century on May 16, 2000. In this agreement, they acknowledged "the strength of their long, historical friendship and geographical proximity in order to advance the fundamental interests of their two peoples." They also expressed hopes that this agreement would "contribute to peace, security, stability, sustained growth, and development in Asia and the rest of the world." To pursue these aspirations, Manila and Beijing also expressed their interests to widen the scope and deepen the level of their cooperation in the defense and security areas. Among the features of this agreement with defense and security implications are the following:

> They agree "to make further exchanges and cooperation in the defense and military fields, strengthen consultations between their military and defense personnel and military diplomatic officials on security issues, to include exchanges between their military establishments on matters relating to humanitarian rescue and assistance, disaster relief and mitigation, and enhance cooperation between their respective strategic and security research institutes."
>
> They agree "to explore new areas for cooperation among their law enforcement, judicial, security, and defense agencies in order to address the serious threats posed by organized transnational crimes."

The Philippine–China Joint Statement on the Framework of Bilateral Cooperation in the Twenty-First Century is the only document signed by both countries that contains provisions on defense cooperation. With the signing of this joint statement, both countries provided a written basis to enhance their Confidence Building Measure (CMB) activities through middle- and high-level exchanges of defense and military officials. In October 2000, for example, then AFP Chief of Staff Angelo Reyes visited China to meet his Chinese counterpart, General Fu Qangyou, chief of the PLA general staff. General Reyes also met then Chinese Defense Minister Chi Haotian and key members of the Central Military Commission. In January 2001, then Defense Secretary Orlando Mercado paid an official visit to China to meet his Chinese counterpart, Minister Chi Haotian. Both defense leaders explored the possibility of strengthening their defense and military cooperation to address security issues of mutual concern.

Immediately after the September 11, 2001, terrorist attacks on the United States, China hosted the Ninth Summit of the Asia–Pacific Economic Cooperation in October 2001. The Philippines and China took this opportunity to sign three important Memoranda of Understanding, namely:

1. Treaty of Extradition between the Republic of the Philippines and the People's Republic of China
2. Memorandum of Understanding between the Government of the Republic of the Philippines and the Government of the People's Republic of China on Cooperation against Illicit Traffic and Abuse of Narcotic Drugs, Psychotropic Substances, and Precursor Chemicals
3. Memorandum of Understanding between the Government of the Republic of the Philippines and the Government of the People's Republic of China on Cooperation in Combating Transnational Crime

These three MOUs provided opportunities for both countries to intensify their defense and military cooperation. But the lack of a clear and coherent operational framework has prevented both countries from moving forward. When General Reyes replaced Mercado as the secretary of national defense, one of the first countries that Reyes visited was China, where he met for the second time General Chi Haotian in April 2002. During this visit, both leaders cultivated a deeper personal friendship that facilitated official discussions for the enhancement of their defense cooperation. They agreed to intensify their strategic defense and military dialogues through their annual intelligence exchange program and occasional exchange of visits of their defense and military colleges. They even explored, albeit very cautiously, the possibility of conducting joint military training and exercises in accordance with their respective constitutional requirements.

General Chi Haotian reciprocated this visit when he met General Reyes in Manila in September 2002. Secretary Reyes underscored during his meeting with Minister Chi that it is in the interest of the Philippine Government to develop a "healthy, comprehensive, and long-term relationship" with China. Interestingly, the main theme of Chi's visit to the Philippines was "sustaining friendship, enhancing cooperation," which demonstrated the interest of the DND to really establish closer defense ties with Beijing.[18] President Gloria Macapagal Arroyo even issued Proclamation No. 148 in 2002, declaring June 9th of every year as "Philippine–China Friendship Day" to raise their bilateral relations, including defense and security, to a more mature and enduring level.

## Current Situation in Philippines–China Defense and Military Cooperation: Cautious Cooperation?

The 2002 visit of Minister Chi was a turning point in Philippines–China relations, for it provided a fertile ground to define the direction of their countries' defense relations in the post-9/11 era. The personal friendship that Minister Chi and Secretary Reyes cultivated also provided a constructive environment to take a candid stock of their bilateral relations and to identify areas where they could enhance their defense ties in the post-9/11 world.[19] They even made an understanding to shelve territorial issues in the South China Sea in order to move their defense relations forward.

During Chi's visit, President Arroyo stressed that the "South China Sea is the sea that unites rather than divides the Philippines and China,"[20] to convey a message that the Philippine government was very serious about establishing defense relations with China. Arroyo even strongly articulated a benign view of China when she repeatedly pronounced that China was not a threat but rather an opportunity for the Philippines. Like the Chinese government, the Arroyo government expressed willingness to shelve sovereignty issues in the South China Sea. The main intention of the Philippines was to promote closer relations with the PRC and take advantage of China's rise as an economic power.[21] In fact, entering into bilateral defense relations with China was part of the Philippine government's comprehensive engagement with the PRC.[22] When she was still the Vice President, Arroyo said, "Comprehensive engagement is indeed what the Philippines needs to pursue its relations with China. China is not only our closest neighbor to the north. It is also a very important player in the regional and world economy as well as in international politics."[23]

The *Policy Paper on China*, made by the Department of Foreign Affairs in the aftermath of 9/11, also recommended to "engage China and enhance relations in all aspects."[24] The policy of comprehensive engagement embraces all aspects of Philippine relations with China. For the DND, a policy of comprehensive engagement may enhance Philippines–China relations in defense and military fields to promote Philippine national security.[25] The DND even drafted the Philippines' Engagement Plan with China on Defense and Security "to strengthen and institutionalize RP-China security and defense relations in order to best optimize relations for mutual gains."[26]

Economic consideration is the primordial factor that encouraged the Philippine government to constructively engage China in all aspects. In her speech at the 30th anniversary celebration of Philippine–China diplomatic relations held at the Manila Hotel, Arroyo underscored that "China has become a major trading partner of the country." She added, "Aside from being a vigorous and generous trading partner, China is an investor in our industries, in our mines, in our oil exploration." She proudly announced that Philippine trade with China exceeded US$13 billion in 2004 and "the future of the two countries' trade partnership looks even brighter." [27]

Establishing defense cooperation with China is a political decision of the Philippine government to take advantage of China's economic prosperity and to benefit from growing Philippines–China economic relations. In fact, China has wanted to have defense cooperation with the Philippines as indicated by the various pronouncements of its defense and military leaders. But the Philippine government was initially reluctant to pursue this type of cooperation because of security anxieties associated with the rise of China. When the PRC assured its neighbor that China would rise peacefully as a great power,[28] the Philippine government maintained an open mind on the issue and gave China the benefit of the doubt.

Thus, when Arroyo was reelected president in May 2004, the first country that she visited was China. Arroyo visited China on September 1–3, 2004, at the invitation of President Hu Jintao. It was during this visit when both leaders seriously discussed the strengthening of their defense ties by setting up a framework for defense cooperation.[29] It was also during this visit when the Philippine government accepted China's offer of loan assistance to implement the now controversial North Luzon Train Project. Also in September 2004, then AFP Chief of Staff Narciso Abaya visited China and witnessed the military exercise "Iron Fist 2004." Abaya and his party were impressed by the modern military hardware and equipment of the PLA, and they expressed the desire to learn lessons from the exemplary practice of China on military modernization.

Philippines–China defense relations took a much clearer direction when Defense Secretary Avelino Cruz, Jr., visited China on November 7–14, 2004. Cruz stressed the importance of his visit "to build stronger confidence and enhance defense cooperation between the two countries."[30] He congratulated China for hosting the ASEAN Regional Forum Security Policy Conference on November 4–6, 2004, and said that the hosting of the forum demonstrated China's positive role in regional security. Cruz also emphasized that the Philippines welcomed all initiatives aimed at further strengthening and expanding defense and military ties and would "sustain its efforts in exchange visits between defense and military officials."[31] More importantly, Cruz's visit to China led to the signing of an MOU on defense cooperation.

The MOU on defense cooperation was signed amid international debate on the regional implications of the Anti-Secession Law passed by the Chinese People's

Congress.[32] To convey to the Chinese government that the Philippines was not alarmed by the passage of the Anti-Secession Law, Foreign Affairs Secretary Alberto Romulo said in the official statement that the Philippines "certainly don't see China as a threat," arguing that "we see China as a partner in the East Asian community." Romulo even visited China from February 28 to March 2, 2005, to ratify the Philippines–China MOU on defense cooperation.

The MOU on defense cooperation is an important document that provides the framework for defense and military cooperation between China and the Philippines. It contains provisions on how to intensify their military-to-military contacts and to promote security cooperation in nontraditional security areas, particularly in counterterrorism. The MOU also calls for the annual conduct of defense and security dialogue to exchange views on their countries' defense policies and on national and security issues of mutual interests.

Based on the MOU, the two countries formally signed the US$1.2 million military assistance of China to the Philippines and proposed a military exchange program between their armed forces. During the holding of the PCDSD, China offered five military training slots for Filipino officers and invited the Philippines to participate in joint naval exercises, particularly in the areas of search-and-rescue operations. They also agreed to promote closer cooperation on counterterrorism and maritime security and to intensify their port visits. At the conclusion of the PCDSD, they signed a protocol agreement to provide more details on their annual defense and security dialogue to be held alternately between the two countries. But the MOU on defense cooperation is very hard to sustain because it is not anchored on a strong legal footing. The MOU is just an executive "mutual understanding" that is even short of an executive agreement that can be abrogated anytime a new executive comes into office. Moreover, implementing the MOU is contingent on Philippines–American security alliance, China–US strategic competition, the South China Sea disputes, and Cross-Strait Conflict.

# Problems in Philippines–China Defense and Military Cooperation

Despite the optimism of the Philippines and China to pursue their defense and military cooperation, there are problems on how to sustain and operationalize this cooperation in the context of the following considerations.

## The Philippines–American Security Alliance

The Philippines' overall defense diplomacy remains anchored on its security alliance with the United States. The United States continues to be a treaty ally by virtue of the Mutual Defense Treaty (MDT) of 1951. The MDT is still in effect and "shall remain in force indefinitely."[33] Though the Philippines and the United States terminated the Military Bases Agreement (MBA) in 1991, they signed the Visiting Forces Agreement (VFA) in 1999 to provide a legal framework for the resumption of their joint military exercises. When the Philippine Senate ratified the VFA, one major justification of the senators who voted in favor of the agreement was China's perceived military advancement in the South China Sea.[34] In the aftermath of the 9/11 terrorist attacks on the United States, the Philippines used the VFA as the legal cover for the conduct of Balikatan military exercises against terrorist threats posed by the Abu Sayyaf Group.

But Beijing was suspicious of Balikatan exercises because of the perception that these exercises were strategically aimed at China.[35] Although the Pentagon officially denies this perspective, there is a prevailing perception in China that the United States is reestablishing its presence in the Philippines to regain its foothold in Southeast Asia and strategically encircle China.[36] There is a view in China that the United States is using the Philippines to regain its dominant position in Southeast Asia and prevent China's regional influence from rising. According to a prominent professor of Beijing University's School of International Studies, "If it's just anti-terrorism, China won't be too worried, but if fighting terrorism will lead to a stepping up of military exchanges between the United States and Southeast Asian countries, then China would be worried."[37] He also argues that "China doesn't want to see the United States using the fight against terrorism to set up military bases in Southeast Asia and have troops stationed there" because such action would be interpreted by Beijing as a threat and as partly targeted at China. But the Philippine government explained that its military exercises with the United States are not aimed at other countries, particularly China.

On November 21, 2002, the DND and the U.S. Department of Defense (DOD) signed the Mutual Logistics Support Agreement (MLSA). The main purpose of the MLSA is to establish "basic terms, conditions, and procedures to facilitate the reciprocal provision of logistic support, supplies, and services," between the two countries' armed forces during the following:

> Combined exercises and training, operations and other deployments undertaken under the Mutual Defense Treaty, the Visiting Forces Agreement or the Military Assistance Agreement as agreed upon between the Parties; and,
> Other cooperative efforts, such as humanitarian assistance, disaster relief and rescue operations, and maritime anti-pollution operations, within Philippine territory, or outside Philippine territory in cases where either Party, or both, have decided to participate.[38]

The MLSA also contributes to the strengthening of Philippines–American relations in the fight against terrorism. Because of Manila's ardent support of the global campaign against terrorism, President George W. Bush declared the Philippines as a major non-NATO (North Atlantic Treaty Organization) ally in May 2003.[39] Bush said that making the Philippines a major non-NATO ally "will allow our countries to work together on military research and development, and give the Philippines greater access to American defense equipment and supplies."[40] In September 2003, the DND released the *RP–U.S. Joint Defense Assessment Update*. As the title suggests, it is an update of the *Joint Defense Assessment Report* of April 2001. The Joint Defense Assessment (JDA) aims to strengthen the Philippines–U.S. defense alliance based on the MDT.[41] The JDA also aimed "to provide a comprehensive assessment of Philippine defense capabilities, and assist the DND in developing a comprehensive defense program and plan for improving prioritized Philippine defense capabilities."[42]

As a defense ally, the United States continues to provide security assistance to the Philippines in the form of the following: (1) foreign military financing, (2) Foreign Sales Program, (3) excess defense articles, (4) international military education and training, and (5) presidential drawdown authority. In 2004, the total U.S. military assistance to the Philippines amounted to US$62.18 million.[43] With this kind of assistance and the nature of their bilateral ties, the cornerstone of Philippine defense diplomacy is still the Philippine–American defense alliance.

Thus, the United States has expressed concerns on the strengthening of Philippines–China defense relations. The U.S. government has called the attention of the Philippine government to the country's "important, delicate bilateral and political relationship with China."[44] The United States was eager to know the extent of Philippines–China security dialogue and "how it was in the national interests of the Philippines to expand defense relations with all countries, including China."[45] There is no doubt that China is a factor in Philippine–American relations.[46] In order not to faze the United States, the Philippine Government explained that its improving defense relations with China was not meant to jeopardize the Philippine–American security alliance. In his speech before the Heritage Foundation on May 18, 2005, Secretary Romulo stressed:

> Like the United States, we are developing constructive relations with China. We believe that Beijing should come forward in reassuring its neighbors on matters of security, especially given the steady growth in its defense spending. At the same time, China's commerce can boost the prosperity of all.
>
> The Philippines is a living example of how China's growth can fuel progress and development in neighboring countries. China's increasing wealth propelled our bilateral trade to grow by an average of 41 percent since 2003. Total trade with China last year was at $13.3 billion, in favor of the Philippines.
>
> A friendly, prosperous and increasingly open China is a powerful stabilizing force for the region and the world....

> Encouraging Beijing to expand its external contacts and to be more involved in regional cooperation with other Asia-Pacific nations is the way forward.[47]

In this speech, Romulo also conveyed an explicit message to the U.S. government that "Filipinos and Americans have been friends for more than a century. Americans have enjoyed longer, closer and more cordial relations with Filipinos than with any other people in Asia. These ties are firmly based on shared historical experiences, on a common commitment to democracy, and on the heritage of free and open societies."[48] This message was meant to allay the fear of the United States on the recent developments in Philippines–China defense and military relations.

Because of the U.S. factor, it is very difficult for the Philippines to broaden its defense ties with China. Though there is a perception that the Philippines is playing the China card against the United States, the government in Manila still values its long-standing "special" relations with the United States. In fact, the United States is actively involved in providing technical assistance to the Philippines in the implementation of the Philippine Defense Reform Program, which aims to provide "the framework for introducing a comprehensive, institutional, structural and systemic reform package at the strategic level for the defense and military establishment."[49]

## China–U.S. Strategic Competition

American concerns of the direction of Philippines–China defense relations can also be attributed to the China–United States strategic competition. For the United States, the Philippines has an important role to play in U.S.–China relations.[50] As a security ally, the United States expects the Philippines to side with Washington on difficult international issues like the rise of China. Thus, the Philippines' current engagement of China in defense and military areas is causing some concerns in the United States.

In his "The Geography of Peace: East Asia in the Twenty-First Century," Robert S. Ross describes East Asian regional order in the aftermath of the cold war as bipolar, divided into continental and maritime regions. This bipolar regional structure, he says, "is characterized by Chinese dominance of mainland East Asia and U.S. dominance of maritime East Asia."[51] Ross contends that in the midst of this bipolar regional order, smaller Asian states tend to compensate for their own vulnerability by clearly aligning with either China or the United States.[52] As a maritime state and by virtue of Philippine–American security alliance, the Philippines is expected to strictly align with the United States to balance China in the post–cold war era.

However, recent developments have shown that Manila is strengthening its defense ties with Beijing while maintaining its security relations with Washington. Rather than aligning strictly with the United States, the Philippines has opted to cooperate with China in defense and military areas. The United States finds this problematic not only within the framework of Philippine–American security relations but also in the context of U.S.–China strategic competition.

In its 2005 Annual Report to the U.S. Congress on the Military Power of the PRC, the DOD welcomes the peaceful rise of China. But it expresses anxieties "about the basic choices China's leaders will make as China's power and influence grow, particularly its military power."[53] Though U.S.–China relations remain "cooperative, candid and constructive," the United States is wary of China's growing economic and military power because there are forces "that could divert China from a peaceful pathway," to wit:

- Nationalistic fervor bred by expanding economic power and political influence.
- Structural economic weaknesses and inefficiencies that could undermine economic growth.
- An inability to accommodate the forces of an open, transparent market economy.
- A government that is still adapting to great power roles.
- An expanding military-industrial complex that proliferates advanced arms.[54]

For the United States, China is a formidable power to contend with in the present and in the future. In fact, American security analysts have viewed China to be the "great American foreign policy problem in the 21st century"[55] and a "potential peer competitor to the United States in world affairs."[56] It is also argued that "China will be a persistent competitor of the United States."[57] The U.S. Commission on National Security/21st Century warns, "The potential for competition between the United States and China may increase as China grows stronger."[58] Even Global Trends 2015, prepared under the direction of the National Intelligence Council, argues that the implications of the rise of China "pose the greatest uncertainty" in East and Southeast Asia.[59] The Commission on America's National Interests describes China as "America's major potential strategic adversary in East Asia."[60]

The most revealing perspective on the American view of China is the one articulated by the U.S.–China Security Review Commission. The commission argues that U.S.–China security relations "is one of the most important and most difficult bilateral relationships" of the United States.[61] It describes China as an emerging global power that has the potential of defeating a superior power.[62] This promoted Bill Gertz to argue, "The People's Republic of China is the most serious national security threat the United States faces at present and will remain so into the foreseeable future."[63]

Analysts have enumerated several factors contributing to the idea of a China threat in the United States and among China's neighbors.[64] But the most compelling factor is the fear of the unknown or the idea of uncertainties associated with China's growing power. The 2005 Annual Report of the DOD on the military power of China laments, "secrecy envelops most aspects of Chinese security affairs." This creates American distrust of China's strategic intentions. Based on the neo-realist theory of international relations, distrust of other states creates a security dilemma, which exists when military preparations of one state create an unresolvable uncertainty in the mind of another as to whether those preparations are for "defensive" purposes only or for "offensive" purposes (a "guessing game").[65] If the current trend of China's military modernization persists, the DOD warns, "PLA capabilities could pose a credible threat to other modern militaries operating in the region."[66]

These American perspectives on the uncertainties of China's growing power pose tremendous challenges to the pursuance of Philippines–China defense and military relations. The United States is suspicious of Chinese strategic intention in strengthening military relations with countries in Southeast Asia. There is a dominant thinking in the United States that China is actively engaging Southeast Asia to enhance its regional influence and pursue its plan to control the world.[67] There is a view in the United States that the rising power of China, if not checked and managed, will most likely result, over the very long term, in a more assertive China.[68] This explains serious concerns of the United States on the recent developments in Philippines–China defense relations. U.S. strategic analysts have already raised worries on the presumed decline of American influence in Southeast Asia as China increasingly gains recognition as an Asian dominant power.[69] It is therefore alarming for the United States to see the Philippines, its security ally, relating closely with China on defense and military issues. Though the Philippines is not prevented from relating with China to have an effective counterweight to the well-entrenched strategic influence of the United States in Philippine foreign and security policy,[70] Washington is wary to see the enhancement of Philippines–China defense relations being used at its expense in the U.S.–China strategic competition.

## The South China Sea Dispute

Another issue that can pose a formidable challenge to the strengthening of Philippines–China defense relations is the territorial dispute in the South China Sea. Various authors have already covered the many ramifications of the dispute.[71] But the issue has not been fully analyzed in the context of Philippines–China defense relations.[72]

There is optimism that Philippines–China defense relations can provide opportunities to manage conflicts in the South China Sea. As explained in Chapter 2, the Mischief Reef and Scarborough issues created a dent in Philippines–China security relations and even resulted in the feeling of distrust in Philippine military thinking toward China.

The PRC states that it is shelving the South China Sea dispute, for the time being, to promote cooperation in the area. Shelving the sovereignty issue, however, does not really solve the issue. It only postpones discussions on "hard" security issues to allow cooperation in less controversial aspects, or "soft" security issues, of the South China Sea conflict. Thus, the sovereignty issue remains a contested issue. Moreover, the phrase "for the time being" implies that China may raise the sovereignty issue when the time is ripe in the future. It has already been asserted that conflicting sovereignty claims can trigger military conflicts in the South China Sea. In this situation, the credibility of Philippines–China defense relations will really be put to the test.

To demonstrate China's willingness to promote cooperation in the settlement of the South China Sea dispute, it signed the ASEAN-China Declaration on the Conduct of Parties in the South China Sea (DOC) on November 4, 2002. This declaration urges all parties to promote "dialogues and exchange of views as appropriate between their defense and military officials." China's participation in the DOC is considered a radical departure from its previous bilateral approach. China is now opening its options to multilateral approaches to deal peacefully with the South China Sea issue.[73] To convert the South China Sea from military flashpoint to "sea of friendship and cooperation," the Philippine National Oil Company, the China National Offshore Oil Company, and the Vietnam Oil and Gas Corporation signed an agreement on March 14, 2005, to conduct a joint marine seismic survey.

Despite the signing of the DOC and the Trilateral Agreement, tensions continue to pervade in the area. When Vietnam promoted tourist activities to visit Vietnam military outposts in the South China Sea, it irked Beijing, which called it an infringement on China's territorial sovereignty. Philippine military intelligence reports continue to monitor poaching of Chinese fishermen in Philippine territorial waters in the South China Sea. It was even suspected that some of the Chinese fishermen were actually military men in civilian attire tasked to protect China's interests in the area.[74] Mutual suspicions on the territorial conflicts in the South China Sea are major stumbling blocks in Philippines–China defense relations.

## The Taiwan Issue

Though the Philippines upholds a one-China policy, Manila continues to have relevant interactions with Taiwan on economic, trade, commercial, cultural, and social areas. The one-China policy prohibits any official military engagements with Taiwan. But the one-China policy has not prevented defense contacts between Taiwan and the Philippines.

As described in Chapter 2, the issue in the Taiwan Strait affects the direction of Philippines–China defense and military cooperation. It was even raised by an American security analyst: "By reinvigorating its military alliance with the United States, the Philippines may be in the undesirable position of having to choose between security cooperation with the United States and economic cooperation with China in the event of a confrontation between the two over Taiwan. The Philippines hopes to avoid having to make such a choice."[75] This situation is confounded by the fact that "there remains an influential group within the Philippines' political elite, especially in the Senate, that is committed to establishing ties with

Taiwan for a combination of ideological or personal economic reasons."[76] Because of the Taiwan issue, the Philippines is pursuing very cautious relations with the PRC. Chapter 11 provides a more detailed analysis on how the Taiwan issue affects Philippines–China security relations.

# Prospects for Cooperation after 9/11

Despite all the aforementioned problems identified, there are nontraditional security issues that can provide opportunities for the two countries to define the scope of their defense and military cooperation after 9/11. These nontraditional security issues are "soft" security issues that are less controversial and can promote broader cooperation between the Philippines and China toward the resolution of their bilateral conflicts in "hard" security issues. The functionalist theory of international relations states that cooperation in low or soft politics of security can lead to "a change in attitudes in favor of even greater cooperation over a widening spectrum of issues"[77] including hard security issues. Chapter 8 of this book explains how the functionalist approach can improve Philippines–China security relations, particularly in the context of managing disputes in the South China Sea.

It is expected that Philippines–China defense cooperation in nontraditional security issues can yield positive results in their overall bilateral relations even in traditional security areas. Among the nontraditional, soft security issues that the Philippines can implement in their defense and military relations are international terrorism, maritime security, and transnational crimes.

## *International Terrorism*

The Philippines and China have a common interest to address "terrorist problems" posed by Muslim separatism. The Philippines has Muslim separatist problems in the Autonomous Region in Muslim Mindanao, while China has its own problems in the Xinjiang-Uighur Autonomous Region. Among Muslim separatist groups, the Philippines has labeled the Abu Sayyaf Group (ASG) as a terrorist organization.[78] China, on the other hand, "labels as terrorists those who are fighting for an independent state in the northwestern province of Xinjiang, which the separatists call Eastern Turkestan."[79] The Philippines and China supported the United States in the global campaign against terrorism and signed all UN resolutions on counter-terrorism. Both countries even explored the possibility of forming an Asian antiterrorism alliance to combat international terrorism.[80]

Because of their common desire to combat terrorism, the Philippines and China can pursue bilateral cooperation to share their experiences in counterterrorism. During the visit of Minister Chi to the Philippines in 2002, the Philippines raised the possibility of having intelligence exchange on terrorism as one area of defense cooperation. During the first Philippines–China Defense and Security Dialogue in May 2005, one of the major areas tackled was terrorism. Though both countries have recognized that countering terrorism cannot be solved by military approach alone, they find it imperative to promote military-to-military cooperation against terrorism through regular intelligence exchange and information sharing. Joint-military training on counterterrorism can also be explored to operationalize their defense cooperation. This area of cooperation is less problematic because of inter-national understanding to combat terrorism.

## Maritime Security

Maritime security is also an area where the Philippines and China can operationalize their defense and military cooperation. Though it is so broad a concept that it includes panoply of notions such as maritime safety, port security, freedom of navigation, security of the sea lines of communications, security from piracy attacks including armed robberies against ships, and most recently, security from maritime terrorism, maritime security is a common issue of both countries that they have to address.[81]

As an archipelago, the Philippines' concern of maritime security is inherently important. China is also considered as a maritime nation that heavily depends on the sea for commerce, trade, and resource supplies. China is broadening its cooperation with ASEAN countries in the area of maritime security. A Chinese military official even proposed joint maritime military exercises between China and ASEAN coun-tries.[82] In November 2004, the Philippines and China — along with other ASEAN members plus South Korea, Japan, Bangladesh, India, and Sri Lanka — signed the Regional Cooperation Agreement on Combating Piracy and Armed Robbery against Ships in Asia. This agreement indicates the prospects for maritime security coopera-tion in Southeast Asia.[83] During the first Philippines–China Defense and Security Dialogue in Manila on May 22–25, 2005, China strongly encouraged the Philippines to conduct a joint maritime security exercise, particularly in the area of search-and-rescue operations. The idea of strengthening maritime security cooperation between the Philippines and China was reiterated during the second Philippines–China Defense and Security Dialogue in Beijing on October 9–13, 2006.

Maritime security is therefore a viable area where the Philippines and China can operationalize their defense and military cooperation. Maritime security coopera-tion can even provide opportunities to promote trust and confidence between the Philippines and China in the management and avoidance of conflicts in the South China Sea.[84]

## Transnational Crimes

The Philippines and China have common concerns in combating transnational crimes. The Philippine Center on Transnational Crime considers this problem as one of the major nontraditional security concerns of the country. In China's

National Defense 2004, Beijing stressed the importance of international cooperation to combat transnational crimes. In fact, there are Chinese organized crime groups in cahoots with other crime groups in Southeast Asia, which includes the Philippines. These crime groups are involved in narcotic trade, human trafficking, and money laundering.[85] The attendant social costs of transnational crimes are serious security concerns of both countries. In fact, transnational crime has become a major threat to domestic security, inter-state relations, and global security.[86] This menace has "already begun to undermine the foundations of the state and the fabric and values of societies as well as to strain relations among states and threaten the stability of the international community."[87] Thus, the Philippines and China have converging interests in combating transnational crimes.

The Philippines and China have signed two documents that can promote defense cooperation to combat transnational crimes. These are (1) the Memorandum of Understanding on Cooperation against Illicit Traffic and Abuse of Narcotic Drugs, Psychotropic Substances and Precursor Chemicals, and (2) the Memorandum of Understanding on Cooperation in Combating Transnational Crime. When President Arroyo visited China in September 2004, she underscored the need to improve the security cooperation mechanism between the two countries and to promote judicial assistance in order to combat transnational crimes more effectively. When President Hu Jintao made a reciprocal visit to the Philippines in April 2005, he urged the Philippine government to increase their bilateral cooperation in security in order to combat transnational crimes. In their joint statement following the visit of President Jintao, the Philippines and China expressed their willingness to strengthen cooperation in nontraditional security areas such as combating drugs and transnational crimes. China and the Philippines can operationalize their cooperation in this area through deeper intelligence exchange, frequent joint training, and meaningful information sharing.

# Conclusion

The Philippines and China began to cooperate in defense and military areas after 30 years of their diplomatic relations. The MOU on defense cooperation signed in 2004 was a turning point in their bilateral ties. Though the two countries are optimistic that their defense cooperation can elevate their bilateral ties to a higher plane, there are realities in inter-state relations that they have to face. Philippines–China defense and military cooperation is cumbersome to situate in the context of Philippines–American security alliance and China–U.S. strategic competition. Territorial issues in the South China Sea and the ongoing conflict in the Taiwan Strait are hard security issues that the Philippines and China have to inevitably contend with in the future to test the viability of their defense relations.

However, there are nontraditional security issues that can make Philippines–China defense relations less controversial and problematic. Issues of international terrorism, maritime security, and transnational crimes provide opportunities for the Philippines and China to pursue their defense and military cooperation without causing fears among its neighbors, particularly the United States.

For the Philippines, managing its relations with China and the United States in the area of hard politics is a dilemma in its strategic policy. But rather than being "torn between two lovers," the challenge for the Philippines is how to get the best of both worlds without necessarily offending either one of them. Managing Philippines–China defense relations and Philippines–American security alliance is a real test of diplomatic skills for the Philippines. To maintain good relations and to maximize its trade with China, the Philippines may strategically bandwagon with China but not at the expense of its security relations with the United States. The most common approach to Southeast Asian countries to a rapidly growing power of China is "low-balancing" with the United States, "combined with efforts to assure and engage China."[88]

For China, the challenge is how to effectively convince the Philippines and the United States that its strategic intention as a rapidly growing power is benign. Though China is presently adopting the principle of "peaceful rise," there are still doubts among its neighbors regarding whether China will continue to peacefully rise in the future. Uncertainties associated with the rise of China are still causing regional and global apprehensions. China has to exert greater effort to assure its neighbors that its strategic intention as a major Asian power, and eventually a global power, is peaceful and responsible now and in the future.

## Endnotes

1. Milton Walter Meyer, *A Diplomatic History of the Philippine Republic* (Honolulu: University of Hawaii Press, 1965), p. 60.
2. Jose Ingles, *Philippine Foreign Policy* (Manila: Lyceum of the Philippines Press, 1982), p. 141.
3. Jose G. Syjuco, *Military Education in the Philippines* (Quezon City: New Day Publishers, 1977. Reprinted by St. Pancratius Print, Inc., 2001).
4. Jose Ma. Sison even wrote an ideological book propagating Maoism in the Philippines. See Amado Guerrero, *Philippine Society and Revolution* (Oakland: International Association of Filipino Patriots, 1979). For excellent discussions on the history and dynamics of the Communist movement in the Philippines, see Kathleen Weekley, *The Communist Party of the Philippines, 1968–1993: A Story of Its Theory and Practice* (Quezon City: University of the Philippines Press, 2001); Patricio N. Abinales, *Fellow Traveler: Essays on Filipino Communism* (Quezon City: University of the Philippines Press, 2001); Joel Rocamora, *Breaking Through: The Struggle within the Communist Party of the Philippines* (Pasig City: Anvil Publishing, Inc., 1994); Alfredo B. Saulo, *Communism in the Philippines: An Introduction* (Quezon City: Ateneo de Manila University Press, 1990); and Greg R. Jones, *Red Revolution: Inside the Philippine Guerilla Movement* (Boulder, San Francisco, London: Westview Press, 1989).

5. Aileen San Pablo-Baviera, "Perceptions of a China Threat: A Philippines Perspective," in Herbert Yee and Ian Storey (eds.), *The China Treat: Perceptions, Myths and Reality* (New York and London: Routledge Curzon, 2002), p. 249.
6. For a collection of excellent articles on the status of ethnic Chinese in Southeast Asia, see Teresita Ang See and Go Bon Juan, *The Ethnic Chinese* (Manila: Kaisa Para sa Kaunlaran, Inc., 1994).
7. Kenneth W. Allen and Eric A. McVadon, *China's Foreign Military Relations* (Washington, DC: Henry L. Stimson Center, 1999), p. 3.
8. Kenneth Allen, "China's Foreign Military Relations with Asia–Pacific," *Journal of Contemporary China*, Vol. 10, No. 29 (2001), p. 647.
9. Melissa G. Curley and Hong Liu (eds.), *China and Southeast Asia: Changing Socio-Cultural Interactions* (Hong Kong: Centre of Asian Studies, the University of Hong Kong, 2002).
10. R. Tasker, "A Line in the Sand," *Far Eastern Economic Review* (April 6, 1995). Also see Koong Pai Ching, "Southeast Asian Countries' Perceptions of China's Military Modernization," (The Cigur Center Conference Paper) at: http://www.gwu.edu/AsiaPapers/koong.htm (accessed on April 17, 2004), p. 7.
11. "Ramos Shift Military Role to External Threats," *Foreign Broadcast and Information Service* (April 24, 1995).
12. Ibid.
13. Armed Forces of the Philippines, *AFP Modernization Program Primer* (Quezon City: General Headquarters, 1998). Also see Ian James Storey, "Creeping Assertiveness: China, the Philippines and the South China Sea Dispute," *Contemporary Southeast Asia*, Vol. 21, No. 1 (April 1999), pp. 95–118.
14. For the author's detailed discussion of this issue, see Rommel C. Banlaoi, "The ASEAN Regional Forum and the Management of Conflicts in the South China Sea" in James K. Chin and Nicholas Thomas (eds.), *China-ASEAN: Changing Political and Strategic Ties* (Hong Kong: Centre of Asian Studies, the University of Hong Kong, 2005), pp. 181–209.
15. See pertinent BBC reports at: http://news.bbc.co.uk/1/hi/world/asia-pacific/352214.stm (accessed on December 12, 2003).
16. Ibid.
17. "Scarborough Shoal — The Next Mischief Reef?" Virtual Information Center Press Summary at: http://www.vic-info.org/regionstop.nsf/0/5dfb865fb0f31fbf8a2568b10 0094a0f?OpenDocument (accessed on March 16, 2004).
18. See Rommel C. Banlaoi, "Philippines–China Defense Relations: Sustaining Friendship, Enhancing Cooperation?" (Paper presented to the Centre of Asian Studies, University of Hong Kong, April 19, 2004).
19. For a serious analysis of their defense ties after 9/11, see Armando S. Rodriguez, "An Analysis of RP–China Defense Relations After 9/11" (MA Thesis: National Defense College of the Philippines, 2003).
20. "South China Sea Unites Not Divides China, RP: Arroyo," *The Philippine Star* (September 28, 2002).
21. Rommel C. Banlaoi, "Philippine Defense Policy Perspectives on the South China Sea and the Rise of China," *Journal of Asia Pacific Studies*, No. 2 (2002), pp. 10–15.
22. Aileen S.P. Baviera, *Comprehensive Engagement: Strategic Issues in Philippines–China Relations* (New Manila: Philippine–China Development Resource Center, 2000).
23. Gloria Macapagal Arroyo, "Foreword."

24. Department of Foreign Affairs, *Policy Paper on China* (Pasay City: DFA Office of Policy Planning and Coordination, October 2001).

25. Rommel Banlaoi, "Philippines–China Defense Relations: Implications for Philippine National Security" (A policy paper included in the Reference Folder of Secretary of National Defense's visit to China on November 7–14, 2004).

26. Department of National Defense, *Philippines' Engagement Plan with China on Defense and Security* (A draft policy paper, 2004).

27. "Philippines–China Trade Exceeds 13 Billion U.S. Dollars," *Philippine Star* (June 12, 2005).

28. For the author's view on the rise of China, see Rommel C. Banlaoi, "Southeast Asian Perspectives on the Rise of China: Regional Security after 9/11," *Parameters: U.S. Army War College Quarterly*, Vol. 37, No. 2 (Summer 2003), pp. 98–107.

29. See Virtual Information Center, "GMA Visits China (September 1–3, 2004)—A Special Press Summary" at: http://www.vic-info.org/RegionsTop.nsf/0/8ed4a606eb71 85250a256f09007bb0a1?OpenDocument (accessed on October 3, 2005).

30. Department of National Defense, *Reference Folder: SND's Visit to PROC* (Office of the Assistant Secretary for Policy and Special Concerns, November 7–14, 2004).

31. Ibid.

32. Rommel C. Banlaoi, "China's Anti-Secession Law: Implications for Philippines–China Defense Relations" (Paper delivered to the Roundtable Discussion on "China's Anti-Secession Law: Implications for Philippines–China Relations" held at the Social Science Building of the Ateneo De Manila University, June 17, 2005).

33. *Mutual Defense Treaty between the Republic of the Philippines and the United States of America* (August 30, 1951), Article VIII.

34. The Senate of the Philippines, *The Visiting Forces Agreement: The Senate Decision* (City of Pasay: The Office of the Philippine Senate Publication, 1999).

35. For an elaboration of this argument, see Rommel C. Banlaoi, "American Strategic Intentions in the War on Terrorism in Southeast Asia" in Wang Xinsheng, Yu Changsen and Cao Yunhua (eds.), *International Anti-Terrorism and Asia Pacific Security* (Guangzhou: Center for Asia–Pacific Studies, 2003), pp. 1–64. Also see Rommel C. Banlaoi, *The War on Terrorism in Southeast Asia* (Quezon City: Strategic and Integrative Studies Center, 2003), Chapter 4. The full copy of this book is also available at: http:// www.apan-info.net/terrorism/banlaoiBook/index.htm.

36. Zhai Kun, "What Underlies the U.S.–Philippine Joint Military Exercises," *Beijing Review* (March 14, 2002), p. 9. Also cited in J. Mohan Malik, "Dragon on Terrorism: Assessing China's Tactical Gains and Strategic Losses after September 11," *Contemporary Southeast Asia*, Vol. 24, No. 2 (August 2002), p. 273.

37. See quotes at: http://taipeitimes.com/news/2002/07/29/print/0000158149 (accessed on August 1, 2002).

38. *Mutual Logistics Support Agreement* (November 21, 2002), Chapter III.

39. Rommel C. Banlaoi, "The Role of Philippine–American Relations in the Global Campaign against Terrorism: Implications for Regional Security," *Contemporary Southeast Asia*, Vol. 24, No. 2 (August 2002), pp. 294–312.

40. American Forces Information Service, "Philippines to Become Major non-NATO Ally, Bush Says" at: http://www.defenselink.mil/news/My2003/n05192003_200305193. html (accessed on October 3, 2005).

41. *RP–U.S. Joint Defense Assessment Update* (September 3, 2003).

42. *Report of the U.S.–Philippine Joint Defense Assessment* (April 2001).

43. Office of the Assistant Chief of Staff for Plans and Programs of the Armed Forces of the Philippines, *Status of U.S. Security Assistance to the Philippines* (Quezon City: Armed Forces of the Philippines General Headquarters, 2005).

44. Volt Contreras, "China Military Assist to RP Does Not Faze US, says Exec," *Philippine Daily Inquirer* (June 27, 2005).

45. Ibid.

46. Aileen S.P. Baviera, "The U.S. Factor in U.S. Alliances in East Asia and the Pacific," *Australian Journal of International Affairs*, Vol. 57, No. 2 (2003), pp. 339–352.

47. Speech of Dr. Alberto G. Romulo, Secretary of Foreign Affairs, at the Heritage Foundation, Washington, D.C., May 18, 2005. For a complete copy of the speech, see http://www.manilatimes.net/national/2005/may/26/yehey/opinion/20050526opi5. html.

48. Ibid.

49. Department of National Defense, "Philippine Defense Reform Program" (PDR) at: http://www.dnd.gov.ph/DNDWEBPAGE_files/html/pdrpge.htm (accessed on October 5, 2005).

50. For a detailed analysis of this issue, see Rommel C. Banlaoi, "The Philippines in China–U.S. Relations: A Strategic Assessment" (Lecture delivered to the Chinese Academy of Social Sciences, Institute of Asia Pacific Studies, Beijing, China, on August 11, 2003).

51. Robert S. Ross, "The Geography of Peace: East Asia in the Twenty-First Century," *International Security*, Vol. 23, No. 4 (Spring 1999), pp. 81–118.

52. Shannon Tow, "Southeast Asia in the Sino–U.S. Strategic Balance," *Contemporary Southeast Asia*, Vol. 26, No. 3 (December 2004), pp. 434–459.

53. Office of the Secretary of Defense, *Annual Report to Congress: The Military Power of the People's Republic of China, 2005* (Washington, DC: Department of Defense, 2005).

54. Ibid., p. 8.

55. Joseph Grieco, "China and American in a New World Polity" in Carolyn W. Pumphrey (ed.), *The Rise of China in Asia: Security Implications* (Carlisle, PA: Strategic Studies Institute, 2002) p. 21.

56. Marvin C. Ott, "Southeast Asia and the United States: Policy without Strategy," *PACNET Newsletter*, No. 21 (May 28, 1999). Also at: http://www/csis.org/pacfor/pac2199.html.

57. Robert G. Kaiser, "2025 Vision: A China Bent on Asian Dominance," *Washington Post* (March 17, 2000), p. A25.

58. The United States Commission on National Security/21st Century, *Seeking a National Strategy: A Concert for Preserving Security and Promoting Freedom* (April 15, 2000), p. 9.

59. National Intelligence Council, *Global Trends 2015: A Dialogue about the Future with Nongovernment Experts* (National Foreign Intelligence Board, NIC 2000-02, December 2000), p. 63.

60. The Commission on America's National Interests, *America's National Interests: A Report of the Commission on America's National Interests* (July 2000), p. 64.

61. *Report to Congress of the U.S.–China Security Review Commission* (Washington, DC: U.S.–China Economic and Security Review Commission, July 2002).

62. Ibid.

63. Bill Gertz, *The China Threat: How the People's Republic Targets America* (Washington, DC: Regnery 2000), p. 199.

64. Herbert Yee and Ian Storey (eds.), *The China Threat: Perceptions, Myths and Reality* (New York and London: Routledge Curzon, 2002), pp. 2–6.

65. Nicholas J. Wheeler and Ken Booth, "The Security Dilemma" in John Baylis and N.J. Rennger (eds.), *Dilemmas of World Politics: International Issues in a Changing World* (Oxford: Clarendon Press, 1992), pp. 29–60. Also see Jack Snyder, "Perceptions of the Security Dilemma in 1914," in Robert Jervis, Richard Ned Lebow, and Janice Gross Stein (eds.), *Psychology and Deterrence* (Baltimore: The John Hopkins University Press, 1985), p. 155.

66. Office of the Secretary of Defense, *Annual Report to Congress: The Military Power of the People's Republic of China, 2005*, "Executive Summary."

67. Geoff Metcalf, "China's Plan to Control the World," *World Net Daily* (October 8, 2000). Also at: http://www.mvcf.com/news/cache/00154/.

68. Michael D. Swaine and Ashley J. Tellis, *Interpreting China's Grand Strategy: Past, Present, and Future* (Santa Monica, CA: RAND, 2000), pp. 232–233.

69. Denny Roy, "Southeast Asia and China: Balancing or Bandwagoning?" *Contemporary Southeast Asia*, Vol. 27, No. 2 (August 2005), p. 320.

70. Rommel C. Banlaoi, "The War on Terrorism in Southeast Asia: Strategic Implications for Philippines–China–U.S. Relations" (Paper presented to the Institute of Southeast Asian Studies, Zhongshan University, Guanzhou China, January 7, 2003).

71. See for example *Bilateral Confidence Building with China in Relation to the South China Sea Disputes: A Philippine Perspective* (Ontario, Canada: Department of Foreign Affairs and International Trade, 2001); Michael Studeman, "Calculating China's Advances in the South China Sea: Identifying the Triggers of Expansionism," *Naval War College Review* (Spring 1998); Ian James Storey, "Creeping Assertiveness: China, the Philippines and the South China Sea Dispute," *Contemporary Southeast Asia*, Vol. 21, No. 1 (April 1999); Mark J. Valencia, Jon M. Van Dyke, and Noel A. Ludwig, *Sharing the Resources of the South China Sea*, Paperback edition (Honolulu: University of Hawaii Press, 1999); Shee Pon Kim, "The South China Sea in China's Strategic Thinking," *Contemporary Southeast Asia*, Vol. 19, No. 4 (March 1998); Ralph A. Cossa, "Security Implications of Conflict in the South China Sea: Exploring Potential Triggers of Conflict," *A Pacific Forum CSIS Special Report*," PacNet Newsletter #16 (April 17, 1998); Daniel Dzurek, *The Spratly Islands Disputes* (Durham: International Boundaries Research Uni, 1996); Chen Jie, "China's Spratly Policy: With Special Reference to the Philippines and Malaysia," *Asian Survey*, Vol. 34, No. 10 (October 1994); and Julius C. Parrenas, "Geopolitical Dimensions of the Spratly Islands Dispute," *Foreign Relations Journal*, Vol. VIII, No. 1 (March 1993).

72. For an attempt, see Natalio C. Ecarma III, *Strengthening Philippines–China Defense Relations* (Master's Thesis: National Defense College of the Philippines, 2005).

73. *Kuik Cheng-Chwee*, "Multilateralism in China's ASEAN Policy: Its Evolution, Characteristics, and Aspiration," *Contemporary Southeast Asia*, Vol. 27, No. 1 (April 2005).

74. An interview with a high-ranking naval officer assigned to monitor the situation in the South China Sea (November 7, 2005).

75. Carl Baker, China–Philippines Relations: Cautious Cooperation" in Satu Limaye (ed.), *Asia's Bilateral Relations* (Honolulu: Asia Pacific Center for Security Studies, 2004.).

76. Ibid.

77. David Mitrany, "The Functionalist Approach to World Organization," *International Affairs*, XXIV (July 1948).

78. To read some existing literatures on the ASG, see Djanicelle J. Berreveld, *Terrorism in the Philippines: The Bloody Trail of Abu Sayyaf, Bin Laden's East Asian Connection* (San Jose: Writers Club Press, 2001); Maria Ressa, *Seeds of Terror: An Eyewitness Account of Al-Qaeda's Newest Center of Operations in Southeast Asia* (New York: Free Press, 2003); and Zachary Abuza, *Militant Islam in Southeast Asia: The Crucible of Terror* (London: Lynne Rienner Publishers, Inc., 2003). For an insightful analysis on the evolution of ASG, see Rohan Gunaratna, "The Evolution and Tactics of the Abu Sayyaf Group," *Janes Intelligence Review* (July 2001). For an excellent historical analysis, see Graham H. Turbiville, Jr., "Bearer of the Sword," *Military Review* (March/April 2002), pp. 38–47. For an analysis of ASG and civil society, see Alfredo Filler, "The Abu Sayyaf Group: A Growing Menace to Civil Society," *Terrorism and Political Violence*, Vol. 14, No. 4 (Winter 2002). Also see Larry Niksch, "Abu Sayyaf: Target of Philippine–U.S. Anti-Terrorism Cooperation," *CRS Report for Congress* (January 25, 2002); and Mark Turner, "Terrorism and Secession in the Southern Philippines: The Rise of the Abu Sayyaf," *Contemporary Southeast Asia*, Vol. 17, No. 1 (June 1995), pp. 1–19. Also see Rommel C. Banlaoi, "Maritime Terrorism in Southeast Asia: The Abu Sayyaf Threat," *Naval War College Review*, Vol. 58, No. 4 (Autumn 2005), pp. 63–80; Eusaquito P. Manalo, *Philippine Response to Terrorism: The Abu Sayyaf Group* (MA Thesis: Naval Post Graduate School, Monterey, California, December 2004).
79. *Chien-Peng Chung,* "China's 'War on Terror': September 11 and Uighur Separatism," *Foreign Affairs* (July–August 2002).
80. Paolo Romero "RP, China to Push Formation of Asian Anti-Terror Alliance, *The Philippines Star* (September 1, 2003), at: http://Www.Newsflash.Org/2003/05/Hl/Hl018695.htm (accessed on October 6, 2005).
81. Rommel C. Banlaoi, "Maritime Security Outlook for Southeast Asia," in Joshua Ho and Catherine Zara Raymond (eds.), *The Best of Times, The Worst of Times: Maritime Security in the Asia Pacific* (Singapore: World Scientific, 2005), pp. 59–79.
82. Lee Kim Chew, "China Could Play Part in ASEAN's Maritime Security," *Strait Times* (June 24, 2004).
83. John Bradford, "The Growing Prospects for Maritime Security Cooperation in Southeast Asia," *Naval War College Review*, Vol. 58, No. 3 (Summer 2005), pp. 63–86.
84. Aileen S.P. Baviera, "Maritime Security in Southeast Asia and the South China Sea: A View from the Philippines" (Paper presented at the International Conference on "Promoting Trust and Confidence in Southeast Asia: Cooperation and Conflict Avoidance" held at the Manila Hotel on October 17–18, 1997).
85. Glen Curtis, Seth Ellan, Rexford Hudson, and Nina Kollars, *Transnational Activities of Chinese Crime Organizations* (Washington, DC: Library of Congress, 2003), p. 37.
86. Carolina G. Hernandez and Gina R. Pattugalan (eds.), *Transnational Crime and Regional Security in the Asia Pacific* (Quezon City: Institute for Strategic and Development Studies, Inc., 1999).
87. Ibid., p. ii.
88. Roy, "Southeast Asia and China: Balancing or Bandwagoning?" p. 319.

# Chapter 10

# Broadening Philippine–Australia Defense Relations in the Post-9/11 Era: Issues and Prospects*

## Introduction

Since the Bali terrorist bombings in October 2002, Australia has been initiating various strategic initiatives to strengthen its web of bilateral defense relations in Southeast Asia. Canberra has signed an antiterrorism agreement with Southeast Asian countries like Indonesia, Malaysia, the Philippines, and Thailand. This is part of Australia's overarching strategy of expanding its bilateral relations in Southeast Asia to advance its national interests, which are perceived to be threatened by traditional and nontraditional security issues in Asia, particularly the specter of international terrorism.[1] Among countries in the region, the Philippines has the potential to forge a defense partnership with Australia in Southeast Asia due in large part to geographic proximity and cultural familiarity. Yet, the deeper basis for broadening their defense ties lies in their shared regional security perspectives.

This chapter examines the state of Philippine–Australia defense relations since September 11 and identifies some issues and prospects for expanding their defense

---

* This chapter is taken from *Contemporary Southeast Asia*, Vol. 25, No. 3 (December 2003), pp. 473–488. Reproduced here with the kind permission of the publisher, Institute of Southeast Asian Studies, Singapore, http://bookshop.iseas.edu.sg.

relations. It argues that besides geographic proximity and cultural familiarity, the more pressing convergence lies in their security interests in the region, especially in the context of the global campaign against terrorism. It concludes that the broadening of Philippine–Australia defense ties can contribute to the web of bilateral defense relations of like-minded states in Southeast Asia necessary for the promotion of regional peace and stability.

## The Origin of Philippine–Australia Defense Relations

Although the Philippines and Australia have robust interactions in various multilateral forums such as the ASEAN Regional Forum (ARF), the Asia–Pacific Economic Cooperation, and the ASEAN Australia Dialogue, among others, broadening their bilateral relations is still a more manageable and efficient way to advance their common security interests. In fact, security studies theory argues that sovereign states adopt bilateralism because there are interests that are better advanced by maintaining separate relationships with other actors.[2] Moreover, bilateralism creates a "hub and spokes" pattern of alliance development and maintenance for states to pursue their common security interests.[3]

Philippine official sources trace the origin of Philippine–Australia bilateral relations to the 19th century when Australian missionaries came to the Philippine Islands to proselytize the inhabitants. Although commercial relations were already recorded during that period, the scale of bilateral trade between both countries was very modest.[4] Trade relations only improved in the early part of the 20th century when Australia became the Philippines' fifth largest source of imports, particularly of coal and beef.[5]

Australia became an important part of Philippine history when President Manuel L. Quezon established his government-in-exile in Australia at the height of the Japanese occupation of the Philippines in the 1940s. During World War II, Australia, as an American ally in the Asia–Pacific, deployed some troops to the Philippines to help liberate the country from the Japanese imperial forces. When the Philippines achieved its independence, Canberra opened a consular office in Manila in 1946 and assisted the economic reconstruction of the Philippines within the framework of the Colombo Plan established in 1951.

The defense relationship of both countries officially started in 1954 when they joined the Southeast Asia Treaty Organization (SEATO). The formation of SEATO was an American experiment of alliance strategy in Southeast Asia using the North Atlantic Treaty Organization (NATO) of Europe as its model.[6] The Philippines and Australia joined the organization because both shared the perception of common threat posed by Communist expansionism in Southeast Asia. Moreover, the Philippines and Australia had close defense ties with the United States.

SEATO suffered its demise in 1977 when the organization failed to pursue constructive intervention in Indochina. As a result, Philippine–Australia defense relations became practically moribund while bilateral relations were increasingly shaped by diplomatic and economic imperatives. Their diplomatic relations started to improve when the Philippines opened its embassy in Canberra in 1962, and further developed when Australia joined the Philippines Assistance Program established in 1989. Filipino migration to Australia increased to 103,942 as of 2001.[7] According to the Philippine Bureau of Immigration, Filipinos ranked eighth among the source of migrants to Australia,[8] making the country another land of milk and honey for Filipinos.

When both countries signed the Philippine–Australia Trade Agreement in 1975, their two-way trade also dramatically improved. In 1998 alone, Australia ranked 17th as an export destination for Philippine exports and 11th as a source of Philippine imports.[9] Their economic relations further grew when both signed the Philippine Investment Promotion and Protection Agreement in 1994. In view of the success of their bilateral relations in the diplomatic and economic spheres, they decided to widen the scope of their cooperation by signing a Memorandum of Understanding (MOU) on Defense Cooperation in 1995. The MOU established the foundation for the development of Philippine–Australia defense relations.

## The State of Philippine–Australia Defense Relations

The 1995 MOU on defense cooperation is a landmark for the defense relations of both countries because it formalizes their defense cooperation, which had long been neglected since the demise of SEATO. The 1995 MOU served as a useful basis to strengthen defense relations in the wake of strategic uncertainties emerging in the Asia–Pacific as a consequence of the end of the cold war and the demise of the Soviet Union. The MOU provides the overarching mechanism in the exploration of various opportunities to intensify their defense ties such as the mutual benefits inherent in cooperative defense activities and exchanges between their respective military establishments. Specifically, both countries agreed to cooperate in the following areas:

- Mutual access by units and personnel to each others' defense facilities, including facilities for refueling and replenishment of ship and aircraft, diversion airfields for aircraft, and planned and emergency repair and maintenance of ships and aircraft.
- Participation in joint training and military exercises.
- Access by defense personnel, including exchanges of students and instructors, to training facilities and training courses in the country of the other party.
- Exchange of information on defense matters.
- Cooperation in defense science and technology matters especially in areas where defense research and development can benefit from the unique environment possessed by each country.

■ Identification of common or similar requirements for defense-related goods and services as well as opportunities for Philippine and Australian companies to participate in meeting those requirements.

To provide policy direction and to initiate, coordinate, and monitor the different activities carried out under the MOU, both countries established the Republic of the Philippines–Australia Joint Defense Cooperation Committee cochaired by a senior representative from each country. The joint committee is authorized to establish subcommittees to effectively address and implement their specific projects on defense matters. Thus, the Philippine–Australia Defense Cooperation Working Group was created to undertake programs and projects on defense-related matters. However, most of the projects implemented were largely in the area of "soft" defense, primarily dominated by confidence-building measures (CBMs). The most robust area of defense cooperation between the two countries is in the education and training of Filipino military officers and defense officials in Australia. Because of the MOU, Australia has become the major source of training and education of Filipino military officers and defense personnel. The quota for Filipino military officers undergoing training and education in Australia has increased tremendously (300%) since 1995. Australia is, in fact, replacing the United States as the biggest provider of military education to the Armed Forces of the Philippines (AFP).

As part of their CBMs on security issues, both countries have also conducted track-two activities. Both countries conduct the annual security dialogues called Philippine–Australia Defense Dialogue on Security (PADS), initiated by their respective foreign affairs departments.[10] PADS has also provided a forum for their respective defense offices to discuss Philippine–Australia defense diplomacy. PADS pursued mutual sharing of perspectives on various security issues facing both countries, ranging from regional conflicts like the South China Sea disputes, the Korean problem, the China–Taiwan conflict, and the Kashmir dispute to other regional security concerns like the rise of China, the role of major powers, and the creation of the ARF.

Although PADS provided a venue for Manila and Canberra to level off their expectations and to explore other avenues of defense and security cooperation, the conduct of PADS was rather moot and academic because no tangible bilateral defense cooperation matter was discussed beyond CBMs. In fact, PADS participants were reluctant to discuss controversial issues of their relations and were discreet in their articulation of security issues confronting them. Frank and candid discussions were avoided except for the enunciation of their official lines.

At the track-two level, both countries also conducted the Philippine–Australia Strategic Forum (PASFOR) held at the National Defense College of the Philippines November 26–29, 2001.[11] Like the PADS, the PASFOR dialogue has provided the two countries excellent forums to discuss their respective security concerns and to exchange views on various strategic issues facing the Asia–Pacific region. Unlike PADS, however, PASFOR discussions were more frank and candid due to the principle of nonattribution and academic freedom. PASFOR discussed "hard" security issues like defense industry and procurement reforms, defense planning, defense budgeting, and even the territorial limits of the Philippines. PASFOR also tackled "soft" security issues like transnational crime, maritime security, peacekeeping operations, and the regional security outlook, among others.[12] In fact, Australian participants in PASFOR were noted academics reflecting the strategic importance of the Philippines for Australia.[13] Unfortunately, the PASFOR initiative was not sustained due to some changes in the priorities of both countries as a result of the global campaign against terrorism.

The PADS and the PASFOR initiatives could have served as valuable instruments in shaping the two countries' bilateral defense diplomacy programs, had they been sustained. Unfortunately, the global campaign against terrorism and the American return to Southeast Asia halted the momentum of Philippine–Australia exchanges on regional security because the Philippines concentrated on reinvigorating its security alliance with the United States. As a result, Philippine–Australia defense exchanges have been marginalized and relegated to the periphery of Philippine defense diplomacy programs. Since 9/11 the Philippines has been focusing its energy on reviving its defense alliance with the United States in order to build its capacity not only in countering terrorism but also in addressing various threats to its security, particularly the defense of the Kalayaan Island Group in the South China Sea. Thus, Philippine bilateral defense diplomacy since September 11 has been largely shaped by its relations with the United States, marginalizing Philippine defense relations with other countries, including Australia. Indeed, the cornerstone of Philippine defense diplomacy since September 11 is the strengthening of Philippine–American defense relations.

The reinvigoration of Philippine–American defense relations is, therefore, diminishing Canberra's role in Philippine defense diplomacy. This is quite unfortunate considering the fact that, after the American withdrawal from the Philippines in 1991, Australia extended various forms of assistance to the Philippine defense establishment. When the United States downgraded its military and defense relations with the Philippines after its withdrawal from Clark and Subic Bays, Canberra expressed willingness to enhance its defense relations with Manila. When the United States disengaged itself from the AFP defense capability development programs, the Australian Ministry of Defense signified its interest in supporting the Philippines in the implementation of the AFP Modernization Program.[14] When the United States reduced its slots for Filipinos in the International Military Education and Training Program, Canberra increased its slots for Filipinos undergoing defense education and training in various institutions in Australia. In short, Australia came to the rescue of the Philippines during the lowest point of Manila's bilateral defense diplomacy with the United States.

To sustain their strategic exchanges and to explore the future direction of Philippine–Australia defense relations after September 11, Manila's National Defense Office for Strategic Assessment and International Policies organized the

Philippine–Australia Defense Engagement Talks on May 6–7, 2003, in Camp Aguinaldo, Quezon City.[15] At these talks, both countries reaffirmed their common values and shared interests in regional security and expressed their commitment to conduct strategic dialogues on a regular basis to broaden their defense ties. Although both countries have robust exchanges on various strategic concerns as part of the CBMs, there is a felt need to move forward and enhance their defense relations beyond the area of education and training. Geographic proximity and cultural familiarity are arguably factors conducive to a stronger relationship. Nevertheless, the most enduring basis on which to build broader defense relations is their shared perspective on regional security.

## Geographic Proximity

Although Australia belongs to Oceania, its immediate strategic space is Southeast Asia. Canberra's 2000 Defense White Paper articulates the importance of Southeast Asia in Australia's strategic interests and objectives and describes the region as its immediate neighbor.[16]

By virtue of geographic proximity, Australia is conceivably a part of the Southeast Asian security complex "whose major security perceptions and concerns are so interlinked that their national security problems cannot reasonably be analyzed or resolved apart from one another."[17] The October 2002 Bali bombings have demonstrated that an insecure Southeast Asia also means an insecure Australia. The 2003 Australia Defense Update even reiterated the importance of Southeast Asia in the security of the country and stressed anew that Southeast Asia is Australia's immediate region. The Philippines can be a reliable strategic partner of Australia in regional security due to geographic proximity. Although Indonesia is the nearest neighbor of Australia in the strictest geographic sense, the two countries have not overcome their historic animosities. Australia–Indonesia relations rapidly deteriorated in the wake of the 1999 East Timor crisis.[18] Moreover, Australia's very close relationship with the United States is also complicating Canberra's relations with Jakarta. Like Australia, the United States heavily criticized Indonesia's handling of the East Timor problem, resulting in the termination of their military ties. The fallout in Australia–Indonesia relations and U.S.–Indonesia relations in the wake of the 1999–2000 East Timor intervention[19] has left an indelible mark in Indonesia's defense diplomacy vis-à-vis the two countries. This situation makes it difficult for Canberra to build closer and deeper defense ties with Jakarta.

## Cultural Familiarity

As a former colony of the United States, the Philippines has long exposure to Western culture. This exposure to Western culture also created a profound impact on Philippine political culture. Like the West, the Philippines embraces the values of political and economic freedom; these similarities have helped the broadening of Philippine–Australia defense relations. The Australian embassy in Manila recognized this factor when it stated, "The Philippines, as a democratic, predominantly Christian country with a long exposure to western culture and a relatively well-educated, English-speaking population, has much in common with Australia."[20]

## Shared Regional Security Perspectives

The most enduring basis on which to broaden Philippine–Australia defense relations is their shared perspective on regional security.[21] The Philippines and Australia have common security interests in the peace and stability of Southeast Asia. Both countries regard their bilateral relations with the United States as an important factor for regional security. They have a convergence of interests in fighting terrorism in Southeast Asia, have common interests in the freedom of navigation in the South China Sea, share common security concerns in the maritime security of Southeast Asia, and regard China as a great security challenge to peace and prosperity in Southeast Asia.

### *Relations with the United States*

Both countries' defense and security policies are strongly based on their defense alliances with the United States. Their defense alliances with the United States are potential common denominators in the broadening of Philippine–Australia defense relations. Australia's Defense Update 2003 emphasizes that Canberra's defense relationship with Washington "remains a national asset."[22] Australia has, in fact, intensified its security alliance with the United States, especially in the aftermath of the October 2002 Bali terrorist bombings. The white paper produced by the Department of Foreign Affairs and Trade has even stressed that "the depth of security, economic and political ties that we have with the United States makes this a vital relationship."[23]

The 1998 Philippine Defense Policy Paper, on the other hand, states that the Philippine–American defense alliance as mandated by the Mutual Defense Treaty (MDT) enhances not only Philippine national defense and security but also contributes to regional stability.[24] In fact, the Philippines has revitalized its defense alliance with the United States as a result of its unwavering support for the American-led global campaign against terrorism.[25]

As American allies in the Asia–Pacific, the Philippines and Australia welcome the American presence in the region as a stabilizing factor. Both regard the continued commitment of the United States to regional stability as an important factor in the advancement not only of their national security interests but also for the maintenance of the prevailing balance of power in the Asia–Pacific region. The

Philippines and Australia also regard the return of the U.S. strategic presence in Southeast Asia after September 11 as one of the most significant developments in the security of the region.

## Terrorism in Southeast Asia

The Philippines and Australia share the same perspectives on the threat of terrorism in Southeast Asia. Thus both countries strongly support the global "war on terrorism." Because of the convergence of their strategic perspectives on terrorism, they signed a Memorandum of Understanding to Combat International Terrorism during the visit to Australia by Philippine Foreign Secretary Blas Ople on March 2–5, 2003. The MOU on terrorism is an important milestone in the broadening of their defense relations, as it reaffirms the commitment of both countries "to strengthen and expand" their cooperation to fight international terrorism and articulates the determination of both countries "to prevent, suppress and eliminate international terrorism in all its forms."[26] In the MOU, the Philippines and Australia decided to intensify their cooperation in the following areas:

- Information and intelligence assessment.
- Law enforcement, including the prevention and investigation of terrorist activities.
- Money laundering and the financing of international terrorism.
- The development of appropriate and effective counterterrorism legal, regulatory, and administrative regimes.
- Smuggling and border-control issues, including document and identity fraud.
- Illegal trafficking in weapons, ammunition, explosives and other destructive materials or substances.
- Defense cooperation relating to international terrorist activities.

To implement their cooperation in these areas, both countries decided to undertake the following forms of cooperation:

- Exchange of information and intelligence.
- Joint training exercises and activities.
- Assistance in the prevention, investigation, and prosecution of acts of terrorism.
- Collaboration of projects with mutual interest.
- Capacity-building initiatives, including training and education programs, convening of meetings, seminars, workshops, and conferences.
- Sharing best practices and procedures to strengthen cooperation.
- Consultation through regional and multilateral fora on issues relating to international terrorism and transnational organized crime.

## The South China Sea Disputes

The Philippines and Australia also have a convergence of strategic perspectives on the territorial disputes in the South China Sea. Although Australia is not a claimant state, it has a stake in the issue because of its interest in the freedom of navigation in the area.[27] Australian commerce and trade with Asian countries depend on freedom of navigation in the South China Sea. Australia's Asia–Pacific Security Outlook submitted to the ARF states that although Australia "does not take a position on competing claims in the South China Sea, which are a matter for the parties concerned to resolve," Australia is wary of "heightened tensions and rivalry between claimants" because "shipping routes important to Australia" pass through the South China Sea.[28]

Apparently, the Philippines' stake in the South China Sea is much greater than Australia's because of the issue of territorial sovereignty. However, like Australia, the Philippines is also cognizant of the implications of the South China Sea disputes for the freedom of navigation in the area. Because Australia is a mere interested observer in the South China Sea disputes, broadening Philippine–Australia defense relations will give Australia a louder voice in the Philippines to articulate Canberra's strategic interests in the South China Sea. The Philippines, on the other hand, can use its defense relations with Australia to leverage against China, which is the most powerful claimant state in the South China Sea.

## Maritime Security

The Philippines and Australia also share strategic perspectives on maritime security issues. Being an archipelagic state of more than 7,100 islands located between the South China Sea and the Pacific Ocean, the Philippines is a maritime state. Thus, maritime security is one of its foremost security concerns. Australia, on the other hand, is an island continent in a maritime region whose area of strategic interests is vast. Australia adjoins the Pacific Ocean in the east, the Indian Ocean in the west, the Southeast Asian archipelago in the north, and — sometimes forgotten — the Southern Ocean.[29] Maritime security issues are therefore in Australia's national interest.

One major maritime security concern of the Philippines is the perplexing problem of maritime jurisdiction. The Philippines has maritime claims overlapping with the exclusive economic zones of neighboring countries Indonesia, Malaysia, Vietnam, China, and Taiwan.[30] The passage of the 1992 Laws on Territorial Waters by the Beijing government declaring the whole South China Sea as part of Chinese territorial waters is also causing maritime security anxieties in the Philippines. The confirmed reports of the existence of terrorist networks in Southeast Asia have also increased the vulnerability of the region to maritime terrorism.[31]

Australia has also expressed anxieties over maritime issues in Southeast Asia because it regards Southeast Asia and its maritime security environment as part of its strategic space.[32] Broadening its defense relations with the Philippines can widen

Australia's network of bilateral relations in Southeast Asia to advance its maritime security interests in the region.

### The Rise of China

The rise of China is another factor in the broadening of Philippine–Australia defense relations. Although both countries have very good diplomatic and trade relations with China, they are wary of China's growing economic power because of its spill-over effects on China's growing military power. From being one of the world's least developed countries in the 1970s, China has developed one of the largest economies in the world.[33] The World Bank and the International Monetary Fund reported that from 1979 to 1997, China's gross domestic product grew at an average rate of 9.8%.[34] This phenomenal economic growth has enabled a significant expansion of China's defense budget.[35] In view of the burgeoning economic and military power of China, the Philippines and Australia are affected by the specter of a "China threat."[36]

The China threat, however, is not officially articulated by the defense officials of the Philippines and Australia. The Philippines has publicly declared China as a regional opportunity, with concomitant challenges, rather than a threat.[37] The Australian official line, on the other hand, states that policy toward China "should be built not on apprehensions but on a positive desire to incorporate China as a valued participant in regional security affairs."[38] Nevertheless, both countries are apprehensive of the growing power of a presumably aggressive China even as they express confidence that China will remain a benign and responsible Asian power.

## Broadening Philippine–Australia Defense Relations: Implications for Regional Security

Broadening Philippine–Australia defense relations would have some implications for regional security. Beijing will view the broadening of Philippine–Australia defense relations with suspicion because China does not want to see its neighbors "ganging up" against Beijing, particularly on the issue of the South China Sea. Although the ARF can provide a forum for the Philippines and Australia to strengthen their leverage vis-à-vis China, there are still many challenges that need to be overcome in enabling the ARF to function effectively as a multilateral security mechanism capable of enforcing its decisions on detractors. The ARF is still very much at the incipient stage of confidence building and has yet to move concretely toward the second and third stages, respectively, of preventive diplomacy and conflict resolution. Major powers have even expressed impatience over the ARF process because China wants the ARF to move forward only at a pace most comfortable to all participants (which also means at a pace most comfortable to China).[39]

The United States will welcome the broadening of Philippine–Australia defense relations as a complement to their bilateral alliances with Washington. But Washington would not be too keen to see Philippine–Australia defense relations evolve as a substitute to Philippine–American defense relations. In the case of Japan, as a major Asian power aspiring to be a normal state, Tokyo is watching all developments in bilateral defense relations of countries in Asia. However, Japan would not stand in the way of Philippine–Australian defense relations getting closer as long as that development does not affect its aspiration of becoming a normal Asian power.

Broadening Philippine–Australia defense relations will also matter to India because of its "Look East" policy. There is a strategic perception in New Delhi that China's strategy is to encircle India. Thus, India wants to establish friendships with Australia and Southeast Asian countries to counter China in the region. India will welcome the broadening of Philippine–Australia defense relations because of their common security interests to check China's growing influence in Southeast Asia. In fact, India is also rebuilding its defense ties with Australia because of common security interests.[40]

Southeast Asian countries will welcome the broadening of Philippine–Australia defense relations for purposes of regional stability. In general, Southeast Asia views a strong web of complementary rather than competitive bilateral defense relations in the region as a positive factor for regional security. Because the Philippines and Australia tend to share common values, strategic space, and regional security perspectives, there is a need to intensify their defense relations to effectively address their common security interests. Intensifying defense relations should not be limited to education and training and CBMs. It is in their mutual interest to start discussing "hard" defense issues to lend credence to their burgeoning defense ties.

In the short term, the Philippines and Australia will continue to strictly implement the provisions of their MOU on defense cooperation. In the September 11 context, the opportune moment could well have arrived to elevate this MOU into a full-blown bilateral agreement to enhance defense cooperation, especially in such areas as defense procurement, institutionalization of defense planning, and acquisition systems.

There is a need to elevate the status of their MOU on counterterrorism into a workable plan of action. The MOU does not have any provision for military cooperation, except for a token provision identifying the defense sector as one of the implementing agencies of the MOU. Although Australia sought to widen the scope of the document to include "joint military operations," the Philippine government did not accept the idea because of constitutional constraints. Thus, the final terms of the MOU referred only to joint training.[41]

In the medium term, both countries could explore the possibility of entering into a status of forces agreement (SOFA) similar but not necessarily identical to the Philippine–American Visiting Forces Agreement.* In comparison to the United

---

* On November 26, 2006, Australia and the Philippines agreed to sign a pact on status of forces to be ratified by the Philippine Senate. The agreement was similar to status of forces agreements among members of the North Atlantic Treaty Organization. Then Philippine Defense Secretary Avelino Cruz said that the agreement with Australia could also be used as a template for similar arrangements with Southeast Asian states, such as Brunei, Indonesia, Malaysia, and Singapore.

States, a Philippine–Australia SOFA would be less controversial because of the absence of colonial baggage. Through SOFA, the Philippine–Australian forces can work together well to address their mutual defense concerns. Their shared experiences in East Timor are good examples of how Australian and Filipino forces can work together to maintain regional peace and stability. In the long term, the Philippines and Australia could also consider exploring the possibility of entering into a mutual defense agreement. Their shared perspectives on regional security, cultural familiarity, and geographic proximity can foster a closer security relationship. This agreement can complement their existing mutual defense agreements with the United States to advance their mutual security interests.

Broadening the framework of Philippine–Australia relations has enormous potential to advance their common security interests. The Philippines and Australia do not have serious conflicts with each other. More importantly, both do not pose threats to each other. Since the establishment of diplomatic relations, their cooperation in various fields has been productive, long-standing, and strong. Australia and the Philippines are even described by their respective foreign affairs departments as "partners in development."[42] The strengthening of their partnership is reinforced by close people-to-people contacts.

In view of the fact that their relations are already robust in functional areas, there is a strong need to strengthen these relations to defense and security areas. As stressed by Minister Alexander Downer, "the goodwill engendered through the continuing development partnership will remain an important part of our relationship."[43] This relationship must necessarily include the broadening of their defense relations, which can contribute ultimately toward a stronger security architecture in Southeast Asia necessary for the promotion of regional peace and stability.

## Endnotes

1. See Department of Foreign Affairs and Trade, Advancing the National Interests: Australia's Foreign and Trade Policy White Paper (Canberra: Department of Foreign Affairs and Trade, 2003).
2. Brian L. Job, "Bilateralism and Multilateralism: Achieving the Right Balance in Security Relations," *Strength through Cooperation: Military Forces in the Asia-Pacific Region* (Washington, DC: Institute for Strategic Studies, National Defense University, 1997) at: http://www.ndu.edu/inss/books/Books%20-%201997/ Strength%20Through%20 Cooperation%201997/stcch13.html.
3. William T. Tow, "Assessing Bilateralism as a Security Phenomenon: Problems of Underassessment and Application (In an Asia–Pacific Context)" (Paper prepared for the Hawaii International Conference on Social Sciences, Honolulu, June 12, 2003), p. 2.
4. See Philippine Embassy in Canberra, "Overview of Relations," at: http://www. philembassy.au.com/bil-oview.htm.
5. Ibid.

6. For more discussion about SEATO and alliance strategy, see Leszek Buszynski, *The Failure of an Alliance Strategy* (Singapore: Singapore University Press, 1983).

7. Philippine Embassy in Canberra, "Overview of Relations," at: http://www.philembassy.au.com/bil-oview.htm. Also see Australian Department of Foreign Affairs and Trade, "Republic of the Philippines Country Brief" (March 2003) at: http://www.dfat.gov.au/geo/philippines/philippines_brief.html.

8. Philippine Embassy in Canberra, "The Filipino Community in Australia," at: http://www.philembassy.au.com/bil-filcom.htm.

9. Philippine Embassy in Canberra, "Trade Relations," at: http://www. philembassy.au.com/bil-trade.htm.

10. The author was a participant at the Third Philippine–Australia Dialogue on Security held on October 6, 2000 at the Century Park Hotel, Manila, as the official representative of the National Defense College of the Philippines.

11. The author was instrumental in the conduct of PASFOR when he proposed the project to Dr. Anthony Bergin during their meeting in Malaysia at the 15th Asia–Pacific Roundtable in 2001.

12. Australian Defense Studies Center and the National Defense College of the Philippines, "Philippine–Australia Strategic Forum (PASFOR): Australian Delegation Background Papers" (November 26–29, 2001).

13. Australian participants to PASFOR were Ainslie Barron, Anthony Bergin, Chris Chung, James Cotton, Alan Dupont, Sandy Gordon, Stefan Markowski, John McFarlane, Hugh Smith, Russel Trood, and Derek Woolner.

14. For a discussion on American disengagement in the Philippines, see Doug Bandow, "Instability in the Philippines: A Case Study for U.S. Disengagement," Foreign Policy Briefing, No. 64 (Cato Institute, March 21, 2001). Available at: http:// www.cato.org/pubs/fpbriefs/fpb64.pdf.

15. The author is a participant in this activity as consultant of the Department of National Defense, Office of the Assistant Secretary for Plans and Programs.

16. Commonwealth of Australia, Defense 2000: Our Future Defense Force (Canberra: Commonwealth of Australia, 2000), p. x.

17. Barry Buzan popularized the idea of the security complex. See Barry Buzan, Ole Waever, and Jaap de Wilde, *Security: A New Framework for Analysis* (London: Lynne Rienner Publishers, 1998), p. 12.

18. For more discussions on Australia–Indonesia relations, see Peter Chalk, *Australian Foreign and Defense Policy in the Wake of the 1999/2000 East Timor Intervention* (Santa Monica, California: RAND, 2001), Chapters 2–4.

19. Ibid.

20. Quoted in Australian Embassy in Manila, "Australia–Philippine Relations" at: http://www.philippines.com.au/resources/philippines/ausphilrell.htm.

21. For a good reading on Australia's strategic perspective on regional security and Philippine–Australia relations, see Jaime Ramon T. Ascalon, "Australian Perspective on Regional Security and Prospects for RP-Australian Security Cooperation," Foreign Affairs Quarterly 1, No. 1 (January–March 1999), pp. 1–12.

22. Commonwealth of Australia, Australia's National Security: A Defense Update 2003 (Canberra: Commonwealth of Australia, 2003), p. 9. Also see Jonathan O. Gackle, "U.S.–Australian Defense Cooperation: A Model for 21st Century Security Arrangements," *Defense & Security Analysis*, Vol. 18, No. 1 (2002), pp. 39–49.

23. Department of Foreign Affairs and Trade, Advancing the National Interests: Australia's Foreign and Trade Policy White Paper (Canberra: Department of Foreign Affairs and Trade, 2003), p. 28.

24. Department of National Defense, In Defense of the Philippines: 1998 Defense Policy Paper (Quezon City: Department of National Defense, 1998), p. 66. This document serves as the defense white paper of the Philippines. Since 1998, this white paper has not been updated nor revised. A draft Philippine defense white paper was circulated for comments in January 2003 but has not been approved for public circulation to date. The author is privy to the preparation of the 2003 Philippine defense white paper.

25. See Rommel C. Banlaoi, "The Role of Philippine–American Relations in the Global Campaign against Terrorism: Implications for Regional Security," *Contemporary Southeast Asia,* Vol. 24, No. 2 (August 2002), pp. 294–312. Also see Paolo Pasicolan, "Strengthening U.S.–Philippine Alliance for Fighting Terrorism," Heritage Foundation Executive Memorandum, No. 815 (May 13, 2002).

26. "Memorandum of Understanding between the Government of the Republic of the Philippines and the Government of Australia on Cooperation to Combat International Terrorism" (March 17, 2003), p. 3.

27. For detailed analysis of Australian interests in the South China Sea, see Christopher Chung, "The South China Sea Dispute: Themes, Developments and Implications for Australia's Interests," Australian Defense Studies Centre Working Paper No. 69 (May 2002).

28. See "Australia," Annual Security Outlook 2002 (ASEAN Regional Forum, 2003) at: http://www.aseansec.org/12665.htm.

29. RAN Sea Power Centre, Australian Maritime Doctrine (Royal Australian Navy, 2000). Also at: http://www.navy.gov.au/seapowercenter/maritimedoctrine.htm.

30. See Edgar L. Abogado and Reynaldo L. Yoma, "Development of a Philippine Maritime Surveillance Capability," in David Wilson (ed.), *Issues in Regional Maritime Strategy* (Papers by Foreign Visiting Military Fellows with Royal Australian Navy Maritime Studies Program, 1998), p. 30.

31. For a detailed discussion on the war on terrorism in Southeast Asia, see Rommel C. Banlaoi, *War on Terrorism in Southeast Asia* (Quezon City: Rex Book Store International, 2004). Online version of this book is available at: http://www.apaninfo.net/terrorism/banlaoiBook/index.htin.

32. I share the view of Robyn Lim on this issue. See Robyn Lim, "Australia and Maritime Security" at: http://www.glocomnet.or.jg/okasaki-inst/robyn.ansmari.htmlx.

33. Carolyn W. Pumprey (ed.), *The Rise of China in Asia: Security Implications* (Carlisle, Pa: Strategic Studies Institute, U.S. War College, 2002), p. 1.

34. Fei-Ling Wang, "China's Self Image and Strategic Intentions: National Confidence and Political Insecurity" (Paper presented at the conference War and Peace in the Taiwan Strait, sponsored by the Program in Asian Studies, Duke University, and Triangle Institute in Security Studies, February 26–27, 1999).

35. See the Annual Report on the Military Power of the People's Republic of China (Report to the Congress Pursuant to the FY2000 National Defense Authorization Act) at: http://www.defenselink.mil/news/Jun2000/p06232000_p111-00.html.

36. This whole paragraph including its note is from Rommel C. Banlaoi, "Southeast Asian Perspectives on the Rise of China: Regional Security after 9/11," Parameters (Summer 2003).

37. For more discussions on Philippine perspectives of China, see Aileen S.P. Baviera, *Strategic Issues in Philippine–China Relations: Comprehensive Engagement* (New Manila: Philippine–China Development Resource Center, 2000).

38. Stuart Harris, "The Role of China in Australia's Regional Security Environment," in Jonathan D. Pollack and Richard H. Yang (eds.), *China's Shadow: Regional Perspectives on Chinese Foreign Policy and Military Development* (Santa Monica, California: RAND, 1998), p. 132.

39. For an excellent reading on the development of the ARF, see Michael Leifer, "The ASEAN Regional Forum," Adelphi Paper No. 302 (London: International Institute of Strategic Studies, 1996). Also see Carlyle A. Thayer, "Multilateral Institutions in Asia: The ASEAN Regional Forum," Asia–Pacific Center for Security Studies Seminar Series (December 2000); and Raymund Jose G. Quilop, "Institution Building in the Asia–Pacific: The ARF Experience," OSS Research Series (Quezon City: Armed Forces of the Philippines Office of Strategic and Special Studies, 2002).

40. Jenelle Bonnor, "Australia–India Security Relations: Common Interests or Common Disinterests?" Working Paper No. 67 (Australian Defense Studies Centre, April 2001).

41. Agence France-Presse, "Philippines, Australia Sign Anti-Terrorism Pact," *Philippine Daily Inquirer*, March 4, 2003.

42. Australian Agency for International Development (AusAID), *Australia and the Philippines: Partners in Development* (Canberra: AusAID, 1998).

43. Ibid.

# GLOBAL, REGIONAL, AND MULTILATERAL SECURITY ISSUES

# Chapter 11

# Global Security Issues and Concerns after 9/11: Threats and Opportunities for the Philippines*

## Introduction

Before the September 11, 2001, terrorist attacks, the global security discourse focused on various strategic uncertainties unleashed by the end of the cold war. Global security analysts talked about the "rise and fall of great powers", the "end of history", the demise of nation–state and the rise of regional economies, the "clash of civilizations", the "Asia Megatrends", the dawning of the Asia–Pacific century, the "call for multilateralism," the advent of globalization, the "emergence of uni-

---

* Revised and updated version of a paper prepared for the Pre-Departure Training of the Philippine delegates to the 29th Ship for Southeast Asian Youth Program held at the Gems Hotel and Conference Center, Antipolo City, on June 15, 2002. Earlier version of this paper was presented on April 13, 2002 at the Asian Institute of Management for the Technical Working Group of the All-Parties Conference organized by the Office of the Speaker, Philippine House of Representatives. Also published in *Strategic and Integrative Studies Center Occasional Paper* (July 2002).

polarism," the "formation of a single Europe," the "menace of rogue states," the "challenges of failed states," and the "rise of China."

In the midst of these issues, the United States, the sole global power and police-man, viewed the global security situation before 9/11 as "favorable" because no organized global coalition seemed to be challenging the democratic core states.[1]

After the 9/11 attacks, however, the United States described the global secu-rity situation as seriously threatened by the specter of an organized global network of terrorists, the al Qaeda, headed by Osama bin Laden. President George W. Bush described global terrorism as a grave threat to the survival of "civilized" nations and underscored:

> The attack took place on American soil, but it was an attack on the heart and soul of the civilized world. And the world has come together to fight a new and different war, the first, and we hope the only one, of the 21st century. A war against all those who seek to export terror, and a war against those governments that support or shelter them.[2]

While the scourge of international terrorism greatly affected the American percep-tion of the global security situation, has the world really changed after 9/11? What are the new global security issues and concerns unleashed by 9/11? What are the threats and opportunities facing the Philippines in light of the 9/11 incidents?

## Global Security Issues and Concerns after 9/11

This chapter argues that nothing has fundamentally changed in global security architecture since 9/11. The security concerns before 9/11 are the same security concerns that the global community is facing after 9/11. What has changed is a tendency of nation–states to focus on the threat of international terrorism to band-wagon with American strategic priority in the global security agenda.

### *Terrorism as a Paramount American Global Agenda*

Because the attacks occurred in the territory of the sole superpower, the scourge of global terrorism is now at the apex of American global agenda. The attacks have attracted global attention because they were the largest and the most devastating the global community has ever witnessed.[3] Al Qaeda's network of terrorists is also believed to have established a strategic global reach affecting the security of many states including the Philippines. It is forecast that the problem of terrorism will continue to dominate the global agenda. According to the study made by the U.S.-based National Intelligence Council, between now and 2015, terrorist tactics will become "increasingly sophisticated and designed to achieve mass casualties."[4]

In Southeast Asia, however, terrorism is not really at the apex of its security agenda, though it regards terrorism as a threat to regional stability. To effectively recover from the long-term repercussions of the 1997 financial crisis, to implement the Association of Southeast Asian Nations (ASEAN) Free Trade Area, to face the challenges of the rise of China, to finalize the concept of the ASEAN+3, to manage territorial disputes, and to maintain ASEAN cohesiveness in the light of the completion of the ASEAN-10 and the possible accession of East Timor greatly shape the security agenda of Southeast Asia. Though Southeast Asia regards terrorism as a continuing low-level threat requiring strategic attention, it does not view terrorism as the defining security issue in the region.[5] In fact, the willingness of Southeast Asian states to become part of the American-led war on terrorism significantly varied.[6] The Philippines was the only ASEAN state that was quick to give higher priority on terrorism in its security agenda because of its attempt to reinvigorate its security alliance with the United States.

## *The Advent of Globalization*

The 9/11 attacks did not undermine the security relevance of the advent of globalization. Globalization remains to be the buzzword of the 21st century that affects growth and governance of many nation–states. Globalization is still regarded as the most powerful force shaping the present era.[7] It is a force that has created a new global order expanding the scale and speed of global flows of capital, goods, services, people, and ideas as well as crimes and terrorism across national borders; thus, increasing the complex interdependence and interconnectedness of states and nonstate players in the global community.[8]

As stated in Chapter 2, there is a view that globalization signals the demise of the nation–state and the rise of regional economies.[9] Others regard globalization as heralding the rise of a virtual state undermining the traditional role played by the territorial state.[10] Despite the process of globalization, the global system remains dominated by nation–states. The nation–state continues to be the most powerful player in global politics. While there may have been a proliferation of nonstate global players and the emergence of nontraditional global security issues that undermine the state's ability to fulfill its function of delivering services to the people, the state continues to throw its weight around and to influence the course of global events.[11]

The role of the state in managing the economy may have significantly reduced due to the dominance of capital in the global market. Yet, the state continues to be the central player when the world faces issues with defense and security implications. While state sovereignty seems to have been eroding because of the porousness of global boundaries, state sovereignty is still being fought for. There are still a lot of people willing to die on the altar of sovereignty.

Indeed, globalization has changed state behavior, "but they are not disappearing. State sovereignty has eroded, but it is still vigorously asserted."[12] The state continues to be the main although admittedly not necessarily the sole unit of analysis in global and domestic politics.

## The World Trade Organization (WTO)

Another related issue with globalization is the WTO issue. The aftermath of 9/11 did not diminish the importance of WTO as a global security issue. The WTO is the reflection of the triumph of free-market global economy that even a socialist state like China accedes to.

The formation of the WTO is based on the economic assumption that trade liberalization triggers economic activities and boosts greater economic productivity. There is a view that the WTO means "more jobs, higher wages, lower prices and more choices for consumers."[13] It is also said that international trade rules and WTO disciplines may give the poorer countries the mechanism to defend themselves against pressures from powerful trading partners.[14]

The WTO is a major global security issue because of sovereignty implications associated with WTO accession. Compliance with multilateral trade rules and regulations implies the limitation of discretionary power for government entities to establish and manage their respective trade policies.[15] There is also a view that the WTO only promotes free trade but not fair trade. It is argued that the WTO may cause the marginalization of some sectors and the widening of income gaps between those who can adjust to the new requirements and those who cannot.[16]

## Weapons of Mass Destruction (WMD)

The massive proliferation of (WMD) is a global security concern. WMD are in fact regarded as a serious global menace because of their capability to cause massive casualties through nuclear, chemical, biological, and radiological means. Intelligence sources confirm the continued increase in number, accuracy, range, and destructive capabilities of WMD. It has been reported that Middle East countries increase their stockpiles of WMD. North Korea, China, and the former Soviet republics have also been producing WMD. Even the United States and other advanced nations of the world are stockpiling WMD despite the strong global call for nonproliferation. When put in the hands of so-called rogue states or terrorist groups, WMD are powerful weapons not only for global deterrence but also of global terror. Thus, the 9/11 incidents made the issue of WMD more serious and threatening.

## The Rise of China

The rise of China as a global power is fast becoming a reality. China is a major power in the Asia–Pacific, playing a vital role in the management of peace and security in the region. It is the biggest country in East Asia in terms of population and land area. It has the largest reservoir of cheap but productive labor in Asia and the largest single market in the Asia–Pacific. China's seemingly unstoppable economic growth, its entry into the WTO, and the rise of its military forces make China the potential competitor of the United States in shaping the global security environment.

The inevitable rise of China is causing concerns in the global community because of the perceived hegemonic intentions of Beijing. China is vocal in criticizing the unipolar moment being enjoyed by the United States. China wants to establish a multipolar world that recognizes China as a "responsible" power. Some American security analysts have viewed China as an Asian power that has the potential of being the American strategic adversary in the Asia–Pacific region.[17] Although the 9/11 attacks have had some positive impact on U.S.–China relations, having increased bilateral contacts through phone calls and meetings, the United States still considers China as a threat at the strategic level, and thus a global security concern.[18]

# Regional Issues and Trends after 9/11

Having discussed these global issues, it is also equally important to discuss the following regional issues and trends after 9/11 that have implications for Philippine foreign and security policy.

## *Europe*

Europe used to be the region dominating the global security system. In the 19th and 20th centuries, Europe was the most important region in the world because of the vital role played by major European powers (like Germany, France, and the United Kingdom) in the maintenance of world peace and management of international conflicts.

Europe continues to play that role within the context of the Transatlantic Alliance with the United States. The North Atlantic Treaty Organization (NATO) is the cornerstone of Euro–Atlantic relations. In the American-led global campaign against terrorism, Europe is playing a vital role through NATO. While Europe seems to be achieving greater unity and "ever closer union" through the European Union (EU), the region's security is being challenged by the situation in the Balkan and Baltic areas. The 9/11 incidents did not change the security landscape of Europe insofar as the Balkan and the Baltic security issues are concerned.

The most important strategic trend happening in Europe is the enunciation of a Common European Security and Defense Policy (CESDP), which indicates the strong desire of Europe to have deeper political integration in the area of defense and security.[19] The launching of the CESDP has been regarded as a serious European effort to establish a European military union after accomplishing the European economic union. One analyst contends, "European military union is fast becoming the successor to monetary union as the next big idea of Europe."[20] When this happens, the EU would have a stronger bargaining tool to deal with the members of the international community.

In the aftermath of 9/11, the EU urged all its member states to jointly combat terrorism. The EU has also adopted a strategy that is comprehensive, covering a wide range of measures. The EU's counterterrorism strategy aims at increasing cooperation in fields ranging from intelligence sharing to law enforcement and the control of financial assets in order to make it easier to find, detain, and bring to justice terror suspects.[21] It also required the criminal law of the 25 EU member states to be aligned so that terrorism is prosecuted and punished in the same manner throughout the EU.[22] The union even appointed Gijs de Vries as the first EU counterterrorism coordinator. In the wake of the terrorist attack in Madrid on March 11, 2004, the European Council endorsed the revised EU Plan of Action on Combating Terrorism to improve its counterterrorism strategy.

## The Asia–Pacific

While Europe dominated world politics in the 19th and 20th centuries, the Asia–Pacific has become a very important and dynamic region in the 21st century. This has prompted many analysts to describe the 21st century as the Asia–Pacific century. The Asia–Pacific is a place of enormous economic opportunity, now accounting for over a quarter of the world's gross domestic product.[23] The 9/11 terrorist attacks did not alter the strategic importance of the Asia–Pacific in global security affairs. In fact, 9/11 has made the Asia–Pacific more vital because of various terrorist groups in the region with historic and financial links with al Qaeda.

Managing peace and security remains the primordial concern of many stakeholders in the Asia–Pacific because the region is host to various territorial disputes. The Spratly Islands dispute; the China–Taiwan conflict; the Russia–Japan conflict over the Northern Territories; the Japan–China conflict over Senkaku Islands; the Philippines–Malaysia dispute over Sabah; the Japan–South Korea dispute over the Liancourt Rocks; the India-Pakistan conflict over Kashmir; the border disputes between China and Vietnam, between Thailand and Burma, between Thailand and Malaysia, between Malaysia and Vietnam, between Vietnam and Indonesia; and the division of the Koreas are just examples of many sources of conflict in the Asia–Pacific region.[24]

The continuing arms buildup in Southeast Asia, the nuclear race between India and Pakistan, the nuclearization of North Korea, the modernization of Chinese Armed Forces, and the strengthening of Japan's Self-Defense Forces have also been identified as triggers to build serious conflict and instability in the region.[25] The resurgence of transnational crimes, the rise of religious revivalism, the threat of international terrorism, and the persistence of separatist movements in various countries in the Asia–Pacific have also been identified as potential sources of instability in the region.[26] These seemingly insurmountable security threats prompted one analyst to argue that instead of building a security community, states in the Asia–Pacific are, in fact, building conflict.[27]

Despite these various sources of insecurities, there are prospects for the development of a security community in the Asia–Pacific as nation–states agree that the region must be protected and secured by ruling out the threat or the use of force in dealing with one another. The ASEAN Regional Forum (ARF) can play a vital role in the development of a security community in the Asia–Pacific. Although ways and means to protect and secure the region may vary among nation–states in the Asia–Pacific, ARF's commitment to renounce force as a way of settling disputes is a positive building block of developing a security community in the region.[28]

## The Middle East

The Middle East is the one of the most troubled regions of the world. The ongoing Palestinian-Israeli conflict is providing the climate of instability in this troubled region. Many types of conflicts have also dominated the Middle East security architecture like the conflicts between Arab states and neighboring countries (for example, Iran and Turkey) and conflict within Arab states (e.g., Lebanon, Sudan, and Iraq).[29]

There is also a serious problem of terrorism in Algeria, Jordan, Egypt, and Palestine. The American-led global war on terrorism has complicated the problem of terrorism in the region. But the strongest potential trigger of serious conflicts in the region is water security, particularly in the areas within the Tigris and Euphrates rivers, the Jordan River, the Nile River, and the Persian Gulf.

The main concern of the international community in this troubled region is the politics of oil. Access to oil resources of the Middle East dominates the agenda of many states in the global community. Because some Middle East states are reported to have been producing various WMD, controlling the proliferation of WMD is also a major global concern in the region. The Middle East also remains the world's largest market of arms, making the region a problematic area of the world.[30] Moreover, the Western world has perceived the Middle East as the main place where the axis of evil exists, thus it is a region of serious concern after 9/11.

## Africa

Africa remains the most neglected region in the global community. The 9/11 events did not alter the global status of Africa. It continues to experience uneven economic growth with worsening poverty. But it has a very strong economic potential because it represents very huge and untapped markets.[31] Although African countries are moving toward more democratic regimes, the weakness of the African states is giving them difficulty in managing their ethnic, socioeconomic, and religious diversities. Some states in Africa have collapsed, for example Somalia and Rwanda.

Understanding the complex security situation in Africa is a major challenge to the international community.

## Latin America

Like Africa, Latin America has been described as the backwater of global security affairs. Latin America continues to face the persistence of a weak and fragmented state institution that undermines government capacity to effectively establish peace and order conducive for economic growth. The weakness of state institutions in Latin America has unleashed tremendous international repercussions, like the case of Peru and Ecuador in 1995. While Latin America attempts to democratize its polity, it continues to suffer the rocky process of democratization with the persistence of insurgency and civil violence. The most serious security concern in Latin America with international repercussion is the prevalence of drug trafficking, arms flows, and organized crime, especially in Colombia, Peru, and Mexico.[32]

# Threats and Opportunities for the Philippines

In midst of these global and regional trends, what are the threats and opportunities facing the Philippines after 9/11?

Global security threats that could unleash tremendous repercussions on the Philippines have already been discussed. There are also some opportunities that can provide the Philippines the wherewithal to overcome these security threats. These opportunities are some prospects for multilateralism and the significance of bilateralism in advancing the security interests of the Philippines.

## Philippine–American Security Relations*

Among our bilateral relations, Philippine relations with the United States have very deep historical, cultural, political, and cultural links. During the height of the cold war, the Philippines served as the linchpin of American security policy in Southeast Asia in containing the spread of communism. But after the cold war, Philippine–American relations hit their lowest point as result of the termination of the Philippine–American Military Bases Agreement (MBA) and the senate rejection of the proposed Treaty of Friendship, Security and Cooperation in 1991.

Philippine–American relations were revitalized when the United States called for global support to combat terrorism in light of the 9/11 attacks. The Philippines immediately responded to the call by quickly granting the United States flight rights as well as offering logistics support and medical personnel to American troops fighting terrorism in Afghanistan.[33] American officials praised the Philippine

---

* See Chapter 8 of this book for detailed discussion on Philippine–American relations.

government's contribution to the antiterrorism coalition efforts in Afghanistan and even described the Philippine initiative as "outstanding." The Americans even commended Philippine President Gloria Macapagal Arroyo for being "very quick to speak up, very quick to take action" to help the United States fight global terrorists.[34] The Philippines now serves as the American "front-line state in the war on terrorism."[35]

The 9/11 terrorist attacks have apparently provided the Philippines and the United States the *raison d'état* to restore and strengthen their security alliance within the framework of the Mutual Defense Treaty (MDT) . The American decision to send troops to Basilan for the antiterrorism military exercise in the context of *Balikatan* is a strong indication of a reinvigorated Philippine–American security alliance.

The Philippines must take advantage of this opportunity because the presence of American troops in the Philippines not only deters global terrorism but it also deters the perceived Chinese assertive activities in the South China Sea. Revitalizing Philippine bilateral ties with the United States also reestablishes deterrence vis-à-vis China, thus strengthening Philippine defense posture in the South China Sea.

However, the revitalization of Philippine–American relations will not prevent the Philippines from strengthening its bilateral relations with China.

## Philippine–Australia Security Relations*

Although an American ally in the Asia–Pacific, Australia is wary of the American presence in the Philippines, not because Sydney does not welcome Washington. In fact, Australia fully supports American activities in the region because of their converging strategic interests. There is a perceived fear, however, in Australia that Philippine–Australian strategic engagement and dialogue might diminish as a result of the reinvigorated Philippine–American relations.

During the 1990s, Australia played the role of a mentor to some Filipino military officers. Australia served as the major destination of Filipino military officers and civilian defense officials undergoing defense training and education. Australia and the Philippines were even involved in an annual regional dialogue on regional security issues to build more confidence between them to hopefully deepen and widen their defense cooperation. Two months after 9/11, Australian and Filipino strategic analysts and scholars even held their Philippine–Australia Strategic Forum (PASFOR) at the National Defense College of the Philippines (NDCP) to increase their interactions and enhance Philippine–Australia cooperation.

Australia was therefore confident that Philippine–Australia relations would not be altered by the 9/11 incident. In fact, Australia has been considering the Philippines as a highly potential strategic partner in the region by virtue of close

---

* See Chapter 10 of this book for detailed discussion on Philippine–Australia security relations.

affinity of the Philippines with the Western world in terms of language and strategic perspectives.[36]

## Philippine–China Security Relations*

The aftermath of 9/11 and the heightened American presence in the Philippines have unleashed some repercussions on China's strategic posture in Southeast Asia. After 9/11, China has reportedly changed its security calculus and was forced to reevaluate its geopolitical position vis-à-vis its relations with the United States and with the claimant states in the South China Sea.[37] In response to the shifting strategic landscape, Beijing has reportedly been launching an uncharacteristically concerted diplomatic effort toward her neighbors.[38]

The Philippine security alliance with the United States will not prevent the Philippines from pursuing a deeper relationship with China. Like Washington, Manila shall establish a constructive cooperative relationship with Beijing because of China's strong potential as trade and strategic partner in the region.

Although the Philippines has an irritant issue with China regarding the territorial disputes in the South China Sea, the Philippines has to establish lasting and enduring relations with China, being the country's strongest permanent neighbor in Asia. The South China Sea is not the sea that divides the Philippines and China but rather the sea that links them.[39] Thus, the South China Sea issue shall not be the issue of conflict between the Philippines and China but the issue that links the two countries. There are functionalist options that provide ways to manage peacefully the territorial issues in the South China Sea.[40]

## Philippine–Japan Relations

Japan is presently suffering some difficulties in maintaining its current position as the world's third largest economy. The Japanese economic recession punctuated by bickering among politicians makes Japan unable to regain its influence as a major economic power. The Japanese relative importance in the global economy is continuously declining.

Despite the economic and political challenges facing Japan, it continues to be an important bilateral partner of the Philippines. Japan remains the Philippines' top bilateral source of Official Development Assistance (ODA). In the year 2000 alone, Japan's total ODA to the Philippines amounted to $1.31 billion. Furthermore, Japanese investment continues to trigger economic growth in Southeast Asia.

Japan's role in the global economy might have been diminishing. But it is not disappearing. Japan continues to contribute to regional stability.

---

* See Chapter 9 of this book for detailed discussion on Philippine–China Security Relations. Also see Rommel C. Banlaoi, *Security Aspects of Philippine–China Relations: Bilateral Issues and Concerns in the Age of Global Terrorism* (Quezon City: Rex Book Store International, 2007).

## Philippine–Association of Southeast Asian Nations (ASEAN) Relations

ASEAN is the most successful regional body in Asia. ASEAN has provided a regime of cooperation in Southeast Asia advancing the economic prosperity and political cooperation of its members. While ASEAN members have territorial conflicts with each other, these conflicts are being effectively managed through the ASEAN Way of managing conflicts, which becomes the inspiration of the ASEAN Regional Forum.

In the midst of globalization and complexity of global security issues, the Philippines can deal with major powers of the world through the ASEAN. The ASEAN provides a loud voice for the Philippines to articulate its security concerns not only in the region but also in the world.

ASEAN has also provided the Philippines the appropriate venue to actively participate in world affairs. Thus, the Philippines shall maintain ASEAN as the cornerstone of Philippine foreign policy. ASEAN is the major instrument where the Philippines can go regional to overcome the challenges of globalization. In fact, ASEAN is complementing the Philippines in its support to the American-led global campaign against terrorism. Thus, the Philippines shall continue supporting various ASEAN initiatives to create a climate of cooperation in the region that promotes trade and investment liberalization and enhanced political cooperation in the spirit of transparency and confidence building.

## Philippine–ASEAN Regional Forum (ARF) Relations

The ARF is an extension of the ASEAN model of regional security.[41] So far, the ARF is the only viable regionwide multilateral security forum that addresses the complexities of security problems in the Asia–Pacific despite the many security challenges it is facing. Bringing together 22 diverse nation–states with varying security perceptions of the world, the ARF aims to promote the security of the Asia–Pacific through constant dialogue and confidence among its members using track-one and track-two mechanisms. The ARF has also agreed on a gradual three-stage evolution of confidence building, preventive diplomacy, and in the longer term, common approaches to conflict resolution.

The Philippines is an active participant of the ARF. Like the ASEAN, the ARF provides the Philippines a venue to actively engage with major powers in the Asia–Pacific on an equal footing. The ARF serves as a powerful multilateral instrument where the Philippines can articulate and advance its security concerns in the region. Thus, it is in the interest of the Philippines to support ARF. Like ASEAN, the ARF serves as the Philippines' tool to go regional in the midst of globalization.

## Philippine–Middle East Relations

The Middle East continues to be the Philippines' largest destination of Filipino overseas workers and the major traditional source of its oil requirements. The

Middle East, through the Organization of Islamic Conference (OIC), is also helping the Philippines in managing the Muslim challenges in the Mindanao. Thus, the Philippines has to continue enhancing its cooperation with Middle East countries because of its strategic interests in this region.

In light of the ongoing Palestinian Israeli Conflict, the Philippines has to uphold United Nations resolutions on this matter. The Philippines has to maintain its support in recognizing the inalienable rights of the Palestinian people for self-determination and the rights of the Jewish people to enjoy their homeland in Israel.

## Philippine–European Union (EU) Relations

The Philippines has strategic interests in EU. The primordial interest of the Philippines in Europe is largely dictated by economic imperatives. Members of the EU continue to be the Philippines' largest donor countries and trading partners.

Compared with ASEAN, however, Philippine economic ties with Europe are very weak. Although the Philippines' trade and investment relations with Europe have grown in recent years, the Philippines continues to occupy the smallest ASEAN economic space in Europe. There is therefore a strong need for the Philippines to reinvent our ties with Europe for future benefits of the Philippines. The Asia-Europe Meeting is a very important venue where the Philippines can strengthen its economic ties with Europe. On the political side, on the other hand, the ARF and ASEAN can serve as a venue for the Philippines to establish a strategic dialogue with Europe.

# Conclusion

Although the dominant issue confronting the global community at present is the issue of global terrorism, the global security fundamentals have not changed. The global security issues that the world faced before 9/11 are the same security issues facing the world after 9/11. Though the threat of terrorism affects the strategic outlook of many players in the international community, the advent of globalization, the global impacts of WTO, proliferation of WMD, and the rise of China continue to be the main drivers of the global security environment.

Compared with the last century, however, this chapter argues that the 21st century has become the Asia–Pacific century. The Philippines, being an Asia–Pacific state, may take this as an opportunity to advance its national interests in the midst of globalization. Hence, the Philippines must go regional to overcome the many security challenges of globalization and other global security issues. The formation of the ARF is one venue where the Philippines can go regional in the midst of globalization.

While going regional, the Philippines must also strengthen and revitalize its bilateral relations with the United States being the sole superpower and the

Philippines' long-time security ally. Strengthening bilateral ties with the United States, however, shall not prevent the Philippines from exploring a strategic partnership with China, the rising Asian power that has the potential of becoming one of the world's superpowers.

# Endnotes

1. Institute for National Strategic Studies, *Strategic Assessment 1999* (Washington, DC: National Defense University, 1999), p. 1.
2. See speech of President George W. Bush, at: http://usinfo.state.gov/products/pubs/.
3. Peter Chalk, "Militant Islamic Extremism in Southeast Asia" (Paper presented in the conference "Transnational Violence and Seams of Lawlessness in the Asia-Pacific: Linkages to Global Terrorism" sponsored by the Asia–Pacific Studies Center on February 19–21, 2002 in Honolulu, Hawaii), p. 1.
4. National Intelligence Council, *Global Trend 2015* (National Foreign Intelligence Board, December 2000), p. 50.
5. Jim Rolfe, "Security in Southeast Asia: It's Not about the War on Terrorism," *Asia–Pacific Center for Security Studies*, Vol. 1, No. 3 (June 2002), p. 2.
6. Sheldon W. Simon, "Mixed Reactions in Southeast Asia to the U.S. War on Terrorism," *Comparative Connections: An E-Journal on East Asian Bilateral Relations* (4th Quarter 2001), p. 1.
7. Jeffrey Frankel, "Globalization of the Economy," in Joseph Nye and John Donahue (eds.), *Governance in a Globalizing World* (Washington, DC: Brookings Institution Press, 2000), p. 45.
8. See Robert O. Keohane and Joseph S. Nye, Jr., "Globalization: What's New? What's Not? (And So What?)," *Foreign Policy*, No. 118 (Spring 2000), pp. 104–119. Also see Pippa Norris, "Global Governance and Cosmopolitan Citizens," in Nye and Donahue, p. 155.
9. Kenichi Ohmae, *The End of Nation States and the Rise of Regional Economies* (New York: The Free Press, 1995).
10. Richard Rosecrance, *The Rise of Virtual State: Wealth and Power in the Coming Century* (New York: Basic Books, 1999).
11. Based on Rommel C. Banlaoi, "Globalization and Nation-Building in the Philippines: State Predicaments in Managing Society in the Midst of Diversity" (Paper presented at the conference "Growth and Governance in Asia," sponsored by the Asia–Pacific Center for Security Studies, Honolulu, Hawaii on March 12–14, 2002).
12. See James N. Rosenau, "Many Damn Things Simultaneously: Complexity Theory and World Affairs," in David S. Alberts and Thomas J. Czerwinski (eds.), *Complexity, Global Politics and National Security* (Washington, DC: CCRP Publication Series, 1999).
13. Rizalino Navarro, "Fight Hard for Philippine Interests within WTO," *Philippine Daily Inquirer* (March 27, 2002).
14. Ibid.
15. See Arthur E. Appleton, "China in WTO: Implications for Regional Economies" (Paper presented at the 15th Asia–Pacific Roundtable organized by ASEAN–ISIS and ISIS Malaysia in Kuala Lumpur on June 6, 2001), p. 3.
16. Navarro, p. 2.

17. Graham T. Allison and Robert Blackwill, *America's National Interests* (A Report from The Commission on America's National Interests, 2000), p. 24.

18. Yu Bin, "United States–China Relations and Regional Security after September 11," *Issues and Insights*, No. 2-02 (Honolulu: Pacific Forum CSIS, April 2002).

19. See Rommel C. Banlaoi, "The European Union's Common Foreign and Security Policy and the Idea of a Common European Security and Defense Policy: Lessons for the ASEAN Regional Forum," in his *Security Cooperation in the ASEAN Regional Forum and in the European Union: Lessons Learned* (Quezon City: National Defense College of the Philippines Monograph No. 1, 2001), pp. 31–59.

20. Richard Medley, "Europe's Next Big Idea: Strategy and Economics to a European Military," *Foreign Affairs,* Vol. 78, No. 5 (September–October 1999), p. 18.

21. For more details, see "EU Fights against Terrorism" at: http://www.consilium.europa. eu/cms3_fo/showPage.asp?id=406&lang=en.

22. Ibid.

23. See "Annual Strategic Outlook" at: http://www.aseansec.org/menu.asp?action=3& content=2.

24. For an excellent listing on the various territorial conflicts in the region, see Desmond Ball, "Arms and Affluence: Military Acquisition in the Asia–Pacific Region," *International Security*, Vol. 18, No. 3 (Winter 1993–1994), pp. 88–89.

25. Ibid.

26. See Alan Dupont, "Transnational Crime, Drugs, and Security in East Asia," *Asian Survey*, Vol. 39, No. 3 (May–June, 1999), pp. 433–455, and his "New Dimension of Security" (Paper presented for the Joint SDSC and IISS Conference on "The New Security Agenda in the Asia–Pacific Region" on May 1–3, 1996).

27. See Robert Manning, "Building Community or Building Conflict? A Typology of Asia–Pacific Security Challenges," in Ralph A. Cossa (ed.), *Asia–Pacific Confidence and Security Building Measures* (Washington, DC: The Center for Strategic and International Studies, 1995), pp. 19–40.

28. Based on Rommel C. Banlaoi, "The ASEAN Regional Forum and Security Community Building in the Asia–Pacific: Lessons from Europe," in his *Security Cooperation in the ASEAN Regional Forum and in the European Union: Lessons Learned* (Quezon City: National Defense College of the Philippines Monograph No. 1, 2001), pp. 1–30. See Chapter 13 of this book.

29. Kamal S. Shehadi, "Middle East," in Paul B. Stares (ed.), *The New Security Agenda: A Global Survey* (Tokyo: Japan Center for International Exchange, 1998), p. 138.

30. For more information about Middle East see The Middle East Research and Information Project at: http://www.merip.org.

31. Institute for National Strategic Studies, "Sub-Saharan Africa: Progress or Drift," in *Strategic Assessment 1999* (Washington, DC: National Defense University, 1999), pp. 153–168.

32. Monica Serrano, "Latin America," in Paul B. Stares (ed.), *The New Security Agenda: A Global Survey* (Tokyo: Japan Center for International Exchange, 1998), p. 162.

33. Transcript: Assistant Secretary Kelly's "Dialogue" Broadcast November 16, 2001 (U.S. official praises Philippine anti-terrorism efforts), at: http://usinfo.state.gov/ regional/ea/easec/philip.htm.

34. Ibid.

35. Angel M. Rabasa, "Southeast Asia after 9/11: Regional Trends and U.S. Interests" (Testimony presented to the Subcommittee on East Asia and the Pacific House of Representatives Committee on International Relations on December 12, 2001), p. 10.
36. See Chapter 10 of this book for more detailed discussions of Philippine–Australia security relations.
37. Dan Ewing, "China's Changing Security Calculus," *Korea Herald* (January 21, 2002). Also at: http://www.nixoncenter.org/publications/articles/011602China.htm.
38. Ibid.
39. See Rommel C. Banlaoi, "Philippine Defense Policy Perspectives on the South China Sea and the Rise of China" (Lecture delivered on June 26, 2002 at Sun Yat Sen University, Guangzhou, China). Also in Rommel C. Banlaoi, *Security Aspects of Philippines–China Relations: Bilateral Issues and Concerns in the Age of Global Terrorism* (Quezon City: Rex Book Store International, 2007), Chapter 5.
40. See Rommel C. Banlaoi, *The ASEAN Regional Forum, the South China Sea Disputes and the Functionalist Option* (Quezon City: National Defense College of the Philippines Monograph No. 3, 2001).
41. Michael Leifer, "The ASEAN Regional Forum: Extending ASEAN's Model of Regional Security," *Adelphi Paper* 320 (London: Oxford University Press, 1996).

*Chapter 12*

# Maritime Security Outlook for Southeast Asia in the Post-9/11 Era*

## Introduction

It is not easy to come to grips with the issue of maritime security in Southeast Asia because the term *maritime security* encompasses such a broad concept that it includes a panoply of notions such as maritime safety, port security, freedom of navigation, security of the sea lines of communications, security from piracy attacks including armed robberies against ships, and most recently, security from maritime terrorism. Although many experts have spoken on the topic of maritime security, there is still the absence of a commonly accepted definition of maritime security that will serve as the firm basis for regional cooperation.

Despite the lack of a workable definition, the growing concerns on maritime security have led to the issuing of the *Statement on Cooperation against Piracy and other Threats to Maritime Security* at the 36th Association of Southeast Asian Nations (ASEAN) Ministerial Meeting (AMM) and the 10th ASEAN Regional Forum (ARF) Post Ministerial Conferences in Cambodia on June 16–20, 2003.

* Originally published as Chapter 3 in Joshua Ho and Catherine Zara Raymond (eds.), *The Best of Times, The Worst of Times: Maritime Security in the Asia–Pacific* (Singapore: Institute for Defense and Strategic Studies and World Scientific Publishing Co., Ltd., 2005), pp. 59–80. Original version of this paper was presented to the Maritime Security Conference organized by the Institute of Defense and Strategic Studies at the Marina Mandarin Hotel, Singapore, May 20–21, 2004.

The statement does not have a clear definition of maritime security and only regards maritime security as "an indispensable and fundamental condition for the welfare and economic security of the ARF region."[1] The statement goes on to say that ensuring maritime security "is in the interests of all countries"[2] and even attempts to limit the issue of maritime security to "piracy and armed robbery against ships and the potential for terrorist attacks on vulnerable sea shipping" as a form of quasi-definition.[3]

The lack of a workable definition has also not deterred ASEAN from issuing its own communiqué at the conclusion of the 37th Ministerial Meeting held on June 29–30, 2004, in Jakarta where members reaffirmed their commitment to the establishment of an ASEAN Security Community (ASC). In this communiqué, ASEAN ministers stressed that maritime cooperation is vital to the evolution of a security community in the region, and they urged each other to explore the possibility of establishing a maritime forum in Southeast Asia. The communiqué thus hints at the increasing awareness of Southeast Asian countries on the importance of regional security cooperation, particularly in the area of piracy and maritime terrorism. Despite the issuance of the communiqué, regional cooperation to promote maritime security in Southeast Asia still remains limited. There is even a view that maritime security in Southeast Asia is "inconsistent and largely ineffective"[4] and as a result encourages intervention by extraregional powers to improve regional maritime security.

Having said that, because Southeast Asia is a maritime region, maritime security is inevitably one of its vital security concerns, and enhancing maritime security in Southeast Asia is arguably an integral component of an overall regional security agenda. Therefore, discussion of maritime security in the region will be broad and not deal only with piracy, sea robbery, and maritime terrorism, as what the ARF document suggests. This is because the issue of maritime security in Southeast Asia has always been comprehensive and multifaceted and includes traditional security issues like territorial disputes in the South China Sea (and to a certain extent the territorial issues in the Taiwan Straits and the Korean Peninsula) and the security impact of major power rivalries.[5] It also includes nontraditional security issues like environmental degradation, weapons proliferation, as well as arms, drugs, and human smuggling.[6]

Although maritime security must be viewed in its various dimensions and nuances in order to have a holistic understanding of maritime security in Southeast Asia, this chapter will not take the comprehensive approach in dealing with the issue of maritime security in Southeast Asia. Instead, the central aspect of this chapter is to describe the maritime security outlook for Southeast Asia in the area of piracy and maritime terrorism and to analyze these issues in the context of shipping and force modernization trends in the region after 9/11. This chapter contends that piracy and maritime terrorism in Southeast Asia have root causes that predate 9/11, and addressing these root causes is crucial to promoting regional maritime security. This chapter concludes with the advocacy that defense development is imperative to increase the capacity of Southeast Asian countries to surmount the gargantuan challenges of maritime security in the age of global terrorism.

## Southeast Asia: A Piracy Hot Spot?

Despite the constant denial by Southeast Asian countries of the existence of piracy,[7] Southeast Asia had the long-standing reputation of being the piracy hot spot of the world. It became the region most prone to acts of piracy, accounting for around 50% of all attacks worldwide. Indonesian waters were the world's most dangerous in terms of piracy attacks. According to the 2003 report of the International Maritime Bureau, out of 445 actual and attempted piracy attacks on merchant ships, 189 attacks occurred in Southeast Asian waters. Of these 189 attacks, 121 attacks occurred in Indonesian waters, with 35 occurring in the waterways around Malaysia and Singapore, particularly in the congested Strait of Malacca. The data represent an increase of 18 piracy attacks recorded in 2002 for Indonesian waters alone, with an increase of 33 attacks for the whole region. Thus, piracy attacks in Southeast Asian waters are high when compared with the incidence of piracy attacks in other regions of the world like Africa and Latin America. But as presented in Chapter 13, piracy incidents declined in 2006 until 2009.

A study has shown that acts of piracy in Southeast Asia occur mostly in ports or anchorages, and pirates range from opportunistic fishermen and common criminals to members of sophisticated Asian crime syndicates.[8] In 2002, it was reported that 95 of the 123 actual reported piracy attacks in Southeast Asia occurred in ports, representing 77% of all attacks.[9] Although the proportion of attacks in Southeast Asia ports dropped to 50% in 2003, ports remained prone to piracy attacks. In fact, ports that were not targets in 2002 became hot targets in 2003.[10] In 2003 alone, acts of piracy were reported in 10 anchorages in Southeast Asia as compared with the 27 anchorages worldwide.[11] Acts of piracy also range from the classic boarding and hijacking of a merchant vessel on high seas to the more common act of stealing from a ship while it is anchored.[12] Thus, three types of piracy have been identified: harbor/anchorage attacks, attacks against vessels on high seas of territorial waters, and hijacking of commercial vessels on high seas.[13]

### Cost of Piracy

Besides the high number of incidents of piracy in Southeast Asia, the cost attributed to acts of piracy is also alarming. James Warren of the Asia Research Institute at the National University of Singapore has claimed that piracy in the region is costing the world economy a staggering amount of US$25 billion a year.[14] Alan Chan, a vocal antipiracy advocate and an owner of Petroships in Singapore, has also said that piracy is costing the region around US$500 million a year.[15] Despite the high number of incidents and the cost resulting from attacks, ship owners have not taken much action due to the high cost of preventive measures. The Organization for Economic Cooperation and Development, for example, has stated that new maritime security measures to counter the threat of attacks will require an initial investment by ship operators of at least US$1.3 billion, and will increase annual operating costs by US$730 million.[16] Despite the high cost of piracy now, the cost of piracy is projected to increase in the future, as the incidents become more bloody, ruthless, and sophisticated.

## Causes of Piracy

The problem of piracy in the region remains a concern, despite serious efforts to combat piracy in Southeast Asia, because of the failure of concerned states to really address the root causes of piracy. Pervasive poverty, the low level of economic development, and the poor quality of governance has helped make piracy an alternative means of livelihood for some people in Southeast Asia. On top of this, the huge coastlines of affected countries, lax port security measures, weak maritime security forces, and limited regional antipiracy cooperation also make the region highly vulnerable to piracy. In particular, countries in Southeast Asia do not have adequate funds and strong political will to fight piracy.[17] Adding insult to injury is the fact that despite the mouthful of rhetoric, there is very limited regional maritime security cooperation in Southeast Asia. As a result of the myriad of factors that has resulted in the high piracy rates, resolving the issue is both difficult and complex. Each issue will now be examined in turn to unearth the root causes of piracy.

The first cause of piracy is pervasive poverty in the region. Poverty incidences in the region range from 16% to 55%,[18] and it is this poverty in Southeast Asia that has prompted people to resort to piracy as an alternative means of livelihood. The harsh economic and development impact of the 1997 Asian financial crisis aggravated the poverty situation in Southeast Asia because many people lost their jobs. The deteriorated situation encouraged people in Southeast Asia, particularly those from the coastal areas, to return to "old ways" of finding a living, one of which is resorting to piracy to supplement income. Resorting to piracy acts as a source of livelihood in Southeast Asia is not very difficult since piracy in the region "was thought to be an acceptable part of the local culture, a normal but illegal means of making money."[19]

The second cause of piracy is weak governance. For example, the high incidences of piracy in Indonesian and Philippine waters could be attributed to political instabilities and weak institutions of governance in these two countries. Weak institutions of governance make these countries unable to effectively protect and control their huge territorial waters. Although Singapore has relatively strong governance among countries in Southeast Asia, weak governance in its neighbors also makes Singapore's waters highly vulnerable to piracy attacks. A compounding factor is the sad reality that countries in Southeast Asia just do not have adequate funds and strong political will to fight piracy.[20]

The third cause of piracy in Southeast Asia is the huge coastline and weak port security in the countries of concern. Southeast Asian countries have a combined coastline length of 92,451 km, which is 15.8% of the world's total. The archipelagos of Indonesia and the Philippines alone (the two largest in the world, with more than 20,000 islands combined) contribute 59% and 24%, respectively, to the region's coastlines.[21] Such coastline makes ensuring port security in Southeast Asia highly difficult and very expensive. Kenneth Button, an American academic, said that Britain and the United States alone spent billions to protect their coastlines. If this is the case, then most Asian countries will not have the money to protect their coastlines because their coastlines are longer than the United States' and Britain's, and their countries poorer. The long coastline in Southeast Asia provides ample hideouts for pirates and is a source of vulnerability for many coastal states in the region.

The fourth cause of piracy in Southeast Asia is the relatively weak maritime forces of Southeast Asian countries. Weak maritime security forces attract pirates to operate in Southeast Asia because the existing maritime armed forces in the region do not have the effective wherewithal to deter, prevent, and preempt pirates in their acts. Cindy Vallar argues, "Once pirates meet little or no resistance from their victims and aren't pursued by law enforcement authorities, they are more likely to strike again."[22] Indonesia, the largest archipelago in the world, has a weak maritime force and its defense budget is the lowest in Southeast Asia.[23] With the scourge of the Asian financial crisis, the value of the Indonesian defense budget also declined by 65% from 1997 to 1998. This worsened the already tight fiscal problems and prevented the country from allocating more to its maritime security force.[24] The Philippines, the world's second largest archipelago, has one of the most ill-equipped maritime forces in Asia. The American military withdrawal in 1991 aggravated the already poor state of Philippine maritime forces. Though the Philippine military ventured into a force modernization program in 1995, the 1997 Asian financial crisis prevented its implementation and prompted even one naval officer to lament that the Philippine Navy "lags both in quality and quantity among the other navies in the region."[25]

Underpaid members of the maritime security forces in Southeast Asia (coast guards, port guards, naval guards) also encourage officers and rank and file to seek other sources to supplement their income. One of these sources is piracy. An analyst observed that most of the personnel employed in Southeast Asia's maritime security forces "are grossly underpaid."[26] With a very limited budget allocated for defense, the military forces in Southeast Asia often cannot afford "to provide sufficient pay to officers and lower ranking members, who then resort to off-budget sources of income."[27]

The fifth cause of piracy in Southeast Asia is the limited instances of maritime security cooperation in the region. As an attempt at gathering more information on regional piracy, a Piracy Reporting Centre was established in Kuala Lumpur, Malaysia, under the auspices of the International Chamber of Commerce's

International Maritime Bureau. However, one shortfall is that the center is non-governmental and acts only as a central information reporting and warning center. It does not coordinate regional maritime patrols and operations to combat regional piracy.

Regional cooperation against piracy in Southeast Asia is predominantly bilateral in nature rather than multilateral. Indonesia, Malaysia, the Philippines, and Singapore have entered into bilateral agreements to coordinate naval patrols and antipiracy exercises. For example, the Philippines and Malaysia have a border-crossing agreement to protect their maritime borders. Indonesia and Singapore also have an agreement to coordinate their maritime patrols and a regime for hot pursuit to combat piracy. Indonesia and Malaysia also have similar arrangements to deal with maritime issues arising out of a common border.[28] Singapore and Malaysia have their own bilateral cooperative mechanisms to discuss common maritime issues.

Besides bilateral arrangements, Southeast Asia also adopted multilateral responses in the campaign against piracy, and an example is the adoption by ARF members on June 16–20, 2003, of the Statement on Cooperation against Piracy and other Threats to Maritime Security. The statement recognizes that maritime security is an indispensable and fundamental condition for the welfare and economic security of the ARF region. Despite the adoption of the statement, actual regional efforts continue to be limited. Singapore Deputy Prime Minister and Defense Minister Tony Tan observed that Southeast Asian states have taken action to combat piracy, with some success, but more can be done. Although ASEAN has taken a lot of initiatives to suppress regional piracy, one of which is the adoption of the work program to implement the Plan of Action to Combat Transnational Crimes signed in Malaysia on May 17, 2002, regional cooperation remains limited due to various domestic considerations.

Why then is cooperation among ASEAN countries to combat the piracy threat so poor? In response, some analysts contend that the ASEAN principle of noninterference in internal affairs is a major obstacle in the regional efforts to combat piracy and other threats to regional maritime security. And because the principle of noninterference is so central to the existence of ASEAN, deeper levels of cooperation are difficult.[29] So central is the principle of noninterference that the signing of Bali Concord II in 2003, which declared the development of an ASEAN Security Community, again reaffirms the principle of noninterference.

Despite this, it is noteworthy that Indonesia, Malaysia, and Singapore have decided to come together to promote maritime security in the Straits of Malacca through coordinated patrols that observe the territorial sovereignty of each country. The port authorities of the Philippines and Indonesia have also decided to establish a coordination system that would advance the maritime security interests of both countries.[30] These initiatives are important developments to promote maritime security cooperation in Southeast Asia.

# Piracy, Maritime Terrorism, and Shipping Trends

A concomitant security issue of piracy problems in Southeast Asia is the specter of maritime terrorism. It is possible for terrorists to use piracy as a cover to conduct acts of maritime terrorism because of the high incidences of piracy in Southeast Asian waters. Although the different motives of the pirate and the terrorist will make them strange bedfellows, with the former pursuing economic gain and the latter pursuing political gain,[31] terrorists still have the ability to either adopt pirate tactics or "piggyback" on pirate raids.[32] Maritime terrorists, rather than simply stealing, "could either blow up the ship or use it to ram into another vessel or a port facility."[33] As such, security experts have observed the blurring of the line between piracy and terrorism. These experts stress that "not only do pirates terrorize ships' crews, but terror groups like al Qaeda could also use pirates' methods either to attack ships, or to seize ships to use in terror attacks at megaports, much like the September 11 hijackers used planes."[34]

A more sinister scenario is the threat that a small but lethal biological weapon could be smuggled into a harbor aboard ship and released into the port.[35] In fact, terrorist groups regard seaports and international cruise lines as very attractive targets because they "reside in the nexus of terrorist intent, capability and opportunity."[36] It may be even asked: "If pirates can act with such impunity, what is stopping terrorists?"[37]

The increasing trends of commercial shipping in Southeast Asia make the challenges of piracy and maritime terrorism in the region even more acute. As early as 1999, the U.S. Coast Guard Intelligence Coordinating Center forecast that the world commercial shipping activities will enormously increase by 2020 and this will also trigger the proliferation of transnational crimes at sea.[38] It also forecast that tremendous growth in the cruise line industry and the emergence of high-speed ferries would be the key developments in the maritime passenger transport business through 2020.[39]

Shipping has long been the major form of transport and communication connecting Southeast Asia and the rest of the world.[40] Four of the busiest international commercial shipping routes are in Southeast Asia, namely, the Malacca, Sunda, Lombok, and Makassar straits.[41] More than 50% of the world's annual merchant fleet tonnage passes through these straits, and more than 15% of the value of world trade passes through Southeast Asia yearly.[42] As a result of rapid expansion of global trade, this trend has been projected to grow in the years to come unless major disasters occur in the region. The Malacca Strait alone carries more than a quarter of the world's maritime trade each year. More than 50,000 large ships pass through the strait annually, not to mention that 40 to 50 oil tankers sail in the said strait daily.[43] Because the strait is the region's maritime gateway between the Indian Ocean and the Pacific Ocean, its present status as the world's center of maritime activities will inevitably persist in the future. If terrorists hijack one of the ships passing through the Malacca Strait and turn it to a floating bomb to destroy ports or oil refineries, the effects will be undoubtedly catastrophic. This kind of incident will not only cripple world trade and slow down international shipping, but it will also sow awesome fear — greater than what happened in 9/11.

Though an analyst argues that it is difficult for terrorists to disrupt shipping in the strait by sinking a ship in a precise spot,[44] the possibility of these kinds of maritime incidents is not very remote. Container shipping is very vulnerable, and the possibility of their being used as weapons of mass destruction (WMD) by maritime terrorists has already been properly documented.[45] Thus, maritime terrorism in Southeast Asia is no longer a question of if, but rather of when and where.[46] A maritime security expert even asserts that maritime terrorism, regionally speaking, is not a question of when, but how often and what are we going to do about it.[47]

Al Qaeda and its operatives in Southeast Asia have a keen awareness of maritime trade and have a deep understanding of its significance to global economy.[48] Al Qaeda also knows the impact of maritime terrorist attacks on maritime commerce and has therefore planned to conduct seaborne attacks to wage maritime terrorism.[49] Al Qaeda's maritime terrorist capability has already been demonstrated by suicide attacks on the destroyer *USS Cole* in 2000 and the French oil tanker *Limburg* in 2002. The intelligence community has, in fact, identified 15 cargo ships believed to be owned by al Qaeda, and these ships could be used for future maritime terrorist attacks.[50] Al Qaeda operatives are also learning about diving with a view to attacking ships from below.[51]

What is more bothersome is the fact that Southeast Asia, as a maritime region, is home to some indigenously based terrorist groups with maritime traditions.[52] The Abu Sayyaf Group (ASG), the *Moro* Islamic Liberation Front (MILF), the Gerakan Aceh Merdeka, and the Jemaah Islamiyah (JI) have been identified as terrorist groups with tremendous intention and capability to wage maritime terrorism. In the Strait of Malacca, for example, the Aegis Defense Services, a London-based security organization, said that the robbery of a chemical tanker, *Dewi Madrim*, appeared to be the work of terrorists "who were learning how to steer a ship, in preparation for a future attack at sea."[53] In Singapore, intelligence and law enforcement forces have uncovered the JI plot planning to bomb a U.S. naval facility in the Island State (Singapore). In the Philippines, the ASG claimed responsibility for the explosion and fire on the ship *Superferry 14* carrying 899 passengers on February 27, 2004. Although the Philippine government belittled the capability of ASG to wage such kind of maritime attacks, ASG spokesperson Abu Soliman said the attack on *Superferry 14* was a sample of things to come and treated the *Superferry 14* incident as a revenge for the ongoing violence in Mindanao. A reliable source from the Philippine intelligence office said that the Marine Board Inquiry in charge of investigating the incident confirmed that the ASG masterminded the *Superferry 14* explosion.[54]

With the sinister linking of terrorists and pirates, Southeast Asia has become the focal point of maritime fear.[55] This led Singapore Home Affairs Minister Wong Kan Seng to declare that pirates roaming the waters of Southeast Asia should be regarded as terrorists.[56] In an interview, the home minister argued, "Although we talk about piracy or anti-piracy, if there's a crime conducted at sea sometimes we do not know whether it's pirates or terrorists who occupy the ship so we have to treat them all alike."[57]

However, exact definitions for piracy and terrorism are problematic because many experts and policymakers are unsure at which point piracy becomes terrorism.[58] A maritime security analyst even stressed that the distinction between piracy and terrorism is becoming blurred because "pirates collude with terrorists, terrorists adopt pirate tactics and policymakers eager for public support start labeling every crime as maritime terrorism."[59]

## The Regional Maritime Security Initiative

As a result of the growing incidences of piracy and the possibility of the conduct of maritime terrorism in Southeast Asia, Admiral Thomas Fargo, Commander in Chief of the U.S. Pacific Command, spoke of the concept of a Regional Maritime Security Initiative (RMSI) during his testimony before the U.S. House of Representatives Armed Services Committee on March 31, 2004.[60] Fargo introduced the concept of RMSI as a means to combat transnational threats in Southeast Asia, and based on the principle of a coalition of the willing. Fargo mentioned that the RMSI was meant to operationalize both the Proliferation Security Initiative (PSI) and the Malacca Straits Initiative (MSI) in order to promote regional security in the midst of growing threats to maritime security.

The RMSI specifically aims to promote cooperation among navies of the region in order "to assess and then provide detailed plans to build and synchronize interagency and international capacity to fight threats that use the maritime space to facilitate their illicit activity."[61] It was widely reported in the media that the RMSI intended to combat transnational crimes in the Straits of Malacca through the mobilization of U.S. marines.[62] Although Fargo testified that he found this concept "well received by our friends and allies in the region," Malaysia and Indonesia — the two main littoral states in the Straits of Malacca — expressed objections to the RMSI, arguing that the concept could violate their national sovereignty. Marty Natalegawa, spokesman of the Indonesian foreign ministry, stressed that the security of the Malacca Straits was the joint responsibility of Indonesia and Malaysia. Deputy Prime Minister of Malaysia, Najib Razak, supported this view when he told the Bernama news agency that Malaysia and Indonesia were responsible for ensuring security in the straits.[63] Razak underscored that Indonesia and Malaysia "do not propose to invite the U.S. to join the security operations we have mounted there [Malacca Strait]" and "even if they wish to act, they should get our permission as this touches on the question of our national sovereignty."[64]

Given the strong sentiments expressed by both Indonesia and Malaysia, Fargo provided further clarification of the RMSI during the Military Law and Operations

Conference on May 3, 2004, in Vancouver, British Columbia.[65] Mindful of the national sensitivities of concerned states in Southeast Asia, Fargo explained that the goal of RMSI was "to develop a partnership of willing regional nations with varying capabilities and capacities to identify, monitor, and intercept transnational maritime threats under existing international and domestic laws."[66] U.S. Naval Pacific Fleet Commander Admiral Walter F. Doran further explained that the RMSI would focus predominantly on intelligence sharing rather than on the deployment of troops. The U.S. Assistant Secretary of State for East Asia and Pacific Affairs even recognized the capability of Malaysia and Indonesia to safeguard the Malacca Straits and stressed that the United States would not deploy troops without the approval of the littoral states.[67]

## Building National Capacities to Combat Piracy and Maritime Terrorism: Force Modernization through Defense Development

Apparently, one major challenge to regional cooperation against piracy and maritime terrorism in Southeast Asia is the issue of national sovereignty. Strong sentiments of nationalism and sensitivity to sovereignty issues make cooperation in maritime security even among countries in Southeast Asia utterly difficult. In addition, most countries in Southeast Asia are also reluctant to deeply involve extraregional powers in the security affairs of their respective countries. Indonesia and Malaysia, particularly, are not willing "to grant an extra-regional power the freedom to conduct patrols and law enforcement at will in their backyard," even in the name of regional maritime security.[68] Therefore, the only way to combat piracy and other transnational maritime security threats in Southeast Asia is to build the national capacities of the respective littoral states through force modernization to confront these threats[69] since territorial integrity is paramount and the principle of noninterference so sacred.

But how do we go about building up national capacities? As highlighted earlier, piracy abounds in Southeast Asia because the national capacity to combat the threat is limited. The Philippines and Indonesia, the two archipelagic states in the region, "have not merely very limited resources in policing their coastlines, but the maritime area and length of coastlines they have to keep under surveillance are extremely large."[70] Indonesia alone needs enormous resources to protect its very long maritime zones. This is in stark contrast with the tiny states of Singapore and Brunei with enough economic resources to ably police their short coastlines.

Although Southeast Asian countries ventured into force modernization programs to varying degrees in the mid-1990s, this does not equate, however, with military effectiveness to address various threats, including maritime, to their national security.[71] The 1997 Asian financial crisis aborted most of these force modernization efforts, particularly in Indonesia, the Philippines, and Thailand. Although Singapore, Brunei, Myanmar, and to a certain extent Malaysia are pushing ahead with their force modernization programs in the aftermath of the financial crisis,[72] present capabilities of littoral states in Southeast Asian remain limited to address the growing maritime security problems in the region. These limitations will be reflected in the present quality and quantity of their maritime forces.[73]

To build the capacities of armed forces in the region to combat threats to maritime security, it may be better for extraregional powers like the United States, Japan, and Australia to intensify their assistance to Southeast Asian countries and build up their capacities through force modernization to address the maritime security threats that confront them.

An excellent example in capacity building is the cooperation between the United States and the Philippines. The United States is assisting the Philippines in the area of counterterrorism through the Philippine Defense Reform (PDR) initiative to enhance the capacity of the Armed Forces of the Philippines (AFP) and other security sectors to address various threats to the country's internal security, which include the ASG, the MILF, and the New People's Army (NPA), among others. U.S. assistance is broad based and extends beyond the conduct of joint military exercises. It includes defense strategic planning, defense programming and budgeting, human resource development, defense acquisition, and military capability building.[74] With the help of Australia, the United States also plans to assist the Philippines in building its national capability to address its maritime security problems. In fact, Australia is broadening its defense ties with the Philippines because of the convergence of their mutual interests in maritime security given that both countries are maritime nations.

Besides assisting the Philippines, the United States also provides assistance to Malaysia in the area of counterterrorism. Despite Malaysia's criticisms of U.S. actions against Afghanistan and Iraq, the United States continues to intensify their bilateral security relationship after 9/11. Malaysia's consent to the setting up of the Regional Counter-Terrorism Centre in Kuala Lumpur with U.S. assistance has been regarded as a clear manifestation of closer security ties between the two countries.[75] These evolving security ties may yet spill over to the area of maritime security.

Indonesia also receives assistance from the United States in the building up of its national capacity to confront both land-based and maritime terrorism. The United States is rebuilding its defense ties with Indonesia and has openly pursued the restoration of full military-to-military relations with Jakarta[76] as a result of its global campaign against terrorism.[77] In the campaign against piracy and maritime terrorism in Southeast Asia, the United States and Indonesia can forge greater cooperation to promote maritime security in the region, especially in the pirate-infested Straits of Malacca.

## Regional Responses

Aside from the United States, other regional powers can also help in building the capacities of Southeast Asian countries to address their maritime security problems. Japan has long been involved in maritime security cooperation in Southeast Asia by hosting various workshops on piracy and conducting maritime security training.[78] Japan has even introduced the idea of "ocean governance" to strengthen maritime security management in the Asia–Pacific.[79]

China, on the other hand, is broadening its cooperation with ASEAN countries to include maritime security. A Chinese military official even proposed joint maritime military exercises between China and ASEAN countries.[80] Although ASEAN countries are concerned about China's expanding maritime ambitions,[81] they see the role of China as an opportunity, with concomitant security challenges, rather than a threat.[82] China's accession to the 1976 Treaty of Amity and Cooperation in Southeast Asia is a positive indication of China's peaceful rise in the region. The signing of the China–ASEAN strategic partnership agreement in October 2003 also provides several opportunities for China and Southeast Asia to promote their common maritime security interests.

Australia is presently strengthening its ties with Southeast Asian countries to advance its maritime security interests in the region,[83] as Australia regards Southeast Asia as an integral part of its strategic space. Thus, it is in the interest of Australia to assist Southeast Asian countries in the promotion of maritime security in the region. In its recent white paper, Australia has enumerated its efforts in promoting maritime security in Southeast Asia by providing financial assistance to countries that are presently strengthening their capabilities in port security. For example, Australia has provided US$1.3 million to the port security capacity-building project in the Philippines to help the Philippine government strengthen its port security arrangements and comply with the security requirements of the International Maritime Organization.[84] Australia has to sustain these efforts to build the capacities of Southeast Asian countries in the fight against piracy and maritime terrorism.

India's "Look East" policy also provides opportunities for maritime security cooperation with Southeast Asian countries. Individual ASEAN countries have enhanced their bilateral ties with India.[85] With the signing of the Framework Agreement on Comprehensive Economic Cooperation between the Association of Southeast Asian Nations and the Republic of India on October 8, 2003, hopes were high that their scope of cooperation will spill over to maritime security.

Assistance of major powers, however, shall not be limited to training of law enforcement agencies like the coast guard or marine police. Assistance must also be comprehensive to address the root causes of piracy and maritime terrorism in Southeast Asia. Assistance therefore must be extended to other reform initiatives like security sector reforms, governance reforms, and socioeconomic reforms to produce a virtuous cycle. Without a comprehensive reform package, the region will continue to face the vicious cycle of maritime security threats.

An interesting component of a comprehensive reform package to address maritime security threats is national defense development — a new approach that aims to reform the national defense sectors in the developing world.[86] Developing national defense sectors increases the capacity of states to address security threats. Otherwise known as defense sector reform, the defense development approach claims that underdeveloped defense sectors "endanger neighboring states, contaminate domestic politics and markets, engage in transnational crimes, such as piracy and maritime terrorism, and even fail in their assigned mission: to provide adequate national security."[87] In this context, defense development is inextricably linked with economic and political development. Successful reform in the national defense sector in the developing world can facilitate economic growth and good governance as well as promote regional and international security. Thus, international donor agencies and development organizations are urged to make defense an integral part of their overall development agenda. Defense development can enhance national capacities of Southeast Asian states to address not only maritime threats but also other threats to their security.

## Conclusion

Piracy and maritime terrorism will continue to plague Southeast Asian waters if the root causes of their conduct are not effectively addressed. If national capacities to combat piracy and maritime terrorism are not built into the littoral states of Southeast Asia, these maritime security threats may escalate as the recent increase in piracy attacks in Southeast Asia shows. However, piracy and maritime terrorism are just two of the many maritime security concerns in Southeast Asia. The comprehensiveness and complexity of maritime security concerns in the region are gargantuan challenges that Southeast Asia countries have to face in the years to come. Thus, assistance of major powers is needed to increase the capacity of littoral states to address their maritime security concerns; and the development of the defense sectors, which includes force modernization, of the affected Southeast Asian countries is one way to enhance the national capacity to combat the transnational security challenges that have already risen and may yet arise in the future. The development of the defense sectors also has the secondary effect of boosting national confidence, and stronger national confidence can open the gate for greater regional and international security cooperation without the anxiety of sacrificing national sovereignty.

## Endnotes

1. ARF Statement on Cooperation against Piracy and other Threats to Maritime Security, Phnom Penh, Cambodia, June 16–20, 2003.
2. Ibid.
3. Ibid.

4. Tamara Renee Shie, "Ports in a Storm? The Nexus between Counterterrorism, Counterproliferation, and Maritime Security in Southeast Asia," *Issues and Insights*, Vol. 4, No. 4 (Pacific Forum CSIS, July 2004), p. 1.

5. See S. Enders Wimbush, "Maritime Security in East Asia in 2025: Critical Uncertainties," and Joshua Ho, "Prospective Maritime Challenges in East Asia: A Singaporean Perspective" (Papers prepared for presentation for the Conference on Maritime Security in East Asia organized by the Center for Strategic and International Studies and American–Pacific Sealanes Security Institute, Inc., held at Hilton Hawaiian Village, Honolulu, Hawaii on January 19–20, 2004).

6. See Andrew T.H. Tan and J.D. Kenneth Boutin (eds.), *Non-Traditional Security Issues in Southeast Asia* (Singapore: Select Publishing Pte Ltd., 2001); and Ralf Emmers, *Non-Traditional Security in the Asia–Pacific: The Dynamics of Securitization* (Singapore: Eastern Universities Press, 2004).

7. Shie, p. 33.

8. Mark Valencia, "International Cooperation in Anti-Piracy Efforts in Asia: Some Considerations," at: http://www.apan-info.net/maritime/key_piracy_view.asp (accessed April 27, 2004).

9. Shie, p. 13.

10. Ibid.

11. Ibid.

12. Dana Robert Dillon, "Piracy in Asia: A Growing Barrier to Maritime Trade," *The Heritage Foundation Backgrounder*, No. 1379 (June 2000), p. 2.

13. See Peter Chalk, "Threats to the Maritime Environment: Piracy and Terrorism" (Presented to the RAND Stakeholder Consultation at Ispra, Italy, October 28–30, 2002).

14. See "Asia Piracy Costs $25 bln a year, says experts," Reuters News Service, Singapore (December 11, 2002) at: http://www.planetark.com/dailynewsstory.cfm/newsid/18987/newsDate/11-Dec-2002/story.htm (accessed April 27, 2004).

15. Bintan Eric Ellis, "Piracy on the High Seas Is on the Rise in Southeast Asia," Fortune (September 29, 2003). Also at: http://www.singapore-window.org/sw03/030919fo.htm (accessed April 27, 2004).

16. See Report of the Organisation for Economic Cooperation and Development, "Price of Increased Maritime Security Is Much Lower than Potential Cost of a Major Terror Attack" at: http://www.oecd.org/document/30/0,2340,en_2649_201185_4390494_1_1_1_1,00.html (accessed April 27, 2004).

17. "Asia Lacks Fund and Will to Fight Piracy: U.S. Academic," *Business Times*, March 10, 2004.

18. "Globalization and Poverty in Southeast Asia: NGO Response" available at: www.asia-caucus.net.ph/resources/poverty_research.doc (accessed May 6, 2004).

19. For more discussions on this topic, see Stuart W. Smead, "A Thesis on Modern Day Piracy," at: http://www.angelfire.com/ga3/tropicalguy/piracymodernday.html (accessed May 4, 2004).

20. "Asia Lacks Fund and Will to Fight Piracy: U.S. Academic," *Business Times*, March 10, 2004.

21. For more discussions, see "Southeast Asia as the Global Center of Marine Biodiversity" at: http://www.pemsea.org/info%20center/articles/tropcsts0797_globlcntrmrnbiodiversity.htm" (accessed May 4, 2004).

22. Cindy Vallar, at: "The Cost of Modern Piracy," at http://www.cindyvallar.com/modern3.html (accessed May 4, 2004).

23. Dillon, p. 1.

24. Ibid.

25. Cdr. Jose Renan C. Suarez, "Towards a Navy of Substance: A Modernization Program," *Navy Digest*, Vol. 3, No. 1, January–June 2003, p. 32. Also see Lt. Antonio F. Trillanes, "An Implementation Analysis of the Philippine Navy Modernization Program," *Navy Digest*, Vol. 3, No. 1, January–June 2003, pp. 21–28. Trillanes is one of the principal actors in the July 2003 Oakwood Mutiny. He is presently in military custody awaiting court-martial.

26. Dillon, p. 2.

27. Ibid.

28. Hasjim Djalal, "Piracy in Southeast Asia: Indonesian and Regional Responses" (Paper prepared for presentation for the Conference on Maritime Security in East Asia organized by the Center for Strategic and International Studies and American-Pacific Sealanes Security Institute, Inc., held at Hilton Hawaiian Village, Honolulu, Hawaii on January 19–20, 2004), p. 6.

29. For more discussions on the author's view on this issue, see Rommel C. Banlaoi, "Security Cooperation and Conflict in Southeast Asia after 9/11" (Paper presented at the 1st Congress of the Asian Political and International Studies Association on November 27–30, 2003, Oriental Hotel, Singapore).

30. Allen V. Estabillo, "RP, Indonesia Want Strong Maritime Security System," *Minda News*, January 16, 2004.

31. Shie, p. 13.

32. Patrick Goodenough, "Maritime Security Takes Center Stage in Southeast Asia," *CNSNews.com*, June 29, 2004. Available online at: http://www.cnsnews.com/ (accessed 27 July 2004).

33. Ibid.

34. Ibid.

35. Richard Halloran, "Link between Terrorists, Pirates in SE Asia a Growing Concern," HonoluluAdvertiser.com, March 7, 2004. Available at: http://the.honoluluadvertiser.com/article/2004/Mar/07 (accessed July 28, 2004).

36. Tanner Campbell and Rohan Gunaratna, "Maritime Terrorism, Piracy and Crime," in Rohan Gunaratna (ed.), *Terrorism in the Asia–Pacific: Threat and Response* (Singapore: Eastern University Press, 2003), p. 72.

37. Zachary Abuza, "Terrorism in Southeast Asia: Keeping al-Qaeda at Bay," *Terrorism Monitor*, Vol. II, Issue No. 9 (May 6, 2004), p. 4.

38. Office of Naval Intelligence, *Threats and Challenges to Maritime Security 2020* (U.S. Coast Guard Intelligence Coordination Center, March 1, 1999), Chapter III. Also see electronic version of the report at: http://www.fas.org/irp/threat/maritime2020/CHAPTER3.htm.

39. Ibid.

40. H.R. Vitasa and Nararya Soeprapto, "Maritime Sector Developments in ASEAN" (Paper presented in the Maritime Policy Seminar organized by the United Nations Conference on Trade and Development and the Ministry of Communications of Indonesia, Jakarta, October 11–13, 1999).

41. For a good reference on this topic, see John Noer and David Gregory, *Chokepoints: Maritime Economic Concerns in Southeast Asia* (Washington, DC: National Defense University, 1996).
42. U.S. Pacific Command, "Shipping and Commerce" at: www.pacom.mil/publications/apeu02/s04ship7.pdf (accessed August 6, 2004).
43. Abuza, p. 5.
44. Joshua Ho of the Singapore-based Institute of Defence and Strategic Studies gave this analysis in an interview with the Economist. See "Shipping in Southeast: Going for the Jugular," *The Economist* (June 10, 2004). Also at: http://www.economist.com/World/asia/displayStory.cfm?story_id=2752802 (accessed August 6, 2004).
45. Michael Richardson, *A Time Bomb for Global Trade: Maritime-Related Terrorism in the Age of Weapons of Mass Destruction* (Singapore: Institute of Southeast Asian Studies, 2004).
46. This is the main theme of the session "The Terrorist Threat to the Maritime Sector in Southeast Asia and the Straits of Malacca," at the International Maritime and Port Security Conference held in Singapore on August 4–5, 2004.
47. John F. Bradford, "Maritime Terror in Southeast Asia: Will the Fire Spread in a Region Already Ablaze?" (Paper presented at the International Maritime and Port Security Conference held in Singapore on August 4–5, 2004).
48. "First Sea Lord Warns of Al-Qaeda Plot to Target Merchant Ships," *Lloyd's List Daily News Bulletin* (August 5, 2004). Available at: http://www.lloydslist.com/bulletin (accessed August 6, 2004).
49. Associated Press, "Expert: Al Qaeda Planning Seaborne Attack," Fox News Channel (March 17, 2004). Available at: http://www.foxnews.com (accessed August 6, 2004).
50. Abuza, p. 5.
51. See "Al-Qaeda Plans High-Sea Terror," WorldNetDaily, October 13, 2003. Available at: http://www.worldnetdaily.com/news/printer-friendly.asp?ARTICLE_ID=35047 (accessed August 6, 2004).
52. Watkins, p. 7.
53. Goodenough, p. 2.
54. As of this writing, however, the Philippine government continues to deny the involvement of ASG in the *Superferry 14* explosion.
55. Halloran, p. 1.
56. "Piracy Equals Terrorism on Troubled Waters: Minister," *Agence France Presse* (December 21, 2003).
57. Ibid.
58. Bantarto Bandoro, "When Piracy becomes Terrorism in the Strait," *The Jakarta Post*, (July 29, 2004).
59. Rubert Herbert-Burns and Lauren Zucker, *Malevolent Tide: Fusion and Overlaps in Piracy and Maritime Terrorism* (Washington, DC: Maritime Intelligence Group, July 30, 2004), p. 1.
60. For an excellent commentary on the RMSI, see Joshua Ho, "Operationalising the Regional Maritime Security Initiative," *IDSS Commentaries* (May 27, 2004).
61. Testimony of Admiral Thomas B. Fargo, U.S. Navy Commander, U.S. Pacific Command, before the House Armed Services Committee, U.S. House of Representatives regarding U.S. Pacific Command Posture, March 31, 2004. Also available at: http://www.pacom.mil/speeches/sst2004/040331housearmedsvcscomm.shtml (accessed July 27, 2004).
62. Shie, p. 23.

63. Goodenough, p. 2.
64. Quoted in Vijay Sakhuja, "Who will safeguard the Malacca Straits?" *Strategic Trend*, Vol. 2, No. 30 (August 2, 2004), p. 1.
65. "Regional Maritime Security Initiative (RMSI): The Idea, The Fact," at: http://www.pacom.mil/rmsi/ (accessed July 28, 2004).
66. Ibid.
67. Shie, p. 23.
68. Ho, p. 1.
69. Rommel C. Banlaoi, "Regional Cooperation against Maritime Terrorism and Proliferation in Southeast Asia" (Discussion paper presented at the Conference on Maritime Security in East Asia organized by the Center for Strategic and International Studies and American–Pacific Sealanes Security Institute, Inc., held at Hilton Hawaiian Village, Honolulu, Hawaii on January 19–20, 2004).
70. Joon Nam Mak, "Piracy in Southeast Asia: Priorities, Perspectives and the Hierarchy of Interests" (Paper prepared for presentation for the Conference on Maritime Security in East Asia organized by the Center for Strategic and International Studies and American–Pacific Sealanes Security Institute, Inc., held at Hilton Hawaiian Village, Honolulu, Hawaii on January 19–20, 2004), p. 1.
71. Andrew Tan, "Force Modernization Trends in Southeast Asia," *IDSS Working Paper*, No. 59 (January 2004), p. 1.
72. Ibid., p. 37.
73. For an excellent analysis of conventional military balance in Southeast Asia, see Anthony H. Cordesman, *The Conventional Military Balance in Southeast Asia: An Analytic Overview: A Comparative Summary of Military Expenditure; Manpower; Land, Air, and Naval, Forces; and Arms Sales* (Washington, DC: Center for Strategic and International Studies, February 27, 2000). Also see Sheldon Simon, "Asian Armed Forces: Internal and External Tasks and Capabilities," *NBR Analysis*, Vol. 11, No. 1 (2000), pp. 1–19 and Derek Da Cunha, "ASEAN Naval Power in the New Millennium," in Jack McCaffire and Alan Hinge (eds.), *Sea Power in the New Century: Maritime Operations in the Asia–Pacific Beyond 2000* (Canberra: Australian Defense Studies Centre, 1998), pp. 73–83.
74. The Philippine Department of National Defence (DND) and United States Army in the Asia–Pacific (USARPAC) cohosted a strategic planning workshop at Oakwood Premier Ayala Center on March 5–7, 2002. As a follow-through, the DND, USARPAC, and the Australian Department of Defence conducted another workshop at Oakwood Premier Ayala Center on August 6–8, 2002. The purpose of this workshop was to learn the best practices in defense planning, programming and budgeting of the United States, Australia, and the Philippines. To make defense procurement as an integral part of the annual DND planning, programming, and budgeting, the three countries held another workshop on defense acquisition system at Oakwood on December 3–5, 2002. The workshop identified some constraints in defense procurement system in the Philippines. The three countries held another workshop on December 9–11, 2003 at Oakwood to exchange ideas on career management system. On July 13–15, 2004, the three countries held the trilateral strategic defense capability planning symposium.
75. Pamela Sodhy, "U.S.–Malaysian Relations during the Bush Administration: The Political, Economic, and Security Aspects," *Contemporary Southeast Asia*, Vol. 25, No. 3 (December 2003), pp. 363–386.

76. International Crisis Group, "Resuming U.S.–Indonesia Military Ties," *Indonesia Briefing* (May 21, 2002). Also see Reyko Huang, "Priority Dilemmas: U.S.–Indonesia Military Relations in the Anti-Terror War," *Center for Defence Information Terrorism Project* (May 23, 2002).

77. Anthony L. Smith, "A Glass Half Full: Indonesia–U.S. Relations in the Age of Terror," *Contemporary Southeast Asia*, Vol. 25, No. 3 (December 2003), pp. 449–472.

78. Shie, p. 31.

79. Masahiro Akiyama, "Prospect for Change in the Maritime Security Situation in Asia and the Role of Japan" (Paper read at the IIPS International Conference on Maritime Security in Southeast and Southwest Asia on December 11–13, 2001 at Ana Hotel, Tokyo, Japan) at: http://www.iips.org/Akiyama_paper.pdf (accessed July 29, 2004).

80. Lee Kim Chew, "China Could Play Part in ASEAN's Maritime Security," *Strait Times* (June 24, 2004).

81. See Lee Jae-Hyung, "China's Expanding Maritime Ambitions in the Western Pacific and Indian Ocean," *Contemporary Southeast Asia*, Vol. 24, No. 3 (December 2002), pp. 549–568.

82. Rommel C. Banlaoi, "Southeast Asian Perspectives on the Rise of China: Regional Security after 9/11," *Parameters: U.S. Army War College Quarterly*, Vol. 33, No. 2 (Summer 2003), pp. 98–107.

83. Commonwealth of Australia, *Australian Maritime Doctrine* (Canberra: Commonwealth of Australia, 2000).

84. Commonwealth of Australia, *Transnational Terrorism: The Threat to Australia* (Canberra: Commonwealth of Australia, 2004), p. 94.

85. Satu Limaye, "India's Relations with Southeast Asia Take a Wing," *Southeast Asian Affairs 2003* (Singapore: Institute of Southeast Asian Studies, 2003), p. 50.

86. Rand Corporation, "Defense Development: A New Approach to Reforming Defense Sectors in the Developing World," *Research Brief* (2004.) Available online at: http://www.rand.org (accessed August 5, 2004).

87. David C. Gompert, Olga Oliker, and Anga Timilsina, "Clean, Lean and Able: A Strategy for Defense Development," *RAND Occasional Paper*, No. 101 (January 2004), p. 2.

# Chapter 13

# Nontraditional Security Issues in the Southeast Asian Maritime Domain: Implications for the Indian Ocean[*]

## Introduction

Though issues of nontraditional security (NTS) have become more prominent in the 21st century security studies discourse, Southeast Asia has always viewed security in nontraditional sense. Since its establishment in 1967, the Association of Southeast Asian Nations (ASEAN) has already interpreted security in a comprehensive manner, which includes panoply of issues that are presently labeled nontraditional. Although the word *security* is not explicitly mentioned in the 1967 Bangkok Declaration, the scope of ASEAN cooperation has always been in the area of security viewed arguably in a nontraditional perspective. The idea that security goes

[*] Originally published in V.R. Raghavan and W. Lawrence Prabhakar (eds.), *Maritime Security in the Indian Ocean Region: Critical Issues of Debate* (New Delhi: Tata McGraw Hill, 2008), pp. 239–262. This is drawn from a paper presented to the International Symposium "The Changing Oceanic Landscape in the Indian Ocean Region: Issues and Perspectives of Debate," organized by the Centre for Security Analysis (CSA), Chennai, India (December 14, 2006).

beyond the traditional domain of the military sector has been widely recognized in Southeast Asia and put into practice in varying degrees by member countries of ASEAN.[1] But the international politics of the cold war formidably marginalized these NTS concerns as major powers concentrated on hard issues of state security through military deterrence. During the cold war, major international security issues were all deliberated within the context of superpower rivalry.

The aftermath of the cold war and the increasing globalization marked by rapid technological change led painstakingly to the resolute rethinking of the traditional notion of security. At present, the agenda of security has broadened and deepened to include myriad issues that are now labeled nontraditional. This resulted in the tremendous growth of discussions on the NTS concerns of Southeast Asia, particularly in the context of human security and Asia's emerging regional order.[2] The growing problem of terrorism unleashed by 9/11 has also confounded these concerns, particularly in the maritime domain.

This paper intends to examine the policies and operational issues of NTS in maritime Southeast Asia as a contiguous region of the Indian Ocean. It aims to describe state responses to NTS threats facing the Southeast Asian maritime domain and assess cooperative and convergent security responses in the wider regional security framework of Southeast Asia in pursuance of a human security agenda. This paper also argues that when viewed from the lens of Maritime Regional Security Complex (MRSC), NTS issues in Southeast Asia inevitably affect the security of the Indian Ocean. Issues of maritime security therefore make the waters of Southeast Asia and the Indian Ocean in the same MRSC where South Asia and Southeast Asia inevitably converge to promote human security.

## Southeast Asia and the Concept of Maritime Regional Security Complex (MRSC)

It is widely acknowledged that regions are now more salient features of international politics in the 21st century.[3] Among the regions of the world, Southeast Asia has taken on increased importance because of its pivotal role in the creation and operation of the ASEAN Regional Forum (ARF).[4] Al Qaeda's reported operations in the region through the Jemaah Islamiyah (JI) even made Southeast Asia the "second front" in the global campaign against terrorism.[5] Its strategic location for international trade and commerce has also made Southeast Asia one of the most important regional security complexes in the world.[6]

Barry Buzan originally developed the concept of a regional security complex (RSC) to describe "a group of states whose primary security concerns link together sufficiently closely that their national securities cannot realistically be considered apart from one another."[7] There are two defining characteristics of an RSC: (1) the distribution of powers among states, and (2) the patterns of amity and enmity.

The first characteristic echoes the neo-realist logic of power balancing. The second characteristic is Buzan's innovation. The concept of amity is characterized by trust and cooperation among states. The concept of enmity, on the other hand, is defined by fear and rivalry generated by the states. Amity involves all types of security relationships ranging from genuine friendship to expectations of mutual protection or support, while enmity covers all forms of security relationships set by mutual suspicions and fears.[8] In his later works, Buzan reformulated the concept of RSC to mean "a set of units whose major processes of securitization, desecuritization, or both are so interlinked that their security problems cannot be reasonably analyzed or resolved apart from one another."[9] Despite the reformulation, the salient feature of an RSC is the observation that states are enmeshed in a complex web of security interdependence, which tends to be regionally focused.

As a region, Southeast Asia is in essence an MRSC "dotted with thousands of islands and islets amid larger landmasses and peninsulas."[10] As an MRSC, states in this maritime region have a high level of interdependence on various maritime security issues confronting them. But the MRSC of Southeast Asia also extends to the Indian Ocean. The South China Sea and the Malacca Straits provide a key maritime link to the Indian Ocean. NTS issues in the South China Sea and the Malacca Straits push South Asia and Southeast Asia closer as interdependent regions. The maritime domain intensifies the security convergence between Southeast Asia and South Asia.

## Nontraditional Security (NTS) in Maritime Southeast Asia

As a maritime region, Southeast Asia is beset by various NTS issues that are largely maritime in nature. The NTS concept was developed as a result of the broadening and deepening of the concept of security, which is a very problematic concept in political science and international relations because scholars and practitioners do not have a shared understanding of the meaning of "security."[11] There are scholars advocating a *limited* or bounded definition, while there are those advancing a *broader* or more *expanded* definition.

A limited definition of security is based on the traditional notion that the state is central to the whole concept of security.[12] The state is the primary political community and player and therefore the main referent of security.[13] The limited definition of security is apparently anchored on the realist school, which views the state as the principal player in domestic and international politics.[14] From this perspective, the security of the state rests on its ability to develop a strong external defense defined in terms of military power, which, on the other hand, is measured in terms of possession of a huge arsenal of weapons as well as recruitment and training of troops for war-fighting missions.

In short, scholars traditionally define security in geopolitical terms, encompassing issues of nuclear deterrence, balance of power, and military strategy.[15] Scholars adhering to the narrow definition of security are those interested in military statecraft and strategic studies. Other scholars, however, have challenged this limited definition of security arguing that security is a broad concept that goes beyond its military dimension.[16] Security also means the security of the environment (environmental security), the security of the people (human security), and security from hunger (economic security), among others. Southeast Asian countries call this concept of security "comprehensive security."[17] Comprehensive security regards the traditional definition of security as an insufficient conceptual tool to describe the security predicaments of developing countries.

An important contribution to the broadening of the concept of security is the Copenhagen School of security. This school emanates from the work *Security: A New Framework for Analysis*, written Barry Buzan, Ole Waever, and Jaap de Wilde of the Conflict and Peace Research Institute (COPRI) based in Copenhagen, Denmark.[18] This school regards security as a particular type of politics applicable to a wide range of issues: social, economic, military, economical, and ecological. It even argues that all security is political because all threats and defenses are constituted and defined politically.[19]

A major intellectual innovation of the Copenhagen School is its differentiation of nonpoliticization, politicization, and securitization. A public issue is nonpoliticized when an issue is not elevated to public debate. An issue is politicized when it becomes "part of public policy, requiring government decision and resource allocations or, more rarely, some other form of communal governance."[20] When an issue "is presented as an existential threat, requiring emergency measures and justifying actions outside the normal bounds of political procedure," it becomes securitized. Issues hitherto regarded as mere public or social issues that have been securitized belong to the concept of NTS.

The succeeding sections of this paper intend to describe NTS issues in the Southeast Asian maritime domain that are now incorporated in the region's security agenda. This paper aims to examine the implications of these issues for the security of the Indian Ocean. This paper argues that NTS issues in the maritime domain are inherently human security issues because they deeply affect the security of individual human beings in both regions.

For purposes of brevity, NTS issues covered in this chapter include (1) piracy and armed robberies against ships, (2) people smuggling and human trafficking, (3) small arms trafficking, (4) drug trafficking, and (5) maritime terrorism. These issues are usually called transnational crimes in many academic and policy-oriented literatures.[21] This paper focuses on these issues because they are usually committed in the maritime domain and they also affect human conditions of concerned states. Other equally important NTS issues such as environmental degradation, illegal fishing, natural disasters, economic crises, money laundering, communal conflicts, internal armed conflicts, and internal governance challenges are better left to other scholars.[22]

## Piracy and Armed Robberies against Ships

Piracy has been a maritime security concern in Southeast Asian since the ancient times. It continues to be "an enormous problem in Southeast Asia especially in Indonesian waters along the Straits of Malacca and Singapore."[23] In fact, Southeast Asia has the long-standing reputation of being the piracy hotspot of the word. It remains the most prone region to acts of piracy and has accounted for around 50% of almost all attacks worldwide.[24]

During the third quarter of 2006, however, the International Maritime Bureau noted with enthusiasm the decline of reported piracy attacks worldwide from 205 in 2005 to only 174 in 2006.[25] Piracy incidents in Southeast Asia also declined from 84 during the third quarter of 2005 to only 65 during the same period of 2006 (see Table 13.1). This prompted Lloyds Maritime Intelligence Unit to drop the Strait of Malacca from the list of dangerous waterways of the world, which only accounted for 8 attacks in 2006 compared with 10 in 2005. It is sad to note that though piracy attacks in Indonesia declined from 61 to 40 during those periods, the country still accounted for more attacks than any other country in the world. Thus, the bureau still warned mariners worldwide "to be extra cautious and to take necessary precautionary measures" when transiting to waterways of Southeast Asia.[26]

**Table 13.1   Actual and Attempted Piracy Attacks in Southeast Asia, 2001–2006**

| Location | 2001 | 2002 | 2003 | 2004 | 2005 | 2006 |
|---|---|---|---|---|---|---|
| Cambodia | — | — | — | — | — | — |
| Indonesia | 71 | 72 | 87 | 70 | 61 | 40 |
| S. Malacca | 14 | 11 | 24 | 25 | 10 | 8 |
| Malaysia | 15 | 9 | 5 | 8 | 3 | 9 |
| Myanmar | 1 | — | — | 1 | — | — |
| Philippines | 7 | 7 | 12 | 3 | — | 3 |
| Singapore | 6 | 4 | — | 8 | 7 | 3 |
| Thailand | 6 | 2 | 1 | 4 | 1 | 1 |

*Source:* ICC International Maritime Bureau, *Piracy and Armed Robbery against Ships* (Report for the period January 1 to September 30, 2006).

There are two major types of pirates operating in Asia, in general, and Southeast Asia, in particular. One type is composed of common sea robbers operating in hit-and-run fashion. The attacks on ships last no longer than 15 to 30 minutes and their operations require a minimum level of organization and planning.[27] Though they engage in simple armed robberies against ships, they have the ability to engage in a high level of violence.

The other type is more organized and virulent. It is composed of pirates involved in organized crimes. They are organized pirate gangs or syndicates that attack medium-sized vessels, including cargo ships, bulk carriers, and tankers.[28] This validates the earlier observation that pirates in Southeast Asia range from opportunistic fishermen and the common criminal to members of sophisticated Asian crime syndicates.[29] Piracy also occurs mostly in ports or anchorages. Though piracy is largely a criminal issue, it has been securitized because of its nexus with maritime terrorism. The successful comeback of the piracy problem after the end of the cold war and the rise of terrorism after 9/11 make piracy in the age of global terrorism a serious national, regional, and global security issue.[30] Its impact on human security also led to the securitization of piracy.

The cost of piracy in Southeast Asia on human security is very alarming.[31] James Warren of the Asia Research Institute at the National University of Singapore (NUS) claims that piracy in the region is costing the world economy a staggering amount of US$25 billion a year.[32] Alan Chan, a vocal antipiracy advocate and an owner of Petroships in Singapore, states that piracy is costing the region around US$500 million a year.[33] The Organization for Economic Cooperation and Development, on the other hand, says that new maritime security measures to counter the threat of attacks will require an initial investment by ship operators of at least US$1.3 billion and will increase annual operating costs by US$730 million thereafter.[34] The cost of piracy in Southeast Asia is projected to increase in the future, as the trend in modern piracy becomes more bloody, ruthless, and terrifying.

Piracy abounds in Southeast Asia because of concomitant human security issues connected with poverty. Prevalent poverty in the coastal areas of Southeast Asia encourages people to resort to piracy activities as sources of livelihood. Poverty incidences in the region range from 16% to 55%.[35] Piracy in Southeast Asia "was thought to be an acceptable part of the local culture, a normal but illegal means of making money."[36]

## People Smuggling and Human Trafficking

People smuggling and human trafficking are serious NTS challenges facing Southeast Asia. Issues of people smuggling and human trafficking are part and parcel of human security discourse. A study shows that Southeast Asia has emerged as a key transit region for human smuggling from Iraq and Afghanistan to Australia and elsewhere.[37] Most of the victims involved are women and children who are forced to work as sex workers. Thus, people smuggling and human trafficking are also associated with sex trafficking or white slavery, child prostitution, and forced labor. They are also linked with the issue of illegal migration.

According to the International Organization for Migration, at least 200,000 to 225,000 people are trafficked from Southeast Asia annually.[38] From around 45,000 to 50,000 women and children being trafficked into the United States each year, 30,000 are believed to have come from Southeast Asia (see Figure 13.1).[39] The "Third Wave" of Chinese illegal migration to the United States, Australia, Japan, and even Europe uses Southeast Asia as a transit point.[40] Based on the 1998 report of the International Labor Organization, much of the human trafficking in Southeast Asia centers around the coastal areas of Thailand, where the sex trade accounts for between 2% and 14% of the gross national product.[41]

Though people smuggling, human trafficking, and illegal migration are old criminal problems in the region, the aggravation of the problem in the aftermath of the cold war has led to the securitization of the issue. Australia, for example, has securitized the issue of people smuggling from Southeast Asia because of the threat it poses to Australian national security and Southeast Asian regional security.[42] The shocking escalation of violence in Southeast Asian countries with ongoing internal armed conflicts and the prevalence of poverty have been identified as some of the factors leading to people smuggling, human trafficking, and illegal migration.

The United Nations has estimated that the business of human smuggling and trafficking generates US$8 billion to US$10 billion every year.[43] Based on the study made by the Global Commission on International Migration, the cost of human smuggling and trafficking worldwide ranges from US$203 to US$26,041 for each

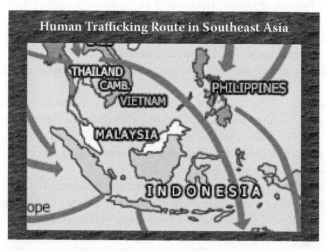

**Figure 13.1    Human trafficking routes across Southeast Asia. (Public Broadcasting Service,** *Dying to Leave, Handbook: The Business of Human Trafficking,* **2003, at: http://www.pbs.org/wnet/wideangle/shows/dying/handbook.html (accessed November 27, 2006.)**

person, depending on the point of origin and point of destination.[44] In Asia, the average cost is US$15,000. The involvement of organized criminal groups with links with corrupt immigration officials makes human smuggling and trafficking obviously a serious human security concern.[45]

## Small Arms Trafficking

Illicit trafficking of small arms and light weapons has been a regional menace and decades-long criminal problem in Southeast Asia.[46] Illegal arms transfers have been pervasive, causing human security concerns in Southeast Asia. The region is viewed as the international hub for small arms trafficking. [47]

There is no reliable source on the exact quantity of small arms and light weapons (SALW) being trafficked in the region. As Peter Chalk laments, "There is, as yet, no estimate of even the rough value of the illicit light arms trade in Southeast Asia."[48] But there are at least 639 million small arms in the world today, nearly 60% of which are legally held by civilians.[49] If 40% are illegally acquired, around 256 million small arms may have been involved in trafficking.

It has been estimated that SALW accounts for around 60% to 90% of more than 100,000 human deaths involved in violent conflict each year and tens of thousands of additional deaths outside of war zones.[50] There is a view that SALW causes more human damage than weapons of mass destruction, making small arms trafficking a nagging human security issue. SALWs are not only weapons of choice of people involved in organized crimes, they are also weapons of choice of terrorist organizations. The *Patterns of Global Terrorism* of the U.S. State Department states that out of 175 terrorist attacks worldwide, approximately half were committed with SALW.[51] The International Action Network on Small Arms laments that Southeast Asia has been very sluggish in taking effective action to curb illegal arms transfers.[52] But three factors make Southeast Asia susceptible to small arms trafficking:

1. The region is the scene of numerous intrastate conflicts, including in Indonesia, Burma, and the Philippines, that draw the demand for weapons from nonstate actors. Unable to afford new arms or find sellers on the legal arms market, nonstate actors often turn to arms dealers and brokers who will supply used or "surplus" arms.

2. Southeast Asia has ready stockpiles of existing weapons. The region has several postconflict states, where vast numbers of military SALW can easily be obtained. Postwar estimates are between 500,000 and 1 million military small arms in Cambodia alone, although this has certainly dropped today due to some in-country collection and destruction, and outflow from the country onto the black market. Weapons left over from the wars in Vietnam and Laos as well as imported arms from China and the Middle East are also finding their way to insurgents, criminals, and terrorists throughout the region.

3. Southeast Asia is a region with long maritime and continental frontiers that are extremely difficult to monitor and police. Many of ASEAN's members are also "weak states" and lack the capacity to effectively control their borders and interdict arms traffickers. Such states also often store national inventories of legally owned small arms in insecure and poorly managed facilities, making theft, loss, and consequently smuggling, possible. Many also lack adequate domestic gun control legislation and enforcement. Sales from Thai Army arsenals feature in the local papers on a somewhat regular basis, and those are only the ones caught by the police.[53]

## Trafficking in Illicit Drugs

Drug trafficking is known to be the largest international crime problem in the world, with an estimated value of US$400 billion annually.[54] Around 200 million people reportedly consume illegal drugs worldwide, mostly cannabis.[55] The United Nations Office on Drugs and Crime has reported that around 15 million people worldwide have used opium and heroin.[56]

Southeast Asia, which has grown and sold narcotics for centuries, serves not only as one of the major transits of illegal drug trade in the world but also as one of the major factories of global narcotics production. Two-thirds of the world's opium production was reportedly based in Southeast Asia through the Golden Triangle of Thailand, Myanmar, and Laos (see Figure 13.2). In fact, the Golden Triangle is in reality a "Quadrangle" because the Yunan Province of China, which produces more opium than anywhere else in the world, represents the fourth side of the illegal drug trade network in Southeast Asia. The Golden Triangle has an opium trade network with the Golden Crescent of Afghanistan, Iran, and Pakistan and opium-producing countries of Mexico and Colombia.

Cannabis grows widely in Cambodia, and amphetamine-type stimulants are produced mostly in Eastern Myanmar and Northern Laos. Thailand has been the most favored route for drug trafficking in Southeast Asia, prompting the Thai government to declare the drug problem as a threat to national security.[57]

The cost of drug trafficking in Southeast Asia on human security is very alarming. Drug abuse contributes to the rapid spread of HIV/AIDS, raises the incidence of violent crimes, aggravates the problem of juvenile delinquency, and even undermines family structures.[58] Illegal drug trade also involves other transnational crimes like arms smuggling and human trafficking, confounding the human security challenge.

## Maritime Terrorism

Being a maritime region, Southeast Asia is vulnerable to the problem of maritime terrorism. Because of the burgeoning threat of terrorism posed by JI (with its ambitious desire to establish a pan-Islamic state in Southeast Asia) and the high incidence

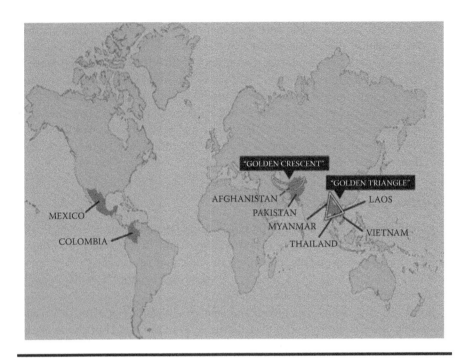

**Figure 13.2 Major world drug trafficking centers. (Wikipedia, at: http://en.wikipedia.org/wiki/Golden_Triangle_[Southeast_Asia], accessed on November 28, 2006.)**

of piracy, maritime terrorism has become a serious challenge to the region's maritime security.[59]

It has been argued that because of the high incidence of piracy in Southeast Asian waters, terrorists could use piracy as a cover for maritime terrorist attacks.[60] There is no doubt that the motives of pirates and terrorist are arguably different. Pirates pursue economic gains, but terrorists advance political objectives.[61] But terrorists have developed the ability to either adopt pirates' tactics or "piggyback" on pirates' raids.[62] Analysts contend that maritime terrorists, rather than simply stealing, could either blow up the ship or use it to ram into another vessel or a port facility.[63] Thus, security experts have raised the blurring line between piracy and terrorism. They stressed "Not only do pirates terrorize ships' crews, but terror groups like Al-Qaeda could also use pirates' methods either to attack ships, or to seize ships to use in terror attacks at megaports, much like the Sept. 11 hijackers used planes."[64]

Southeast Asia has already experienced the scourge of maritime terrorism. In the Strait of Malacca, for example, the Aegis Defense Services, a London-based security organization, said that the robbery of a chemical tanker, *Dewi Madrim*, appeared to be the handiwork of terrorists.[65]

Specifically in Singapore, intelligence and law enforcement forces have uncovered the JI plot to bomb the U.S. Naval Facility in the Island State. In Indonesia, the Gerakan Aceh Merdeka has also been engaged in maritime terrorism[66] and has been accused of masterminding several attacks in the Malacca Straits.[67] In the Philippines, the Abu Sayyaf Group (ASG) claimed responsibility for the explosion of *Superferry 14* carrying 899 passengers on February 27, 2004. The *Superferry 14* explosion resulted in the death of 116 passengers and wounding of at least 300 others.[68] The death toll caused by maritime terrorism is very telling of its impact on human security.

With the growing nexus of terrorism and piracy, Southeast Asia is becoming the focal point of maritime fear.[69] This has prompted Singapore Minister for Home Affairs Wong Kan Seng to aptly declare pirates roaming the Southeast Asian waters as terrorists.[70] He argued, "Although we talk about piracy or anti-piracy, if there's a crime conducted at sea sometimes we do not know whether it's pirates or terrorists who occupy the ship so we have to treat them all alike."[71]

# Association of Southeast Asian Nations (ASEAN) Policies and Operational Responses to NTS Threats

ASEAN is rich with numerous declarations aiming to promote regional cooperation on NTS. Since 1967, the bulk of ASEAN cooperation has always been in the area of NTS. Though discussion on NTS became more popular only in the aftermath of 9/11, ASEAN regional security cooperation as stated earlier has always been nontraditional and comprehensive.

## Regional Cooperation on NTS the ASEAN Way

ASEAN has two major types of cooperation on NTS. One is cooperation in functional areas that include cooperation in culture and information, disaster management, drugs and narcotics, education, health and nutrition, HIV/AIDS, labor, rural development and poverty eradication, severe acute respiratory syndrome (SARS), science and technology, women, youth, and children, as well as ASEAN University Network.[72] The other is cooperation on transnational issues that include environment, transboundary haze, transnational crime and terrorism, legal cooperation, migration, drugs, and civil services.[73] In the past, ASEAN regarded these issues as public, social, criminal, or political issues. Because these issues affect the security of human beings, they have been securitized in the context of human security.

At the policy level, each of these types of cooperation has produced various declarations, agreements, plans of action, and working groups. But at the heart of all these types of cooperation in Southeast Asia is the ASEAN Way of noninterference in the domestic affairs of member states enshrined in the 1976 Treaty of Amity and Cooperation in Southeast Asia. The ASEAN Way is a diplomatic norm in Southeast Asia upholding the practice of intense dialogues and exhausting consultations (*musyawarah*) to generate consensus (*mufakat*) on contentious issues facing the region. This practice, called *musyawarah dan mufakat*, encourages all ASEAN members to cooperate on various areas through informal and incremental mechanisms.

The idea of ASEAN Security Community (ASC) in the Bali Concord II signed in October 2003 is a clear demonstration of its members' strict adherence to the ASEAN Way. Instead of challenging the ASEAN Way of noninterference, the concept of ASC strongly affirms it by stressing that "ASEAN shall continue to promote regional solidarity and cooperation. Member Countries shall exercise their rights to lead their national existence free from outside interference in their internal affairs."[74] The Bali Concord II also reaffirms the principle of the sovereign rights of each member of ASEAN by dismissing the speculation that ASEAN is building a defense pact or military alliance. To promote regional security, the Bali Concord II states that:

> The ASEAN Security Community, recognizing the sovereign right of the member countries to pursue their individual foreign policies and defense arrangements and taking into account the strong interconnections among political, economic and social realities, subscribes to the principle of comprehensive security as having broad political, economic, social and cultural aspects in consonance with the ASEAN Vision 2020 rather than to a defense pact, military alliance or a joint foreign policy.[75]

One very important characteristic of the ASC is the strong recognition of ASEAN as a regional security complex where the security of one state is inextricably linked with the security of other states. The Bali Concord II vividly underscores:

> The ASEAN Security Community is envisaged to bring ASEAN's political and security cooperation to a higher plane to ensure that countries in the region live at peace with one another and with the world at large in a just, democratic and harmonious environment. The ASEAN Security Community members shall rely exclusively on peaceful processes in the settlement of intra-regional differences and regard their security as fundamentally linked to one another and bound by geographic location, common vision and objectives.[76]

Based on NTS issues covered in this paper, the major ASEAN document that defines the parameters of regional cooperation is the ASEAN Declaration on Transnational Crimes, signed as early as December 20, 1997, in Manila, Philippines. This declaration was a response to the 29th ASEAN Ministerial Meeting (AMM) in Jakarta in July 1996, which stressed the need "to focus attention on such issues as narcotics, economic crimes, including money laundering, environment and illegal migration which transcend borders and affect the lives of the people in the region." The declaration was also in pursuance of the 30th AMM in Kuala Lumpur in July 1997, which stressed the need for sustained cooperation in addressing transnational concerns including the fight against terrorism, trafficking in people, illicit drugs and arms and piracy.

Apparent in this declaration is the urgent need to combat transnational crimes that affect human security. Table 13.2 lists some of the major declarations, joint communiqué, and other documents signed by ASEAN to combat transnational crimes and promote regional cooperation in NTS.

Because transnational crimes and NTS threats are also committed at sea, ASEAN issued a communiqué at the conclusion of the 37th Ministerial Meeting held on June 29–30, 2004, in Jakarta, where ASEAN foreign ministers urged the need to "explore the possibility of establishing a maritime forum" in Southeast Asia. The ASEAN, through the ARF, also issued the Statement on Cooperation against Piracy and Other Threats to Maritime Security at the 36th ASEAN Ministerial Meeting and the 10th ARF Post Ministerial Conferences in Cambodia on June 16–20, 2003. This statement aims to promote maritime security cooperation not only in Southeast Asia but also in the entire Asia–Pacific region.

Beyond the ASEAN Way, Admiral Thomas Fargo of the U.S. Pacific Command launched the controversial concept of Regional Maritime Security Initiative (RMSI) during his testimony before the U.S. House of Representatives Armed Services Committee on March 31, 2004.[77] Fargo introduced the RMSI to address transnational threats in Southeast Asia. Fargo argued that the RMSI aimed to operationalize the Proliferation Security Initiative (PSI) and the Malacca Straits Initiative (MSI) to promote regional security in the midst of the growing maritime security threats. But ASEAN did not accept the RMSI, PSI, and MSI because of the strong objection of Indonesia and Malaysia, who are cautious of American strategic intentions.

## Operational Responses to NTS Threats in Southeast Asia

To address NTS threats in Southeast Asia at the operational level, ASEAN signed the ASEAN Plan of Action to Combat Transnational Crime (2001) followed by the Work Program to Implement the ASEAN Plan of Action to Combat Transnational Crime (May 17, 2002). Indonesia, Malaysia, and the Philippines signed in May 2002 the Agreement on Information Exchange and Establishment of Communication Procedures, otherwise known as the Trilateral Agreement, to enhance regional cooperation and promote the interoperability among participating countries in curbing transnational crimes and other illegal activities occurring within their territories. Participating countries have started the formulation of standard operating procedures to vigorously implement the Trilateral Agreement. The Trilateral Agreement also inspired the drafting of the proposed ASEAN Counter-Terrorism Convention,

**Table 13.2  Major Declarations, Joint Communiqué, and Other Documents Signed by ASEAN to Combat Transnational Crimes and Promote Regional Cooperation in Nontraditional Security, 1998–2005**

| |
|---|
| Manila Declaration on the Prevention and Control of Transnational Crime (1998) |
| Joint Communiqué of the 2nd ASEAN Ministerial Meeting on Transnational Crime (AMMTC), Yangon, June 23, 1999 |
| Joint Communiqué of the 3rd ASEAN Ministerial Meeting on Transnational Crime (AMMTC), Singapore, October 11, 2001 |
| 2001 ASEAN Declaration on Joint Action to Counter Terrorism, Bandar Seri Begawan, November 5, 2001 |
| Joint Communiqué of the Special ASEAN Ministerial Meeting on Terrorism (AMMTC), Kuala Lumpur, May 20–21, 2002 |
| Declaration on Terrorism by the 8th ASEAN Summit, Phnom Penh, November 3, 2002 |
| Joint Declaration of ASEAN and China on Cooperation in the Field of NTS Issues, Phnom Penh, November 4, 2002 |
| Joint Declaration on Co-Operation to Combat Terrorism, 14th ASEAN-EU Ministerial Meeting, Brussels, January 27, 2003 |
| Joint Communiqué of the 4th ASEAN Ministerial Meeting on Transnational Crime (AMMTC), Bangkok, January 8, 2004 |
| Joint Communiqué of the 1st ASEAN Plus Three Ministerial Meeting on Transnational Crime (AMMTC+3), Bangkok, January 10, 2004 |
| Joint Communiqué of the 24th ASEAN Chiefs of Police Conference, Chiang Mai, Thailand, August 16–20, 2004 |
| Joint Communiqué of the 25th ASEAN Chiefs of Police Conference, Bali, Indonesia, May 16–20, 2005 |
| Joint Communiqué of the Second ASEAN Plus Three Ministerial Meeting on Transnational Crime (AMMTC+3), Ha Noi, November 30, 2005 |
| Joint Communiqué of the 5th ASEAN Ministerial Meeting on Transnational Crime (AMMTC), Ha Noi, November 29, 2005 |

*Source:* ASEAN Secretariat Web site at: http://www.aseansec.org.

which will be presented for approval at the 12th ASEAN Summit in Cebu City, Philippines. Laos and Thailand have acceded to the Trilateral Agreement.

Aside from numerous multilateral mechanisms found in ASEAN, the region also has a complex web of bilateral cooperation among Southeast Asian countries aiming to combat transnational crimes and NTS threats. There have been bilateral maritime border security agreements between Indonesia and Malaysia, the Philippines and Malaysia, Singapore and Malaysia, and the Philippines and Indonesia.[78] These maritime border agreements not only aim to promote maritime security against NTS threats in Southeast Asia but also to ease bilateral tensions in the post–cold war ASEAN.[79]

To strengthen operational response against transnational crimes and NTS threats in the maritime domain, Singapore even proposed the holding of maritime security exercises among navies in Southeast Asia. But among all initiatives in Southeast Asia, the implementation of round-the-clock coordinated patrols of the Malacca Straits by Malaysia, Indonesia, and Singapore is the most encouraging. With the code name Operation Malsindo (Malaysia, Singapore, Indonesia) launched in July 2004, it is thus far the biggest patrolling exercise in the Malacca Straits by the three littoral states. Though there has been no concrete evidence to suggest that Malsindo has directly reduced the scale of piracy in the Malacca Straits,[80] the initiative is an exemplary operational response that can contribute to the reduction of NTS threats in Southeast Asian waters.[81] Malsindo's best practices can provide useful lessons for future initiatives of claimant states in the South China Sea. As stated earlier, piracy attacks in the Malacca Straits were reduced in the third quarter of 2006. Moreover, the Malsindo presents an ASEAN alternative to the American-proposed RMSI. There is a need to emphasize, however, that the Malsindo is still hampered by the sensitivity of littoral states' overprotecting sovereignty and a lack of real operational capacity.[82]

# Implications for the Indian Ocean

What are the implications of this whole gamut of issues for the Indian Ocean? As stated earlier, this paper argues that the waters of Southeast Asia and the Indian Ocean are the waters that unite rather than divide South Asia and Southeast Asia. The maritime states of these two regions constitute the MRSC of Southeast Asia and the Indian Ocean (Figure 13.3). This MRSC is a product of 2,000 years of maritime activities. Though the colonial years and the cold war diverted the attention of South Asia and Southeast Asia away from each other, the Indian Ocean and two major waters of Southeast Asia (the Malacca Straits and the South China Sea) continued to link the two regions together. Maritime and historical links even strongly facilitated the dialogue partnership of India and ASEAN.[83] As a result, India is viewed as the "second wing" of ASEAN.[84] The Indian Ocean is India's strategic connection with Southeast Asia. The shipping lane transiting the Indian

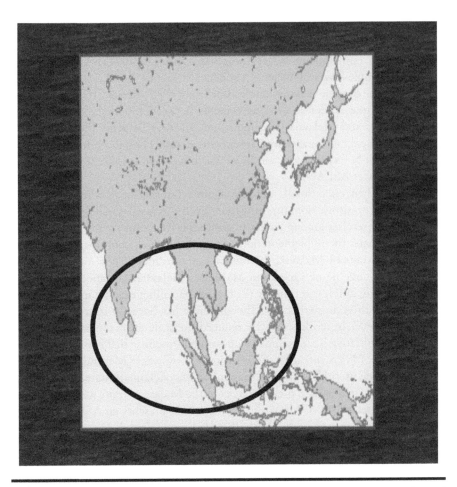

**Figure 13.3  A maritime regional security complex of the Southeast Asia and Indian Ocean regions. (C-Map at: http://80.239.21.90/ntplus/asia.asp.)**

Ocean and entering the strategic choke point of Southeast Asia further makes it an MRSC. Sudhir Devare provides a very succinct analysis of an inevitable link between the Indian Ocean and the waters of Southeast Asia when he writes:

> The forefathers of the people from India and Southeast Asia clearly did not regard the seas around them as dividing factors. Due to the long coastlines of their countries, they had developed maritime traditions and were adept at sailing the ocean and the seas around them for trade and business. Travel across the seas was the best means of communication, which was much developed before the European navigators started sailing around the world. This was prior to globalization becoming a universal phenomenon. Indian ships, not only from the

east coast but also from faraway western coastal regions of Malabar and Gujarat, crossed the Indian Ocean to the fabled islands of Yawadipa of Suvarnadwipa in pursuit of trade. They would travel to the Burmese ports and even further south, anchoring on the Kra peninsula. Goods from India would then be carried across the narrow stretch of land to the Gulf of Siam and onwards to the kingdom of Funan and beyond the South China Sea. Indian ships sailed regularly through the Malacca Strait and traveled to the Vietnamese and Chinese ports. They seemed to have known the route to the islands of the present-day Indonesian archipelago very well.[85]

In this context, NTS in the Southeast Asian maritime domain also affects the NTS of the Indian Ocean and vice versa.

In the area of piracy, for example, the hijacking of the *Alondra Rainbow* in 1999 by pirates operating in the Malacca Straits was solved by the Indian Coast Guard after several days of chase. The Piracy Reporting Centre in Kuala Lumpur gave a worldwide alert prompting the Indian Coast Guard to act decisively.[86] In the area of drug trafficking, the Indian Ocean region is home to more than two-thirds of the world's narcotic supplies with the Golden Triangle of Southeast Asia. Waters of Malaysia and Indonesia are being used as transit points for this illegal activity.[87] The Indian Ocean and the waters of Southeast Asia also provide maritime transit of drug trade between the Golden Triangle and the Golden Crescent.[88] As argued by Vijay Sakhuja:

> The Indian Ocean, by virtue of its geographic location, is home to the narcotic trade from the "Golden Triangle" and the "Golden Crescent." The ocean has emerged as an important transit route for the dispatch of large consignments of narcotics to the Western world as also to the Far East. [89]

There is also a symbiotic relationship between drug trafficking and arms smuggling activities happening in the Indian Ocean that involve Southeast Asian criminal groups.[90] Arms smuggling by sea is the preferred means of criminals because it is by far the "safest method." Even human smugglers regard the sea as the cheapest and easiest form of illegal transportation of migrants.[91] Drug, human, and arms smugglers use the Indian Ocean and the waters of Southeast Asia to operate. These are just some of many examples of interconnectedness of the Indian Ocean and the maritime domain of Southeast Asia.

## Toward Interregional Maritime Security Cooperation

Being in the same MRSC, it is only imperative for the Indian Ocean region[92] and the region of Southeast Asia to pursue interregional maritime security cooperation. Peter Lehr took stock of various proposals to promote regional maritime security cooperation in the Indian Ocean.[93] John Bradford undertook the same project to examine the growing prospects for maritime security cooperation in Southeast Asia.[94] But literature promoting interregional maritime security cooperation between Southeast Asia and the Indian Ocean region is lacking if not absent. Though ASEAN and the South Asian Association for Regional Cooperation (SAARC) promote interregional cooperation,[95] maritime security cooperation between the two associations is still wanting. Countries of Southeast Asia and the Indian Ocean regions pursue maritime security cooperation in the ARF. But cooperation is confined to confidence building.

In March 1997, Australia, Bangladesh, India, Indonesia, Iran, Kenya, Madagascar, Malaysia, Mauritius, Mozambique, Oman, Singapore, South Africa, Sri Lanka, Tanzania, Thailand, United Arab Emirates, and Yemen formed the Indian Ocean Rim Association for Regional Cooperation (IOR-ARC). But the main objective of IOR-ARC is to promote economic cooperation in the Indian Ocean region, particularly on trade and investment, rather than maritime security cooperation. In fact, the IOR-ARC even deliberately ignored issues of maritime security cooperation. Australia attempted to put security in the agenda of IOR-ARC but to no avail. The IOR-ARC mimics the principle of open regionalism of the Asia–Pacific Economic Cooperation (APEC).

As a dialogue partner, India has existing agreements with ASEAN that promote maritime security cooperation. On October 8, 2003, India and ASEAN signed the Joint Declaration for Cooperation to Combat International Terrorism. India and ASEAN also signed on November 30, 2004, the Partnership for Peace, Progress and Shared Prosperity, which aims to promote cooperation in combating the menace of international terrorism and other transnational crimes. A plan of action was even made for this purpose. But the cooperation is limited between ASEAN and India only, and it does not include other countries of the Indian Ocean region. Thus, there is no existing interregional cooperation between the ASEAN and the Indian Ocean regions on maritime security.

Interregional cooperation, or interregionalism, has become a phenomenon in international relations after the end of the cold war.[96] Interregional cooperation occurs between ASEAN and the European Union through the APEC, Asia-Europe Meeting, and dialogue partnership and between Asia and Latin America through the Forum for East Asia–Latin America Cooperation. But interregional cooperation has not been happening between ASEAN and the Indian Ocean regions.

Being in the same MRSC, the ASEAN and the Indian Ocean regions can promote interregional cooperation in the area of maritime security. One major step in a thousand-mile journey is to establish a maritime security forum among countries of ASEAN and the Indian Ocean regions. This forum may initially promote confidence building on maritime security issues. But eventually, the forum shall evolve into a mechanism that aims to prevent the escalation of, and even collectively combat, NTS threats in the maritime domain to consequentially advance human security.

# Conclusion

Southeast Asia has always defined security in a nontraditional sense. As a maritime region, Southeast Asia has always been beset with NTS problems. But the international politics of the cold war marginalized the NTS issues facing the region. The end of the cold war and the aftermath of 9/11 have made NTS one of the prominent regional security issues.

Many NTS threats in the Southeast Asian maritime domain are not confined to the region. They also extend to the vast Indian Ocean. NTS threats in maritime Southeast Asia inexorably affect the security of the Indian Ocean. As maritime regions, the Indian Ocean and Southeast Asia constitute an MRSC where the maritime security concerns of one are inextricably linked with the maritime security concerns of the other. Thus, there is a need to promote interregional maritime security cooperation between the two in order to ensure the maritime security of both regions for the betterment of their people. The security of both regions' maritime domains inescapably promotes human security.

# Endnotes

1. Muthiah Alagapa, "Comprehensive Security: Interpretations in ASEAN Countries," in Robert A. Scalapino, Seizaburo Sato, Jusuf Wanandi, and Sung-joo Han (eds.), *Asian Security Issues: Regional and Global* (Berkeley: University of California Institute of East Asian Studies, 1988), p. 50.
2. William Tow, Ramesh Thakur, and In-Taek Hyun (eds.), *Asia's Emerging Regional Order: Reconciling Traditional and Human Security* (New York, Paris, and Tokyo: United Nations University Press, 2000).
3. David A. Lake and Patrick M. Morgan (eds.), *Regional Orders: Building Security in a New World* (University Park, PA: The Pennsylvania State University, 1997), p. 6.
4. For excellent references on the ARF, see Ralf Emmers, Cooperative Security and Balance of Power in ASEAN and the ARF (London: Routledge, 2003); A New Agenda for the ASEAN Regional Forum, IDSS Monograph No. 4, A Report of the IDSS Project on the Future of the ASEAN Regional Forum (Singapore: Institute of Defense and Strategic Studies, 2002); Carl Thayer, *Multilateral Institutions in Asia: The ASEAN Regional Forum* (Honolulu: Asia–Pacific Center for Security Studies, 2000); Sorpong Peou, The ASEAN Regional Forum and Post–Cold War IR Theories: A Case for

Constructive Realism (Singapore: Institute of Southeast Asian Studies, 1999); Amitav Acharya, The ASEAN Regional Forum: Confidence-Building (Ottawa: Department of Foreign Affairs and International Trade, 1997); Michael Leifer, The ASEAN Regional Forum: Extending ASEAN's Model of Regional Security, Adelphi Paper 302 (London: International Institute for Strategic Studies, 1996). Also see Rommel C. Banlaoi, Security Cooperation in the ASEAN Regional Forum and in the European Union: Lessons Learned (Quezon City: National Defense College of the Philippines, 2001); and Udai Bhanu Sing, ASEAN Regional Forum and Security of the Asia–Pacific, Delhi Papers No. 15 (New Delhi: Institute for Defense Studies and Analyses, 2001).

5. Rommel C. Banlaoi, *War on Terrorism in Southeast Asia* (Quezon City: Rex Book Store International, 2004).

6. It was Barry Buzan who first described a Southeast Asian security complex. See Barry Buzan, "The Southeast Asian Security Complex," *Contemporary Southeast Asia*, Vol. 10, No. 1 (1988), pp. 1–16.

7. Barry Buzan, *People, States and Fear: An Agenda for International Security Studies in the Post-Cold War Era*, 2nd. ed. (London: Harvester Wheastsheaf, 1991).

8. Barry Buzan, "Third World Security in Structural and Historical Perspective," in Brian Job (ed.), *The Insecurity Dilemma: National Security of Third World States* (London: Lynne Reiner, 1992), pp. 167–189.

9. Barry Buzan and Ole Waever, *Regions and Powers: The Structure of International Security* (Cambridge: Cambridge University Press, 2003), p. 44.

10. Eric Koo, "Terror on the High Seas: Southeast Asia's Modern Day Pirates," *Asia Times Online* (October 19, 2004).

11. Muthiah Alagappa, "Rethinking Security: A Critical Review and Appraisal of the Debate," in his *Asian Security Practice: Material and Ideational Influences* (Stanford California: Stanford California Press, 1998), p. 29.

12. See Barry Buzan, "National Security and the Nature of the State," in his *People, States and Fear: An Agenda for International Security Studies in the Post Cold War*, 2nd edition (London: Harvester Wheatsheaf, 1991), Chapter 2.

13. Alagappa, "Rethinking Security: A Critical Review and Appraisal of the Debate," p. 30.

14. The most popular textbook on realism in the Philippines is Hans Morgenthau, *The Politics among Nations: The Struggle for Power and Peace* (New York: Alfred A. Knopft, Inc., 1948). For a classic book on realism, see Edward H. Carr, *The Twenty-Year's Crisis, 1919–1939: An Introduction to the Study of International Relations* (London: McMillan, 1939) and Edward Schwarzenberger, *Power Politics* (London: Cape Publishers, 1941).

15. Ralf Emmers, *Non-Traditional Security in the Asia–Pacific: The Dynamics of Securitization* (Singapore: Eastern Universities Press, 2004), p. 1.

16. Keith Krause and Michael Williams, "Broadening the Agenda of Security Studies: Politics and Methods," *Mershon International Studies Review*, Vol. 40, No. 2 (October 1996), pp. 227–254.

17. Muthiah Alagappa, "Comprehensive Security: Interpretations in ASEAN Countries," in Robert Scalapino, Seizaburo Sato, Jusuf Wanandi, and Sung-joo Han (eds.), *Asian Security Issues: Regional and Global* (Berkeley: University of California Institute of East Asian Studies, 1988), pp. 50–78.

18. Barry Buzan, Ole Waever, and Jaap de Wilde, *Security: A New Framework of Analysis* (Boulder and London: Lynne Rienner Publishers, 1998).

19. Ibid., p. 141.
20. Ibid., p. 23.
21. For an earlier examination of transnational crimes in the context of security studies, see Carolina Hernandez and Gina Pattugalan (eds.), *Transnational Crime and Regional Security in the Asia–Pacific* (Quezon City: Institute for Strategic and Development Studies, 1999).
22. Andrew T.H. Tan and J.D. Kenneth Boutin (eds.), *NTS Issues in Southeast Asia* (Singapore: Select Publishing for the Institute of Defence and Strategic Studies, 2001).
23. Graham Gerald Ong, *Ships Can Be Dangerous Too: Coupling Piracy and Maritime Terrorism in Southeast Asia's Maritime Security Framework*, ISEAS Working Paper No. 1 (Singapore: Institute of Southeast Asian Studies, 2004), p. 1.
24. For the author's elaborate thoughts on this issue, see Rommel C. Banlaoi, "Maritime Security Outlook for Southeast Asia," in Joshua Ho and Catherine Zara Raymond (eds.), *The Best of Times, The Worst of Times: Maritime Security in the Asia–Pacific* (Singapore: World Scientific for the Institute of Defence and Strategic Studies, 2005), pp. 59–80.
25. ICC International Maritime Bureau, *Piracy and Armed Robbery against Ships* (Report for the Period: January 1–September 30, 2006).
26. Ibid., p. 15.
27. For elaboration, see Carolin Liss, *Private Security Companies in the Fight against Piracy in Asia*, Working Paper No. 120 (Asia Research Centre, Murdoch University, Australia, September 2005), p. 2.
28. Ibid.
29. Banlaoi, "Maritime Security Outlook for Southeast Asia," p. 61.
30. For an excellent examination of the nexus of piracy and maritime terrorism, see Peter Lehr (ed.), *Violence at Sea: Piracy in the Age of Global Terrorism* (New York and London: Routledge, 2007).
31. This is based in Banlaoi, "Maritime Security Outlook for Southeast Asia," op. cit.
32. See "Asia Piracy Costs $25 bln a year, says experts," Reuters News Service, Singapore (December 11, 2002) at: http://www.planetark.com/dailynewsstory.cfm/newsid/18987/newsDate/11-Dec-2002/story.htm (accessed April 27, 2004).
33. Bintan Eric Ellis, "Piracy on the High Seas is on the Rise in Southeast Asia," *Fortune* (September 29, 2003). Also at: http://www.singapore-window.org/sw03/030919fo.htm (accessed April 27, 2004).
34. See Report of the Organisation for Economic Cooperation and Development, "Price of Increased Maritime Security Is Much Lower than Potential Cost of a Major Terror Attack," at: http://www.oecd.org/document/30/0,2340,en_2649_201185_4390494_1_1_1_1,00.html (accessed April 27, 2004).
35. "Globalization and Poverty in Southeast Asia: NGO Response," at: www.asiacaucus.net.ph/resources/poverty_research.doc (accessed May 6, 2004).
36. See Stuart W. Smead, "A Thesis on Modern Day Piracy," at: http://www.angelfire.com/ga3/tropicalguy/piracymodernday.html (accessed May 4, 2004).
37. Asia–Pacific Center for Security Studies, "Executive Summary Transnational Violence and Seams of Lawlessness" (February 19–21, 2002), at: http://www.apcss.org/core/Conference/CR_ES/020219ES.htm (accessed November 27, 2006).
38. Annuska Derks, *Combating Trafficking in Southeast Asia: A Review of Policy and Programme Response* (Geneva: International Organization for Migration, 2000), p. 5.

39. Ibid.

40. Bertil Lintner, "Illegal Aliens Smuggling To and Through Southeast Asia" (Budapest: The European Science Foundation, Asia Committee and the Economic and Social Research Council, May 26–27, 2000), p. 1.

41. Public Broadcasting Service, *Dying To Leave, Handbook: The Business of Human Trafficking* (2003), at: http://www.pbs.org/wnet/wideangle/shows/dying/handbook.html (accessed November 27, 2006).

42. Ralf Emmers, NTS in the Asia–Pacific: The Dynamics of Securitization (Singapore: Eastern Universities Press, 2004), pp. 61–81.

43. Public Broadcasting Service, Dying To Leave, Handbook: The Business of Human Trafficking, op. cit.

44. Melanie Petros, "The Cost of Human Smuggling and Trafficking," Global Migration Perspectives, No. 31 (April 2005), pp. 4–5.

45. For more discussions, see Hamisch McCulloch, "Assessing the Involvement of Organized Crime in Human Smuggling and Trafficking," 122nd International Training Course at: http://www.unafei.or.jp/english/pdf/PDF_rms/no62/UK(2).pdf (accessed November 27, 2006).

46. *Small arms* refers to revolvers and self-loading pistols, rifles and carbines, submachine guns, assault rifles and light machine guns. *Light weapons* refers to heavy machine guns, hand-held, under-barrel, and mounted grenade launchers, portable antiaircraft guns, portable antitank guns and recoilless rifles, portable launchers of antitank missiles and rocket systems, portable launchers of antiaircraft missile systems and mortars of calibers of less than 100-mm caliber. See Gina R. Pattugalan, "Small Arms Proliferation and Misuse: Human Security Impact and Policy Actions in Southeast Asia," *Kasarinlan: Philippine Journal of Third World Studies*, Vol. 19, No. 1 (2004), pp. 62–91.

47. For an excellent reference, see Philips Jusario Vermonte and Philips Jusario Vermonte (eds.), *Small Is (not) Beautiful: The Problem of Small Arms in Southeast Asia* (Jakarta: Center for Strategic and International Studies, 2004).

48. Peter Chalk, "Light Arms Trading in SEA," *Jane's Intelligence Review* (March 1, 2001).

49. For more information on this topic, see UN Security Council, "Press Release on Small Arms Debate Support Action Programme" (November 10, 2002), at: http://www.un.org/News/Press/docs/2002/sc7528.doc.htm (accessed November 27, 2006).

50. Small Arms Survey, Small Arms Survey 2005: Weapons at War (Geneva, Switzerland: Small Arms Survey, 2005).

51. See for example U.S. Department of State, Patterns of Global Terrorism 2003 (Washington, DC: Department of State, April 2004). Also see Federation of American Scientist, "Illicit Arms Trade," at: http://www.fas.org/asmp/campaigns/smallarms/IssueBrief3ArmsTrafficking.html (accessed November 27, 2006).

52. International Action Network on Small Arms, "Small Arms in Southeast Asia and the Pacific," at http://www.iansa.org/regions/asiapacific/asiapacific.htm (accessed on November 27, 2006).

53. David Capie, Small Arms Production and Transfers in Southeast, Paper No. 146 (Canberra: Australian National University, 2002).

54. Emmers, *NTS in the Asia–Pacific: The Dynamics of Securitization*, p. 9.

55. Ibid.

56. United Nations Office on Drugs and Crime, *Global Illegal Drug Trends 2003* (New York and Vienna: UNODC, 2003), p. 11.

57. Ralf Emmers, "Securitisation of Drug Trafficking: A Study of Thailand" in his NTS in the Asia–Pacific: The Dynamics of Securitization, pp. 9–34.
58. Ibid., p. 12. Also see Kongpetch Kulsudjarit, "Drug Problem in Southeast and Southwest Asia," Annals of the New York Academy of Sciences, Vol. 1025 (October 2004), p. 446.
59. Rommel C. Banlaoi, "Maritime Terrorism in Southeast Asia: The Abu Sayyaf Threat," Naval War College Review, Vol. 58, No. 4 (Autumn 2005), pp. 63–80. Also see Catherine Zara Raymond, "Maritime Terrorism in Southeast Asia: Potential Scenarios," Terrorism Monitor, Vol. 4, No. 7 (April 6, 2006), pp. 1–3.
60. Based in Banlaoi, "Maritime Security Outlook for Southeast Asia," op. cit.
61. Tamara Renee Shie, "Ports in a Storm? The Nexus between Counterterrorism, Counterproliferation, and Maritime Security in Southeast Asia," *Issues and Insights*, Vol. 4, No. 4 (Pacific Forum CSIS, July 2004), p. 1.
62. Patrick Goodenough, "Maritime Security Takes Center Stage in SE Asia," CNSNews. COM (June 29, 2004), at: http://www.cnsnews.com/ (accessed July 27, 2004).
63. Ibid.
64. Ibid.
65. Ibid., p. 2.
66. See Jeffrey Chen, "The Emerging Nexus between Piracy and Maritime Terrorism in Southeast Asia Waters: A Case Study on the Gerakan Aceh Merdeka (GAM)," in Lehr (ed.), *Violence at Sea: Piracy in the Age of Global Terrorism*, pp. 139–154.
67. Robert Snoddon, "Piracy and Maritime Terrorism: Naval Responses to Existing and Emerging Threats to the Global Seaborne Economy" in Lehr (ed.), *Violence at Sea: Piracy in the Age of Global Terrorism*, p. 230.
68. For an elaborate discussion on this issue, see Rommel C. Banlaoi, "The Abu Sayyaf Group: Threat of Maritime Piracy and Terrorism" in Lehr (ed.), *Violence at Sea: Piracy in the Age of Global Terrorism*, pp. 121–137.
69. Richard Halloran, "Link Between Terrorists, Pirates in SE Asia a Growing Concern," HonoluluAdvertiser.com (March 7, 2004), at: http://the.honoluluadvertiser.com/article/2004/Mar/07 (accessed July 28, 2004).
70. "Piracy Equals Terrorism on Troubled Waters: Minister," *Agence France Presse*, No. 21 (Singapore, 2003).
71. Ibid, p. 1.
72. See ASEAN Cooperation on Functional Areas, at: http://www.aseansec.org/8558. htm.
73. See ASEAN Cooperation on Transnational Issues, at: http://www.aseansec.org/4916. htm.
74. *Declaration of ASEAN Concord II* (October 7, 2003).
75. Ibid.
76. *Declaration of ASEAN Concord II* (October 7, 2003).
77. For an excellent commentary on the RMSI, see Joshua Ho, "Operationalising the Regional Maritime Security Initiative," *and IDSS Commentaries* (May 27, 2004).
78. For an earlier study, see Amitav Acharya, "Regional Military–Security Cooperation in the Third World: A Conceptual Analysis of the Relevance and Limitations of ASEAN (Association of Southeast Asian Nations)," *Journal of Peace Research*, Vol. 29, No. 1 (January 1992), pp. 7–21.
79. N. Ganesan, *Bilateral Tensions in the Post-Cold War ASEAN* (Singapore: Institute of Southeast Asian Studies, 1999).

80. Graham Gerard Ong-Webb, "Piracy in Maritime Asia: Current Trends" in Lehr (ed.), *Violence at Sea: Piracy in the Age of Global Terrorism*, p. 79.

81. On 14 July 2005, the Singapore-based Institute of Southeast Asian Studies held a seminar to assess the implementation of Malsindo after one year. The title of the seminar was "One Year after MALSINDO: Regional Developments, Accomplishments and Further Challenges in the Malacca Straits." See: http://www.iseas.edu.sg/14jul05.html.

82. Chris Rahman, "The International Politics of Combating Piracy in Southeast Asia" in Lehr (ed.), *Violence at Sea: Piracy in the Age of Global Terrorism*, p. 194.

83. See G.V.C. Naidu, *India and ASEAN*, Delhi Papers No. 8 (New Delhi: Institute for Defense Studies and Analyses, 1998).

84. Satu Limaye, "India's Relations with Southeast Asia Take a Wing," *Southeast Asian Affairs 2003* (Singapore: Institute of Southeast Asian Studies, 2003), p. 50.

85. Sudhir Devare, *India and Southeast Asia: Towards Security Convergence* (Singapore: Institute of Southeast Asian Studies, 2006), pp. 89–90.

86. W. Lawrence S. Prabhakar, "Regional Maritime Dynamics in Southern Asia in the 21st Century" in Ho and Raymond (eds.), *The Best of Times, The Worst of Times: Maritime Security in the Asia–Pacific*, p. 105.

87. Mat Taib Yassin, "Indian Ocean Region: Malaysia's perspective" (Paper presented at the Indian Ocean Conference held in Honolulu, Hawaii on August 19–21, 2003), p. 10.

88. P. K. Ghosh, "Maritime Security Challenges in South Asia and the Indian Ocean: Response Strategies" (Paper presented at the Conference on Maritime Security in East Asia organized by the Center for Strategic and International Studies and American–Pacific Sealanes Security Institute, Inc., held at Hilton Hawaiian Village, Honolulu, Hawaii on January 19–20, 2004), p. 6.

89. Vijay Sakhuja, "Indian Ocean and the Safety of Sea Lines of Communication," *Strategic Analysis*, Vol. 25, No. 5 (August 2001).

90. See Jérôme Lauseig, "New Security Challenges in the Indian Ocean: Instigators, Flows and Factors of Instability," *African Security Review*, Vol. 8, No. 1 (1999), p. 20.

91. Sakhuja, "Indian Ocean and the Safety of Sea Lines of Communication," op. cit.

92. On the debate on whether the Indian Ocean constitutes a region or not, see Peter Lehr, "Prospects for Multilateral Security Cooperation in the Indian Ocean: A Skeptical View," *Indian Ocean Survey*, Vol. 1, No. 1 (January–June 2005), pp. 1–15.

93. Ibid. also see Peter Lehr, "The Challenge of Security in the Indian Ocean in the 21st Century: Plus ca Change…?" Working Paper No. 13 (Heidelberg Papers in South Asian and Comparative Politics, November 2002).

94. John Bradford, "The Growing Prospects for Maritime Security Cooperation in Southeast Asia," *Naval War College Review*, Vol. 58, No. 3 (Summer 2005), pp. 63–86.

95. See Faizal Yahya, "Pakistan, SAARC and ASEAN Relations." Contemporary Southeast Asia, Vol. 26, No. 2 (August 2004), pp. 346–375.

96. Heiner Hänggi, Ralf Roloff, and Jürgen Rüland (eds.), *Interregionalism and International Relations* (Abingdon, New York: Routledge, 2005).

## Chapter 14

# The ASEAN Regional Forum and Security Community Building in the Asia–Pacific after 9/11: Lessons from European Integration*

## Introduction

Nation–states in the Asia–Pacific have been embarking on building a "security community" in the region to deal with the various threats unleashed by the end of the cold war. The complexities of the post–cold war security environment have prompted nation–states to "go regional" in search of a lasting solution to their multifaceted security problems. Building a security community at the regional level gives nation–states within that region a sense of relative peace and security in an environment of complexities and uncertainties. The aftermath of the September 11,

* Revised and updated version of the paper entitled "The ASEAN Regional Forum and Security Community Building in the Asia–Pacific: Lessons from Europe," published in Rommel C. Banlaoi, *Security Cooperation in the ASEAN Regional Forum and in the European Union: Lessons Learned* (Quezon City: National Defense College of the Philippines, 2001), pp. 1–30.

2001, attacks made the complexities of the regional security situation even more difficult to grasp because of the growing threat posed by international terrorism.

Considering the diversities of economic and political systems, culture, geography, and social structure in the Asia–Pacific, can nation–states in the region build a security community? What is a security community? What is the prospect of building a security community in the Asia–Pacific after 9/11? Can the ASEAN Regional Forum (ARF) serve as a security community in the Asia–Pacific? What lessons can the ARF learn from the security community building in Europe?

## Security Community: An Analytical Framework

Scholars and practitioners of international politics regard security community building as a remedy to the problem of international conflict.[1] They believe that building a security community not only prevents the occurrence of war among nations but also makes the prospect of war among nations utterly impossible.

As an analytic framework, Karl Deutsch and his associates carefully examine the notion of a security community by viewing it as a product of human communication flows. Deutsch defines a security community as a group of states whose members "share dependable expectations of peaceful change" and rule out "the use of force as a means of problem solving."[2] Together with his associates, he identifies two types of security community: *amalgamated security community* and *pluralistic security community*. Deutsch argues that it is the building of a security community that can eliminate "war and expectation of war" within the boundaries of participating nation–states.[3]

According to Deutsch, an amalgamated security community is a political and security arrangement where previously independent units formed a single unit with a common government. He cites the United States as an example of an amalgamated security community. He also provides the following conditions for the formation of an amalgamated security community:

- Mutual compatibilities of values.
- A distinctive way of life.
- Expectations of joint rewards timed so as to come before the impositions of burdens from the amalgamation.
- A marked increase in political and administrative capabilities of at least some participant units.
- Superior economic growth on the part of some participating units and the development of so-called core areas around which are grouped comparatively weaker areas.
- Unbroken link of social communication, both geographically between territories and between social strata.
- Broadening of the political elite.

- Mobility of persons, at least among the politically relevant strata.
- Multiplicity of communications and transactions.[4]

A pluralistic community, on the other hand, is a political and security arrangement where participating states or units retain their legal independence. The North Atlantic Treaty Organization (NATO) and the security arrangement between the United States and Canada are examples of this kind of a security community. Deutsch identifies the following conditions for the formation of a pluralistic security community:

- Comparability of values among decision makers.
- Mutual predictability of behavior among decision makers of units to be integrated.
- Mutual responsiveness of government to actions and communications of other governments.[5]

Although the Deutschian notion of security communities may have an explanatory appeal in Europe and in North America, other scholars in the field are challenging the applicability of the Deutschian framework of security communities in developing countries.[6] Amitav Acharya, for example, proposed an alternative security community framework applicable for developing countries. Examining the prospects of building a security community in Southeast Asia, Acharya identified the following basic requirements:

- Total absence of armed interstate conflict, or prospects for such conflict within a region.
- Absence of a competitive military buildup or arms race involving the regional actors.
- Existence of formal or informal institutions and practices.
- Existence of a high degree of political and economic integration as a necessary precondition of a peaceful relationship.[7]

Acharya also differentiated the idea of a security community from the idea of a defense community. The latter "implies an alliance relationship which is usually conceived and directed against a pre-recognized and commonly perceived external threat."[8] The former identifies no such threat nor has the function "of organizing joint defense" against external threat.[9] Acharya also underscored the difference between a security community and a security regime. Borrowing the idea of Janice Gross Stein,[10] Acharya wrote:

> A security regime, as Stein points out, normally describes a situation in which the interests of the actors "are neither wholly compatible nor wholly competitive." Indeed, a security regime may develop within an otherwise adversarial relationship in which the use of force is inhibited

by the existence of a balance of power or mutual deterrence situation....
A security community, on the other hand, must be based on a fundamental, unambiguous and long-term *convergence* of interests among the
actors in the avoidance of war.[11]

Acharya concluded that despite the formation of the Association of Southeast
Asian Nations (ASEAN), a security regime rather than a security community is
more appropriate in describing the security system in Southeast Asia. This view
revised his previous idea when he regarded ASEAN as a security community.[12]
But Acharya revived his concept of a security community to describe ASEAN in
his latest piece on the subject.[13] Acharya regards ASEAN's collective identity as an
important aspect of community building in the region. This collective identity is
anchored on what he calls the "we feeling" in ASEAN, which is not based on the
logic of economic interdependence and democracy but based on the cultural and
social process within the region.[14] Chapter 15 of this book discusses security community building in ASEAN after 9/11. Readers are strongly encouraged to read this
chapter for detailed discussions on ASEAN security community building in the age
of global terrorism.

For Carlyle Thayer, ASEAN has indeed gradually evolved into a security community since its creation in 1967.[15] Thayer describes a security community as a
grouping of states whose members "have ruled out the use or threatened use of force
to resolve matters in dispute, including conflicting territorial claims."[16]

Paridah Abdul Samad and Mohktar Mohammad also regard ASEAN as a "security community" in a sense that "no member would seriously consider to use force
against another to settle disputes."[17] They stress, however, that with the absence
of a common threat and with the presence of actual and potential conflicts in the
region, they describe ASEAN as a community that "has not reached the stage of
a security community," in a Deutschian sense, although ASEAN has come a long
way in reducing tensions between its members.[18]

As used in this chapter, a security community refers to an imagined community of state and nonstate players adhering to the habit of peaceful management of
conflict among them. This paper borrows the concept of an imagined community
from Benedict Anderson, who uses the idea to describe the process of nation building. He argues:

A nation is an imagined political community... It is imagined as a community, because regardless of the actual inequality and exploitation that
may prevail in each, the nation is always conceived as a deep horizontal
comradeship. Ultimately, it is this fraternity that makes it possible, over
the past two centuries, for so many millions of people, not so much to
kill, as willingly to die for such limited imaginings.[19]

Like a nation, a security community is an imagined community because despite the complex diversities of players in the Asia–Pacific, there is a general perception, or shared imagination, so to speak, that relative peace and security may be attained by cooperating with one another and by ruling out the threat or the actual use of force in settling their disputes. This security community may be in the form of a formal organization of states with a permanent secretariat or an informal grouping of states with no permanent secretariat but with a regular process of constant dialogues and consultations. Since a security community may be viewed as an imagined community, it is also socially constructed, which takes time.

The presence of a security community, however, does not imply the eradication of disputes among nations. The existence of disputes is a reality in every community. A security community aims to prevent disputes to escalate into war or any form of armed confrontation between and among states. The bottom line of a security community is a relative perception of being secure if they cooperate with each other. The existence of a security community can assuage the fear of nation–states of a possible violent confrontation among them.

## Attempts to Develop a Security Community in the Asia–Pacific

In the Asia–Pacific, there have been various attempts to develop a security community. But most of these attempts were utter failures and were done at the subregional level.

Before the outbreak of World War II, the Japanese imperial government made an ambitious design of Greater East Asia Co-Prosperity Sphere. This design, however, was a product of Japanese colonization rather than a product of voluntary integration among states in the region.

In 1951, Australia, New Zealand, and the United States tried to form a security community when they signed the Australian, New Zealand, United States (ANZUS) Alliance Treaty. The treaty came into force on April 29, 1952, when its members ratified the document. The ANZUS then served as a smaller multilateral military alliance in the Asia–Pacific pursuing the idea of collective defense. This strengthened further U.S.–New Zealand relations as enshrined in the Radford-Collins Agreement of 1951, which provided for the implementation of allied naval control and protection of shipping in the Pacific and Indian oceans.[20] But when the New Zealand government announced in 1985 that it would not grant port access to those American warships carrying nuclear weapons, it irked Washington because of American policy of neither affirming nor denying the presence of nuclear weapons on specific U.S. vessels. As a result, the United States suspended its defense obligations to New Zealand in 1986.

As result of the crisis in U.S.–New Zealand relations, the ANZUS treaty was never invoked. Nonetheless, Australia and the U.S. continued to cooperate bilaterally under the terms of ANZUS. Although ANZUS created some tensions between Australia and New Zealand, military ties between the two countries also continued but outside the ANZUS parameter.[21]

Another attempt to build a security community in the Asia–Pacific was the formation of the Southeast Asia Treaty Organization (SEATO) in Manila on September 8, 1954. It was initially composed of the United States, the United Kingdom, France, Australia, the Philippines, New Zealand, Pakistan, and Thailand.

The SEATO was compared to NATO because of its anticommunist stance. Unlike NATO, however, SEATO did not obligate its members to assist each other in case of military attack against any of its members. Because its membership was composed of only two states in Southeast Asia, the Philippines and Thailand, SEATO failed to strictly establish a security community in the region.

For purposes of containment, SEATO included Laos under its umbrella. SEATO members signed a protocol to their treaty unanimously designating Laos, for purposes of Article IV, the operational article that commits members "to act to meet the common danger" in the event of aggression against any of its members.[22]

The Vietnam War (1965–1973) served as an acid test to the credibility of SEATO as a security alliance. Although SEATO members criticized U.S. military efforts in Vietnam, and although several SEATO members sent troops to fight there, SEATO as an alliance played no direct role in the war.[23] SEATO started to disintegrate when France ceased active participation in SEATO in 1967. Pakistan followed suit when it officially withdrew in 1972. With the U.S. withdrawal from Vietnam and the Communist victories throughout Indochina in 1975, it was said that SEATO had become an anachronism.[24] By mutual consent of its members, the organization suffered demise on June 30, 1977.[25] This prompted Leszek Buszynski to argue that SEATO demonstrated the failure of an alliance strategy.[26]

Two years after the formation of SEATO, the United Kingdom spearheaded the formation of a loose multilateral alliance-type defense formation through the signing of the Anglo-Malayan Defense Agreement in 1957. With the disintegration of the Malayan Federation, another agreement was formed in 1971 when Australia, Malaysia, New Zealand, Singapore, and the United Kingdom signed the Five-Power Defense Agreement (FPDA). Like SEATO and ANZUS, the FPDA has never been invoked. Its activities are confined mostly on annual joint exercises, regular consultations, and exchanges of military personnel.[27]

In 1961, the Philippines, Thailand, and Malaysia formed the Association for Southeast Asia (ASA) to pursue regional cooperation. But ASA suffered its demise in 1962 when the Philippines pursued its claim to Sabah. To revive the spirit of community building in Southeast Asia, Malaysia, the Philippines, and Indonesia formed the MAPHILINDO in July 1963. It was dissolved three months after, amid the *Konfrontasi* between Malaysia and Indonesia. Nonetheless, ASA and MAPHILINDO became the forerunners of ASEAN, which was formed initially in 1967 by the Philippines, Thailand, Singapore, Malaysia, and Indonesia. To date, ASEAN comprises 10 members with the accession of Brunei in 1984, Vietnam in 1995, Laos and Myanmar in 1997, and Cambodia in 1999.

In the South Pacific, participants established the South Pacific Forum (SPF) in 1969. Currently comprising Australia, Cook Islands, Federated States of Micronesia, Fiji, Kiribati, Nauru, New Zealand, Palau, Papua New Guinea, Marshall Islands, Samoa, Solomon Islands, Tonga, Tuvalu, and Vanuatu, the SPF aims to promote the security of the region by improving their living standards and ensuring sustainable development, among other things.[28] Like ASEAN, the SPF has its "Pacific Way" of reducing tensions among its members through constant dialogues and consultations.

In South Asia, the founding members established the South Asian Association for Regional Cooperation (SAARC) on December 8, 1985.[29] This signified the intention of its members to build a regional community in accelerating their economic and social development through collective action. Presently composed of Bangladesh, Bhutan, India, Maldives, Nepal, Pakistan, and Sri Lanka, the SAARC also aims to promote the welfare of the peoples of the region through economic, social, and cultural development and to contribute to "mutual trust, understanding and appreciation of one another's problems."[30] Because of internal and external conflicts within and between member states, the SAARC remains a "symbol of Eastern Promise — golden opportunities yet to be realized."[31] Nonetheless, the SAARC remains the only viable regional organization in South Asia aiming to reduce tensions among the nation–states in the region.

It may be observed from the foregoing that since the end of the Second World War II, attempts at security community building in the Asia–Pacific were done at the subregional level. The only regionwide attempt at security community building during the cold war was the establishment of Asia–Pacific Council (ASPAC) in 1966. The ASPAC was formed at the height of U.S. involvement in the Vietnam War.[32] The council, however, was more of a regional grouping of anti-Communist states in the region scared of the domino effect of communism in Vietnam. The council was allowed to lapse in 1972 as it failed to solicit widespread support from other countries in the region.[33]

In the aftermath of the cold war, Australian Foreign Minister Gareth Evans proposed in 1990 the concept of a Conference on Security and Cooperation in Asia (CSCA) to address the post–cold war security dilemma of the countries in the Asia–Pacific. Inspired by the Conference on Security and Cooperation in Europe (CSCE), the proposal to establish the CSCA did not successfully materialize because countries in the Asia–Pacific rejected the CSCE model.[34] Nonetheless, nongovernmental organizations in the region formed the Council for Security Cooperation in the Asia–Pacific (CSCAP), a track-two mechanism aiming to provide "a more structured regional process of a non-governmental nature.... To contribute to the efforts towards regional confidence building, enhancing regional security through dialogues, consultation and cooperation."[35]

It is viewed that the establishment of CSCAP is "one of the most important milestones in the development of institutionalized dialogue, consultation and cooperation" tackling the post–cold war security concerns of the region.[36] Although the efforts of CSCAP are nonofficial in nature, it provides several venues for confidence-building measures in the Asia–Pacific.[37]

Strictly speaking, among the subregional groupings in the Asia–Pacific, only ASEAN experienced a relative success in regional cooperation.[38] ASEAN did not envision the creation of a security community in the region as understood in Deutschian sense. Its main goal was economic, social, and cultural cooperation to reduce tensions among Southeast Asia's non-Communist states.[39] In the Bangkok Declaration, the five founding fathers affirmed their determination to "ensure their stability and security from external interference" and to "preserve their national identities."[40] Its main principle of conflict management — the ASEAN Way — is confidence and consensus building and noninterference in internal affairs.

Despite the existence of various disputes among its members, ASEAN has prevented the occurrence of serious armed confrontation among them. The 1971 Zone of Peace, Freedom and Neutrality (ZOPFAN), 1976 Treaty of Amity and Cooperation, and the 1976 Declaration of ASEAN Concord are instrumental in making ASEAN a viable organization in the region.[41] Its success in handling the Cambodian crisis gave ASEAN credibility as a security community in Southeast Asia. Thus, ASEAN is viewed as a security community because its members have ruled out the threat or the use of force for settling their disputes.[42] The expansion of ASEAN to include Laos, Cambodia, and Myanmar has enhanced the credibility of ASEAN as a security community in Southeast Asia.

Because of the relative success of the ASEAN Way,[43] especially the way ASEAN handled the Cambodian crisis, countries in the Asia–Pacific adopted the ASEAN method when they formed the Asia–Pacific Economic Cooperation (APEC) in 1989 and the ARF in 1994.[44]

The main goal of APEC is to pursue the economic security of the region through deeper economic cooperation guided by the principle of "open regionalism."[45] While it has the vision of developing an "Asia–Pacific Economic Community" as articulated by APEC's Eminent Persons Group, it has no ambition of forming a "defense or a security community" as used in the Deutschian or Acharyan sense. In fact, APEC has not considered political and strategic issues to be included in its mandate, despite an American proposal.[46]

The ARF fills that gap. Extending the ASEAN model of regional security, in 1994 ARF initially put together 18 countries in the Asia–Pacific: Australia, Brunei, Canada, China, the European Union, Indonesia, Japan, Laos, Malaysia, New Zealand, Papua New Guinea, the Philippines, Russia, Singapore, South Korea, Thailand, United States, and Vietnam. In 1995, Cambodia entered the ARF, and India and Myanmar entered in 1996. With Mongolia as the latest member of the organization, the ARF has its criteria in accepting new members, which include: (1) commitment to key ARF goals and previous ARF decisions and statements; (2)

relevance to the peace and security of the ARF "geographical footprint" (Northeast and Southeast Asia and Oceania); (3) gradual expansion; and (4) consultation and consensus by all ARF members on all future membership decisions.[47]

The ARF's main goal is to promote the security of the Asia–Pacific through constant dialogue and confidence among its members using track-one and track-two mechanisms. The ARF has also agreed on a gradual three-stage evolution of promoting confidence building, preventive diplomacy, and in the longer term, common approaches to conflict resolution. There are talks that the first two stages can proceed in tandem.[48] In fact, the ARF Working Group on Preventive Diplomacy has developed proposals for the eventual adoption of preventive diplomacy.[49] Academicians in the region have also explored the possibility of moving ARF from confidence building to preventive diplomacy, but the process remains contentious.[50]

But is the ARF a step toward the building of a security community in the Asia–Pacific?

## The ASEAN Regional Forum (ARF) and Constraints to "Security Community" Building in the Asia–Pacific

The Asia–Pacific beyond doubt is facing tremendous challenges in its attempt to build a security community. Though Admiral Dennis Blair, former commander of the United States Command in the Asia–Pacific, advocated the idea of security communities as a "way ahead" in the region,[51] it fails to receive support from other stakeholders because of their wariness of American strategic intentions, particularly when applied in the context of the global campaign against terrorism. Only ASEAN has reached the status of a security community when its members signed the ASEAN Concord II during their summit in Bali, Indonesia, on October 7–8, 2003.[52]

Following the Deutschian notion of an amalgamated security community, building this type of a security community in the Asia–Pacific is not just difficult but also impossible at this juncture because all countries in the region are very protective of their national sovereignty. Even applying the Deutschian notion of a pluralistic security community is also difficult because of apparent differences of values among decision makers in the Asia–Pacific. Strictly using the Acharyan notion of a security community is also inconceivable because his four requirements cannot be applied in the Asia–Pacific considering the present security situation in the region.

If we mean a security community as a grouping of state and nonstate players with the aim of securing the region through constant dialogues and with the goal of promoting peace and stability in the region by ruling out the threat or actual use of force to solve their conflicts, the ARF may be considered as a step toward the development of a security community in the Asia–Pacific.

In its attempt to build a security community in the region, the ARF has to confront various security challenges. The Asia–Pacific at present is marred by a lot of insecurities.[53] Western analysts argue that the absence of a formal security organization to address security problems in the region is one of the causes of these insecurities.[54] The ARF is not yet a formal security institution compared with European institutions because the ARF at present is more interested in the "process" rather than in the "institution." As its name suggests, the organization aims to primarily serve a forum for security dialogues and confidence-building measures among its members with a long-term vision of eventually adopting a common approach to conflict resolution.

The ARF is also facing a gargantuan task, as the Asia–Pacific is host to various territorial disputes threatening the security of the region. The Spratly Islands dispute; the China–Taiwan conflict; the Russia–Japan conflict over the Northern Territories; the Japan–China conflict over Senkaku Islands; the Philippines–Malaysia dispute over Sabah; the Japan–South Korea dispute over the Liancourt Rocks; the India–Pakistan conflict over Kashmir; the border disputes between China and Vietnam, between Thailand and Burma, between Thailand and Malaysia, between Malaysia and Vietnam, and between Vietnam and Indonesia; and the division of the Koreas are just a few examples of many sources of conflicts in the Asia–Pacific region.[55] The continuing arms buildup in Southeast Asia, the nuclear race between India and Pakistan, the nuclearization of North Korea, the modernization of Chinese Armed Forces, and the strengthening of Japan's Self-Defense Forces have also been identified as triggers to build serious conflict and instability in the region.[56] The resurgence of transnational crimes, the rise of religious revivalism, the threat of international terrorism, and the persistence of separatist movements in various countries in the Asia–Pacific have also been identified as potential sources of instability in the region.[57]

These seemingly insurmountable security threats prompted Robert Manning to argue that instead of building a security community, states in the Asia–Pacific are, in fact, building conflict.[58]

Despite these various sources of insecurities, there are prospects for the development of a security community in the Asia–Pacific as nation–states agree that the region must be protected and secured by ruling out the threat or the use of force in dealing with one another. Although ways and means to protect and secure the region may vary among nation–states in the Asia–Pacific, ARF's commitment to renounce force as a way of settling disputes is a positive building block of developing a security community in the region.

Although there may be a lot of challenges being confronted by the ARF in its attempt to build a security community in the Asia–Pacific, these challenges are not unusual. Europe has faced these challenges in its own context. Thus, it is useful to discuss the European experience of security community building to guide nations in the Asia–Pacific in its attempt to build its own security community.

It is very important to note that there is a tendency among Asian scholars and policymakers to be wary and suspicious of the "European model" in grappling with the ramifications of security issues in the Asia–Pacific. Many Asians contend that the security environment in the Asia–Pacific is apparently different from the European security environment.[59] Geography alone gives Europe and the Asia–Pacific different security concerns, Europe being predominantly land oriented and the Asia–Pacific being predominantly maritime oriented.[60] Because nation–states in the Asia–Pacific are culturally more heterogeneous and ethnically more diverse compared with Europe, building a security community in the Asia–Pacific is said to be more difficult than in Europe.[61]

Despite these apparent differences, it is very important to present here the European experience in security community building because Europe has one of the rare examples of a "successful process of community building at the regional level."[62] The case of the European Union (EU) is just an excellent example of a successful security community building at the regional level. The EU's success in building a security community in Europe, however, only applies to its 15 member states. The EU has failed to prevent conflict from taking place in its neighbors, especially in the Balkan areas.[63] Indeed, the EU has its share of ups and downs. As argued by Nikolas Busse and Hanns W. Maull, "The history of European integration has been full of disappointments, problems and setbacks."[64]

The purpose of this section is not to apply in the Asia–Pacific the European model of security community building but to demonstrate the painful process experienced by Europe in security community building so that policymakers in the Asia–Pacific will get useful insights from this experience. By knowing this painful but successful process of security community building, countries in the Asia–Pacific will be more optimistic in building their own security community.

## Security Community Building: Lessons from European Experience

The idea of a European security community may be traced to the proposal of Duke Maximilien de Bethune of Sully during the 17th century.[65] The duke envisioned the creation of a common European army, which he regarded as very instrumental in the attainment of peace and prosperity in the region. Intense intra-European wars did not lead to the realization of this vision. After the Napoleonic War, Austria, Prussia, Britain, Russia, and later Bourbon France formed in 1815 the Concert of Europe aimed to manage security problems facing the region at that time. The Crimean War of 1854 led to the collapse of the concert.[66]

After the end of World War II, France proposed the establishment of the European Defense Community (EDC) in 1950. Formally created in 1952, the EDC laid down rules for the establishment of a common European defense through a common European army with a centralized procurement of military facilities and a high degree of collective decision making in the areas of defense, foreign and security policies.[67] But it suffered demise in 1954 partly because the United Kingdom refused to join and partly because of the French paranoia of possible German domination of Western Europe.[68] Moreover, other Western European states found the EDC offensive to their national sovereignty. Instead of EDC, Western Europe formed the Western European Union (WEU) aimed among other reasons to control stocks of certain armaments of all member countries, viewing that the control of armaments is one of the mechanisms to maintain the "balance of power" in Europe, thus avoiding the possibility of another intra-European War. The WEU also ensured "transparency" in arms buildup in Western Europe.

To protect Western European states from Soviet communist aggression, they formed NATO with the very active participation of the United States. NATO has been providing Western Europe a security umbrella since the end of World War II. The end of the cold war did not change this security setup. In fact, Western Europe relied heavily on NATO when a crisis broke out in Yugoslavia and Kosovo.

The only viable security community in Western Europe was the European Coal and Steel Community (ECSC), formed in 1951 by the Benelux States, Italy, Germany, and France. Unlike the EDC, the ECSC was not a defense community. The ECSC only integrated the production and distribution of coal and steel among its member states. Because coal and steel are important requirements for the production of arms, the ECSC indirectly regulated the production of arms in the region. Member states believed that cooperation in the area of "low politics" such as coal and steel would assuage their fear of possible conflict among them, thus maintaining peace and harmony in Western Europe.

In 1957, the founders of the ECSC formed the European Economic Community (EEC) and the European Atomic Energy Community (EURATOM), deepening the economic integration of member states. Then, all three communities existed in Western Europe: the ECSC, EEC, and the EURATOM. In 1965, they signed the Merger Treaty, resulting in the formation of the European Community (EC). To widen the scope of their cooperation, they formed the European Political Cooperation (EPC) in 1970 to tackle issues of "high politics" confronting the EC.

The EPC, however, was merely an intergovernmental forum for foreign and security policy coordination working outside the EC framework. Despite that, the EC attracted other European states to join the community. In 1973, it had its first enlargement when it acceded to the United Kingdom, Denmark, and Ireland. Greece joined the EC in 1981.

To improve their security policy coordination and to deepen their political cooperation, member states signed the Single European Act in 1986, bringing the EPC within the sphere of the Community. It was also during this year when the EPC accepted Spain and Portugal as new members.

Despite bringing the EPC within the sphere of the Community, it remained strictly intergovernmental in nature, operating under the cardinal rule of consensus.

After the end of the cold war, the member states embarked on having a common foreign and security policy (CFSP) to have a single European voice in the international community. In 1992, they signed the Maastricht Treaty creating the EU and making the CFSP the second pillar of the union. Because of the promising vision of the EU, other European states were attracted to join the union. In 1995, the EU acceded to Austria, Finland, and Sweden, resulting in the present 15 members of the EU.

Despite having a CFSP, the EU failed to respond effectively to various international crises in the region like the Yugoslavian crisis. The European Parliament vehemently criticized the EU arguing that the CFSP was no different from the EPC and that the EU's three-pillar structure restricted the union's ability to act internationally.[69]

To improve the CFSP, member states signed the Amsterdam Treaty in 1997, which *improved* the provisions pertaining to the CFSP. One of the improvements in the new treaty is the proposal to establish a policy planning and early warning unit in the EU.[70]

Yet, the CFSP remained intergovernmental. Despite its *improvements* and some *innovations*, the EU still failed to respond to the Kosovo crisis. While the EU achieved relative success in the area of economic integration, the union remained backward in its political integration. In fact, the EU is still relying heavily on the security umbrella provided by NATO. The Amsterdam Treaty even strengthens this reliance. Though the EU envisions the WEU as its operational arm, the WEU operations are confined with humanitarian and peacekeeping activities.

In other words, security community building in EU is still confined with "soft security" issues. Even the membership of this security community is still limited to 15 members. Though the EU is open for further enlargement, its stringent enlargement policy prevents other European states from entering the union. Despite these limitations, European security community building in soft areas has contributed immensely to the promotion of peace and stability in Europe.

The only Europe-wide organization in Europe concerned with security issues is the Organization for Security and Cooperation in Europe (OSCE). The OSCE is viewed as the only pan-European security organization whose 55 participating states cover the geographical area from Vancouver to Vladivostok.[71] Evolving from the CSCE created in 1975 through the Helsinki Act, the OSCE serves as a framework for conventional arms control in Europe and a venue for confidence-building measures. It adheres to the sovereign equality of all member states, inviolability of frontiers, territorial integrity of states, peaceful settlement of disputes, nonintervention in internal affairs, and restraint from the threat or use of force, among other things.

## What Lessons Can the Asia–Pacific Learn from the European Experience?

The most important lesson is that there is no shortcut to building a security community. Building a security community cannot be achieved through a quantum leap to politically sensitive areas of security. Security community building is an incremental process starting from confidence building. The OSCE started from a mere forum, the CSCE. Thus, the ARF is doing the careful process of building a security community when it starts from confidence building.

As discussed earlier, the European experience in security community building has gone through a long and painful process. Though they attempted to form a security and defense community as early as the 1950s, it was to no avail because nation–states in Europe were still sensitive of their national sovereignty. They were not yet prepared to surrender their sovereign prerogative in the area of defense and security. The OCSE is acceptable to European states because the organization respects the sovereign rights of participating states. Though Europe has the EU and the WEU, these organizations remained intergovernmental like the ASEAN. In a loose Deutschian sense, the EU and the WEU may be considered "pluralistic security communities."

## The ARF as a Possible Security Community in the Asia–Pacific in the Post–9/11 Era?

Since the ARF was established in 1994, the international security environment has changed enormously, and this calls for a new agenda to make the forum more relevant.[72] The present global campaign against terrorism also provides tremendous pressures for the ARF to reexamine its current role.

Despite its various limitations, the ARF may be developed into a security community in the Asia–Pacific in the post-9/11 world. Its habits of constant dialogue and confidence building are positive processes to assuage the fear of all nation–states in the region of possible occurrence of armed confrontation against one another. The ARF process can draw big nation–states in the Asia–Pacific into cooperative relations with their smaller neighbors. Peer pressure will bind all nation–states in the region to be more peaceful in dealing with one another. The various confidence- and security-building measures, no matter how slow and difficult, may serve as the foundation of a security community building in the Asia–Pacific region.[73] The ARF is the first step in a thousand-mile journey toward the development of a formal security community in the region.

The ARF, however, is likened to a "brick made without the straw" because of its very informal nature.[74] Former Philippine President Joseph Estrada even expressed his "impatience" with the ARF process, arguing that the "Asia–Pacific is the only region in the world that has not yet established instruments for effective political and security cooperation."[75] It has also been viewed that the ARF is "trying to build on sand" and it can "do little to help security in the wider Asia–Pacific region."[76] There was also a view that the rise of China as an economic and military power in the region may undermine the efforts of the ARF. It is argued that the security of the Asia–Pacific will depend not on the ability of the ARF to improve security in the region but in large part on the choice China makes, "whether it chooses to integrate peacefully into a new regional order, or whether it opts to assert hegemony on the basis of size, centrality and history."[77] It is also contended that the ARF "has done nothing to improve security" even in the ASEAN's own front yard[78] when China asserted its claims over the territories in the South China Sea by occupying the Mischief Reef being claimed by the Philippines. Its inability to act decisively during the East Timor crisis aggravated further the ARF's credibility dilemma.

As regards speculation that China might undermine the ARF process because of its sheer economic and military strength, it has to be underscored that when China joined the ARF, it opted to forge cooperation with other members by enhancing trust and transparency among them. While it is true that China is a military and economic power in the region, it is dependent on the region for its economic growth and prosperity.[79] China's cooperative role during the Asian financial crisis dismisses the idea of China as a "threat" in the region and gives China an image of "responsible" power in Asia.[80] In fact, it will be an act of self-flagellation if China opts to be an aggressive power in the region. China cannot afford to be the "Iraq" in the Asia–Pacific because it will destroy the trust of its neighbors, which China is trying to build. China's post–cold war security policy is to build trust and confidence with its neighbors in the Asia–Pacific through bilateral and multilateral dialogues, negotiation, and consultation.[81] President Jiang Zemin himself stressed that "China's stand on security mechanisms in Asia–Pacific is to hold bilateral and regional security dialogues in various forms, on various levels, and through various channels, with the goal of strengthening communication and trust."[82] China's adherence to the principle of the ARF signifies China's enthusiasm to be part of the security community in the region. As contended by Andrew J. Nathan and Robert S. Ross, although China wants to develop the rules of the international community, "Beijing wants to play by the rules of the international community."[83] The challenge to the ARF is how to regulate the behavior of China the way the EU regulates the behavior of Germany.

Europe viewed Germany the way the Asia–Pacific views China today. Because of Germany's aggression during the war, Europeans were scared of possible German domination of Europe when they formed the EC/EU. However, they used EC/EU mechanisms to bind Germany. Nations in the Asia–Pacific can also use the ARF's mechanism to bind not only China but also other potential powers in the region like Japan, India, and Indonesia. The ARF can also serve as venue for smaller states in the Asia–Pacific to articulate their strategic and security interests vis-à-vis great powers with stakes in the region like the United States, Russia, Australia, and Canada. After 9/11, in fact, China has demonstrated a more cooperative and constructive attitude in the ARF process and has enunciated the value of multilateral cooperation in its New Security Concept.[84] Its doctrine of peaceful rise formulated in the aftermath of 9/11 reaffirms China's commitment to build a peaceful and prosperous Asia–Pacific region.[85] Like Germany of the post–World War II era,

China is becoming more benign and responsible as a major power. Through the process of socialization, the ARF provides a mechanism to ensure that China and other participants will behave peacefully and thereby contribute to the construction of a security community in the Asia–Pacific region in the post-9/11 era.

## Conclusion

Despite the absence of a full-blown security community in the Asia–Pacific, the ARF, so far, is the only viable regionwide multilateral security forum that addresses the complexities of security problems in the Asia–Pacific. Bringing together diverse nation–states with varying security perceptions of the world is already the ARF's remarkable achievement.

While other scholars view a "concert of powers" as an alternative to the ARF, China, which is a major power in the region, officially rejects a concert approach. While a concert approach may look relevant in managing the conflict in Northeast Asia, the approach may not work in Southeast Asia because security issues in this region are less central to great-power relations.[86]

States in the Asia–Pacific still view ASEAN's approach as a viable framework for managing tensions in the region. Even in South Asia, it is argued that a concert approach "that seeks to pressure India to abandon the further development of its nuclear arsenal has little chance of being effective."[87] Even though the major powers in the Asia–Pacific may have a shared interest to establish a concert relationship in the region, the individual motivations of great powers differ.[88] In other words, ARF limitations at present do not mean that a concert of great powers would provide a more effective way to address the multifaceted security concerns in the Asia–Pacific.[89]

In its attempt to build a security community after 9/11, the ARF may be taking it slowly, but surely. While the ARF may not have reached the status of a security community in Deutschian or Acharyan's sense, the security regime that it has established provides several opportunities to build a security community in the Asia–Pacific.

Europe and North America took years to build their own security communities, so why should the Asia–Pacific be in a hurry? As argued by Ralph Boyce, "The ARF is still young; other regional organizations have taken decades to reach their current levels of effectiveness. We must recognize the time needed for the ARF to mature."[90]

## Endnotes

1. See Karl Deutsch et al., *Political Community and the North Atlantic Area: International Organization in the Light of Historical Experience* (New York: Greenwood Press Publishers, 1969).

2. Ibid, p. 4.
3. Ibid., p. 5.
4. See Karl Deutsch et al., *Political Community and the North Atlantic Area: International Organization in the Light of Historical Experience* (New York: Greenwood Press Publishers, 1969).
5. Ibid.
6. See for example Ronald J. Yalem, "Regional Security Communities and World Order," in George W. Keeton and Gerge Swanzenberger (eds.), *The Yearbook of International Affairs 1979* (London: Stevens and Sons, 1979).
7. Amitav Acharya, "A Regional Community in Southeast Asia?" in Desmond Ball (ed.), *The Transformation of Security in the Asia–Pacific Region* (London: Frank Cass and Co., Ltd., 1996), pp. 177–178.
8. Ibid.
9. Ibid.
10. Janice Gross Stein, "Detection and Defection: Security Regimes and the Management of International Conflict," *International Journal*, Vol. 40 (Autumn 1985), p. 600.
11. Acharya, p. 179.
12. Amitav Acharya, "The Association of Southeast Asian Nations: 'Security Community' or 'Defense Community'," *Pacific Affairs*, Vol. 63, No. 2 (Summer 1991), pp. 159–178.
13. Amitav Acharya, *Constructing a Security Community in Southeast Asia: ASEAN and the Problem of Regional Order* (London and New York: Routledge, 2001).
14. See Amitav Acharya, *The Quest for Identity: International Relations of Southeast Asia* (Singapore: Oxford University Press, 2000).
15. Carlyle A. Thayer, "Arms Control in South-East Asia," *Defense Analysis*, Vol. 12, No. 1 (1996), p. 78.
16. Ibid.
17. Paridah Abdul Samad and Mokhtar Mohammad, "ASEAN's Role and Development as a Security Community," *The Indonesian Quarterly*, Vol. 23, No. 1 (First Quarter 1995), p. 68.
18. Ibid., p. 72.
19. See Benedict Anderson, Imagined Communities: *Reflections on the Origin and Spread of Nationalism,* revised and expanded edition (London: Verso, 1991).
20. See Thomas-Durell Young, "New Zealand Air Power Requirements and Force Determinants," at: http://www.airpower.maxwell.af.mil/airchronicles/aureview/1986/mar-apr/young.html.
21. See "ANZUS," at: http://www.funkandwagnalls.com/encyclopedia/low/articles/a/a002001942f.html.
22. Arthur J. Dommen, *Laos: Keystone of Indochina* (Boulder and London: Westview Press, 1985), p. 51.
23. See "SEATO," at: http://www.funkandwagnalls.com/encyclopedia/low/articles/s/s024000454f.html.
24. Ibid.
25. Ibid. Also see some discussions in Michael Leifer, "The ASEAN Regional Forum: Extending ASEAN's Model of Regional Security," Adelphi Paper 320 (London: Oxford University Press, 1996), p. 9.
26. Leszek Buszincki, *The Failure of an Alliance Strategy* (Singapore: Singapore University Press, 1983).

27. For a short background on this topic, see Anthony Bergin, "The Five Power Defence Arrangements" in Abdul Razak Baginda and Anthony Bergins (eds.), *Asia–Pacific's Security Dilemma: Multilateral Relations Amidst Political, Social and Economic Changes* (London: ASEAN Academic Press, 1998), pp. 77–85. For a more comprehensive discussion, see P. Metheun, *The Five Power Defense Arrangements and Military Cooperation among the ASEAN States* (Canberra: Australian National University, 1992).

28. For a short background on this topic, see Anthony Bergin, "The Five Power Defence Arrangements" in Abdul Razak Baginda and Anthony Bergins (eds.), *Asia–Pacific's Security Dilemma: Multilateral Relations Amidst Political, Social and Economic Changes* (London: ASEAN Academic Press, 1998), pp. 77–85. For a more comprehensive discussion, see P. Metheun, *The Five Power Defense Arrangements and Military Cooperation among the ASEAN States* (Canberra: Australian National University, 1992).

29. Bangladesh first initiated the idea of regional cooperation in South Asia in 1977. Between 1980 and 1981, consultations among the governments of the seven South Asian countries occurred. In August 1983, foreign ministers met in New Delhi to sign the Declaration on South Asian Regional Co-Operation (SARC) and to formally launch the Integrated Programme of Action (IPA). It was only in 1985 that the founding members signed the Charter of the SARRC. See: http://www.saarc.com/shistory.html.

30. See "South Asian Association for Regional Cooperation," at: http://www.south-asia.com/saarc/.

31. See "South Asian Association for Regional Cooperation," Asia–Pacific Center for Security Studies Regional Reference Guide.

32. See Frank Frost, "ASEAN Since 1967: Origins, Evolution and Recent Developments," in Alison Broinowski (ed.), *ASEAN into the 1990s* (London: MacMillan Press, 1990), p. 3.

33. Ibid.

34. See Geoffrey Wiseman, "Common Security in the Asia–Pacific Region," *The Pacific Review*, Vol. 5, No. 1 (1992), pp. 42–59.

35. Desmond Ball, Richard L. Grant, and Jusuf Wanandi, *Security Cooperation in the Asia-Pacific Region* (Westview Press: Boulder Colorado, 1993), pp. 11–12.

36. Desmond Ball, "CSCAP: The Evolution of Second Track Process in Regional Security Cooperation," in *The Council for Security Cooperation in the Asia–Pacific Region* (CSCP Pro Tem Committee, 1993), p. 50.

37. For more information on the activities of CSCAP, see: http://www.cscap.org/.

38. For more discussion, see Broinowski, op. cit.

39. Jeannie Henderson, "Reassessing ASEAN," Adelphi Paper 328 (London: Oxford University Press, 1999), p. 16.

40. Koro Bessho, "Identities and Security in East Asia," Adelphi Paper 325 (London: Oxford University Press, 1999), p. 41.

41. See "ASEAN," at: http://www.aseansec.org/.

42. Sheldon Simon, "The Regionalization of Defense in Southeast Asia," *Pacific Review*, Vol. 5, No. 2 (1992), p. 122.

43. For a critique of the ASEAN Way, see Kay Moller, "Cambodia and Burma: The ASEAN Way Ends Here," *Asian Survey*, Vol. 38, No. 12 (December 1998), pp. 1087–1104; and Shaun Narine, "ASEAN and the ARF: The Limits of the ASEAN Way," *Asian Survey* (October 1997), pp. 961–978.

44. The 1997 Asian financial crisis, however, challenged ASEAN's credibility as a regional organization. See Amitav Acharya, "Realism, Institutionalism and Asian Economic Crisis," *Contemporary Southeast Asia*, Vol. 21, No. 1 (April 1999), pp. 1–29.
45. See "APEC," at: http://www.apec.org/.
46. Franscois Godement, "Moving from Confidence-Building to Preventive Diplomacy: The Possibilities" (Paper presented during the 13th Asia–Pacific Roundtable on May 30 to June 2, 1999 at Kuala Lumpur, Malaysia), p. 1.
47. "ARF Membership," at: http://www.dfat.gov.au/arf/arfintro.html.
48. See Simon S.C. Tay, "The ASEAN Regional Forum: Preparing for Preventive Diplomacy," *Contemporary Southeast Asia*, Vol. 19, No. 3 (December 1997).
49. "ARF Working Group on Preventive Diplomacy," at: http://www.aseansec.org/politics. arf4xh.htm.
50. Franscois Godement, "Moving from Confidence Building to Preventive Diplomacy: The Possibilities" (Paper read at the 13th Asia–Pacific Roundtable in Kuala Lumpur, Malaysia, on May 30 to June 2, 1999). Also see Ralph A. Cossa, "CSCAP and Preventive Diplomacy: Helping to Define the ARF's Future Role" in the same Roundtable Discussion.
51. Dennis C. Blair and John T. Hanley, Jr., "From Wheels to Web: Reconstructing Asia–Pacific Security Arrangements," *The Washington Quarterly*, Vol. 24, No. 1 (Winter 2001), pp. 7–17.
52. For an analysis of various researches on ASEAN as security community, see Rommel C. Banlaoi, "Research on ASEAN as a Security Community: Strengths and Limitations of Realism and Constructivism in Southeast Asian Security Studies" (Paper prepared for presentation to the Annual Convention of International Studies Association at the Town and Country Resort and Convention Center in San Diego, California, March 22–25, 2006. This paper was also submitted to the Department of Political Science, University of the Philippines in partial fulfillment of the requirements in International Studies 263, "International Security").
53. There have been a lot of studies pertaining to Asia–Pacific security. For a long list of these studies, see: http://www.lib.adfa.oz.au/web/military/infogd17.htm.
54. See Gerald Segal, "How Insecure Is Pacific Asia?" *International Affairs*, Vol. 73, No. 2 (1997), pp. 235–249.
55. For an excellent listing on the various territorial conflicts in the region, see Desmond Ball, "Arms and Affluence: Military Acquisition in the Asia–Pacific Region," *International Security*, Vol. 18, No. 3 (Winter 1993–1994), pp. 88–89.
56. Ibid.
57. See Alan Dupont, "Transnational Crime, Drugs, and Security in East Asia," *Asian Survey*, Vol. 39, No. 3 (May–June, 1999), pp. 433–455; and his "New Dimension of Security" (Paper presented for the Joint SDSC and IISS Conference on The New Security Agenda in the Asia–Pacific Region, May 1–3, 1996).
58. See Robert Manning, "Building Community or Building Conflict? A Typology of Asia–Pacific Security Challenges," in Ralph A. Cossa (ed.), *Asia–Pacific Confidence and Security Building Measures* (Washington, DC: The Center for Strategic and International Studies, 1995), pp. 19–40.
59. Nikolas Busse and Hanns W. Maull, "The Future of the ARF: A European View" (A draft paper prepared for presentation in the Seminar on the Future of the ARF organized by the Institute of Defense and Strategic Studies at the Orchard Hotel, Singapore, April 27–28, 1998), p. 1.

60. Ibid.
61. Ibid.
62. Ibid., p. 11.
63. Godement, p. 5.
64. Busse and Maull, p. 14.
65. My discussion in this section is culled from Rommel C. Banlaoi, *The Amsterdam Treaty and the European Unions' Common Foreign and Security Policy: The Politics of Defense and Foreign Policy Making in the Context of Intergovernmental Conferences* (Quezon City: Center for Asia–Pacific Studies, 1999), Chapter II.
66. For a lengthy discussion on this topic, see Richard Langhorne, *The Collapse of the Concert of Europe: International Politics, 1890–1914* (New York: St. Martin's Press, 1981).
67. Philipp Gummet, "Foreign, Defense and Security Policy," in Martin Rhodes, Paul Heywood, and Vincent Wrights (eds.), *Development in East European Politics* (London: Macmillan Press, Ltd., 1997), p. 209.
68. Ibid., pp. 209–210.
69. Banlaoi, p. 41.
70. Juliet Lodge and Val Flynn, "The CFSP after Amsterdam: The Policy Planning and Early Warning Unit," *International Relations*, Vol. XIV, No. 1 (April 1998), pp. 7–21.
71. "OSCE Fact Sheet: What Is the OSCE?" at: http: //usis-israel.org.il/publish/press/osce/archive/december/os11203.htm, (December 2, 1996), p. 1.
72. Institute for Defence and Strategic Studies, A New Agenda for the ASEAN Regional Forum, IDSS Monograph No. 4 (Singapore: IDSS, 2002).
73. Raymond Quilop, "Confidence and Security Building Measures: Towards a Security Community in the Asia–Pacific," Office of Strategic and Special Studies (OSS) Working Papers (Quezon City: OSS, 1998).
74. Leifer, p. 53.
75. See "Estrada Renews Call for Expansion of ASEAN Security Forum," *Manila Business World* (October 22, 1999), p. 1.
76. Robyn Lim, "The ASEAN Regional Forum: Building on Sand," *Contemporary Southeast Asia*, Vol. 20, No. 2 (August 1998), p. 115.
77. Ibid., p. 116.
78. Ibid., p. 116.
79. Gary Klintworth, "Greater China and Regional Security" in Gary Klintworth (ed.), *Asia–Pacific Security: Less Uncertainty, New Opportunities* (Melbourne: Addison Wesley Longman Australia Pty Limited, 1996), p. 35.
80. Amitav Acharya, "Realism, Institutionalism, and the Asian Economic Crisis," *Contemporary Southeast Asia*, Vol. 21, No. 1 (April 1999), p. 7.
81. Yu Xiaoqiu, "China," in Paul B. Stares (ed.), *The New Security Agenda: A Global Survey* (Tokyo: Japan Center for International Exchange, 1998), p. 205. Also see Hans Binnendijk and Ronald N. Montaperto (eds.), *Strategic Trends in China* (Washington, DC: Institute for National Strategic Studies, National Defense University, 1998).
82. Ibid. Also see Beijing Review, Vol. 36, No. 34 (1995), pp. 8–9.
83. Andrew J. Nathan and Robert S. Ross, *The Great Wall and the Empty Fortress: China's Search for Security* (New York and London: W.W. Norton and Company, 1997), p. 235.

84. See Kuik Cheng Chwee, "China's Participation in the ASEAN Regional Forum (ARF): The Exogenous and Endogenous Effects of International Institutions," in James K. Chin and Nicholas Thomas (eds.), *China and ASEAN: Changing Political and Strategic Ties* (Hong Kong: Centre of Asian Studies, The University of Hong Kong, 2005), pp. 141–170. Also see Rosemary Foot, "China in the ASEAN Regional Forum: Organizational Processes and Domestic Modes of Thought," *Asian Survey*, Vol. 38, No. 5 (May 1998), pp. 425–440.
85. The State Council, China's Peaceful Development Road (Beijing: The State Council Information Office, December 22, 2005). Also see Zheng Bijian, "China's Peaceful Rise to Great Power Status," *Foreign Affairs* (September/October 2005).
86. Amitav Acharya, "A Concert of Asia?," *Survival*, Vol. 41, No. 3 (Autumn, 1999), p. 98.
87. Ibid., p. 95.
88. Ibid., p. 96.
89. Ibid., p. 89.
90. Ralph Boyce, "Moving from Confidence-Building to Preventive Diplomacy: The Possibilities" (Paper presented during the 13th Asia–Pacific Roundtable on May 30–June 2, 1999, Kuala Lumpur, Malaysia), p. 11.

*Chapter 15*

# Security Cooperation and Conflict in Southeast Asia after 9/11: Constructivism, the ASEAN Way, and the War on Terrorism*

## Introduction

To deepen and intensify regional security cooperation and improve the management of inter-state conflicts in Southeast Asia, members of the Association of Southeast Asian Nations (ASEAN) met in Bali, Indonesia, on October 7–8, 2003, for the 9th ASEAN Summit. In this summit, ASEAN leaders signed the ASEAN Concord II, which adopts the concept of security community to bring security cooperation in Southeast Asia to a "higher plane."[1]

---

* Revised version of the paper published in Amitav Acharya and Lee Lai To (eds.), *Asia in the New Millennium* (Singapore: Marshall Cavendish Academic, 2004), pp. 32–55; and in *Indian Ocean Survey*, Vol. 1, No. 1 (January–June 2005), pp. 49–74. Original version of this paper was presented to the 1st Congress of Asian Political and International Studies Association (APISA), Oriental Hotel, Singapore, November 27–30, 2003.

The adoption of an ASEAN Security Community (ASC) is a significant landmark in the history of ASEAN as it formally declares an important mechanism to improve security cooperation in Southeast Asia. It also occurs at the time of a heightened campaign against terrorism in the region[2] and amid criticism lodged against ASEAN as the most successful regional organization in the developing world. Since the 1997 Asian financial crisis[3] and the 1999 East Timor problem,[4] ASEAN's international standing has been under tremendous attack for its limitations to respond decisively on these two critical issues. The accession of Cambodia and Myanmar also created issues against ASEAN. The war on terrorism in Southeast Asia confounds the ASEAN dilemma of building its image as a credible security community.

Using constructivism as a framework, this chapter argues that the adoption of ASC does not challenge ASEAN's approach to regional security. Rather, the ASC affirms the usual ASEAN Way of security cooperation and conflict management. Although the war on terrorism and the emergence of various nontraditional security threats[5] in Southeast Asia are putting tremendous pressure on the organization to reexamine the ASEAN Way, the principle of agreeing not to disagree when faced with actual regional security threats still holds water in the region. ASEAN members' strong attachment to the principle of noninterference is still pervasive in various declarations and concords. The ASEAN principle of noninterference remains the overarching framework of security cooperation and conflict management in Southeast Asia despite the many challenges posed by 9/11.

This chapter also contends that the gravity of terrorist threats in Southeast Asia does not automatically put terrorism at the apex of the ASEAN security agenda.[6] Pre-9/11 security issues like the implications of territorial and border disputes for regional security, the repercussions of the 1997 Asian financial crisis, the challenges of ASEAN enlargement, the prospects of ASEAN+3 project, the implementation of ASEAN Free Trade Area, the independence of East Timor, and the great power rivalry in the region continue to predominate the ASEAN security agenda. These agenda are evident in various declarations and documents adopted by ASEAN after 9/11.

For ASEAN, terrorism is only one of many security issues facing Southeast Asia and is not the defining security issue of the region. ASEAN even regards terrorism as "a continuing low level threat."[7] Southeast Asian countries only pay attention to the threat of terrorism because it can affect the region's long-term stability, which is deemed vital for regional growth and prosperity. But in the absence of a commonly agreed regional definition of terrorism, ASEAN states calculate their individual response to terrorism in order not to encroach upon fellow ASEAN members' sovereign prerogatives on the issue, particularly in those countries with a large Muslim population. There are also domestic political roots to this calculation, making an ASEAN response to terrorism highly problematic despite the declaration of ASC.

Finally, this chapter argues that although ASEAN is adjusting itself to the new geostrategic environment unleashed by the war on terrorism in Southeast Asia,[8] its ability to counter terrorism in the region is restricted by the inherent principle of the ASEAN Way. Because of ASEAN's own process of institution building and identity formation, an ASEAN approach to counterterrorism is still undergoing a difficult process of evolution and gestation. Thus, countering terrorism in Southeast Asia in the short and medium terms depends not on ASEAN's institutional capability to address the threat but on the capability of its member states to coordinate their individual efforts outside but inspired by the ASEAN framework. Although ASEAN can provide a long-term approach to address the problem of terrorism in Southeast Asia, this depends on the construction of the institutional capacity of ASEAN as a potential conflict-preventing and problem-solving regional organization in Southeast Asia.

## Constructivism: Understanding the ASEAN Way of Security Cooperation and Conflict Management

Constructivism offers an alternative theoretical framework in the study of regional security cooperation. Like realism, constructivism regards states as principal units of analysis in international security affairs. But constructivism posits that the identities of states and their concomitant security interests are products of the complex and long process of social constructions. Even the structure of the international system is socially constructed. Cultural norms, social values, and identities shape policy preferences of key players in international politics.

Alexander Wendt is one of the major authorities on constructivism. He advances the following core claims of constructivism: (1) states are the principal units of analysis for international political theory; (2) the key structures in the states' system are intersubjective, rather than material; (3) state identities and interests are in important part constructed by these social structures, rather than given exogenously to the system by human nature or domestic politics.[9]

Wendt also claims that states, as principal players in international politics, have corporate identity defined as the "intrinsic, self-organizing qualities that constitute actor individuality."[10] This corporate identity shapes and determines state pursuance of national security, regional stability, and international recognition. How states fulfill their needs of corporate identities depends on states' social identities, which are understood in terms on how states view themselves vis-à-vis other states in international society.[11] States construct their interests based on these identities.[12]

Like the realist framework, constructivism also describes the international society as the state of international anarchy. But it departs from the realist framework, stating that anarchy is a given state of affairs. For constructivism, international anarchy is also socially constructed. As Wendt contends, "anarchy is what states make of it."[13] He argues that "an anarchy of friends differs from one of enemies, one of self-help from one of collective security, and these are all constituted by structures of shared knowledge."[14] On the basis of this perspective, the state of international anarchy can be converted into a "security community," which Wendt defines as a social structure "composed of shared knowledge in which states trust one another to resolve disputes without war."[15]

Although other scholars of international relations are contesting the explanatory and predictive appeal of constructivism, it serves as an alternative framework for analyzing regional institutions like the ASEAN. Constructivism puts greater emphasis on the importance of institutions to state action. Institutions create norms, rules, and procedures for international interactions and collective actions, which are also socially constructed. State identities and interests also develop with the development and evolution of institutions. These institutions, on the other hand, exist and persist because states produce and reproduce them through sustained practices and habits of interactions. In other words, states and institutions also have dynamic interactions, making "the possibility that each bring about change in the other."[16]

Among the Asian constructivists, Amitav Acharya receives the reputation of the most authoritative scholar in Southeast Asian security studies. Acharya uses constructivism to analyze the strengths and weaknesses of ASEAN as a regional organization.[17] Acharya also examines ASEAN's successes and failures in constructing a security community in Southeast Asia. He describes ASEAN as a security community from a constructivist point of view despite serious attacks by realist scholars.[18] He regards ASEAN's security community status as a social construct, similar with what Benedict Anderson calls "imagined community."[19] Acharya states that ASEAN as a security community is

> sort of an "imagined community" — a vision which preceded rather than resulted from political, strategic and functional interactions and interdependence, and as such it must be understood in non-material terms. ASEAN is a community similar to Benedict Anderson's classic formulation of the nation–state as an "imagined community."[20]

As a security community, Acharya regards ASEAN's collective identity as an important aspect of community building in the region. This collective identity is anchored on what he calls the "we feeling" in ASEAN, which is not based on the logic of economic interdependence and democracy but based on the cultural and social process within the region.[21] Acharya emphasizes that culture alone does not construct collective norms. Rather, "norms also created culture," and this norm, which many scholars describe as the ASEAN Way, is a construction of a long-term process of social interaction, cultural adjustment, and political socialization.[22]

## The ASEAN Way of Building a Security Community: Security Cooperation and Conflict Management after 9/11

The ASEAN Way is a diplomatic norm in Southeast Asia upholding the practice of intense dialogues and exhausting consultations (*musyawarah*) to generate consensus (*mufakat*) on contentious issues facing the region. This practice, called *musyawarah dan mufakat*, encourages all ASEAN members to cooperate on various areas through informal and incremental mechanisms. At the heart of the ASEAN Way is the cardinal principle of noninterference in the domestic affairs of member states enshrined in the 1976 Treaty of Amity and Cooperation in Southeast Asia. The impact of colonial history, the consequences of great power rivalry, interstate disputes, and the emergence of post-colonial nation–states in Southeast Asia are contributory factors to ASEAN's strong attachment to noninterference.[23] The ASEAN Way also upholds the principle of renouncing the threat or use of force to settle differences and to manage disputes. The ASEAN Way is the strong tie that firmly binds all 10 ASEAN members together.

But the ASEAN Way of noninterference has been criticized for its limitations to the resolution of existing conflicts in the region. The ASEAN Way only puts regional conflicts "under the rug" rather than solves them; it only diffuses contentious issues away rather than squarely confronts them. Thus, the ASEAN Way only contains regional problems.[24] This prompted other scholars to describe the ASEAN Way as an obsolete mechanism to address traditional and nontraditional security threats facing the region, particularly the alarming threat of terrorism in Southeast Asia.[25] The ideas of "constructive engagement," "flexible intervention," and "flexible engagement" were proposed to reinvent the ASEAN principle of noninterference.[26] All of these proposals failed due to the rejection of other ASEAN members, particularly Indonesia, the de facto leader in ASEAN. In fact, the idea of flexible engagement was eventually "watered down" to the idea of "enhanced interaction," which according to one scholar is nothing but "a reaffirmation of the sanctity of the ASEAN Way."[27]

Despite its limitations as a model of regional cooperation,[28] the ASEAN Way remains at the core of security cooperation and conflict management in Southeast Asia even after 9/11. The ASEAN Way continues to serve as the overarching principle of regional security cooperation and dispute settlement. Although the war on terrorism is challenging its member states to reexamine the ASEAN Way, there is still paramount adherence to this diplomatic norm.[29]

The idea of a security community in the ASEAN Concord II is a clear demonstration of its members' strict adherence to the ASEAN Way. Instead of challenging the ASEAN way of noninterference, the concept of ASC strongly affirms it by stressing that "ASEAN shall continue to promote regional solidarity and cooperation. Member Countries shall exercise their rights to lead their national existence free from outside interference in their internal affairs."[30] The ASEAN Concord II also reaffirms the principle of the sovereign rights of each member of ASEAN by dismissing the speculation that ASEAN is building a defense pact or military alliance. The ASEAN Concord II states the following:

> The ASEAN Security Community, recognizing the sovereign right of the member countries to pursue their individual foreign policies and defense arrangements and taking into account the strong interconnections among political, economic and social realities, subscribes to the principle of comprehensive security as having broad political, economic, social and cultural aspects in consonance with the ASEAN Vision 2020 rather than to a defense pact, military alliance or a joint foreign policy.[31]

In other words, national sovereignty is still paramount in the ASC. But one very important characteristic of the ASC is the recognition in ASEAN that the security of each member state also depends on the security of the region. The ASEAN Concord II states:

> The ASEAN Security Community is envisaged to bring ASEAN's political and security cooperation to a higher plane to ensure that countries in the region live at peace with one another and with the world at large in a just, democratic and harmonious environment. The ASEAN Security Community members shall rely exclusively on peaceful processes in the settlement of intra-regional differences and regard their security as fundamentally linked to one another and bound by geographic location, common vision and objectives.[32]

In short, the formal declaration of a security community in Southeast Asia in the ASEAN Concord II does not question the ASEAN Way. Instead, the idea of a security community in the region reaffirms the fundamental principle of the ASEAN Way. ASC is a social construct resulting from the ASEAN norms of noninterference, nonuse of force, and avoidance of collective defense.[33] As a social construct, ASC is not the end product of security cooperation but rather still part of the whole process of socialization upholding ASEAN norms, which define and redefine ASEAN's unique identity as a regional community.[34] These norms enshrined in the ASEAN Way guide ASEAN actions in countering terrorist threats in Southeast Asia.

## Security Community, the ASEAN Way, and the War on Terrorism in Southeast Asia

The formal declaration of security community in Southeast Asia does not alter ASEAN's approach to regional security issues, which include the issue of terrorism.

The ASEAN Way remains as the ASEAN overarching framework in responding to the war on terrorism in Southeast Asia.

As a collective body, ASEAN declared its sympathy for the United States in the wake of the 9/11 terrorist attacks. But its members were very cautious in linking terrorism with Muslim radicalism because of the sensitivities of other Southeast Asian states host to Muslim communities. Thus, the willingness of its members to become part of the American global campaign against terrorism has varied depending upon ASEAN members' perception of terrorism and domestic political considerations.[35] Because of the absence of a commonly agreed regional definition of terrorism, ASEAN is facing a tremendous dilemma of designing a collective strategy to combat terrorism in Southeast Asia.[36] Domestic political factors such as the varying role of Islam in each individual Southeast Asia country, specific characteristics of their political systems, and their peculiar domestic policies on terrorism also affect the development of an ASEAN antiterrorist strategy. Thus, ASEAN has to rely on the national ability of its member states to confront the problem and to make the necessary inter-state coordination to address the problem at the regional level.

Although ASEAN has a varying perception of terrorist threats, its members have already recognized the existence of these threats even prior to the 9/11 incident. As early as 1997, ASEAN already paid attention to the terrorist problem in the region when its members signed the ASEAN Declaration on Transnational Crime. Following this declaration was the signing in 1998 of the Manila Declaration on the Prevention and Control of Transnational Crime. This declaration established the ASEAN Center for Combating Transnational Crime in Manila. In 1999, ASEAN members adopted the ASEAN Plan of Action to Combat Transnational Crimes at the 2nd ASEAN Ministerial Meeting on Transnational Crime (AMMTC) in Myanmar. Prior to 9/11, therefore, ASEAN was already cognizant of terrorist problems in the region within the context of transnational crimes.

The first ASEAN declaration after the 9/11 terrorist attacks is the 2001 ASEAN Declaration on Joint Action to Counter Terrorism. In this declaration, ASEAN members condemned in the strongest terms the horrifying terrorist attacks in New York City, Washington D.C., and Pennsylvania and extended their deepest sympathy and condolences to the people and Government of the United States of America and the families of the victims from nations all around the world. This declaration shows ASEAN's vintage use of broad diplomatic language to (1) maintain the principle of noninterference, (2) pursue ASEAN solidarity on the issue, and (3) uphold the exclusive sovereignty of member states in combating terrorism.

ASEAN members also adopted the Joint Communiqué of the Special ASEAN Ministerial Meeting on Terrorism in Kuala Lumpur on May 20–21, 2002. In this joint communiqué, ASEAN members uphold the ASEAN Way of combating terrorism through the following provisions:

- Recognition and respect of sovereignty, territorial integrity, and domestic laws of each ASEAN member country in undertaking the fight against terrorism.
- Recognition of the right of individual ASEAN member countries to continue pursuing practical preventive measures to address the root causes of terrorism.
- Commitment to counter, prevent, and suppress all forms of terrorist acts in accordance with the Charter of the United Nations and other international law, especially taking into account the importance of all relevant UN resolutions.

In May 2002, ASEAN adopted the Work Program to Implement the ASEAN Plan of Action to Combat Transnational Crime. This is one of the longest documents signed by ASEAN members pertaining to the campaign against terrorism. It upholds the importance of information exchange, training, extraregional cooperation, legal measures, and institutional capacity-building not only in combating terrorism but also in preventing the rise of transnational crimes. In the area of antiterrorism, ASEAN members agreed to work toward the criminalization of terrorism in the region.

Like previous ASEAN documents on terrorism, this work program does not endorse a collective response to combat terrorism and other transnational crimes in Southeast Asia. It only provides broad provisions to allow the independent maneuver of member states for interstate coordination at the regional level. But like the issue of haze, an environmental disaster that happened in Indonesia in 1997, the main emphasis of the work program is on the development of national plans and capabilities rather than on the formulation of regional strategies against terrorism.[37]

When U.S. Secretary of State Collin Powell held his Southeast Asian tour in August 2002, the United States and ASEAN members signed the ASEAN-U.S. Joint Declaration for Cooperation to Combat International Terrorism. In this joint declaration, all parties agreed to pursue the following measures:

- Continue and improve intelligence and terrorist financing information sharing on counterterrorism measures, including the development of more effective counterterrorism policies and legal, regulatory, and administrative counterterrorism regimes.
- Enhance liaison relationships among their law enforcement agencies to engender practical counterterrorism regimes.
- Strengthen capacity-building efforts through training and education; consultations between officials, analysts, and field operators; and seminars, conferences and joint operations as appropriate.
- Provide assistance on transportation and on border and immigration control challenges, including document and identity fraud, to stem effectively the flow of terrorist-related material, money, and people.

- Comply with United Nations Security Council Resolutions 1373, 1267, 1390 and other United Nations resolutions or declarations on international terrorism.
- Explore on a mutual basis additional areas of cooperation.

But the main emphasis of this joint declaration remains on liaison, coordination, and information sharing. In fact, the intention of ASEAN in this declaration is more strategic and pragmatic. ASEAN members want to take advantage of the American global war on terrorism to get foreign assistance from the sole superpower. By signing this declaration, ASEAN countries hope to grab the opportunity of getting antiterrorism assistance from the United States to enhance their national capacity to confront the problem, rather than to develop a collective response to counter terrorism. Each one of them does not even want to see the war on terrorism to be capitalized by the United States to justify intervention using the idea of collective action as an excuse.

Southeast Asian countries have also expressed apprehension of the American penchant for its military approach to counterterrorism and to expedite its goal of destroying al Qaeda and its Southeast Asian network. Although all ASEAN states support the American campaign against terrorism in the region, they want this campaign to be launched in the context of noninterference and not on the basis of what a scholar calls U.S. foreign policy of "praetorian unilateralism."[38]

During the 8th ASEAN Summit in Phnom Penh on November 3, 2002, ASEAN members signed the Declaration on Terrorism. In this declaration, ASEAN members expressed determination "to carry out and build on the specific measures outlined in the ASEAN Declaration on Joint Action to Counter Terrorism," which they adopted in Brunei Darussalam in November 2001. They also reiterated their strong resolve to intensify ASEAN efforts, collectively and individually, "to prevent, counter and suppress the activities of terrorist groups in the region." While this document sees the value of collective response to confront the problem of terrorism in Southeast Asia, the document is more of a declaration of intent than a concrete program of action. In fact, ASEAN has been criticized because most efforts it has adopted are plain "declarations" rather than concrete "collective actions." Furthermore, regional security cooperation in countering terrorism in Southeast Asia has not been well coordinated because of conflicting national interests and mutual suspicions of ASEAN members.[39] As observed by scholars of the Heritage Foundation:

> ASEAN as an organization has done relatively little to coordinate the substantial counter-terrorism efforts of its member states—a response to the problem of terrorism that is symptomatic of its chronic inability to coordinate its member states into collective action on any front. Applied military cooperation between ASEAN states is rare and often late in

coming. Yet terrorism is so deeply entrenched in Southeast Asia that uprooting it will require more than local initiatives by each state.[40]

Although ASEAN declarations do not mean endorsement of collective actions, these declarations remain vital in building thrusts and confidence for the development of a mechanism for inter-state coordination against terrorism. Although terrorism really poses clear and present danger to Southeast Asia, ASEAN remains very careful in adopting a collective response to counter terrorism in order not to undermine the sovereign prerogative of its member states on the issue. ASEAN allows its members to pursue regional security cooperation against terrorism bilaterally or multilaterally. But these must be done outside the auspices of ASEAN to maintain solidarity and to protect the identity of ASEAN undergoing the process of continuing social construction. Furthermore, ASEAN respects the corporate identity and national sovereignty of its members in dealing with terrorist threats in Southeast Asia.

The trilateral Agreement on Information Exchange and Establishment of Communication Procedures signed by Indonesia, Malaysia, and the Philippines on May 7, 2002, is an excellent example of regional cooperation against terrorism outside the ASEAN framework. Although ASEAN, as a regional body, regards the trilateral agreement as an important contribution in the campaign against terrorism, it does not regard the trilateral agreement as part of the official ASEAN initiative. The trilateral agreement is the product of sovereign prerogative of three original parties outside the ASEAN framework.

The trilateral agreement, however, has yet to prove itself. Since its signing, contracting parties have not yet operationalized the agreement. The draft terms of reference of the agreement have not been finalized yet. In January 2003, a meeting was held in the Philippines to finalize the terms of reference, but to no avail. Countering terrorism in Southeast Asia, therefore, continues to be based on the usual practice of inter-state coordination. Despite some problems in the implementation, Thailand and Myanmar have acceded to the trilateral agreement. Other ASEAN members have expressed interest to follow suit.

In other words, ASEAN cooperation in the war against terrorism is still based on the ASEAN Way of noninterference in the domestic affairs of its member states. While all ASEAN members recognize the importance of collective action against terrorism, they do not want to use the war on terrorism as an excuse to challenge the principle of noninterference. Some Southeast Asian countries have expressed apprehensions that the war on terrorism might become a justification for later intervention in their domestic affairs.[41] Although ASEAN members acknowledge the need to seek a regional solution of the terrorist problem, they want this regional solution to evolve and to be constructed within the framework of the ASEAN Way. In fact, all ASEAN declarations pertaining to antiterrorism are strict reminders to all member states to abide by the norms, rules, and procedures of the ASEAN Way. As stated earlier, the Joint Communiqué of the Special ASEAN Ministerial

Meeting on Terrorism recognizes and respects the sovereignty, territorial integrity and domestic laws of each ASEAN Member Country in undertaking the fight against terrorism.

## The ASEAN Way, Regional Security Cooperation, and the Individual Country's Response to Terrorism

Since September 11, there has been intensified cooperation at the various levels (bilateral, regional, and international) to fight international terrorism.[42] But ASEAN security cooperation against terrorism remains interstate and intergovernmental rather than regional in Southeast Asia, the second front in the global campaign against terrorism.[43] While ASEAN opposes terrorism, it does not qualify as an antiterrorist coalition in the region because of the restrictions of the ASEAN Way.[44] ASEAN declarations on terrorism are not endorsements of collective response but reaffirmations of the whole process of confidence building on counterterrorism.

Despite the adoption of numerous declarations to fight terrorism and the formal declaration of ASEAN as a security community, ASEAN shall not be viewed as an antiterrorist organization because of (1) each individual country's varying perception of terrorism as a threat to national and regional security, and (2) each individual country's mixed commitment to the American call for global support to combat international terrorism.

### Indonesian Response to Terrorism

Indonesia is the most troubled country in Southeast Asia, having been the victim of two major terrorist bombings: the Bali bombing and the Marriott Hotel (Jakarta) bombing. Although critical of the U.S. global war against terrorism, Indonesia condemned the 9/11 attacks and expressed its readiness to cooperate with any UN collective action against terrorism. President Megawati Sukarnoputri was the first Muslim leader in Asia who visited the White House after 9/11. On September 19, 2001, President Megawati met President Bush, where they exchanged pledges to strengthen existing cooperation in the global effort to combat international terrorism. Bush also promised to lift the embargo on commercial sales of nonlethal military items to Indonesia.[45]

Indonesia, however, demanded that the United States not target a specific country in the campaign against terrorism, arguing that it would affect U.S. investment in that country.[46] As a matter of fact, Jakarta did not officially endorse U.S. military operations against the Taliban government in Afghanistan and called on all parties "to avoid open war." When the United States urged all "civilized states" to block financial support for terrorist movements, Indonesia also displayed a lukewarm reaction because of thousands of Islamic charities in Southeast Asia.[47] To scrutinize those charities in its own country would risk a significant Muslim backlash, not to mention Indonesian ill-capacity to monitor thousands of financial transactions coming from overseas and nongovernmental organizations.[48] One of the major reasons for the critical support of Indonesia to the U.S. war on terrorism is the presence of Islamic radicals in the country. Indonesia is the world's largest Islamic country. Thus, Jakarta is tempering its support to the U.S. antiterrorism campaign to avoid tensions with militant Islamic elements of the Indonesian population.

Despite the critical support of Indonesia, the global campaign against terrorism leads to the improvement of U.S.-Indonesia military relations. In the early 1990s, Indonesian-American military ties were suspended due to the 1992 Santa Cruz massacre in Dili and the perceived human rights violations in East Timor. Driven by the U.S. war on terrorism in Southeast Asia, the American and Indonesian governments have found the opportunity of rebuilding their military ties.[49] The U.S. Department of Defense has openly pursued the restoration of full military-to-military relations with Indonesia.[50] The U.S. Congress even passed a bill in December 2001 allowing Indonesian military to participate in the U.S.-initiated counterterrorism training and programs. Indonesia, on the other hand, regarded the U.S. war on terrorism as an opportunity to resume U.S.-Indonesia military relations, especially in the light of separatist and sectarian violence in Aceh, the Moluccas, Sulawesi, and Irian Jaya. Jakarta knows that the United States can be of great assistance in combating its own terrorism problems. But Jakarta does not want this assistance to justify American intervention in Indonesian domestic affairs.

## Malaysian Response to Terrorism

Malaysia's support to the American-led war on terrorism is quite ambivalent. It supports the ASEAN declaration on antiterrorism but is critical of the U.S.-led war in Southeast Asia. Malaysia has also opposed the U.S.-initiated military campaign in Afghanistan.

Malaysia's ambivalent response is based on the apprehension that the U.S. antiterrorism campaign might trigger militant activities in Kuala Lumpur, considering the presence of militant Muslims in the country. It might be recalled that Prime Minister Mahathir Mohamad used the antimilitant Muslim campaign to crack down on the Islamic Party of Malaysia, the strongest Islamic opposition party in Malaysia.[51] To prevent the unintended consequence of its support to the war on terrorism, Mahathir carefully supported the war on terrorism with no anti-Islamic undertone.

Despite this ambivalent support, the Malaysian government took the lead in Southeast Asia in sponsoring an Islamic Conference on Terrorism in April 2002. Malaysia also ordered its local banks to freeze the assets of organizations found to be sponsoring or connected with terrorism. It arrested around 60 suspected terrorists since 9/11 because of their alleged membership in the Malaysian Militant/Mujahadin Movement. This organization reportedly established a link with al Qaeda. Malaysian police authorities arrested these people on the basis of the Internal Security Act.

Malaysia has implemented stricter measures to crack down on groups with links to extremism and has enforced more rigid policies on visas to deter people from using Malaysia as a transit point for terrorist activities. Malaysia has also formulated a new law prohibiting the use of religious schools as fronts for terrorist activities. It has enforced an integrated curriculum for religious schools to assure that no school curriculum would be used for terrorist indoctrination. Malaysian police authorities, on the other hand, have created Special Forces deployed in various universities to monitor covert terrorist activities in the campuses and to identify foreign students trying to recruit students in the terrorist front organizations. Its immigration office has required all Malaysian students planning to study abroad to register before departure.

The war on terrorism has created an opportunity for Malaysia to improve its strained bilateral relations with the United States. Malaysia–U.S. bilateral ties improved in the aftermath of 9/11 when Mahathir visited President Bush in Washington on May 13–15, 2002. In this meeting, both leaders agreed to enhance their cooperation in combating terrorism in Southeast Asia. They also signed an agreement calling on both countries to coordinate law enforcement, to share intelligence information, and to strengthen border security. The former Malaysian prime minister, Abdullah Ahmad Badawi, called for a more systematic study of the causes of terrorism.

## Philippine Response to Terrorism

The Philippines was the first ASEAN state to declare the strongest support to the U.S. war on terrorism. Manila even expressed willingness to deploy Philippine troops to Afghanistan once approved by the Philippine Congress. The Philippines also offered its territory to the United States as transit points or staging areas of troops fighting the war on terrorism in Afghanistan. When President Gloria Macapagal Arroyo visited the United States in November 2001, she reiterated its administration's full support to the U.S. war on terrorism.

Prior to the visit, the Philippine government formed the Inter-Agency Task Force against International Terrorism on September 24, 2001. This Inter-Agency Task Force aims to coordinate intelligence operations and to facilitate the identification and neutralization of suspected terrorist cells in the Philippines. To freeze the financial assets of international terrorists, the Philippine Congress passed the Anti-Money Laundering Act on September 29, 2001. President Arroyo also announced on October 12, 2001, its 14-pillar approach to combat terrorism. On the basis of the 14-pillar approach to combat terrorism, the Philippine government also issued General Order No. 2 on May 9, 2002, directing the Armed Forces of the Philippines (AFP) and the Philippine National Police to prevent and suppress acts of terrorism and lawless violence in Mindanao. Together with General Order No. 2, the Philippine government also issued on the same day the Memorandum Order No. 61 to provide measures in quelling the acts of terrorism in the Southern Philippines.

Through the Operation Center of the Cabinet Oversight Committee on Internal Security (COCIS), the Philippine government has also drafted the National Plan to Address Terrorism and its Consequences as Annex to the third version of the National Internal Security Plan (NISP). The Philippine government approved the NISP on November 26, 2001, through Memorandum Order 44.

As part of its support to the American-led global campaign against terrorism, the Philippines also hosted the presence of American troops to conduct joint military exercises in the Philippines dubbed as Balikatan 02-1.[52] The Philippines and the United States launched the Balikatan 02-1 in February 2002 with the official goal of enhancing the capability of Philippine and U.S. forces to combat international terrorism. To further express its full support to the global campaign against terrorism, the Philippine government, through its National Security Council Secretariat, hosted the International Conference on Anti-Terrorism and Tourism Recovery on November 8–9, 2002. Eighteen countries including the members of the Association of Southeast Asian Nations and the United States, Britain, China, Japan, South Korea, and Australia, as well as officials from the World Tourism Organization and the International Police Organization participated in the international conference.

The Philippines heavily supports the war on terrorism because it wants to reinvigorate its security ties with the United States for strategic and economic reasons. When the U.S. forces withdrew from Clark Air Base and Subic Bay Naval Base in 1992 as a result of the termination of the Military Bases Agreement (MBA) in 1991, the *once-strong* and *once-special* Philippine–American security relations became practically moribund.[53] The war on terrorism in Southeast Asia revived the *once-ailing* security ties between the two countries.[54]

Because of staunch Philippine support to the war on terrorism, Manila was able to solicit military assistance from Washington. President George W. Bush pledged a total of $100 million in military aid not only to enhance Philippine ability to combat terrorists but also to increase its wherewithal to fight local insurgents.[55] During the conduct of Balikatan 02-1, Filipino troops received training in special operations, air night operations, maritime operations, patrol craft maintenance, and civil-military operations.

During the commemoration of the 50th anniversary of the signing of the Mutual Defense Agreement, the United States promised to assist the Philippines in acquiring new military equipment that would include a C-130 transport plane, 8 Huey helicopters, a naval patrol boat, and 30,000 M-16 rifles plus ammunitions. In addition to training and US $100 million in military aid, the Bush Administration also pledged a US$150 million antiterrorism assistance package to the Philippines. On June 28, 2002, President Bush signed a memorandum ordering the release of $10 million worth of defense articles and services from the inventory of the U.S. Department of Defense (DOD) to the Philippine government. During President Arroyo's stopover in Hawaii on October 25, 2002, on her way to an Asia–Pacific Economic Cooperation (APEC) Summit in Mexico, she met Hawaii Senator Daniel

Inouye, who reassured President Arroyo of the restoration of the U.S. congressional cut on the $30 million military assistance by the U.S. government to the AFP.

Following the May 19, 2003, meeting between Bush and Arroyo in Washington, D.C., the United States designated the Philippines as a major NATO. According to Bush, making the Philippines a major non-NATO ally would allow the two countries "to work together on military research and development, and give the Philippines greater access to American defense equipment and supplies."[56] Having designated a major non-NATO ally also strengthens the Philippine defense posture in the light of the growing power of China in Southeast Asia.[57]

## Singapore Response to Terrorism

As a close strategic partner of the United States in Southeast Asia, Singapore immediately extended its strong support to the U.S.-led war on terrorism. The Singapore Parliament also passed the Anti-Terrorism Regulations Act, which came into force on November 13, 2001. The Anti-Terrorism Regulations Act criminalizes "the direct or indirect provision of economic or financial assistance to the terrorists and provides for specific punishment for perpetrating a hoax of a terrorist act."[58]

To intensify its counterterrorist campaign, the Singapore government formed the Executive Group, a national security secretariat with decision-making power tasked to respond to complex emergency situations. The government also directed its police and armed forces to increase it defensive security measures at vital installations and facilities like airports, border checkpoints, government offices, and commercial buildings. Singapore also imposed strict visa requirements on foreigners coming from Egypt, Iran, Pakistan, Saudi Arabia, and Sudan.

Singapore played a pivotal role in unearthing pertinent information on terrorist activities in Southeast Asia through its arrest of suspected terrorists connected with Jemaah Islamiyah (JI) and al Qaeda. Like its Indonesian and Malaysian counterparts, however, the Singaporean government is careful in its antiterrorist campaign in order not to alienate its Muslim population. In fact, Abdullah Tarmugi, Singapore's minister-in-charge of Muslim affairs, urged Singaporeans not to identify Muslims with terrorism. To date, the Singaporean government is working out a comprehensive national security strategy to fight terrorism.

## Thailand Response to Terrorism[59]

Although Thailand joined the international community in condemning the terrorist attacks on America, the Thai government expressed reluctance in joining the American-led global campaign against terrorism. It even declared neutrality in this global campaign. The Thai parliament also expressed cautions and urged its members to be critical in the antiterrorist campaign of the United States. Despite this expression of reluctance, Thailand has intensified its efforts to implement the UN resolutions related to counterterrorism.

As part of its national counterterrorism measures, the Thai government has set up the Committee of Counter-International Terrorism (COCIT) chaired by the prime minister. The COCIT serves as a focal point for policy formulation on antiterrorism. Thailand also has the Counter International Terrorist Operations Center (CITOC) directed by COCIT. The CITOC is responsible for the coordination between the policy level and operational units on antiterrorism.

To suppress the funding of international terrorist activities, Thailand supported the U.S. call to block the funding of terrorists. As early as 1999, in fact, the Thai government established the Anti-Money Laundering Office (AMLO) to take effective countermeasures against money laundering and other illegitimate financing. On December 11, 2001, the Thai cabinet approved the two draft amendments of the Penal Code and the Anti-Money Laundering Act to proscribe financing of terrorism as a serious offense under the Thai criminal law and to empower the AMLO to freeze terrorist funds as mandated by the United States Security Council (UNSC) Resolution 1373.

To shore up its campaign against international terrorism, the Thai government also intensified its international cooperation program against terrorism. On September 10, 2002, Thailand, the United Kingdom, and the European Commission signed the Memorandum of Understanding on the Asia–Europe Meeting (ASEM) Anti-Money Laundering Project to promote international cooperation against money laundering as a way of combating transnational crime including international terrorism. On October 3, 2002, Thailand and Australia also signed the memorandum of understanding between the two countries to develop more effective counterterrorism policies and legal policies through the exchange of terrorist financing information, training, and education.

Although critical of the American campaign against terrorism, Thailand has been conducting joint military exercises with the United States through the Cobra Gold Exercise, a series of U.S.–Thai military exercises designed to ensure regional peace and strengthen the ability of the Royal Thai Armed Forces to defend Thailand or respond to regional contingencies.[60] On May 14–28, 2002, both forces conducted the Cobra Gold Exercise on antiterrorism. Aside from the Cobra Gold Exercises, Thailand also hosted the Southeast Asia Cooperation against Terrorism (SEA-CAT) held in March 2002. The SEA-CAT aimed to establish a regional coordination infrastructure for information sharing and exchange supporting a multinational response to combat terrorism and other transnational crimes in the region.

## Conclusion

In the midst of a heightened campaign against terrorism in Southeast Asia, ASEAN proclaimed the idea of an ASEAN security community to intensify security cooperation and promote regional solidarity. The idea of a security community, however, maintains the ASEAN Way, which upholds the principle of noninterference. Although the problem of terrorism in Southeast Asia is not only domestic but also regional in scope, ASEAN continues to approach the problem in the ASEAN Way, which respects the sovereignty of states and consensus-based decision-making norm.

Different perceptions of terrorist threats and domestic political factors prompt ASEAN members to continuously embrace the principle of the ASEAN Way in combating terrorism in Southeast Asia. Although the ASEAN Way may not provide an immediate solution to the problem of terrorism in the region, the ASEAN Way allows its members to coordinate their efforts to address this regional menace in the immediate and short-term without offending their respective national sensitivities.

There is no doubt that the idea of a security community is an important milestone in the history of ASEAN as it strongly recognizes that security of every Southeast Asian state is inextricably linked with the security of others. More importantly, the idea of a security community in ASEAN reflects the sharing of common imagining of ASEAN member states that they have achieved a condition where they rule out the use of force to settle differences and to address their interrelated security problems, which include the problem of terrorism.

# Endnotes

1. Declaration of ASEAN Concord II (October 7, 2003).
2. For a detailed discussion of the author's analysis of the war on terrorism in Southeast Asia, see Rommel C. Banlaoi, *The War on Terrorism in Southeast Asia* (Manila: Rex Book Store, 2004). For an excellent analysis of al Qaeda's Southeast Asian network, see Zachary Abuza, "Tentacles of Terror: Al-Qaeda's Southeast Asian Network," *Contemporary Southeast Asia*, Vol. 24, No. 3 (December 2002), pp. 427–465; and "Funding Terrorism in Southeast Asia: The Financial Network of al-Qaeda and Jemaah Islamiyah," *Contemporary Southeast Asia*, Vol. 21, No. 1 (April 1999), pp. 54–73.
3. See, for example, Edmund R. Thompson and Jessie P. H. Poon, "ASEAN after the Financial Crisis," *ASEAN Economic Bulletin*, Vol. 17, No. 1 (April 2000). Also see Michael Wesley, "The Asian Crisis and the Adequacy of Regional Institutions," *Contemporary Southeast Asia*, Vol. 25, No. 2 (August 2003), pp. 169–199.
4. See Alan Dupont, "ASEAN's Response to East Timor Crisis," *Australian Journal of International Affairs*, Vol. 54, No. 2 (July 2000), pp. 163–170.
5. Andrew T.H. Tan and J.D. Kenneth Boutin (eds.), *Non-Traditional Security Issues in Southeast Asia* (Singapore: Institute of Defense and Strategic Studies, 2001).

6. Jim Rolfe, "Security in Southeast Asia: It's Not about the War on Terrorism," *Asia Pacific Security Studies*, Vol. 1, No. 3 (June 2002).

7. Ibid., p. 2.

8. Daljit Singh, "The Post–September 11 Geostrategic Landscape and Southeast Asian Response to the Threat of Terrorism," *ISEAS Working Paper*, No. 9 (September 2002). Available at: http://www.iseas.edu.sg/pub.html.

9. Alexander Wendt, "Collective Identity Formation and the International State," *American Political Science Review*, 88 (June 1994), p. 385.

10. Ibid.

11. Shaun Narine, "Economics and Security in the Asia Pacific: A Constructivist Analysis" (Paper prepared for presentation at the 41st Annual Convention of the International Studies Association, Los Angeles, California, March 14–18, 2000), p. 4. Also available at: http://www.ciaonet.org/isa/nas01/.

12. Ibid.

13. Alexander Wendt, "Anarchy Is What States Make of It: The Social Construction of Power Politics," *International Organization*, Vol. 46, No. 2 (1992), pp. 391–425.

14. See Alexander Wendt, "Constructing International Politics" in Michael Brown et al. (eds.), *Theories of War and Peace* (MA: MIT Press, 1998), p. 423.

15. Ibid., p. 418.

16. See Narine, p. 4.

17. Amitav Acharya, *Constructing a Security Community in Southeast Asia: ASEAN and the Problem of Regional Order* (London and New York: Routledge, 2001).

18. For an excellent review of the debate, see Sorpong Peou, "Realism and Constructivism in Southeast Asian Security Studies Today: A Review Essay," *The Pacific Review* Vol. 15, No. 1 (2002), pp. 119–138. Also see Nikolas Busse, "Constructivism and Southeast Asian Security," *The Pacific Review*, Vol. 12, No. 1 (1999), pp. 39–60. For other frameworks analyzing Southeast Asian security, see Sheldon Simon, "Realism and Neoliberalism: International Relations Theory and Southeast Asian Security," *The Pacific Review*, Vol. 8, No. 1 (1995), pp. 5–24; and, Amitav Acharya, "Realism, Institutionalism and the Asian Economic Crisis," *Contemporary Southeast Asia*, Vol. 21, No. 1 (April 1999), pp. 1–29.

19. Benedict Anderson, *Imagined Communities*, revised and updated version (London: Verso, 1991). Anderson's concept is also used to examine the ASEAN Regional Forum as a potential security community in the Asia Pacific. See Rommel C. Banlaoi, "The ASEAN Regional Forum and Security Community Building in the Asia–Pacific: Lessons from Europe?" *National Security Review*, Vol. 19, No. 2 (2nd Semester 1999), pp. 118–133.

20. Acharya, p. 2.

21. See Amitav Acharya, *The Quest for Identity: International Relations of Southeast Asia* (Singapore: Oxford University Press, 2000). This is cited in Sorpong Peou, p. 132.

22. Ibid., p. 72.

23. Robin Ramcharan, "ASEAN and Non-Interference: A Principle Maintained," *Contemporary Southeast Asia*, Vol. 22, No. 1 (April 2000), p. 81.

24. Shaun Narine, *Explaining ASEAN: Regionalism in Southeast Asia* (Boulder, Colorado, and London: Lynne Reiner Publishers, 2002).

25. One prominent Indonesian scholar even describes the ASEAN Way as a *passe*. See Jusuf Wanandi, "ASEAN's Past and the Challenges Ahead: Aspects of Politics and Security," in Simon C. Tay, Jesus Estanislao, and Hadi Soesastro, (eds.), *Reinventing ASEAN* (Singapore: Institute of Southeast Asian Studies, 2001). Also see Kay Moller, "Cambodia and Burma: The ASEAN Way Ends Here," *Asian Survey*, Vol. 38, No. 12 (December 1998), pp. 1087–1104 and Shaun Narine, "ASEAN and the ARF: The Limits of the ASEAN Way," *Asian Survey*, Vol. 37, No. 10 (October 1997), pp. 961–978.

26. Carlyle A. Thayer, "Re-inventing ASEAN: From Constructive Engagement to Flexible Intervention," *Harvard Asia Pacific Review* (Summer 1999). Also see Surin Pitsuwan, "Future Directions for ASEAN" (Lecture presented at the Forum on Regional Strategic and Political Developments organized by the Institute of Southeast Asian Studies, Singapore, July 25, 2001). Also at: http://www.iseas.edu.sg/pub.html.

27. Ramcharan, p. 65.

28. For an excellent discussion on the limits of the ASEAN Way as a model of regional security cooperation in the Asia Pacific, see Michael Leifer, "The ASEAN Regional Forum: Extending ASEAN's Model of Regional Security," *Adelphi Paper*, No. 320 (London: Oxford University Press, 1996). Also see Narine, "ASEAN and the ARF: The Limits of the ASEAN Way."

29. Hiro Katsumata, "Reconstruction of Diplomatic Norms in Southeast Asia: The Case of Strict Adherence to the ASEAN Way," *Contemporary Southeast Asia*, Vol. 24, No. 1 (April 2003), pp. 104–121.

30. Declaration of ASEAN Concord II (October 7, 2003).

31. Ibid.

32. Ibid.

33. For an elaboration of ASEAN perspectives of collective defense, see Amitav Acharya, "The Association of Southeast Asian Nations: Security Community of Defense Community?" *Pacific Affairs*, Vol. 63, No. 2 (Summer 1991).

34. For a critical appraisal of ASEAN as a regional community, see Tobias Nischalke, "Does ASEAN Measure Up? Post–Cold War Diplomacy and the Idea of Regional Community," *The Pacific Review*, Vol. 15, No. 1 (2002), pp. 89–117.

35. For a detailed account of ASEAN members response to the global campaign against terrorism, see Sheldon W. Simon, "Southeast Asia and the War on Terrorism," *NBR Analysis*, Vol. 13, No. 4 (July 2002), pp. 25–37.

36. For further discussions on these issues, see Barry Desker, "Islam and Society in Southeast Asia after September 11," *IDSS Working Paper Series*, No. 3 (September 2002); Willem van der Geest (ed.), "Mapping Muslim Politics in Southeast Asia After September 11," *The European Institute for Asian Studies Publications*, Vol. 2, No. 5 (December 2002); and Harold Crouch, Ahmad Fauzi Abdul Hamid, Carmen A. Abubakar, and Yang Razali Kassim, "Islam in Southeast Asia: Analyzing Recent Developments," *ISEAS Working Paper Series*, No. 1 (January 2002).

37. Ramcharan, p. 69.

38. Kumar Ramakrishna, "The U.S. Foreign Policy of Praetorian Unilateralism and the Implications for Southeast Asia," in Uwe Johannen, Alan Smith, and James Gomez (eds.), *September 11 and Political Freedom: Asian Perspectives* (Singapore: Select Publishing, 2003), pp. 86–115.

39. Andrew Tan, "The New Terrorism: How Southeast Asia Can Counter It," in Uwe Johannen, Alan Smith, and James Gomez (eds.), *September 11 and Political Freedom: Asian Perspectives* (Singapore: Select Publishing, 2003), pp. 116–141.

40. Dana Robert Dillon and Paolo Pasicolan, "Promoting a Collective Response to Terrorism in Southeast Asia," *Heritage Foundation Executive Memorandum*, No. 825 (July 22, 2002).

41. James Cotton, "Southeast Asia after 11 September," *Terrorism and Political Violence*, Vol. 15, No. 1 (Spring 2003), p. 161.

42. Daljit Singh, "Two Years On: Terrorism in Southeast Asia Remains a Threat," *ISEAS Viewpoints* (September 11, 2003), p. 2. Also available at: http://www.iseas.edu.sg.

43. John Gershman, "Is Southeast Asia the Second Front?" *Foreign Affairs* (July/August 2002). Also see Peter Symonds, "Why Has South East Asia Become the Second Front in Bush's War on Terrorism?" at: www.wsws.org.

44. Dana R. Dillon, "The Shape of Anti-Terrorist Coalitions in Southeast Asia," *Heritage Lectures*, No. 773 (December 13, 2002), p. 1.

45. Kurt Biddle, "Indonesia–U.S. Military Ties: September 11th and After," *Inside Indonesia*, (April–June 2002), p. 1. Also at: http://www.insideindonesia.org/edit70/kurtedit_a.htm (accessed on July 25, 2002).

46. Christoffersen, "The War on Terrorism in Southeast Asia: Search for Partners, Delimiting Targets," *Center for Contemporary Conflict Strategic Insights: East Asia* (March 2002) at: http://www.ccc.nps.navy.mil/rsepResources/si/mar02/eastAsia.asp (accessed July 11, 2002).

47. Sheldon Simon, "Mixed Reactions in Southeast Asia to the U.S. War on Terrorism," *Comparative Connections* (4th Quarter 2001).

48. Ibid.

49. International Crisis Group, "Resuming U.S.–Indonesia Military Ties," *Indonesia Briefing* (May 21, 2002), p. 1.

50. Reyko Huang, "Priority Dilemmas: U.S.–Indonesia Military Relations in the Anti-Terror War," *Center for Defense Information Terrorism Project* (May 23, 2002), at: http://www.cdi.org/terrorism/priority-pr.cfm (accessed on July 24, 2002).

51. Simon, p. 4.

52. Rommel C. Banlaoi, "The Role of Philippine–American Relations in the Global Campaign against Terrorism: Implications for Regional Security," *Contemporary Southeast Asia*, Vol. 24, No. 2 (August 2002), pp. 278–296.

53. Richard D. Fisher, Jr., "Rebuilding the U.S.–Philippine Alliance," *The Heritage Foundation Backgrounder*, No. 1255 (February 22, 1999).

54. See Rommel C. Banlaoi, "Philippine–American Security Relations and the War on Terrorism in Southeast Asia," at: http://www.apan-info.net/terrorism/terrorism_view_article.asp?id=43.

55. Steven Mufson, "U.S. to Aid Philippines' Terrorism War Bush Promises Military Equipment, Help in Freezing Insurgents' Assets," at: http://www.washingtonpost.com/ (accessed on April 27, 2002).

56. Jim Garamone, "Philippines to Become Major Non-NATO Ally, Bush Says," *American Forces Press Service*, at: http://www.defenselink.mil/news/May2003/n05192003_2003 05193.html.

57. See Rommel C. Banlaoi, "Southeast Asian Perspectives on the Rise of China: Regional Security after 9/11," *Parameters*, Vol. 33 No. 2 (Summer 2003), pp. 98–109.

58. Soo Seong Theng, "New Anti-Terrorism Laws in Singapore" at http://www.lawgazette. com.sg/2002-6/June02-focus2.htm (accessed on March 10, 2003).
59. Based on "Progress Report on Thailand's Implementation of Counter-Terrorism Activities," at: http://www.mfa.go.th/internet/document/Terrorism%20Report.doc (accessed on March 19, 2003).
60. For further information on Cobra Gold 2002, see "Exercise Cobra Gold 2002" at: http://www.cobragold2002.okinawa.usmc.mil/cg2002-news.html. For more updates on Cobra Gold Exercises, see "Cobra Gold Exercises," at: http://www.apan-info.net/ exercises/default.asp.

## Chapter 16

# The Philippines and ASEAN at Forty: Achievements, Challenges, and Prospects in Regional Security Cooperation*

## Introduction

Since its establishment in 1967, the Association of Southeast Asian Nations (ASEAN) has gone a long way in its regional cooperation. From an association of states in Southeast Asia tasked to merely promote economic, social, and cultural cooperation, ASEAN has dramatically metamorphosed into a regional grouping that promotes security cooperation among its member states, particularly in the area of defense and military affairs.

Though security has always been at the core of ASEAN's existence, member states heavily emphasized "soft" security (for example, economic, social, and

---

* Revised and updated version of an article originally published in Mandarin at *Southeast Asian Studies: A Journal of Jinan University, China*, Vol. 4 (2007).

cultural) in its early stages of development in order to build trust among themselves. As it matures at the age of 40, ASEAN has become more confident to discuss defense and military concerns that are considered "hard" security issues. The adoption of an ASEAN Security Community (ASC) in 2003 and the holding of the ASEAN Defense Ministerial Meeting (ADMM) launched in Malaysia in 2006 were crystal-clear indications that ASEAN has daringly brought security cooperation in Southeast Asia to a higher level. Amid these developments is the vital role played by the Philippines in the promotion of security cooperation in ASEAN.

This chapter describes the evolution of security cooperation in Southeast Asia and takes stock of ASEAN achievements in this area spanning four decades of its existence. It also identifies some challenges facing ASEAN as it aspires to become a regional organization with a coherent regional security agenda. Particularly, this chapter examines the role of the Philippines in the pursuance of security cooperation in Southeast Asia using ASEAN as the major platform.

## The Philippines and the Evolution of ASEAN Security Cooperation during the Cold War

The Philippines has always regarded ASEAN as the cornerstone of its foreign and security policy to promote economic development and stability in the region.[1] Thus, the Philippines has been an avid advocate of security cooperation in Southeast Asia. Even prior to the formation of ASEAN, the Philippines hosted the establishment of the Southeast Asia Treaty Organization (SEATO) in Manila on September 8, 1954, to promote collective defense in Southeast Asia against Communist expansionism during the height of the cold war. SEATO attempted to approximate the function of the North Atlantic Treaty Organization (NATO) but to no avail, because SEATO did not obligate its members to assist each other in case of military attack against any of its members. Moreover, SEATO only included two Southeast Asian states: the Philippines and Thailand. Interestingly, both countries have existing military treaty alliances with the United States.

Despite the failure of SEATO, the Philippines formed the Association for Southeast Asia (ASA), with Thailand and Malaysia in 1961 to pursue regional security cooperation. Though it was Malaysia's idea to form the ASA, strong Philippine support for the idea made it happen. In fact, ASA suffered its demise in 1963 when the Philippines suspended its diplomatic relations with Malaysia when they failed to reach a mutual understanding over the issue of Sabah. Like SEATO, ASA also suffered its untimely demise because of conflicting national interests.

To revive the spirit of regional security cooperation in Southeast Asia, the Philippines, with Malaysia and Indonesia, formed the Malaysia–Philippines–Indonesia (MAPHILINDO) association in August 1963. But it was dissolved three months after because of the *Konfrontasi* between Malaysia and Indonesia.

The Philippines tried to keep MAPHILINDO alive in order to preserve the basis of its claim to Sabah,[2] but Philippine efforts did not succeed. Nonetheless, the Philippines continued to advocate for regional security cooperation in Southeast Asia through the establishment of ASEAN.

When the Philippines, together with Indonesia, Malaysia, Singapore, and Thailand, joined together for the formation of ASEAN in 1967, their primordial objective was to promote regional security from the very beginning but to emphasize economic, social, and cultural cooperation. The five original founders of ASEAN defined security in a comprehensive sense consisting of political, economic, social, cultural, and even military factors interacting in all levels of analysis.[3] But the core members gave greater emphasis to cooperation in nonmilitary areas in order not to offend their national sensitivities. They deliberately avoided "hard" security issues of defense and military affairs in its embryonic phase in order to promote closer cooperation in "soft" and less controversial security issues through the principles of good neighborliness and mutual respect of each other's sovereignty, guided by the policy of noninterference in the domestic affairs of members.

The Bangkok Declaration of 1967 was the founding document of ASEAN. The 1967 declaration was very explicit in its goal to promote regional security free from foreign intervention. Amid the backdrop of the cold war, original ASEAN members vigorously excluded military alliance from its objective to assuage the fear of its neighbors that ASEAN was forming a "military bloc." Even founding members themselves did not entertain the idea of collective defense within the ASEAN framework because of the sensitive issue of State sovereignty.

During the formative years of ASEAN, it only saw modest progress in regional security cooperation.[4] One major reason for this limited progress was the failure of its members to reach consensus on how to exactly implement the Bangkok Declaration of 1967, specifically the provision urging its members to ensure the "stability and security" of the region free from "external interference."[5] In fact, ASEAN did not have any clear program on how to achieve its aim of regional security.[6] The Philippine government even expressed disappointment for a slow progress of ASEAN. Nonetheless, the formation of ASEAN some 40 years ago laid the political foundation for regional cooperation among its members by opening excellent channels of communication to manage their differences without resorting to armed confrontation. ASEAN also allowed regional cooperation to sink in amid intense nationalism of its members.

ASEAN has therefore allowed the establishment of the habits of consultation among its members to build greater confidence and diffuse inter-state territorial tensions among them, particularly between the Philippines and Malaysia, Indonesia and Malaysia, and Singapore and Malaysia. This prompted former Philippine President Ferdinand E. Marcos to exclaim, "We have come to the point where the national interests of the Philippines are almost equivalent to the interests of ASEAN itself."[7]

To promote Southeast Asia as a region of peace, freedom, and neutrality in the midst of the cold war between the United States and the former Soviet Union, ASEAN members met in Kuala Lumpur on November 27, 1971, to sign the declaration on the Zone of Peace, Freedom and Neutrality (ZOPFAN). This declaration is still anchored on the 1967 Bangkok Declaration. But the ZOPFAN declaration commits all ASEAN members to "exert efforts to secure the recognition of and respect for Southeast Asia as a Zone of Peace, Freedom and Neutrality, free from any manner of interference by outside powers," and to "make concerted efforts to broaden the areas of cooperation, which would contribute to their strength, solidarity and closer relationship." Though ZOPFAN put the Philippines in an odd position because the Philippines hosted at that time two major American military facilities, ZOPFAN conveyed the message to the United States that the Philippines had identified itself with the interests of ASEAN. In fact, the Philippines became ASEAN's de facto spokesperson with the United States on various aspects of their relations.[8]

The year 1976 was a major turning point in the history of ASEAN. During this year ASEAN held its first summit of heads of government in Bali. It was in Bali where member countries signed the ASEAN Concord I, or the Bali Declaration of 1976, otherwise known as the Bali Concord I. The Philippines drafted the Bali Concord I, which the heads of government signed on February 24, 1976.[9]

The Bali Concord I raised the level of ASEAN cooperation by adopting a program of action in the political, economic, social, cultural, and technical spheres to improve the living standards of the Southeast Asian region as an antidote against Communist insurgency threatening the national security of ASEAN members. The Bali Concord I also created the ASEAN Secretariat with no supranational authority compared to the European Commission in Brussels. The ASEAN Secretariat was also established in Indonesia, regarded by its members as their de facto leader. ASEAN was, in fact, "guided from behind" by Indonesia, whose concept of "national resilience" became the basis for ASEAN's "regional resilience."[10] This concept of regional resilience in ASEAN embraces the values of *flexibility, consensus*, and *mutual understanding* to promote regional security.[11] To extend its brand of regional cooperation, the Bali Concord I also allowed dialogue relations with third countries, particularly major powers.

It was during the meeting in Bali when ASEAN members also signed the 1976 Treaty of Amity and Cooperation in Southeast Asia, or TAC. The TAC allowed the expansion of ASEAN to other states in Southeast Asia. It also officially endorses the ASEAN Way of regional security cooperation among parties. The ASEAN Way is a diplomatic norm in Southeast Asia upholding the practice of intense dialogues and exhausting consultations (*musyawarah*) to generate consensus (*mufakat*) on contentious issues facing the region. This practice, *musyawarah dan mufakat*, encourages all ASEAN members to cooperate on various areas through informal and incremental mechanisms. At the heart of the ASEAN Way is the cardinal principle of noninterference in the domestic affairs of member states enshrined in the TAC.

The impact of colonial history, the consequences of great power rivalry, interstate disputes, and the emergence of postcolonial nation–states in Southeast Asia are contributory factors to ASEAN's strong attachment to noninterference.[12] The ASEAN Way also upholds the principle of renouncing the threat or use of force to settle differences and to manage disputes. This encouraged some major powers to adopt the ASEAN Way when they acceded to the TAC. For example, China signed the TAC, which improved China's relations with ASEAN. India and Australia followed suit.

Since 1967, the ASEAN Way of noninterference has been criticized for its limitations to actually resolve existing conflicts in the region. It is argued that the ASEAN Way only puts regional conflicts "under the rug" rather than solves them; it only diffuses contentious issues away rather than squarely confronts them. Thus, critical analysts have argued that the ASEAN Way only contains, rather than solves, regional problems.[13] This prompted other scholars to describe the ASEAN Way as an obsolete mechanism to address traditional and nontraditional security threats facing the region, particularly the alarming threat of terrorism in Southeast Asia aggravated by the 9/11 incident.[14] Ideas of *constructive engagement, flexible intervention*, and *flexible engagement* were recently proposed to reinvent the ASEAN principle of noninterference.[15] These proposals failed due to the rejection of other ASEAN members, particularly Indonesia. In fact, the idea of flexible engagement, supported by the Philippines, was eventually "watered down" to the idea of "enhanced interaction," which according to one scholar is nothing but "a reaffirmation of the sanctity of the ASEAN Way."[16]

Despite its limitations as a model of regional cooperation,[17] the ASEAN Way remains at the core of security cooperation and conflict management in Southeast Asia to date. The ASEAN Way continues to serve as the overarching principle of regional security cooperation and dispute settlement in the region. Through the ASEAN style of regional cooperation, the association improved the security relations among its members. It even encouraged other Southeast Asian states to join ASEAN to take advantage of the opportunities of regional cooperation. ASEAN admitted Brunei as a new member on January 7, 1984. Though ASEAN was challenged in the aftermath of Communist victories in Indochina in 1975, the association strongly waged a vigorous diplomatic campaign to manage the problem, particularly the refugee issue. ASEAN also faced the challenge of the Vietnamese invasion of Cambodia. But ASEAN used its diplomatic skills to address this challenge by sponsoring a series of dialogues. ASEAN's success in managing the problem in Indochina received extensive international recognition. This prompted some scholars to describe ASEAN as "the third world's most successful experiment in regionalism" and a "diplomatic player capable of intervening on major issues of regional security."[18] The success of ASEAN to promote regional security amid tensions in Indochina encouraged the eventual enlargement of the association.

## Philippine and ASEAN Security Cooperation after the Cold War

The end of the cold war, however, tested ASEAN's relevance as a regional association. When the United States withdrew its troops from the Philippines in November 1991, it created security anxieties, considering the rapid growth of China's power in the post–cold war era. The end of the cold war radically altered the security environment in Southeast Asia with China playing a more prominent role. When China declared in 1992 that the South China Sea was an integral part of its territory, it aggravated ASEAN's apprehension of China. Thus, ASEAN called for the expansion of ASEAN to enlarge its voice vis-à-vis major powers.

The 1992 ASEAN Summit reiterated that the TAC was open for accession by other Southeast Asian states. Founding members staunchly advocated for the enlargement of ASEAN in order to unite Southeast Asia amid China's growing economic and military power in the Asia Pacific region. In July 1992, Vietnam and Laos signed the TAC. ASEAN even facilitated the formation of the ASEAN Regional Forum (ARF) in 1993 to address security uncertainties in the Asia Pacific and to "civilize" China. It was viewed that "ASEAN's central aim in establishing the ARF was to bring China into structures that would encourage it to play a responsible role in the region."[19] The Philippines even used the ARF as a forum to internationalize the South China Sea issue.[20]

In July 1995, Vietnam became the seventh member of ASEAN. For ASEAN, Vietnam's accession gave an opportunity for the association to forge better ties with China. With the sponsorship of the Philippines, Laos and Myanmar were also eventually admitted as new members to help break the perceived "Chinese encirclement" of Southeast Asia.

## Philippine and ASEAN Security Cooperation during the 1997 Financial Crisis

Despite the progress, ASEAN suffered another tremendous setback in regional cooperation during the 1997 Asian financial crisis. ASEAN's failure to prevent the regional economic crisis utterly exposed the limitations of ASEAN and its fragile style of regional cooperation.

But the economic crisis gave China a golden opportunity to improve its ties with ASEAN members when it did not devalue its currency to help affected states to recover from the regional financial crunch. China voluntarily contributed to the rescue packages for Thailand and Indonesia and even promised to increase Chinese investments in the region.[21]

The Philippines, however, expressed caution on Chinese strategic intentions when the Philippine Air Force discovered in 1999 a new concrete building in the

Mischief Reef occupied by China in 1995. The Philippines elevated the issue to the level of ASEAN to strengthen its bargaining position with China. Failing to get ASEAN consensus on the issue, the Philippines signed a Visiting Forces Agreement (VFA) with the United States in 1999 to deter the perceived "Chinese expansionism" in the South China Sea. The signing of the agreement improved the once-ailing Philippine–American security alliance in the post–cold war era. It was also in 1999 when ASEAN completed the ASEAN-10 with the accession of Cambodia.

Although the ASEAN-10 failed to reach consensus on how to respond to the Mischief Reef controversy, the Philippines hailed the completion of the ASEAN-10 as it finally united Southeast Asia as a region. A former Philippine national security adviser stressed that the "unification advances ASEAN's effort to safeguard its sub-region from the interventionism of outside powers – to prevent Southeast Asia from becoming an arena of their strategic competition."[22] But the September 11, 2001 terrorist attacks on the United States posed another challenge to the effectiveness of ASEAN promoting regional security considering that Southeast Asia has become the second front in the global campaign against terrorism, next to Afghanistan.[23]

## Philippine and the ASEAN Security Cooperation after 9/11

As discussed in Chapter 15, ASEAN declared its sympathy for the United States in the wake of the 9/11 terrorist attacks. But its members were very cautious in linking terrorism with Muslim radicalism because of the sensitivities of other Southeast Asian states host to Muslim communities. Thus, the willingness of its members to become part of the American global campaign against terrorism has varied, depending upon ASEAN members' perception of terrorism and some domestic political considerations.[25] Because of the absence of a commonly agreed regional definition of terrorism, ASEAN faced a tremendous dilemma of designing a collective strategy to combat terrorism in Southeast Asia.[26] Domestic political factors such as the varying role of Islam in each individual Southeast Asia country, specific characteristics of their political systems, and their peculiar domestic policies on terrorism tremendously affected the development of an ASEAN antiterrorist strategy.

To deepen and intensify regional security cooperation and improve the management of inter-state conflicts in Southeast Asia, ASEAN members met in Bali, Indonesia, on October 7–8, 2003, for the 9th ASEAN Summit. In this summit, ASEAN leaders signed the ASEAN Concord II, which adopted the concept of a security community to bring security cooperation in Southeast Asia to a "higher plane."[27] The adoption of ASC was a significant landmark in the history of ASEAN because it formally declared an important mechanism to improve security cooperation in Southeast Asia.

## The Philippines and the ASEAN Security Community

The Philippines strongly supported the idea of ASC. The ASC realized the Philippines' original concept of regional security cooperation, which the defunct SEATO failed to implement. The idea of a security community in the ASEAN Concord II is also a clear demonstration of its members' strict adherence to the ASEAN Way. Instead of challenging the ASEAN Way of noninterference, the concept of ASC strongly affirms it by stressing that "ASEAN shall continue to promote regional solidarity and cooperation. Member Countries shall exercise their rights to lead their national existence free from outside interference in their internal affairs."[28] The ASEAN Concord II also reaffirms the principle of the sovereign rights of each member of ASEAN by dismissing the speculation that ASEAN is building a defense pact or military alliance. The ASEAN Concord II states:

> The ASEAN Security Community, recognizing the sovereign right of the member countries to pursue their individual foreign policies and defense arrangements and taking into account the strong interconnections among political, economic and social realities, subscribes to the principle of comprehensive security as having broad political, economic, social and cultural aspects in consonance with the ASEAN Vision 2020 rather than to a defense pact, military alliance or a joint foreign policy.[29]

In other words, national sovereignty is still paramount in the ASC. But one very important characteristic of the ASC is the recognition in ASEAN that the security of each member state also depends on the security of the region. The ASEAN Concord II states:

> The ASEAN Security Community is envisaged to bring ASEAN's political and security cooperation to a higher plane to ensure that countries in the region live at peace with one another and with the world at large in a just, democratic and harmonious environment. The ASEAN Security Community members shall rely exclusively on peaceful processes in the settlement of intra-regional differences and regard their security as fundamentally linked to one another and bound by geographic location, common vision and objectives.[30]

It is very important to note that the formal declaration of the security community in Southeast Asia in the ASEAN Concord II does not question the ASEAN Way. Instead, the idea of a security community in the region reaffirms the fundamental principle of the ASEAN Way. ASC is a social construct resulting from the ASEAN norms of noninterference, nonuse of force, and avoidance of collective defense.[31] As a social construct, ASC is not the end product of security cooperation but rather still part of the whole process of socialization, upholding ASEAN norms, which define and redefine ASEAN's unique identity as a regional community.[32]

With the adoption of ASC, ASEAN launched the holding of ADMM in 2006. The ADMM is another milestone in the history of ASEAN because it provided defense ministers in Southeast Asia the opportunity to see and talk to each other face-to-face in a multilateral setting to discuss sensitive security issues confronting the region. From mere cooperation in economic, social, and cultural areas, ASEAN, through the ADMM, is now talking about defense and military issues, which were considered taboo before. The Philippines considers the holding of the ADMM as an important step toward the realization of ASEAN as a security community. In fact, the Philippines hosted the Second ADMM on January 25–26, 2007, to "galvanize" ASEAN security cooperation. It even supported Indonesia's call to host the ADMM Retreat in Bali, Indonesia, in March 2007 in order to accelerate the implementation of the ASEAN security community. The Philippines also hosted the 13th ASEAN Summit in January 2007. During this summit, ASEAN adopted the ASEAN Counter-Terrorism Convention with the principle of ASC in mind.

## Conclusion

What have we learned after 40 years of ASEAN existence?

The ASEAN at 40 tells us that there is no easy road to security cooperation. There are roadblocks and challenges in security cooperation in ASEAN because of the principles of sovereignty and noninterference in the domestic affairs that continue to dictate the international behaviors of ASEAN member states. There was also a slow phase in ASEAN security cooperation since it was established in 1967 because of strong nationalism of its members. Though all member states agree in general terms on the importance of cooperation to promote regional security, the devil is in the details, particularly in the area of defense and military affairs.

Despite all the challenges of ASEAN security cooperation, its achievements after 40 years of dialogue and consultation may be considered as "record breaking." ASEAN has provided a platform for the creation of ARF that aims to promote regional security in the Asia Pacific. ASEAN has also adopted the idea of developing a security community in Southeast Asia in order to elevate regional cooperation to a higher plane. More importantly, it created the ADMM to put all ASEAN defense ministers together to discuss issues that concern the security of the region that have tremendous impacts on the individual national security of its members. As a matter of fact, ASEAN is now talking about establishing an ASEAN peacekeeping force in 2012 without necessarily transforming ASEAN into a "defense organization." The Philippines is an advocate of this idea given its exemplary practices in peacekeeping duties in Aceh, East Timor, and Cambodia.

Forty years have passed, and we have seen ASEAN slowly moving regional cooperation forward from "soft" to "hard" security issues. Amid this process is the strong resolve of the Philippines to enhance ASEAN security cooperation by introducing innovations that render the principle of nonintervention in Southeast Asia more "flexible." Will the present stage of ASEAN security cooperation through the ASC and ADMM lead to the establishment of a formal defense arrangement?

The answer depends on how ASEAN members will define the "nuts and bolts" of their security cooperation. At present, members maintain their adherence to the ASEAN Way of noninterference in the domestic affairs of states. As such, members also pay attention to the sensitivities of their neighbors, particularly major powers. Thus, establishing a formal defense arrangement within ASEAN is still out of its formal agenda. The ASEAN Concord II is even explicit in its declaration that ASEAN does not intend to establish an ASEAN defense organization or a collective security institution. ASEAN wants to maintain its status as a cooperative security association pursuing the idea of a security community.

What concerns ASEAN at present is the strengthening of ASEAN's organizational structure and capacity in order to enforce compliance of members to implement decisions and agreements. ASEAN also has to further reinvent itself in order to effectively deal with internal security problems of members with regional repercussions. ASEAN also has to open engagement with the civil society in Southeast Asia in order to bring ASEAN security cooperation not only to a higher plane but also to the grassroots. Most importantly, ASEAN has to exercise flexibility in the implementation of its noninterference principle to make the association a stronger institution with the capacity not only to prevent but also to settle disputes in all areas.

There is a saying that life begins at 40. Now is the time for ASEAN to begin reinventing itself to make it more responsive to the security needs of the region and of its members in the 21st century. It is only then when we can really claim that ASEAN is a viable security community in Southeast Asia.[33]

## Endnotes

1. Jose Ingles, *Philippine Foreign Policy* (Manila: Lyceum of the Philippines, 1982), p. 165.
2. Estrella D. Solidum, *Toward a Southeast Asian Community* (Quezon City: University of the Philippines Press, 1974), p. 30.
3. Shaun Narine, "ASEAN and the Management of Regional Security," *Pacific Affairs*, Vol. 71, No. 2 (Summer 1998), p. 196.
4. Frank Frost, "ASEAN since 1967: Origins, Evolution and Recent Developments," in Alison Broinowski (ed.), *ASEAN into the 1990s* (London: Macmillan, 1990), p. 1.
5. Ibid., p. 6.
6. Jeannie Henderson, *Reassessing ASEAN*, Adelphi Paper No. 328 (London: International Institute for Strategic Studies, 1999), p. 15.
7. Quoted in Benjamin Domingo, *The Making of Philippine Foreign Policy* (Manila: Foreign Service Institute, 1982), p. 282.

8. Ibid., p. 284.
9. Ingles, p. 166.
10. Henderson, p. 17.
11. Abbul R. Rais, "ASEAN States Security: Resilience through Security Cooperation," *Air War College Technical Reports* (March 1989).
12. Robin Ramcharan, "ASEAN and Non-Interference: A Principle Maintained," *Contemporary Southeast Asia*, Vol. 22, No. 1 (April 2000), p. 81.
13. Shaun Narine, *Explaining ASEAN: Regionalism in Southeast Asia* (Boulder, Colorado, and London: Lynne Reiner Publishers, 2002).
14. One prominent Indonesian scholar even describes the ASEAN Way as a *passe*. See Jusuf Wanandi, "ASEAN's Past and the Challenges Ahead: Aspects of Politics and Security," in Simon C. Tay, Jesus Estanislao, and Hadi Soesastro (eds.), *Reinventing ASEAN* (Singapore: Institute of Southeast Asian Studies, 2001). Also see Kay Moller, "Cambodia and Burma: The ASEAN Way Ends Here," *Asian Survey*, Vol. 38, No. 12 (December 1998), pp. 1087–1104; and Shaun Narine, "ASEAN and the ARF: The Limits of the ASEAN Way," *Asian Survey*, Vol. 37, No. 10 (October 1997), pp. 961–978.
15. Carlyle A. Thayer, "Re-Inventing ASEAN: From Constructive Engagement to Flexible Intervention," *Harvard Asia Pacific Review* (Summer 1999). Also see Surin Pitsuwan, "Future Directions for ASEAN" (Lecture presented at the Forum on Regional Strategic and Political Developments organized by the Institute of Southeast Asian Studies, Singapore, July 25, 2001). Also at: http://www.iseas.edu.sg/pub.html.
16. Ramcharan, p. 65.
17. For an excellent discussion on the limits of the ASEAN Way as a model of regional security cooperation in the Asia Pacific, see Michael Leifer, "The ASEAN Regional Forum: Extending ASEAN's Model of Regional Security," *Adelphi Paper*, No. 320 (London: Oxford University Press, 1996). Also see Narine, "ASEAN and the ARF: The Limits of the ASEAN Way."
18. Henderson, p. 19.
19. Ibid., p. 28.
20. Rommel C. Banlaoi, *The ASEAN Regional Forum, the South China Sea Disputes, and the Functionalist Option* (Quezon City: National Defense College of the Philippines, 2001).
21. Amitav Acharya, "Realism, Institutionalism and the Asian Economic Crisis," *Contemporary Southeast Asia*, Vol. 21, No. 1 (April 1999), p. 7.
22. Jose T. Almonte, *Toward One Southeast Asia* (Quezon City: Institute for Strategic and Development Studies, 2004), p. 1.
23. Rommel C. Banlaoi, *War on Terrorism in Southeast Asia* (Quezon City: Rex Book Store International, 2004).
24. For an elaborate discussion of this topic, see Rommel "C. Banlaoi, "Security Cooperation and Conflict in Southeast Asia after 9/11: Constructivism, the ASEAN Way and the War on Terrorism," in Amitav Acharya and Lee Lai To (eds.), *Asia in the New Millennium* (Singapore: Marshall Cavendish Academic, 2004), pp. 56–68. Also in Chapter 15 of this volume.
25. For a detailed account of ASEAN members response to the global campaign against terrorism, see Sheldon W. Simon, "Southeast Asia and the War on Terrorism," *NBR Analysis*, Vol. 13, No. 4 (July 2002), pp. 25–37.

26. For further discussions on these issues, see Barry Desker, "Islam and Society in Southeast Asia after September 11," *IDSS Working Paper Series*, No. 3 (September 2002); Willem van der Geest, (ed.), "Mapping Muslim Politics in Southeast Asia after September 11," *The European Institute for Asian Studies Publications*, Vol. 2, No. 5 (December 2002); and Harold Crouch, Ahmad Fauzi Abdul Hamid, Carmen A. Abubakar, and Yang Razali Kassim, "Islam in Southeast Asia: Analyzing Recent Developments," *ISEAS Working Paper Series*, No. 1 (January 2002).

27. *Declaration of ASEAN Concord II* (October 7, 2003).

28. Ibid.

29. Ibid.

30. Ibid.

31. For an elaboration of ASEAN perspectives of collective defense, see Amitav Acharya, "The Association of Southeast Asian Nations: Security Community of Defense Community?" *Pacific Affairs*, Vol. 63, No. 2 (Summer 1991).

32. For a critical appraisal of ASEAN as a regional community, see Tobias Nischalke, "Does ASEAN Measure Up? Post–Cold War Diplomacy and the Idea of Regional Community," *The Pacific Review*, Vol. 15, No. 1 (2002), pp. 89–117.

33. For Philippine perspective on this topic, see Rodolfo Severino, *Toward an ASEAN Security Community*, Trends in Southeast Asian Series, No. 8 (February 2004).

# Index

For Product Safety Concerns and Information please contact our EU
representative GPSR@taylorandfrancis.com Taylor & Francis Verlag GmbH,
Kaufingerstraße 24, 80331 München, Germany

Printed and bound by CPI Group (UK) Ltd, Croydon, CR0 4YY
08/05/2025
01864477-0001